# ARAB ISLAMIC BIBLIOGRAPHY

# ARAB ISLAMIC BIBLIOGRAPHY

## The Middle East Library Committee Guide

Based on Giuseppe Gabrieli's
*Manuale di bibliografia musulmana*

EDITED BY

DIANA GRIMWOOD-JONES

DEREK HOPWOOD

J. D. PEARSON

WITH THE ASSISTANCE OF

J. P. C. Auchterlonie, J. D. Latham, Yasin Safadi

HARVESTER PRESS

HUMANITIES PRESS

First published in Great Britain in 1977 by
THE HARVESTER PRESS LIMITED

*Publisher: John Spiers*
2 Stanford Terrace, Hassocks,
Sussex, England

and in the USA by
HUMANITIES PRESS INC.,
Atlantic Highland, N.J. 07716



Harvester Press
**British Library Cataloguing in Publication Data**

Arab-Islamic bibliography.
Bibl. – Index.
ISBN 0-85527-384-4
1. Grimwood-Jones, Diana 2. Hopwood, Derek 3. Pearson, James Douglas 4. Gabrieli, Giuseppe 5. Middle East Libraries Committee
016.909-04-927 Z6207.A/
Civilization, Arab – Bibliography
Civilization, Islamic – Bibliography

Humanities Press
**Library of Congress Cataloguing in Publication Data**

Arab-Islamic bibliography.
Includes index.
1. Near East – Bibliography. 2. Africa, North – Bibliography. 3. Islam – Bibliography. 4. Civilization, Islamic – Bibliography. I. Grimwood-Jones, Diana. II. Hopwood, Derek. III. Pearson, James Douglas, 1911– . IV. Gabrieli, Giuseppe, 1872–1942.
Manuale di bibliografia musulmana.
Z3013.A66 [DS44] 016.909'04'927 76–51397
ISBN 0-391-00691-6

Printed in Great Britain by
Stephen Austin and Sons Ltd., Hertford

# Contents

ERRATA

Page vi. Section V, Periodicals for Islamic and Middle Eastern studies begins on page 116 and not 161. Section VI, which begins on page 119, is a subsection of Section V. Arabic Geographical Names begin on page 129.

Page vii. Section VI, Studies on individual manuscripts and miniatures begins on page 176.

# Foreword

by J. D. PEARSON

Giuseppe Gabrieli, who deserves to be ranked among the great librarians and bibliographers of all times, died in April 1942, soon after attaining the seventieth anniversary of his birth. His son, Francesco Gabrieli, the distinguished Arabist and Islamic scholar, now occupies the Chair of Arabic in the University of Rome which was once held by his father. Giuseppe Gabrieli (1872–1942) gained distinction as a scholar, librarian and bibliographer. He entered the University of Naples in November 1891 where he studied Arabic under Lupo Buonazia. In 1893 he joined the Istituto di Studi Superiori at Florence where he became a pupil of Fausto Lasinio for Arabic and of David Castelli for Hebrew. He graduated in 1895 with a thesis on the life, times and poems of the Arab poetess al-Khansa, which was published in 1899. In 1899 he successfully completed the requirements for the Diploma of Arabic in the Istituto Orientale at Naples, where his teacher was Carlo Alfonso Nallino to whom he was runner-up in 1900 in the competition for the Chair of Arabic language and literature in the University of Palermo.

In 1902 he became Librarian of the Reale Accademia dei Lincei and later taught Arabic in the University of Rome. During the First World War he began a long-enduring association with Prince Leone Caetani, who dedicated the fifth volume of *Annali dell' Islam* to Gabrieli, acknowledging him as the most faithful and constant of his collaborators in this important work.

The bibliography of Giuseppe's published work compiled by his son, Francesco, runs to 249 items, comprising writings on Oriental subjects (69), Bibliography (12), Local history (21), Documentation of the Lincei academicians (89), Christianity, Religion and Education (31) and miscellaneous topics (27).

Important as are his works of literary and historical scholarship, perhaps his greatest contribution to Islamic studies is the series of reference works and bibliographies that issued from his pen. He compiled indexes of the biographies contained in the *Wāfī bi'l-wafayāt* of al-Safadī, and of the historical sources cited in the *Annali Musulmani* of G. Rampoldi and assembled materials for a bibliography and concordance of the *History of Ibn Khaldūn*. He contributed a lengthy excursus on the Islamic proper name as a preface to the first volume of *Onomasticon Arabicum* on which he collaborated with Caetani. This was also published separately.

In the field of manuscript studies and cataloguing he was also active. His *Manoscritti e carte orientali negli archivi e nelle biblioteche d'Italia* (1930), supplemented by *Documenti Orientali* (1933) is a unique work wherein are enumerated collections of manuscripts in all the Oriental languages which existed in Italian libraries, with details of their history and catalogues available, which deserves the flattery of imitation in other countries. In another work he tells the story of the Caetani Foundation for Islamic studies and provides a catalogue of its Oriental manuscripts in many languages. He collaborated with his son Francesco in an article describing the manuscripts of the *Shah-Nāma* to be found in Italian libraries.

Of bibliographies proper he contributed the 'Italian fascicle' of the *Post-War Bibliography of the Near Eastern Mandates, 1919–1930*, and in his *Bibliografia degli studi orientalistici del 1912 al 1934* supplied the section covering a period of 22 years in the series of bibliographies which record Italian contributions to Oriental studies from the earliest times until quite recently, an unbroken series which makes Italy unique among European nations, or indeed any other.

The *Manuale di bibliografia musulmana* was published in 1916, in the series 'Manuali Coloniali' issued under the auspices of the Ministero delle Colonie. On the title page, Gabrieli describes himself as Librarian of the R. Accademia dei Lincei and 'Libero docente' of Arabic language and literature in the Royal University of Rome. The volume which has come down to us is described as 'Parte prima, Bibliografia generale', and is the only part ever to have been published. So far as is known, materials collected for the other part of the projected work no longer exist.

In the preface Gabrieli explains the scope of the work and the circumstances of its compilation:

> In compiling the present Manual my first intention was to collect for our young people beginning to study Islamic languages, especially Arabic, the most necessary bibliographical references, scattered here and there in works not always easy of access or which may be learnt only from the lips of the teacher. It was in my mind to provide for the debutant in Islamic studies a work similar to those which already exist, in the Italian language, for classical philology, Italian literature, and the history of mathematics.
>
> But in the course of composition and especially while it was in the press the formerly somewhat modest work underwent a transformation. Since the bibliography of Muslim literature and especially Muslim history is still in the formative period and since there is complete lack of a work surveying the present position reached by these studies it seemed more appropriate to me to aim at a wider rather than a narrower conception of its scope and to contemplate in place of one volume, rather two or three, embracing the whole bibliography of Islamic studies. This first volume (which can stand independent of the others) comprises the general bibliography or general sources for the study of the Islamic disciplines undertaken, whether for philological reasons or for practical purposes. Such a wide scope will inevitably destroy the modest proportions previously contemplated and the order of completeness originally striven for, but may make it the more acceptable not only to students in our Oriental schools and institutes, but also to teachers, Orientalists, librarians and not least, to officials of our colonial administration.
>
> The work has been given, it might be said, a historical character, in that in each section not only are the principal works arranged in chronological order but the earliest works in each field are recorded, even though they may have been completely superseded and are now quite without value. Special attention has been paid to writings by Italian authors through a natural desire to demonstrate the national contribution, however exiguous this may have been, to every branch of Muslim Oriental studies.
>
> I have tried to give here and there in addition to the title of the work,

a brief mention of the contents, value, origin, etc. In various places I have made lists of Orientalists, early translators, exhibitions, schools, institutes, manuscripts, etc., which may be useful also to those who are amateurs in these studies.

Whenever possible, titles have been transcribed and works described from actual copies in libraries to which I have had ready access, the Library of the Lincei, and those of the Prince Leone Caetani and Professor Celestini Schiaparelli. I have always borne in mind the needs of those working in small centres of study less well provided with books, in giving full bibliogrpahical details on which they may rely. For works not accessible to me these details necessarily remain incomplete.

The system of transliteration for works published in scripts other than the Roman is that used in the valuable historical and biobibliographical works of Prince Caetani.

The eleven chapters in the *Manuale* are of unequal length. The first discusses the extent of the Muslim world and defines the scope of the volume; the second enumerates the principal booksellers to deal with for Islamic studies.

Three chapters are concerned with matters other than books, coins, archaeological sources, and the Muslim calendar. The one dealing with archaeological sources contains a section on museums and on 'archaeological classification', subdivided into medals, seals, heraldic devices and amulets. The final chapter in the book provides correspondences between the Muslim era and the Christian beginning with A.H. 1 and extending to A.H. 1340 (A.D. 1922). It marks with an asterisk those lunar Hijri years which fall entirely within a single Christian year – these occur apparently about every 33 years.

One chapter and part of another are concerned with teaching establishments and teachers. In 'Orientalismo ed Orientalisti', he lists works on the history of Oriental studies and provides a list of 519 professional Islamic scholars and amateurs interested in the field, including persons alive at the time, giving their vital dates and indicating where bibliographies of their writings are to be found. One's mind boggles at the thought of extending this list to the present day and the likely dimensions it would have, but a biographical dictionary of Arabists and Islamicists would certainly make a very useful addition to the tools of our trade. In this chapter are also noted the names of interpreters and dragomans in Eastern countries and the early translators of Arabic texts into Latin. Congresses are also noted here. In any revision of this chapter that might be contemplated it would be useful to give directions for the location of information on theses and work in progress.

Part of the chapter headed 'Didattica e Propaedeutica Islamica' – that on didattica – is concerned with teaching and schools in Muslim countries and others. University departments and research institutions and learned societies are named and a list of Madrasahs is given. Most of the section will have been superseded now by Ljunggren and Geddes.

The remaining part of this chapter (Propaedutica) indicates the principal works for the study of Muslim languages and of the history of the various literatures to which Islam gave birth. In addition to this, four other chapters are specifically concerned with books: these are those devoted to bibliographies, periodicals and series, manuscripts, and printed books.

Little needs to be said about the bibliography chapter. It lists general Oriental bibliographies, bibliographies of the Arabs and Arabic, current bibliographies, lists of books published in various cities and countries, and bibliographies of Muslim territories. Subject bibliographies are omitted as they were to have formed part of the projected second volume. This part of the work, so far as Arabic-Islamic bibliography is concerned, was brought up to date by Ahmad Abdel Halim, a Sudanese and former student of the School of Librarianship in London, in a thesis which gained the laureate for the best submitted in his year. A rather surprising inclusion here is a section on encyclopaedias and citionaries – Herbelot's *Bibliothèque Orientale*, Hughes's *Dictionary of Islam* and the *Encyclopaedia of Islam*.

The chapter on periodicals and series furnishes lists of scholarly journals, monograph series, Festschriften and scientific missions; this last-named giving information on the published reports of important expeditions to the East such as the Morgan Delegation en Perse of 1897–1902, the d'Ollone Mission to the Muslims in China, the South Arabian expedition of von Wissmann and others.

Gabrieli listed 236 scholarly journals to which an Islamic scholar might wish to have recourse. Compared with this, about 500 journals were searched for the last published supplement to *Index Islamicus*, but it is fair to say that some of them produced nothing.

In manuscripts, Gabrieli not only includes codexes and their catalogues (a list now entirely superseded by the work in recent years of Vajda, Huisman and Sezgin) but also archives, papyri and inscriptions. Of these, the lists of the early archive publications are most useful and to bring this up to date would certainly be a most valuable contribution. Papyri and inscriptions may be more adequately covered.

Concluding this long catalogue of the contents of Gabrieli, there is the chapter on printed books. This gives us data on libraries and their published catalogues, and on problems which their custodians have to face in transliteration and other aspects of cataloguing. But most interesting and perhaps most worthy of extension and revision is the section giving references to the history of printing in Arabic characters in the East as well as in Europe.

So there we have Gabrieli. Some of it is antiquated, superseded by other works published since this time and this may conveniently be discarded. But much remains that is of the greatest value, certainly to practising librarians (as I can vouch for from my own experience) and I suspect to scholars as well. I have, as I have said, derived great benefit from it but there are many who have been put off using it because it is written in a language not widely known in the East.

The Middle East Library Committee (MELCOM) in Great Britain has shown, in the Bibliography Conference held in 1970 (which prepared an initial bibliography for use in departments of Islamic studies and elsewhere) that it is able to persuade scholars and librarians to work together as a team to produce what will certainly become an indispensable reference book. It now offers this new guide to reference materials for Islamic studies along the same lines as Gabrieli's work, retaining or referring to all that remains useful in the original publication and supplementing this with information on what has been contributed by scholars, librarians, bibliographers and others since the publication of the *Manuale* in 1916.

J. D. PEARSON

# Abbreviations

## PERIODICALS

| | |
|---|---|
| ʿA. al-M. | ʿĀlam al-maktabāt |
| Abh. Kgl. Ges. Wiss. Göttingen | Abhandlungen der Königlichen Gesellschaft |
| Abh. z. Gesch. d. Math. | Abhandlungen zur Geschichte der Mathematik |
| Acta or. | Acta orientalia |
| Acta or. hung. | Acta orientalia hungarica |
| Afr. hist. studies | African historical studies |
| AI | Ars Islamica |
| AIEA | Archivos del Instituto de Estudios Africanos |
| AIEO | Annales de l'Institut des Études Orientales |
| AION | Annali. Istituto Orientale di Napoli |
| AJSL | American journal of Semitic languages and literatures |
| Amer. Num. Soc. Museum notes | American Numismatic Society. Museum notes |
| Amer. pol. sci. rev. | American political science review |
| And. | Al-Andalus |
| Ankara Univ. Dil ve Tarih-Coğ. Fak. derg. | Ankara Üniversitesi. Dil ve Tarih-Coğrafya Fakültesi dergisi |
| Ann. Afr. Nord | Annuaire de l'Afrique du Nord |
| Ann. alg. géog. | Annales algériennes de géographie |
| Ann. Fac. Droit Beyrouth | Annales de la Faculté de Droit de Beyrouth |
| AO | Ars Orientalis |
| Arch. maroc. | Archives marocaines |
| Arch. soc. rel. | Archives de sociologie des religions |
| Arch. stor. sci. | Archivio di storia della scienza |
| BEA | Bulletin des etudes arabes |
| BEO | Bulletin d'etudes orientales |
| Bib. doc. ter. | Bibliography, documentation, terminology |
| BICHS | Bulletin of the International Committee of Historical Sciences |
| BIE | Bulletin de l'Institut Égyptien (d'Égypte) |
| BM qtly | British Museum quarterly |
| Bodl. Lib. record | Bodleian Library record |
| Bol. Asoc. Esp. Or. | Bolletin de la Asociación Española de Orientalistas |
| Bol. de la R. Acad. Hist. | Boletín de la Real Academia de la Historia |
| Bol. Soc. Geogr. Lisboa | Boletim da Sociedade de Geographia de Lisboa |
| Boll. R. Ist. Archeol. e Storia dell'Arte | Bolletino del Reale Istituto di Archeologia e Storia dell'Arte |
| BPP | Bengal past and present |

| | |
|---|---|
| BSEHGIS | Bulletin de la Société d'Études Historiques et Géographiques de l'Isthme de Suez |
| BSOAS | Bulletin of the School of Oriental and African Studies |
| Bull. Com. Afr. Française. Renseignements coloniaux | Bulletin du Comité de l'Afrique Française. Renseignements coloniaux |
| Bull. corresp. afr. | Bulletin de correspondance africaine |
| Bull. écon. soc. Maroc | Bulletin économique et social du Maroc |
| Bull. enseign. publ. Maroc | Bulletin de l'enseignement publique du Maroc |
| Bull. IFAN | Bulletin de l'Institut Français d'Afrique Noire |
| Bull. IFAO | Bulletin de l'Institut Français d'Archéologie Orientale |
| Bull. IHEM | Bulletin de l'Institut des Hautes Études Marocaines |
| Bull. inf. Inst. de Recherches et d'Histoire des Textes | Bulletin d'information. Institut de Recherches et d'Histoire des Textes |
| Bull. Soc. Sci. Nat. Maroc | Bulletin de la Société des Sciences Naturelles du Maroc |
| Cah. civ. med. | Cahiers de civilisation médiévale |
| Cahiers alg. | Cahiers algériennes |
| Cahiers hist. alg. | Cahiers d'histoire algérienne |
| Cahiers de l'or. contemp. | Cahiers de l'orient contemporain |
| Corresp. d'orient | Correspondance d'orient |
| CRAIBL | Comptes rendus des séances. (Académie des Inscriptions et Belles-Lettres) |
| CT | Cahiers de Tunisie |
| Durham Univ. J. | Durham University journal |
| Égypte contemp. | L'Égypte contemporain |
| Études philos. et litt. | Études philosophiques et littéraires |
| Folia or. | Folia orientalia |
| Geog. rev. | Geographical review |
| GLECS Comptes-rendus | Groupe linguistique d'études chamito-sémitiques. Comptes-rendus |
| Hist. J. | Historical journal |
| IBLA | Institut des Belles Lettres Arabes |
| IC | Islamic culture |
| IJMES | International journal of Middle Eastern studies |
| Int. libr. rev. | International library review |
| Int. soc. sci. bull. | International social science bulletin |
| Int. studies | International studies |
| IQ | Islamic quarterly |

| | |
|---|---|
| JA | Journal asiatique |
| J. Amer. folklore | Journal of American folklore |
| JAOS | Journal of the American Oriental Society |
| J. Asiat. Soc. Pakistan | Journal of the Asiatic Society of Pakistan |
| JBBRAS | Journal of the Bombay Branch of the Royal Asiatic Society |
| J. Bombay Nat. Hist. Soc. | Journal of the Bombay Natural History Society |
| JESHO | Journal of the economic and social history of the Orient |
| Jhg. d. Z. f. Math. u. Physik | Jahrgang der Zeitschrift für Mathematik und Physik |
| JNES | Journal of Near Eastern studies |
| JNSI | Journal of the Numismatic Society of India |
| JPASB | Journal and Proceedings of the Asiatic Society of Bengal |
| JPHS | Journal of the Pakistan Historical Society |
| JRAS | Journal of the Royal Asiatic Society |
| JRCAS | Journal of the Royal Central Asian Society |
| JRGS | Journal of the Royal Geographical Society |
| J. Soc. Afr. | Journal de la Société des Africanistes |
| JWH | Journal of world history |
| KSINA | Kratkie soobshcheniya Instituta Narodov Azii |
| MEJ | Middle East journal |
| Mém. Acad. Imp. Sci. St. Pétersbourg | Mémoires de l'Académie Impériale des Sciences de St. Pétersbourg |
| MESA bull. | Middle East Studies Association bulletin |
| MIDEO | Mélanges de l'Institut Dominicaine d'Études Orientales |
| MSOS | Mitteilungen des Seminars für orientalische Sprachen |
| MW | Moslem world (later:) Muslim world |
| NC | Numismatic chronicle |
| Num. Z. | Numismatic Zeitschrift |
| OCP | Orientalia Christiana periodica |
| OLZ | Orientalistische Literaturzeitung |
| OM | Oriente moderno |
| Pakistan lib. rev. | Pakistan library review |
| Philos. Q. | Philosophical quarterly |
| Prilozi orijent. filol. ist. | Prilozi za orijentalni filologiju i istoriju jugoslovenskih naroda pod turkom vladavinom |
| Proc. Egypt. Soc. Hist. St. | Proceedings of the Egyptian Society of Historical Studies |
| Proche-Or. chrét. | Proche-Orient chrétien |
| Przegl. or. | Przeglad orientalistyczny |
| PULC | Princeton University Library chronicle |

| | |
|---|---|
| Quest. dipl. et colon. | Questions diplomatiques et coloniales |
| RA | Revue africaine |
| RAA | Revue des arts asiatiques |
| RAAD | Revue de l'Académie Arabe de Damas |
| RAAM | Revue de l'art ancien et moderne |
| RABM | Revista de archivos, bibliotecas y museos |
| RBN | Revue belge de numismatique et de sigillographie |
| RCAJ | Royal Central Asian journal |
| REI | Revue des études islamiques |
| Rev. alg. | Revue algérienne |
| Rev. arch. | Revue archéologique |
| Rev. de géog. | Revue de géographie |
| Rev. franç. hist. outremer | Revue française d'histoire d'outre-mer |
| Rev. franç. sci. pol. | Revue française de science politique |
| Rev. hist. | Revue historique |
| Rev. hist. civ. Maghreb | Revue d'histoire et de civilisation du Maghreb |
| Rev. hist. maghrébine | Revue d'histoire maghrébine |
| Rev. hist. et philos. rel. | Revue d'histoire et de philosophie religieuses |
| Rev. hist. rel. | Revue de l'histoire des religions |
| Rev. maroc. droit | Revue marocaine de droit |
| Rev. num. | Revue numismatique |
| Rev. quest. hist. | Revue des questions historiques |
| Rev. tunis. sci. soc. | Revue tunisienne des sciences sociales |
| Revista polit. int. | Revista de politica internacional |
| RIE | Revue internationale d'Égypte |
| Riv. coloniale | Rivista coloniale |
| Riv. stor. ital. | Rivista della storia italiana |
| RMM | Revue du monde musulman |
| RO | Rocznik orientalistyczny |
| RSO | Rivista degli studi orientali |
| RT | Revue tunisienne |
| Sitzb. K. Akad. Wiss. | Sitzungsberichte der Königlichen Akademie der Wissenschaften |
| SLJR | Sudan law journal and reports |
| SM | Scientific monthly |
| SNR | Sudan notes and records |
| Sov. etn. | Sovetskaya etnografiya |
| Sp. libs. | Special libraries |
| SPMSE | Sitzungsberichte der Physikalisch-Medizinischen Sozietät in Erlangen |
| Trav. Inst. Rech. Sahar. | Travaux de l'Institut de Recherches Sahariennes |
| Unesco bull. lib. | Unesco bulletin for libraries |
| WI | Die Welt des Islams |
| WZKM | Wiener Zeitschrift für die Kunde des Morgenlandes |

| | |
|---|---|
| YAOC | Yearbook of oriental art and culture |
| ZB | Zentralblatt für Bibliothekswesen |
| ZDMG | Zeitschrift der Deutschen Morgenländischen Gesellschaft |
| Zeits. f. Assyriologie | Zeitschrift für Assyriologie |
| ZKV | Zapiski Kollegii Vostokovedov pri Aziatskom Musee Akademii Nauk SSSR |
| ZN | Zeitschrift für Numismatik |
| ZVO | Zapiski Vostochnago Otdeleniya Imperatorskago Russkago Archeologicheskago Obshchestva |

## OTHER ABBREVIATIONS

| | |
|---|---|
| CAFRAD | Centre Africain de Formation et de Recherches Administratives |
| CERES | Centre d'Études et Recherches Économiques et Sociales |
| EI | Encyclopaedia of Islam |
| IFAO | Institut Français d'Archéologie Orientale |
| IHEM | Institut des Hautes Études Marocaines |
| IHET | Institut des Hautes Études de Tunis |
| RGS | Royal Geographical Society |
| SEHG | Société des Études Historiques et Géographiques |

# Bibliographies

AHMED ABD EL HALIM and J. D. PEARSON

Bibliographies of the Arab Islamic world abound: in the new edition of the Asian and African parts of Besterman some 400 titles on the Arab Near and Middle East alone will be found. In addition, there are *c.* 150 titles on North Africa. It must be borne in mind, too, that Besterman excludes bibliographies embedded in other works, such as periodical articles or chapters or segments of books, and books in Oriental languages without a Western title-page.

In the present chapter, works in the Besterman excluded categories will be found to appear, but the lists given are intended to serve practical purposes and do not, therefore, aim at completeness through the inclusion of antiquated and superseded works.

Wherever possible, the actual works have been examined personally, and to give some idea of the extent of a bibliography, the Besterman device of a figure in brackets is used at the end of the description. If this is lacking, either the work in question has not been accessible or it is not of a type which lends itself to numerical analysis. On occasion the figure quoted is an approximation based on random sampling methods.

## I. GENERAL ORIENTAL

Islamic studies have always been regarded as a branch of Oriental studies in European countries, and the earlier literature in the field is comprehended in the series of bibliographies covering the whole of Asia or Oriental studies. These may be said to begin with the earliest compilations in the field by León Pinelo and Hottinger in the seventeenth century, Ternaux-Compans (1841) and Zenker (1840), continuing through the annual reports made by Jules Mohl to the Société Asiatique, and culminating in the great series of continuing bibliographies produced in Germany, beginning with the *Wissenschaftliche Jahresberichte* issued by the Deutsche Morgenländische Gesellschaft and passing through the stages of the *Bibliotheca orientalis* (1876–83, Friederici) and *Literatur-Blatt für orientalische Philologie* (1883–86, Klatt and Kuhn) to reach their apogee in the monumental never surpassed, *Orientalische Bibliographie* founded by August Müller in 1888 and continued by Kuhn and Scherman until its unfortunate demise in 1928. These last-named are all listed in detail, and described, in Pearson, *Oriental and Asian bibliography* (London, 1966) pp. 129–35, as is the 'Bullettino (Bolletino)' published by the Italian Oriental Society in its journal *Rivista degli studi orientali* from 1907 to 1920.

The older bibliograpies of Oriental studies, from León Pinelo's *Epitome* of 1629 and Hottinger's *Promtuarium* (1658) will be found listed in Besterman, *W.B.B.*, under the rubrics 'Oriental literatures (3. General)' and 'Asia (General)'. To these Gabrieli added the *Repertorium für biblische und morgenländische*

*Literatur* edited by J. G. Eichhorn from 1777 to 1786, but this, with its continuation by Paulus, is a periodical with no special bibliographical content.

With the bibliographies covering Oriental studies in general may be associated those reporting the productions of Orientalists in a particular country, of which the earliest is the *Bibliotheca orientalis et linguistica* of Carl Heinrich Herrmann, published in Halle in 1870 and enumerating 'books, writings and treatises of oriental and comparative linguistic literature published from 1850 to 1868 in Germany'. A list of works in this genre may be found in *OAB*, pp. 140–47; it may be supplemented (for dependent literature) by the titles given in *Index Islamicus*, section I, iv.

## II. ISLAM IN GENERAL. NEAR AND MIDDLE EAST (WITH OR WITHOUT NORTH AFRICA): GENERAL AND SUBJECTS

There seems little point in attempting to separate bibliographies of Islam in general from those of the Arab World or the Near and Middle East in general. Islam may for our purposes be defined as the religion of qllāh and the Prophet Muḥammad, those who adhere to this religion and the countries in which these adherents live. This scope extends considerably beyond the Arab World, which is the totality of countries where Arabic predominates as the spoken language, and which include countries in the Near and Middle East and in North Africa. In practice, bibliographies of the Near and Middle East often include materials relating to non-Arabic speaking countries such as Turkey, Iran, Afghanistan and Pakistan.

### (a) General (all subjects)

GAY, J., *Bibliographie des ouvrages relatifs à l'Afrique et à l'Arabie. Catalogue méthodique de tous les ouvrages français & des principaux en langues étrangères traitant de la géographie, de l'histoire, du commerce, des lettres et des arts de l'Afrique et de l'Arabie.* San Remo &c., 1875. [400]

'Arabie' means all Arabic-speaking countries, not just the Arabian peninsula. The work was reprinted at Amsterdam in 1941.

CHAUVIN, V., *Bibliographie des ouvrages arabes ou relatifs aux Arabes publiés dans l'Europe chrétienne de 1810 à 1885.* 12v. Liège, 1892–1909. [5000]

NEW YORK PUBLIC LIBRARY, *List of works relating to Arabia and the Arabs.* New York, 1911. [2000]

ZWEMER, S. M., 'A working bibliography on Islam'. *MW* **2**, 1912, pp. 32–6. [45]

PFANMÜLLER, C., *Handbuch der Islam-Literatur.* Berlin &c., 1923. [400]

DODD, S. C. *ed.*, *A post-war bibliography of the Near Eastern mandates. A preliminary survey of publications on the social sciences dealing with Iraq, Palestine and Trans-Jordan, and the Syrian states from Nov. 11, 1918 to Dec. 31, 1929. Arranged in alphabetical list by authors, with a limited index by subject matter, presented in the following eight facsimiles by languages.* (A.U.B., Publs. of the Fac. of Arts and Sciences; Soc. sci. ser., 1.) Beirut, 1932–36.

English fasc. Basim A. Faris ed. [4699]

Arabic fasc. Anis Freyha ed. [1941]

DAVISON, R. H., *The Near and Middle East; an introduction to history and bibliography*. (Service center for teachers of history, Publ. 24.) Washington, 1959. [125]

STEEPER, H. F., *Middle East*. (Oce of Education, International Educational Relations; Keep tab on the lab, ii, 2.) Washington, 1960. [150]

RUBIO GARCIA, L., 'Introducción a una bibliografia sobre el Oriente Medio'. *Revista polít. int.* **62–3**, 1962, pp. 511–63. [500]

HOWARD, H. N., 'The Middle East in paperback'. *MEJ* **18**, 1964, pp. 355–66. [226]

WRIGHT, L. C., *The Middle East; an annotated guide to resource materials, 1966*. Greensboro, N. C., 1966. [62]

ANAWATI, G. C., 'Bibliographie islamo-arabe. Livres et articles sur l'Islam et l'arabisme parus en langues occidentales, durant la période 1960–1966'. *MIDEO* **9**, 1967, pp. 143–213. [986]

DURHAM UNIVERSITY. CENTRE FOR MIDDLE EASTERN AND ISLAMIC STUDIES, *Register of current British research in Middle Eastern and Islamic studies*. Durham, 1969 [300]; rev. edn. 1971. [250]

ZEIGLER, H. C., 'A general background bibliography on the modern Middle East'. *Middle East Research Association* 1969–70, ff. 70–86. [100]

GEDDES, C. L., *Islam in paperback*. (American Inst. of Islamic St., Bibliographic ser., 1.) Denver, 1969. [250]

HASHAD, Mahmoud, *Select bibliography on Arab Islamic civilization and its contribution to human progress*. (Kuwait Univ, Libraries Dept., Bibliographic ser., 3.) Kuwait, 1970. [2093]

DOTAN, U., *A bibliography of articles on the Middle East, 1959–1967*. Tel Aviv, 1970. [2902]

HOWARD H. N. and others *eds.*, *Middle East and North Africa; a bibliography for undergraduate libraries*. (Foreign Area Materials Center Occasional Publs., 4.) Williamsport, 1971. [1192]

MIDDLE EAST LIBRARIES COMMITTEE, *Middle East and Islam; a bibliographical introduction*; ed. D. Hopwood and D. Grimwood-Jones. Zug, 1972. [3191]

ZUWIYYA, Jalal, *The Near East (South-West Asia and North Africa); a bibliographic study*. Metuchen, N.J., 1973. [3616]

ATIYEH, G. N., *The contemporary Middle East, 1948–1973; a selective and annotated bibliography*. Boston, Mass., 1975. [6500]

### WORK PUBLISHED IN A PARTICULAR COUNTRY OR LANGUAGE

*British*

BRITISH COUNCIL, *British works on the Arab world; an exhibition arranged by the British Council*. London, 1971. [900]

*Chinese*

OGILVIE, C. L., 'A classified bibliography of books on Islam in Chinese and Chinese-Arabic'. *MW* **8**, 1918, pp. 74–8. [94]

*French*

DAGHER, J. A., *L'Orient dans la littérature française d'après guerre 1919–1933.* Beirut, 1937. [5239]

*German*

REGEL, F., *Die deutsche Forschung in Türkisch Vorderasien.* (Länder und Völker der Türkei, 7.) Leipzig, 1915. [500]

*Israeli*

LANDAU, J. M., 'Israeli studies on the Middle East'. *MEJ* **19**, 1965, pp. 354–62. [123]

*Russian*

LOEWENTHAL, R., 'A bibliography of Near and Middle Eastern studies published in the Soviet Union from 1937 to 1947'. *Oriens* **4**, 1951, pp. 328–44. [260]

—— 'Russian materials on Islam and Islamic institutions: a selective bibliography'. *Der Islam* **33**, 1958, pp. 280–309. Published also as: *External research paper* 133–1, March, 1958. [377]

—— 'Russian materials on Arabs and Arab countries: a selective bibliography'. *Der Islam* **34**, 1959, pp. 174–87. Published also as: *External research paper* 133–3, March, 1958. [163]

BOLTON, A. R. C., *Soviet Middle East studies: an analysis and a bibliography.* 8 pts. London, 1959.

LANDAU, J. M., 'Some Soviet works on Islam'. *MES* **9**, 1973, pp. 358–62.

—— 'Some Soviet bibliographies on the Middle East'. *MES* **9**, 1973, pp. 227–30.

*Spanish*

EPALZA, M. de, 'Bibliografía general árabe e islámica en España, 1960–1964'. *Bol. Asoc. Esp. Or.* **2**, 1966, pp. 131–75. [650]

CURRENT BIBLIOGRAPHIES

'Bulletin des périodiques de l'Islam (1896–1918)'. *Rev. hist. rel.* **35**, 1897–**80**, 1919.

'Islambericht'. *Archiv für Religionsgeschichte* **8**, 1905, pp. 129–43; **11**, 1908, pp. 339–68; **15**, 1912, pp. 530–602.

'Kritische Bibliographie'. *Der Islam* **4**, 1913–21, 1933.

'Abstracta Islamica'. *REI* **1**, 1927–.

'Bibliography of periodical literature on the Near and Middle East'. *MEJ* **1**, 1947–. Reprinted.

'Contribution à un répertoire documentaire de l'Orient contemporain'. *Cahiers de l'or. contemp.* **9–10**, 1947–33, 1955.

'Revue bibliographique'. *Arabica* **1**, 1954–5, 1958.

*Index Islamicus* (1906–). 1958–. Full details given in the chapter on 'Periodicals'.

'Bibliographie 1963'. *Corresp. d'Orient. Études* 1964–.

*Revue bibliographique du Moyen Orient.* Damascus, Nov. 1968–.

*Islam in paperback.* Denver [1969–].

*Orient-press. Bollettino bibliografico di studi orientalistici.* Rome, 1970–.

*Recent publications on the Middle East.* Ed. by J. L. Murray. Durham, 1970–.

## (b) SUBJECTS

(i) Religion; (ii) Law; (iii) Philosophy. Science; (iv) Art. Archaeology, Numismatics; (v) Geography. Travels. Anthropology; (vi) History; (vii) Social sciences; (viii) Language and literature.

### (i) RELIGION

*General*

PICKENS, C. L., *Annotated bibliography of literature on Islam in China*. Hankow, 1950. [350]

KHĀN, Mu'īn ul-Dīn Aḥmad, 'A bibliographical introduction to modern Islamic development in India and Pakistan, 1700–1953'. *J. Asiat. Soc. Pakistan* **4** (appendix), Dacca, 1959. [895]

QUELQUEJAY, Ch., 'Les sources de documentation sur la religion musulmane en Union Soviétique depuis 1945'. *Cahiers monde russe soviétique* **1**, 1959–60, pp. 184–98, 373–81. [216]

O'SHAUGHNESSY, T., 'An annotated list of selected books on Islamism appearing from 1950 to 1960'. *Studia missionalia* **11**, 1961, pp. 201–22.

DÉJEUX, J., 'Connaisance de l'Islam'. *Parole et mission* **22**, 1963, pp. 502–11.

Reviewed by G. C. Anawati in *Rev. thomiste* 1964, p. 284.

HAMPSON, R. M., *Islam in South Africa; a bibliography*. Cape Town, 1964. [230]

FAHD, Toufic, 'L'Islam, chronique bibliographique'. *Rev. hist. et philos. rel.* **5**, 1971, pp. 175–90.

GEDDES, C. L., *An analytical guide to the bibliographies on Islam, Muhammad and the Qur'an*. (American Inst. of Islamic St., Bibliographic ser., **3**.) Denver, 1973. [211]

*See also* Chauvin, *op. cit.*, vol. xii, 1922, *passim*.

*Muḥammad, the Prophet*

HOROVITZ, J., 'The earliest biographies of the Prophet and their authors'. *IC* **1**, 1927, pp. 535–59; **2**, 1928, pp. 22–50, 164–82, 495–526. [50]

KRYMSKII, A. E., *Istochniki dlya istorii Mokhammeda i literatura o nem. I. Ot Orvy do Ibn-Iskhâka s Ibn-Khishamom*. (Trudy po vostokovedeniyu, **13**.) Moscow, 1902. [20]

RODINSON, M., 'Bilan des études mohammadiennes'. *Rev. hist.* **229**, 1963, pp. 169–220. [250]

*See also* Chauvin, *op. cit.*, vol. xi, 1909.

*Qur'ān*

LOBHERZ, J. C., *Dissertatio historico-philologico-theologico de Alcorani versionibus variis, tam orientalibus, quam occidentalibus, impressis et hactenus 'ανεκδοτοις*. Altdorf, 1704.

WOOLWORTH, W. S., 'A bibliography of Koran texts and translations'. *MW* **17**, 1927, pp. 279–89. [118]

NEW YORK PUBLIC LIBRARY. SLAVONIC DIVISION, *The Koran in Slavonic. A list of translations*. New York, 1937. [16]

*See also* Chauvin, *op. cit.*, vol. x, 1907.

*Ḥadīth*

-KATTĀNĪ, Muḥammad b. Ja'far, *Al-risāla al-mustaṭrafa li-bayān mashhūr kutub al-sunna al-musharrafa*. 3rd edn. Beirut, 1964. [1500]

*See also* Chauvin, *op. cit.*, vol. x, 1907.

*Polemics. Islamo-Christian dialogues*

STEINSCHNEIDER, M., *Polemische und apologetische Literatur in arabischer Sprache zwischen Muslimen, Christen und Juden, nebst Anhängen verschiedenen Inhalts. Mit Benutzung handschriftlicher Quellen.* (Abh. f.d. Kunde des Morgenlandes **6**, iii.) Leipzig, 1877. [500]

DÉJEUX, J. & CASPAR, R., 'Bibliographie sur le dialogue islamo-chrétien'. *Proche or. chr.* **16**, 1966, pp. 174–82. [144]

CASPAR, R., 'Le dialogue islamo-chrétien. Bibliographie'. *Parole et mission* **33**, 1966, pp. 312–22; **34**, 1966, pp. 475–81.

*Theologians*

IBN QAYYIM AL-JAWZIYYA, Muḥ. b. Abī Bakr, *Asmā' mu'allafāt Ibn Taymiyya*. Damascus, 1953.

The works of Ibn Taymiyya.

*Modernists*

BAIDAR, Abid Raza, 'Jamal al-Din al-Afghani: a bibliography of source materials'. *Int. studies* **3**, 1961, pp. 99–108. [200]

With a list of the contents of *Al-'urwa al-wuthqā*, of which nine numbers were published in 1884.

KUDSI-ZADEH, A. A., *Sayyid Jamal al-Din al-Afghani: an annotated bibliography*. Leiden, 1970. [688]

A select list by the same author appeared in *MES* **2**, 1965, pp. 66–72. [49]

*Sufism*

KOPF, D., 'Bibliographical notes on Sufism to its Bengali-Indian development'. *Folklore* [Calcutta] **3**, 1962, pp. 113–22. [123]

*Ibn 'Arabī*

AFFIFI, A. E., 'The works of Ibn 'Arabi in the light of a memorandum drawn up by him'. *Bull. Fac. Arts Alexandria* **8**, 1954, pp. 109–17, with the Arabic text on pp. 193–207. [251]

'AWWĀD, Gūrgīs, 'Fihrist mu'allafāt Muḥyī al-Dīn Ibn 'Arabī'. *Maj. al-Majma' al-'Ilmī al-'Arabī* (*RAA*) **29**, 1954, pp. 345–59, 527–36; **30**, 1955, pp. 51–60, 268–80, 395–410. [540]

BADAWĪ, 'Abd al-Raḥmān, 'Autobibliografia de Ibn 'Arabī'. *And.* **20**, 1955, pp. 107–28. [290]

YAHYA, Osman, *Histoire et classification de l'oeuvre d'Ibn 'Arabī. Étude critique.* 2v. Damascus, 1964.

*Shī'a*

KĀẒIMĪ, Ḥasan Ṣadr al-Dīn, *Kitāb al-shī'a wa-funūn al-islām*. Sidon, 1331/1913.

-ṬŪSĪ, Muḥammad b. al-Ḥasan, *Fihrist kutub al-shīʿa aw Fihrist al-Ṭūsī; Tusy's list of Shyʿah books and ʿAlam al-Hoda's notes on Shyʿah biography*, ed. by A. Sprenger and others. (Bibliotheca Indica, 19.) Calcutta, 1853–55. [892 authors]

KANTŪRĪ, Iʿjāz Ḥ., *Kashf al-ḥujūb wa'l-astār ʿan asmā' al-kutub wa'l-asfār; The bibliography of Shiʿa literature* . . . ed. by M. Hidayat Husain. (Bibliotheca Indica, 203.) 2v. Calcutta, 1912–35. [3414]

ĀGHĀ BUZURG AL-TIHRĀNĪ, M. Muḥsin, *Al-dharīʿa ilā taṣānīf al-shīʿa; Bibliographie des ouvrages shiʿites*. Najaf, 1926–.

IBN SHAHRĀSHŪB, Muḥammad b. ʿAlī al-Sarawī, *Kitāb maʿālim al-ʿulamā' fī fihrist kutub al-shīʿa; Maâlim-ul-ulamā. Bibliography of the Shyʿahs (Supplement to Tusy's Fihrist)* . . . ed. by Abbas Eghbal. Tehran, 1934. [990 writers]

*Ismaʿīlīs*

FYZEE, A. A., 'Materials for an Ismaili bibligraphy'. *JBBRAS* N.S. **11**, 1935, pp. 59–65; **12**, 1936, pp. 107–9; **16**, 1940, pp. 99–101. [119]

IVANOW, W., *Ismaili literature: a bibliographical survey*. A second, amplified edition of, *A guide to Ismaili literature*. Tehran, 1963. [929]

*Assassins*

LEWIS, B., 'The sources for the history of the Syrian Assassins'. *Speculum* **27**, 1952, pp. 475–89. [75]

*Qarmatians*

MASSIGNON, L., 'Esquisse d'une bibliographie qarmate'. (In *A volume of Oriental studies presented to E. G. Browne*, Cambridge, 1922, pp. 329–38.)

*ʿIbāḍis*

SMOGORZEWSKI, Z., 'Essai de bio-bibliographie Ibadite-Wahbite. Avant-propos'. *RO* **5**, 1927, pp. 45–57. [20 sources; no more published]

MOTYLINSKY, A. de C., 'Bibliographie du Mzab. Les livres de la secte abadhite'. *Bull. corresp. afr.* **3**, 1885, pp. 15–72. [90]

Also published separately, Algiers, 1885.

BAALI, A., 'Bibliographie ibadhite'. *Rev. alg.* 1943–5, pt. 1, pp. 39–40. [50]

(ii) LAW

PRATT, I. A., *List of works in the New York Public Library relating to Muhammedan law*. New York, 1907. [225]

AGHNIDES, N. P., *Mohammedan theories of finance; with an introduction to Mohammedan law and a bibliography*. (Columbia Univ. st. in hist., econ. and public law, 70.) New York, 1916 (repr. 1969).

PÉRÈS, H., 'La bid'ah du début de l'Islam à nos jours (bibliographie)'. *BEA* **2**, 1942, pp. 150–1. [30]

LIEBESNY, H. J., 'Literature on the law of the Middle East'. *MEJ* **3**, 1949, pp. 461–9. [86]

GODCHOT, J. E., *Les constitutions du Proche et du Moyen-Orient*. Paris, 1957. [575]

SCHACHT, J., *An introduction to Islamic law*. Oxford, 1964, pp. 215–85. [500]

(iii) PHILOSOPHY, SCIENCE

*Philosophy*

CALVERLEY, E. E., 'A brief bibliography of Arabic philosophy'. *MW* **32**, 1942, pp. 60–8. [87]

MENASCE, P. J. de, *Arabische Philosophie*. (Bibliographische Einführung in das Studium der Philos., 6.) Bern, 1948. [500]

WALZER, R., 'A survey of work on medieval philosophy, 1945–52. Part I: Medieval Islamic philosophy. (Philos. surveys, 8.)'. *Philos. Q.* **3**, 1953, pp. 175–81.

*Science*

*General*

CENTRE DE COOPERATION SCIENTIFIQUE - MOYEN ORIENT, *Liste de (des) travaux scientifiques publiés au Moyen Orient*. Cairo, 1948–55.

Continued as:

NATIONAL RESEARCH COUNCIL OF EGYPT, *Résumés analytiques des travaux scientifiques et techniques publiés en Égypte et travaux reçus de l'Afghanistan, Chypre, Iran, Irak, Liban, Pakistan, Soudan et Syrie*. (Bull. of the Scientific and Technical Doc. Centre, part 2.) 1955–.

*Translations into and from Arabic*

WÜSTENFELD, H. F., *Die Übersetzungen arabischer Werke in das Lateinische seit dem XI. Jahrhundert*. Göttingen, 1877. [250]

STEINSCHNEIDER, M., *Die arabischen Übersetzungen aus dem Griechischen:*

I. Abschnitt: 'Philosophie'. 12. Beiheft zum *Centralblatt f. Bibliothekswesen* 1893, pp. 129–240. Also issued separately, Leipzig, 1893. [396]

II. Abschnitt: 'Mathematik'. *ZDMG* **50**, 1896, pp. 161–219, 337–70, 371–417. [139]

III. Abschnitt: 'Die griechischen Ärtzte in arabischen Übersetzungen. Kritische Bibliographie'. *Archiv für pathol. Anat. u. Physiol. u. klin. Med.* **124**, 1891, pp. 115–36, 268–96, 455–87. [33]

A general survey of the whole field was published in the 5. Beiheft zum *Centralblatt f. Bibliothekswesen* 1889, pp. 51–81, also as a *Sonderdruck* in 50 copies. The whole was reprinted at Graz, 1969.

STEINSCHNEIDER, M., *Die europäischen Übersetzungen aus dem Arabischen bis Mitte des 17. Jahrhunderts*. [500]

A. *Schriften bekannter Übersetzer*. (Sitzb. K. Akad. Wiss. Wien, phil.-hist. Kl. **149**, iv, 1904.)

B. *Übersetzungen von Werken bekannter Autoren, deren Übersetzer unbekannt oder unsicher sind*. (*Ibid.* **151**, i, 1905.)

*Einleitung*. (Anzeiger K. Akad. Wiss. Wien, phil.-hist. Kl. **41**. Jhg., 1904.)

Reprinted as a whole at Graz, 1956.

STEINSCHNEIDER, M., *Zur pseudepigraphischen Literatur insbesonders der geheimen Wissenschaften des Mittelalters.* (Wissenschaftl. Blätter aus der Veitel Heine Ephraim'schen Lehranstalt, erste Sammlung **3**.) Berlin, 1862. [8]

KAPP, A. G., 'Arabische Übersetzer und Kommentatoren Euklids, sowie deren math.-naturwiss. Werke auf Grund der Ta'rīkh al-ḥukamā' des Ibn al-Qiftī'. *Isis* **22**, 1934–35, pp. 150–72; **23**, 1935, pp. 54–99; **24**, 1935–36, pp. 37–9. [45]

CARMODY, F. J., *Arabic astronomical and astrological sciences in Latin translation; a critical bibliography.* Los Angeles, 1956. [2000]

PARET, R., 'Notes bibliographiques sur quelques travaux récents consacrés aux premières traductions arabes d'oeuvres grecques'. *Byzantion* **29–30**, 1959–60, pp. 387–446.

'Esquisse d'une bibliographie des traductions d'oeuvres philosophiques de langue arabe (parfois persane) en langues européennes (à l'exclusion du latin, du néerlandais, du russe et du turc)'. *Etudes philos. et. litt.* **3**, 1968, pp. 25–33. [125]

*Individual philosophers and scientists*

-*Bīrūnī*

BOILOT, D. J., 'L'oeuvre d'al-Beruni; essai bibliographique'. *MIDEO* **2**, 1955, pp. 161–256; corrigenda et addenda. *Ibid.* **3**, 1956, pp. 391–6. [180]

This work is based on the earlier work by E. Wiedemann, E. Suter and O. Rescher, 'Ueber al Biruni und seine Schriften', *SPMSE* **52–3**, 1920–21, pp. 55–96.

-BĪRŪNĪ, Muḥammad b. Aḥmad, *Epître de Bērūnī; Risāla fi fihrist kutub Muḥammad b. Zakariyya al-Rāzī*, ed. P. Kraus. Paris, 1936.

Includes the *Fihrist* of his own writings. [138]

IMĀM, M. Kāẓim, *Tarjama-yi aḥvāl va-fihrist-i asār-i Abī Rayḥān Bīrūnī.* Tehran, 1352/1974.

ROZENFEL'D, B. A. and others, *Abu-r-Raykhan al-Biruni, 973–1048.* Moscow, 1973. [189]

In Russian.

*Fakhr al-Din al-Rāzī*

ANAWATI, G. C., 'Fakhr al-Din al-Rāzī; tamhīd li-dirāsat ḥayātihi wa-mu'allafātihi'. (In *Mélanges Taha Husain*, Cairo, 1962, pp. 193–234.) [134]

-*Fārābī*

STEINSCHNEIDER, M., *Al-Farabi (Alpharabius), des arabischen Philosophen Leben und Schriften, mit besonderer Rücksicht auf die Geschichte der griechischen Wissenschaft unter den Arabern.* (Mém. Acad. Imp. Sci. St. Pétersbourg, 7e sér., **13**, iv.) St. Petersburg, 1869. [105]

RESCHER, N., *Al-Farabi; an annotated bibliography.* Pittsburg, 1962. [350]

-*Ghazzālī*

BADAWĪ, 'Abd al-Raḥmān, *Mu'allafāt al-Ghazzālī; Les oeuvres d'al-Ghazâlî; étude bibliographique.* Cairo, 1961. [457]

BOUYGES, M., *Essai de chronologie des oeuvres d'al-Ghazali.* (Recherches de l'Institut des Lettres Orientales, 14.) Beirut, 1959. [404]

*Ḥunayn b. Isḥāq*

GABRIELI, G., 'Hunayn ibn Isḥaq'. [In Italian.] *Isis* **6**, 1923, pp. 282–92. [100]

BERGSTRÄSSER, G., *Ḥunain ibn Isḥāq. Über die syrischen und arabischen Galen-Übersetzungen.* Zum ersten Mal hrsg. und übers. (Abh. f.d. Kunde des Morgenlandes, XVII. Band, 2.) Leipzig, 1925. [129]

MEYERHOF, M., 'New light on Ibn Isḥāq and his period'. *Isis* **8**, 1926, pp. 685–724. [129]

BERGSTRÄSSER, G., *Neue Materialen zu Ḥunain ibn Isḥaq's Galen-Bibliographie.* (Abh. f.d. Kunde des Morgenlandes XIX. Band, 2.) Leipzig, 1932. [50]

*Ibn Rushd*

BOUYGES, M., 'Notes sur les philosophes arabes connus des Latins au Moyen Âge. V.: Inventaire des textes arabes d'Averroes'. *Mélanges Univ. St. Joseph* **8**, i, 1922; additions and corrections, **9**, 1923, pp. 43–8. [84]

GABRIELI, G., 'Averroè (1126–1198). (Biografie e bibliografie di scienzati arabi, 3.)' *Arch. stor. sci.* **5**, 1924, pp. 156–62. [70]

*Ibn Sīnā*

GABRIELI, G., 'Avicenna. (Biografie e bibliografie di scienzati arabi.)' *Arch. stor. sci.* **4**, 1923, pp. 258–70. [64]

ANAWATI, G. C., *Essai de bibliographie avicennienne.* Cairo, 1950. [1250]

NAFICY, Saïd, *Bibliographie des principaux travaux européens sur Avicenne.* (Publs. Univ. Tehran, 173.) Tehran, 1953. [295]

MAHDAVĪ, Yaḥyā, *Fihrist-i nuskhahā-yi muṣannafāt-i Ibn Sīnā; Bibliographie d'Ibn Sina'* (Publs. Univ. Tehran, 206.) Tehran, 1954. [450]

LAZARD, G., 'Publications iraniennes à l'occasion du millénaire d'Avicenne'. *REI* **22**, 1954, pp. 151–63. [38]

VAJDA, G., 'Bibliographie d'Ibn Sina'. *REI* **22**, 1954, pp. 163–6.

ERGIN, O., *Ibni Sina bibliografyası.* (Üniversite Tıp Tarihi Enstitüsü yayınlar, 51.) Istanbul, 1958.

*Jābir b. Ḥayyān (Geber)*

KRAUS, P., *Jābir ibn Ḥayyān, contribution à l'histoire des idées scientifiques dans l'Islam.* Vol. 1: *Le corpus des écrits jābiriens.* (Mém. présentées à l'Inst. d'Égypte, 44.) Cairo, 1943. [2982]

*-Kindī*

McCARTHY, R. J., *Al-taṣānīf al-mansūba ilā failasūf al-'Arab.* Baghdad, 1962. [444]

RESCHER, N., *Al-Kindi, an annotated bibliography.* Pittsburgh, 1964. [300]

*-Rāzī, Muḥammad b. Zakariyā'*

RUSKA, J., 'Al-Bīrūnī als Quelle für das Leben und die Schriften al-Rāzī's'. *Isis* **5**, 1923, pp. 26–50. [184]

—— 'Die Alchemie al-Rāzī's'. *Der Islam* **22**, 1935, pp. 281–319. [26]

KRAUS, P., *Épitre de Bērūnī contenant le répertoire des ouvrages de Muḥammad b. Zakarīyā al-Rāzī*. Paris, 1936.

With a catalogue of 113 works genuinely by Bīrūnī, and some 25 attributed to him.

*Astronomy. Astrology. Mathematics*

SUTER, H., *Die Mathematiker und Astronomen der Araber und ihre Werke.* (Abh. zur Geschichte der mathematischen Wissenschaften mit Einschluss ihrer Anwendung. X. Heft. Zugleich Supplement zum 45. Jhg. d. *Z. f. Math. u. Physik.*) Leipzig, 1900. [538 writers]; *Nachträge und Berichtungen. Ibid.* 1902 (XIV. Heft, pp. 155–85.) [6]

VERNET GINÉS, J., 'Una bibliografía de la historia de las ciencias matemáticas y astronómicas entre los árabes (años 1942–1956)'. *And.* **21**, 1956, pp. 431–40. [89]

Continued as:

'Bibliografia'. *And.* **23**, 1958, pp. 215–36, 465–95. [710]

CARMODY, F. J., *Arabic astronomical and astrological sciences in Latin translation; a critical bibliography.* Berkeley, &c., 1956. [2000]

*Astrolabes*

CRESWELL, K. A. C., 'A bibliography of Islamic astrolabes'. *Bull. Fac. Arts Cairo* **9**, ii, 1947, pp. 1–15.

'AWWĀD, Gūrgīs, 'Al-asṭurlāb wa-mā ūlaf fīhi min kutub wa-rasā'il fī al-'uṣūr al-islāmiyya'. *Sumer* **13**, 1957, pp. 154–78. [187]

Astrolabes and what has been written about them in Islamic times. Also issued separately by Al-Rabita Press, Baghdad, 1957.

*Entomology*

JAY, D., *Annotated bibliography of locusts in South-western Asia.* Coconut Grove, Fla., 1969. [301]

*Geology*

AVNIMELECH, M. A., *Bibliography of Levant geology, including Cyprus, Hatay, Israel, Jordania, Lebanon, Sinai and Syria.* Jerusalem, 1965. [13,500]

*Medicine. Pharmacology*

ANAWATI, G. C., 'Introduction à l'étude des drogues dans l'antiquité et le Moyen Age'. *MIDEO* **5**, 1958, pp. 345–66. [261]

HAMARNEH, Sami Khalaf, *Bibliography on medicine and pharmacy in medieval Islam* . . . (Veröff. d. Int. Ges. f. Gesch. d. Pharmazie, N.F. 25.) Stuttgart, 1964. [1000]

Works in languages other than Arabic which are not included in this bibliography are listed in the author's *Fihrist makhṭūṭāt al-kutub al-Ẓāhiriyya; al-ṭibb wa-al-ṣaydala* (Damascus, 1969), pp. 26–52. [175]

SPIES, O., 'Beiträge zur medizinisch-pharmazeutischen Bibliographie des Islam'. *Der Islam* **44**, 1968, pp. 138–73. [550]

EBIED, Rifaat Y., *Bibliography of medieval Arabic and Jewish medicine and allied sciences* . . . London, 1971. [1972]

(iv) ART. ARCHAEOLOGY. NUMISMATICS

CRESWELL, K. A. C., *A bibliography of the architecture, arts and crafts of Islam to 1st Jan., 1960.* Cairo, 1961. [15,000]; *Supplement, Jan. 1960–Jan. 1972.* Cairo, 1973. [4500]

*Earlier works by Creswell*

'A bibliography of Islamic astrolabes'. *Bull. Fac. Arts Cairo* **9**, ii, 1947, pp. 1–15.

*A bibliography of Muslim architecture in North Africa (excluding Egypt).* Supplément à Hespéris **41**, 1954, Paris, 1954. [597]

*A bibliography of the Muslim architecture of Egypt.* (Publs. de l'I.F.A.O.; Art islamique, 3.) Cairo, 1955. [657]

'A bibliography of the Muslim architecture of Mesopotamia'. *Sumer* **12**, 1956, pp. 51–65. [183]

'A provisional bibliography of the Muhammadan architecture of India'. *Indian antiquary* **51**, 1922, pp. 81–108, 165–79. Also as reprint, Bombay, 1922.

'A provisional bibliography of the Muslim architecture of Syria and Palestine'. *Jerusalem* (London, 1920–22), pp. 70–94. [300]

'A bibliography of glass and rock crystal in Islam'. *Bull. Fac. Arts Cairo* **14**, i, 1952, pp. 1–28.

*A bibliography of arms and armour in Islam.* (James G. Forlong Fund, 25.) London, 1956. [497]

(with E. Gratzl and R. Ettinghausen) *Bibliographie der islamischen Einbandkunst, 1871 bis 1956.* [282]

*A bibliography of painting in Islam.* (Publs. de l'I.F.A.O.; Art islamique, 1.) Cairo, 1953.

*A provisional bibliography of painting in Muhammadan art.* London, 1922. [200]

*Other works*

RONFLARD, A. and others, 'L'art musulman; essai de bibliographie'. *Arch. maroc.* **3**, 1905, pp. 1–95. [1264]

MIGEON, G., 'Orient musulman (et Extrême-Orient); musées, fouilles, publications. (Chroniques.)' *RAAM* **41**, 1922, pp. 71–4, 301–5; **42**, 1923, pp. 197–200.

'Bibliographia 1933/34'. *AI* **1**, 1934, pp. 239–53. [122]

MARÇAIS, G., 'Sur la constitution de collections de photographies, de clichés de projection, de cartes postales représentant des types de maisons et de costumes indigènes'. *RA* **76**, 1935, pp. 437–40.

MAŃKOWSKI, T., 'A review of Polish publications on Islamic art'. *AI* **3**, 1936, pp. 111–15.

*Annual bibliography of Islamic art and archaeology, India excepted.* Vol. 1, 1937–v.3, 1939. Ed. by L. A. Mayer, with the collaboration of [many other scholars]. 3v. Jerusalem, 1937–39.

ADAMS, H. D., *Selective bibliography of Hispano-Islamic art in Spain and North Africa (711–1492).* New York, 1939. [1200]

'Literature on Islamic art, 1939 to 1945'. *AI* **13–14**, 1949, pp. 150–79; **15–16**, 1951, pp. 151–211.

'L'archéologie musulmane en France de 1939 à 1945'. Par J. Sauvaget.

'Literature on Islamic art published in England during the war, 1939–1945'. By L. Ashton.

'Indian studies in Islamic art published during the War, 1935[*sic*]–1945'. By H. and A. Goetz.
'Publications on Turkish and Islamic arts in Turkey, 1939–1945'. By Tahsin Oz.
'Bibliography of contributions on Islamic art published in Germany and Austria during the War years, 1939–1945'. By D. S. Rice.
'Literature on Islamic art published in Palestine, Iraq and Egypt during the War years'. By L. A. Mayer.
'Bibliography of wartime publications in Scandinavia, 1939–1945'. By C. J. Lamm.
'Bibliography of Spanish Muslim art, 1939–1946'. By L. Torres Balbás.
'Bibliographie des publications de l'art islamique parus en Syrie, 1939–1945'. Par Salahud Din Munajjid.
'A selective bibliography of American publications on Islamic, Parthian, Sasanian and Coptic art, published from 1939–1945'. By H. von Erffa.

PEARSON, J. D. & RICE, D. S., *Islamic art and archaeology. A register of work published in the year 1954(–1955)*. Cambridge, 1956–60. [833]

CAIRO. DĀR AL-KUTUB, *Fine arts subject catalogue; Al-funūn al-jamīla fihris mawḍūʿī*. Cairo, 1962–.

SAMMUT, E., 'A handlist of writings on art in Malta'. *Melita historica* **4**, i, 1964, pp. 34ā52. [300]

NATHANSON, P., *Bibliography of Islamic art*. Montreal, 1970.

*Writings of scholars in the field*

M. Aga-Oglu (1896–1949). *AI* **15–16**, 1951, pp. 268–71. [44]
Mehdi Bahrami (1905–51). *AO* **2**, 1957, pp. 625–7. [32]
Ananda K. Coomaraswamy. *AI* **9**, 1942, pp. 125–42. [494]
K. A. C. Creswell. *AO* **2**, 1957, pp. 509–12. [77]
M. M. D'yakonov. *Ibid.*, pp. 512–19. [63]
Halil Edhem Eldem (1861–1938). *AI* **6**, 1939, pp. 198–201. [40]
E. Herzfeld. *Ibid.* **7**, 1940, pp. 82–92; **15–16**, 1951, pp. 266–7. [203]
E. Kühnel. *AO* **1**, 1954, pp. 195–208; *Festschrift E. Kühnel*, Berlin, 1959, pp. 388–404 [382]; *ZDMG* **115**, 1965, pp. 11–13. [24]
L. A. Mayer. *AO* **4**, 1961, pp. 455–62.
U. Monneret de Villard (1881–1954). *RSO* **30**, 1955, pp. 172–88 [140]; *AO* **2**, 1957, pp. 628–33 [170]; *OM* **34**, 1954, pp. 587–90. [65]
J. Sauvaget. *AO* **1**, 1954, pp. 208–13. [90]
J. V. S. Wilkinson. *Ibid.* **3**, 1959, pp. 259–62. [31]

*Music. Theatre*

ʿAWWĀD, Gūrgīs, 'The more important books published on Arab music'. [In Arabic.] *Hunā Baghdād* **148**, 1956, pp. 16–18.

BEN CHENEB, Saadeddine, 'Le théâtre en Orient aux XIXe et XXe siècles. (Bibliographie)'. *BEA* **3**, 1943, pp. 22–4. [52]

DAGHER, J. A., 'Fann al-tamthīl khilāl qarn; Le théâtre à travers un siècle'. *Al-Mashriq* **42**, 1948, pp. 434–60; **43**, 1949, pp. 118–39.
No more published?

-ʿALŪJĪ, ʿAbd al-Ḥamīd (Abdul Hameed al-Alouchi), *Rāʾid al-musīqā al-ʿarabiyya; Guide to Arabic music.* (Silsilat al-kutub al-ḥadītha, 1.) Baghdad, 1964. [1002]

FARMER, H. G., *The sources of Arabian music; an annotated bibliography of Arabic manuscripts which deal with the theory, practice, and history of Arabian music from the eighth to the seventeenth century.* [New edn.] Leiden, 1965. [353]

ṬUʿMA, Ṣāliḥ Jawād (Salih J. Altoma), *Bibliyūghrāfiyyat al-adab al-ʿarabī al-masraḥī al-ḥadīth (1945–1965); A bibliographical survey of Arabic dramatic literature, 1945–1965.* Baghdad, 1969. [1252]

*Archaeology.* See also *Art*

INOSTRANTZEV, K. A. & SMIRNOV, Y. I., *Materialy dlya bibliografii musulmanskoi arkheologii iz bumag Barona V. G. Tizengauzena.* St. Petersburg, 1906. [4000]

*Numismatics*

ELDEM, Halil Edhem, *Islāmī nūmismatikiçin bir biblioğrafi tecrubesi.* Ankara, 1933.

MAYER, L. A., *Bibliography of Moslem numismatics, India excepted.* 2nd edn. (Oriental Translation Fund, 35.) London, 1954. [2092]

KMIETOWICZ, R., 'Supplements to L. Mayer's *Bibliography of Moslem numismatics*'. *Folia or.* **2**, 1960, pp. 259–75. [201]

LEWICKI, T., 'Nouveaux travaux concernant les trésors de monnaies musulmanes trouvés en Europe orientale et en Asie centrale (1919–1963)'. *JESHO* **8**, 1965, pp. 81–90. [35]

MILES, G. C., 'Oriental numismatics'. (In *Survey of numismatic research 1960–1965.* Bd. 2, *Medieval and Oriental numismatics,* Copenhagen, 1967, pp. 273–89.)

*Military arts*

ZAKY, A. Rahman, 'A preliminary bibliography of medieval Arabic military literature'. *Gladius* **4**, 1965, pp. 107–12. [12]

(v) GEOGRAPHY. TRAVELS, ANTHROPOLOGY

*Geography*

OMAN, G., 'Notizie bibliografiche sul geografo arabo al-Idrīsī (XII secolo) e sulle sue opere'. *AION* N.S. **11**, 1961, pp. 25–61; **12**, 1962, pp. 193–4; **16**, 1966, pp. 101–3; **19**, 1969, pp. 45–55. [133]

ANWARI, M. Iqbal, 'Bibliography of works on al-Masʿūdī'. (In *Al-Masʿudi millenary commem. vol.* 1960, pp. 113–16.) [63]

*Travels*

LEVAL, A., *Voyages en Levant pendant les XVIe, XVIIe et XVIIIe siècles. Essai de bibliographie.* Budapest, 1897. [125]

FIELD, H., *Near East travel bibliography.* Washington, D.C., 1947.
On microfilm.

WEBER, S. H., *Voyages and travels in Greece, the Near East and adjacent regions made previous to the year 1801 . . .* Princeton, 1953. [860]

—— *Voyages and travels in the Near East made during the XIX century . . .* Princeton, 1952. [1206]

Both the above works are described as forming part of a larger catalogue of works on geography, cartography, voyages and travels in the Gennadius Library, Athens.

FEDDEN, R., *English travellers in the Near East.* (British book news; Bibliographical ser. of supplements, 97.) London, 1958. [75]

HACHACHO, M. Ali, 'English travel books about the Arab Near East in the eighteenth century'. *WI* N.S. **9**, 1964, pp. 1–206. [164]

BEVIS, R., *Bibliotheca cisorientalia* [*sic*]. *An annotated check list of early English travel books on the Near and Middle East.* Boston, 1973. [2000]

*Anthropology*

SWEET, L. E., *The central Middle East; a handbook of anthropology and published research on the Nile Valley, the Arab Levant, Southern Mesopotamia, the Arabian peninsula and Israel.* (Hraflex books Mi-001.) New Haven, 1968. [1500]

SWEET, L. E. & O'LEARY, T. J. *eds., Circum-Mediterranean peasantry; introductory bibliographies.* New Haven, 1969. [1500]

(vi) HISTORY

*General*

YOVANOVITCH, V. M., *An English bibliography on the Near Eastern question, 1481–1906.* (Servian Royal Acad., Second series of monuments, 48.) Belgrade, 1909. [1521]

NEW YORK PUBLIC LIBRARY, *List of works in the New York Public Library relating to the Near East question and the Balkan states, including European Turkey and modern Greece.* New York, 1910. [5500]

EARLE, E. M., *Problems of the Near East.* (Carnegie Endowment for International Peace, Bibliogr. ser., 2.) New York, 1924. [400]

RIZZITANO, U., 'Studi de storia islamica in Egitto (1940–1952)'. *OM* **33**, 1953, pp. 442–56. [120]

SAUVAGET, J., *Introduction à l'histoire de l'Orient musulman. Éléments de bibliographie.* (Introduction à l'Islam, 1.) Paris, 1943. [1500]

—— Corrections et supplément (juillet 1946). Edition réfondue et complétée par Cl. Cahen. (Initiation à l'Islam, 1.) Paris, 1961.

—— *Jean Sauvaget's Introduction to the history of the Muslim East; a bibliographical guide, based on the second edition as recast by Cl. Cahen.* Berkeley, 1965. [1500]

PÉRÈS, H., 'Histoire générale des Arabes; références essentielles en arabe, en français, et en anglais'. *BEA* **7**, 1947, pp. 199–201. [38]

GABRIELI, F., 'Studi di storia musulmana, 1940–1950'. *Riv. stor. ital.* **62**, 1950, pp. 98–110. [80]

SPULER, B., *Geschichte der islamischen Länder*. (Hdb. d. Orientalistik, I, 6.) Leiden, 1952–59.
(i) Die Chalifenzeit, Entstehung und Zerfall des islamischen Weltreichs, 1952. [110, pp. 125–8]
(ii) Die Mongolenzeit. 1953. [139]
(iii) Neuzeit. 1959. [550]

—— *The Muslim world, a historical survey*; trans. by F. R. C. Bagley. Leiden, 1960–.
(i) The age of the Caliphs. [339]
(ii) The Mongol empire. [183]
(iii) The last great Muslim empires.
(iv) Modern times. (In the press)

MĀJID, ʻAbd al-Munʻim, *Muqaddima li-dirāsat al-taʼrīkh al-islāmī; taʻrīf bi-maṣādir al-taʼrīkh al-ʻarabī*. Cairo, 1953.
Guide to historical research, with list of sources in Arabic and other languages.

'Select works on Islamic history and culture published in Pakistan and India in 1957–1958(–1959?)'. *JPHS* **7**, 1959, p. 53 [47]; **8**, 1960, pp. 82–3. [69]

ḤASAN, ʻAlī Ibrāhīm, *Istikhdām al-maṣādir wa-ṭuruq al-baḥth fī al-taʼrīkh al-islāmī al-ʻāmm wa-fī al-taʻrīkh al-miṣrī al-wasīṭ; An authentic annotated bibliography and methods of research of Islamic and Egyptian medieval history*. Cairo, 1963.

CAIRO. DĀR AL-KUTUB, *The Arab history; a bibliographical list*. Cairo, 1966. [1900]

BAER, G., *Meqoroth le-toledoth ha-mizraḥ ha-tīkhon he-ḥādāsh*. 2nd edn. Jerusalem, 1964. [200]
Sources for the history of the modern Near East, with comments. In Hebrew.

LEWIS, B., 'Sources for the economic history of the Middle East'. (In M. A. Cook ed., *Studies in the economic history of the Middle East*. London, 1970, pp. 78–92.) [75]

*Historiography*

SHAYYAL, J. D., 'A sketch of Arabic historical works published in Egypt and the Near East during the last five years (1945–1950)'. *Proc. Egypt. Soc. Hist. St.* **1**, 1951, pp. 143–74.

'Mā sāhama bihi al-muʼarrikhūn al-ʻarab min miʼat sana al-akhīra min dirāsat al-taʼrīkh al-ʻarab (title varies)'. *Al-Abḥāth* **12**, 1959, Lists: pp. 139–371, 451–65. [500]
Arab historiography in the last hundred years.

*Historians, general*

WÜSTENFELD, F., *Die Geschichtsschreiber der Araber und ihre Werke*. (Abh. Kgl. Ges. Wis. Göttingen, 28–9.) Göttingen, 1882. [2000]

PONS BOIGUES, F., *Ensayo bio-bibliográfico sobre los historiadores y geógrafos arábigo-españoles*. Madrid, 1898. [303]

*Crusades*

MAYER, H. E., *Bibliographie zur Geschichte der Kreuzzüge*. Hanover, 1960. [5362]

ATIYA, A. S., *The Crusade; historiography and bibliography.* (Companion volume to: *Crusade, commerce and culture.*) Bloomington, &c., 1962. [1500]

*Latin Kingdoms*

LA MONTE, J. L., 'Bibliography of works relating to the fiefs and families of the Latin crusading states in Syria, Palestine and Cyprus'. *BICHS* **7**, 1935, pp. 42–55. [276]

*Ibn Khaldūn*

PÉRÈS, H., 'Ibn Khaldoun: sa vie et son oeuvre (bibliographie)'. *BEA* **3**, 1943, pp. 55–60; complément (H. Pérès and R. Brunschvig), *ibid.* pp. 145–6; complément (M. Chemoul), *ibid.* **5**, 1945, p. 201. [128]

GABRIELI, G., 'Saggio di bibliografia e concordanza della storia d'Ibn Haldūn'. *RSO* **10**, 1923–25, pp. 169–211. [50]

PÉRÈS, H., 'Essai de bibliographie de la vie et oeuvre d'Ibn Haldun'. (In *Studi G. Levi della Vida* II, 1956, pp. 304–29.) [314]

FISCHEL, W. J., 'Selected bibliography of Ibn Khaldûn'. (In Ibn Khaldûn, *The Muqaddimah*, trans. by F. Rosenthal, pp. 485–512; also as reprint, New York, 1958.) [450]

BADAWĪ, 'Abd al-Raḥmān, *Mu'allafāt Ibn Khaldūn*. Cairo, 1967.

*Others*

'ABBĀDĪ, Aḥmad Mukhtār, 'Mu'allafāt Lisān al-Dīn bin al-Khaṭīb fī al-Maghrib (712–776h. = 1212–1274m.)'. *Hespéris* **46**, 1959, pp. 247–53. [25]

(vii) SOCIAL SCIENCES

*General*

UNESCO MIDDLE EAST SCIENCE CO-OPERATION OFFICE, *Middle East social science bibliography; books and articles on the social sciences published in Arab countries of the Middle East in 1955–1960.* Cairo, 1961. [1270]

*Economics*

*Point four. Near East and Africa; a selected bibliography of studies on economically underdeveloped countries.* (Dept. of State, Division of Library and Ref. Services, Bibliogr. 56.) Washington, 1951. [2050]

DOST, H., *Bibliography on land and water utilization in the Middle East.* Wageningen, 1953.

*A cumulation of a selected and annotated bibliography of economic literature on the Arabic-speaking countries of the Middle East 1938–1960.* Cumulated . . . from the bibliography prepared by the Economic Research Institute, American University of Beirut. Boston, 1967. [12,000]

FATEMI, Ali M. S. and others, *Political economy of the Middle East; a computerized guide to the literature.* Akron, 1970. [25,000]

*Near East and South Asia; a bibliography. A bibliography of materials dealing with the Near East and South Asia in the Land Tenure Center Library.* Madison, 1971 [925]; *Supplement*, 1972. [475]

*Education*

*Bibliographie zum Erziehungs- und Bildungswesen in den Ländern des muslimischen Orients*. Hamburg, 1967.

*International relations*

HOWARD, H. N., 'Recent books on international relations'. *MEJ* **3**, 1949, pp. 337–41. [47]

U.S. GOVERNMENT, *Middle East; the strategic hub. A bibliographic survey of literature*. Washington, D.C., 1973.

U.S.A. DEPT. OF STATE LIBRARY DIVISION, *The Suez crisis; a chronological reading list*. Washington, D.C., 1956. [150]

*Political science. Politics*

ZIADEH, N. A., 'Recent Arabic literature on Arabism'. *MEJ* **6**, 1952, pp. 468–73. [18]

DAGHER, J. A., *Al-dīmuqrāṭiyya fī al-maktaba al-miṣriyya; Democracy in Arabic literature*. Beirut, 1959. [450]

CHARNAY, J. P., 'Le marxisme et l'Islam. Essai de bibliographie'. *Arch. soc. rel.* **10**, 1960, pp. 133–46.

QUBAIN, F. I., *Inside the Arab mind. A bibliographic survey of literature in Arabic on Arab nationalism and unity*. Arlington, Va., 1960. [1041]

ULE, W., *Bibliographie zu Fragen des arabischen Sozialismus, des Nationalismus und des Kommunismus unter dem Gesichtspunkt des Islams*. Hamburg, 1967.

LANDAU, J. M., 'Soviet studies on workers' movements in the Middle East'. *MES* **6**, 1970, pp. 346–9. [12]

*Public administration*

TEHRAN-REGIONAL COOPERATION FOR DEVELOPMENT, *Bibliography of publications on public administration and management*. Tehran, 1967. [2488]

*Sociology*

NEWMAN, M. M., *Handbook on racial and nationality backgrounds. Section 1: Peoples of the Near East*. New York, 1922. [300]

BENEDICT, B., *A short annotated bibliography relating to the sociology of Muslim peoples*. Montreal, 1955. [500]

*Arab culture and society in change. A partially annotated bibliography of books and articles in English, French, German and Italian*. Compiled by the staff of CEMAM 'Centre d'etudes pour le monde arabe moderne' . . . St. Joseph's University, Beirut, Lebanon. Beirut, 1973. [4954]

UNIVERSITY OF MICHIGAN LIBRARY, *Women in the Near East; a booklist*. Ann Arbor, 1974. [102]

(viii) LANGUAGE AND LITERATURE

*General*

PÉRÈS, H., *Langue et littérature arabes. Notions essentielles de bibliographie*. Algiers, 1932. [395]

AKBARABADI, Sa'id Ahmad, 'Contribution of India to Arabic language and literature since independence'. (In S. Maqbul Ahmed *ed.*, *India and the Arab world*, 1969, pp. 24–8.) [50]

GUTKOWSKI, J., *Guide to Arabic sources*. Montreal, 1973. [82]

*Language*

PÉRES, H., *L'arabe dialectal algérien et saharien; bibliographie analytique avec un index méthodique. Références arrêtées au 31 décembre 1957 avec Addenda pour 1958*. (Bibl. Inst. Et. Sup. Isl. Alger, 14.) Algiers, 1958. [486]

FERGUSON, C. A., 'Syrian Arabic studies'. *MEJ* **9**, 1955, pp. 187–94.

Includes also Lebanon, Palestine and Jordan.

FERGUSON, C. A. & ECHOLS, J., 'Critical bibliography of spoken Arabic proverb literature'. *J. Amer. Folklore* **65**, 1953, pp. 67–83. [128]

SOBELMAN, H., *Arabic dialect studies; a selected bibliography*. Washington, 1962. [600]

'AWWĀD, Gūrgīs, *Al-mabāḥith al-lughawiyya fī mu'allafāt al-'irāqiyyīn al-muḥdathīn (1800–1965)*. Baghdad, 1965. [750]

GHĀLĪ, Wajdī Rizq, 'Arabic dictionaries; an annotated comprehensive bibliography'. *MIDEO* **10**, 1970, pp. 341–66. [208]

—— *Al-mu'jamāt al-'arabiyya; bibliyūjrāfiya shāmila mashrūḥa; Arabic dictionaries; an annotated comprehensive bibliography*. Cairo, 1971. [707]

*Literature*

PÉRÈS, H., 'La poésie populaire en Afrique du Nord'. *BEA* **1**, 1941, pp. 17–19. [53]

—— 'Pour un corpus des poésies populaires de l'Algérie'. *BEA* **1**, 1941, pp. 111–15. [85]

—— 'Bibliothèque arabe-française'. *BEA* **1**, 1941, pp. 142–6; **2**, 1942, p. 52. [150]

The most representative works of Arabic literature.

PÉRÈS, H., 'La poésie en Occident musulman aux XIe et XIIe siècles de notre ère'. *BEA* **2**, 1942, pp. 12–14. [70]

KHEMIRI, T. & KAMPFFMEYER, G., 'Leaders in contemporary Arabic literature: a book of reference. Pt. 1'. *WI* **9**, ii–iv, 1930, pp. 1–41. [76]

With an appendix of selections in Arabic.

PÉRÈS, H., *Littérature arabe moderne; grands courants. Bibliographie*. Algiers, 1940. [400]

HEYWORTH-DUNNE, J., 'Society and politics in modern Egyptian literature; a bibliographical survey'. *MEJ* **2**, 1948, pp. 306–18. [51]

DAGHER, J. A., *Maṣādir al-dirāsa al-adabiyya; Éléments de bio-bibliographie de la littérature arabe conforme aux programmes officiels d'enseignment. Liban-Syrie, Iraq-Egypte*. 3v. Sidon, 1950–56; Beirut, 1972.

GRANJA, F. de la, 'Los estudios sobre poesia arábigoandaluza'. *And.* **18**, 1953, pp. 224–9. [35]

ABDEL-MEGUID, Abdel-Aziz, 'A survey of story literature in Arabic from before Islam to the middle of the nineteenth century'. *IQ* **1**, 1954, pp. 104–13. [15]

-WAHHĀBĪ, Khaldūn, *Marājiʻ tarājim al-udabāʼ al-ʻarab*. Baghdad, 1956–. in progress?

BENCHEIKH, J. E., 'Petite bibliographie des études littéraires arabes'. *Cahiers alg.* **3**, 1968, pp. 101–24. [84]

ṬUʻMA, Ṣāliḥ Jawād (Salih J. Altoma), *A bibliographical survey of Arabic dramatic literature, 1945–1965*. Baghdad, 1969. [1252]

ALWAN, Mohammed Bakir, 'A bibliography of modern Arabic fiction in English'. *MEJ* **26**, 1972, pp. 195–200.

—— 'A bibliography of modern Arabic poetry in English translation'. *MEJ* **27**, 1973, pp. 373–81.

AWWAD, Mikha'il and others, *Arabic poetical works since the beginning of 1971 until the end of March 1972*. Baghdad, 1972. [186]

LANDAU, J. M., 'Some Soviet works on modern Arabic literature'. *MES* **7**, 1971, pp. 363–5.

*Translations*

DAGHER, J. A., 'Jūta fī al-adab al-ʻarabī al-ḥadīth'. *Al-Kitāb* **2**, 1949, pp. 389–97. [42]

Goethe in modern Arabic literature.

ANAWATI, G. C., 'Les traductions de l'arabe et en arabe de l'UNESCO'. *Rev. du Caire* **18** (no. 185), 1955, pp. 300–20. [15]

BEN CHENEB, Mohammed, 'Contribution bibliographiques à l'étude du mouvement de traduction. Les traductions d'oeuvres étrangères en Égypte de 1953 a 1962'. *AIEO* N.S. **1**, 1964, pp. 59–76. [130]

MOENNIG, R., *Uebersetzungen aus der deutschen Sprache: eine Bibliographie; Fihris mutarjam ʻan al-almaniyya ... al-nuskha al-ʻarabiyya*. Göttingen, 1968. [314]

BADRAN, Husain and others, *Al-thabt al-bibliyūjrāfī li-al-aʻmāl al-mutarjama 1956–1972*. Cairo, 1972. [5000]

Works translated into Arabic and published in Egypt, 1956–72.

*Individual writers*

*Abū Nuwās*

PÉRÈS, H., 'Abû Nuwâs et la poésie bachique'. *BEA* **1**, 1941, pp. 49–51. [90]

*-Fāsī*

-FĀSĪ, Muḥammad, 'Ta'līf Abī Zaid ʻAbd al-Raḥmān bin ʻAbd al-Qādir al-Fāsī kamā dhakarahā ibnuhu Abū ʻAbd Allāh fī kitābihi Al-lu'lu' wa-al-murjān; Une liste complète des oeuvres du grand polygraphe marocain ʻAbd ar-Raḥmān al-Fāsī'. *Hespéris* **29**, 1942, pp. 67–78. [196]

*-Ḥarīrī*

PÉRÈS, H., 'Traductions françaises des Maqâmât (séances ou assemblées) d'al-H'arîrî'. *BEA* **2**, 1942, pp. 151–2. [50]

*Ibn al-Jawzī*

ʻALŪJĪ, ʻAbd al-Ḥamīd, *Mu'allafāt Ibn al-Jawzī*. (Silsilat al-kutub al-ḥadītha, 9.) Baghdad, 1965. [519]

*Ibn al-Muqaffa'*

GABRIELI, F., 'L'opera di Ibn al-Muqaffa''. *RSO* **13**, 1931–32, pp. 197–247; additions, P. Kraus, *ibid.* **14**, 1934, pp. 1–20. [15]

*Ibn Qutayba*

ḤUSEINI, Isḥāq Mūsā, *The life and work of Ibn Qutayba*. (Oriental ser., 21.) Beirut, 1950. [15]

*-Jāḥiẓ*

-SANDŪBĪ, Ḥasan, *Adab al-Jāḥiẓ (baḥth taḥlīlī fī ḥayāt al-Jāḥiẓ wa-sīratihi . . .)*. Cairo, 1250/1921.

PELLAT, Ch., 'Jāḥiẓiana III. Essai d'inventaire de l'oeuvre Jāḥiẓien'. *Arabica* **3**, 1956, pp. 147–80. [193]

*-Ma'arrī*

MARGOLIOUTH, D. S., 'Index librorum Abu'l-'Alae Ma'arrensis'. (In *Centenario della nascita di Michele Amari*, vol. **1**, Palermo, 1910, pp. 217–31. [73]

DAGHER, J. A., *350 maṣdaran fī dirāsat Abī al-'Alā al-Ma'arrī*. Beirut, 1944. [424]

SALEH, Moustapha, 'Abū'l-'Alā al-Ma'arrī, bibliographie critique'. *BEO* **22**, 1969, pp. 133–204; **23**, 1970, pp. 197–309. [588]

*Mayy Ziyāda*

HADDAD, Haroun, 'Les amours de Mayy Ziyada. Étude suivie d'un "Guide bibliographique succinct établi selon les sujets" '. In *Atti 3, Cong. studi arabi e islamici, 1966*, Naples, 1967, pp. 373–84.

*-Shābbī*

BERNARDINI-MAZZINI, A., 'Abu'l -Qāsim al-Šābbī; bibliographie et oeuvres'. *IBLA* **131**, 1973, pp. 97–117.

*-Suyūṭī*

JAUNPURĪ, 'Abd al-Awwal, *Shakl al-mu'tī al-hāfil bi-mu'allafāt al-Suyūṭī*. Jaunpur, 1893. [496]

See also Ḥājjī Khalīfah, *Kashf al-ẓunūn*, below.

*Ṭāhā Ḥusayn*

NALLINO, M., 'Notizie bibliografiche su Ṭāhā Ḥusain . . .'. *OM* **30**, 1950, pp. 83–7. [35]

SCHOONOVER, K., 'Contemporary Egyptian authors. II: Ṭāhā Ḥusayn'. *MW* **45**, 1955, pp. 359–70. [28]

BADAWĪ, 'Abd al-Raḥmān, Mu'allafāt; Travaux de Taha Husain'. (In *Mél. Taha Husain*, Cairo, 1962, pp. 19–28 of Arabic section.) [52]

*Tawfīq al-Ḥakīm*

PAPADOPOULO, A., 'Tewfik el-Hakim et son oeuvre'. *Rev. du Caire* **40** (no. 212), 1958, pp. 257–79. [25]

*Thousand and one nights*

BROCKWAY, D., 'The MacDonald collection of Arabian Nights; a bibliography'. *MW* **61**, 1971, pp. 256–66. [103]

English translations only. Lists of editions and translations in 30 other languages will appear in future issues of *MW*.

## III. INDIVIDUAL COUNTRIES AND AREAS

(i) Arabian Peninsula; (ii) Palestine, Jordan; (iii) Syria. Lebanon; (iv) Iraq; (v) Egypt. U.A.R.; (vi) Sudan; (vii) North Africa; (viii) Libya; (ix) Tunisia; (x) Algeria; (xi) Morocco; (xii) Muslim Spain.

### (i) The Arabian Peninsula

*General*

GAY, J., *Bibliographie des ouvrages relatifs à l'Afrique et à l'Arabie.* San Remo, &c., 1875 (repr. Amsterdam, 1941). [400]

NEW YORK PUBLIC LIBRARY, *List of works relating to Arabia and the Arabs.* New York, 1911. [2000]

LIBRARY OF CONGRESS. REFERENCE DEPARTMENT, DIVISION OF ORIENTALIA, NEAR EASTERN SECTION, *The Arabian Peninsula; a selected, annotated list of periodicals, books and articles in English.* Washington, D.C., 1951 (repr. New York, 1969). [719]

UNITED NATIONS. FOOD AND AGRICULTURE ORGANIZATION, *Bibliography and reading guide to Arabia.* (FAO/32/4/2183) Rome, 1952? [146]

Also issued as:

HEYWORTH-DUNNE, J., *Bibliography and reading guide to Arabia.* (Muslim World ser., 1.) Cairo, 1952. [146]

MOUBARAC, Y., 'Éléments de bibliographie sud-sémitique. (Appendix final: L'Arabie contemporaine)'. *REI* **23**, 1955, pp. 121–76. [180]

HAZARD, H. W., *Bibliography of the Arabian Peninsula.* Prepared by the American Geographical Society for the Human Relations Area Files. New Haven, 1956.

MACRO, E., *Bibliography of the Arabian Peninsula.* Coral Gables, Fla., 1958. [2380]

CAIRO. DAR AL-KUTUB, *A bibliographical list of works about the Arabian Peninsula.* Cairo, 1963. [450]

GEDDES, C. L., *Analytical guide to the bibliographies on the Arabian Peninsula.* (Amer. Inst. of Islamic St., Bibliographic ser., 4.) Denver, 1974. [70]

*Regions*

DE GAURY, G., 'An Arabian bibliography. (A list of some books on that part of Arabia now ruled by Ibn Saud, on the pilgrimage to Mecca and Medina and on closely connected subjects.)' *JRCAS* **31**, 1944, pp. 315–20. [172]

RENTZ, G., 'Literature on the Kingdom of Saudi Arabia'. *MEJ* **4**, 1950, pp. 244–9. [50]

—— 'Recent literature on the Hadramaut'. *MEJ* **5**, 1951, pp. 371–7. [50]

CUCINOTTA, E., 'L'opera degli italiani per la conoscenza del Yemen'. *Riv. coloniale* **21**, 1926, pp. 414–26.
'Gli studi italiani sul Yemen'. *Levante* **52**, 1953, pp. 18–22. [28]

MACRO, E., 'The Yemen'. *RCAJ* **45**, 1958, pp. 43–51. [200]
—— *Bibliography of Yemen with notes on Mocha.* Coral Gables, Fla., 1960. [1894]

U.S. DEPT. OF STATE, *The tribes of Yemen; a list of Western language books and periodical articles containing information on the tribes of Yemen.* (External research paper, 146.) Washington, D.C., 1964. [102]

KABEEL, Soraya, *Selected bibliography on Kuwait and the Arabian Gulf.* (Kuwait Univ. Libraries Dept., Bibliographic ser., 1.) Kuwait, 1969. [1300]
Also an Arabic version. [813]

HOPWOOD, D., 'Some Western studies of Saudi Arabia, Yemen and Aden'. (In D. Hopwood *ed.*, *The Arabian peninsula*, London, 1972, pp. 13–27.)

-ḤABASHĪ, 'Abd Allāh M., *Marājiʿ taʾrīkh al-Yaman.* Damascus, 1972. [2000]
Sources for the history of Yemen.

KING, R. & STEVENS, J. H., *A bibliography of Oman, 1900–1970.* (Centre for Middle Eastern and Islamic Studies, Occasional papers ser., 2.) Durham, 1973. [172]

STEVENS, J. H. & KING, R., *A bibliography of Saudi Arabia.* (Centre for Middle Eastern and Islamic Studies, Occasional papers ser., 3.) Durham, 1973. [1079]

UNESCO REGIONAL OFFICE, BEIRUT, *A bibliography on the Arabian Peninsula.* 1974. [12]
—— *A bibliography on Bahrain.* 1973. [86]
—— *A bibliography of Oman and Muscat.* 1974. [80]
—— *A bibliography on Qatar.* 1974. [56]
—— *A bibliography on United Arab Emirates.* 1974. [200]

### (ii) Palestine. Jordan

RÖHRICHT, R., *Bibliotheca geographica Palestinae. Chronologisches Verzeichniss der auf die Geographie des Heiligen Landes bezüglichen Literatur von 333 bis 1878 und Versuch einer Cartographie.* Berlin, 1890. [4000]; *Verbesserte und vermehrte Neuausgabe mit einem Vorwort* von D. H. K. Amiran. Jerusalem, 1963. [4262]

THOMSEN, P., *Die Palästina-Literatur. Eine internationale Bibliographie in systematischer Ordnung mit Autoren- und Sachregister.*
Band A: Die Literatur der Jahre 1878–1894. Berlin, 1957–60. [12,818]
I. 1895–1904 [Entitled *Systematische Bibliographie der P.L.*] Leipzig, &c., 1908. [2918]
II. 1905–1909. 1911. [3755]
III. 1910–1914. 1916. [3754]
IV. 1915–1924. 1927. [8437]
V. 1925–1934. 1936. 1938. [11,252]
VI. 1935–1939. 1956. [9189]
VII. 1940–1945. 1969–72. [11,506]

KONIKOFF, A., *Select bibliography of Eastern Palestine.* Jerusalem, 1946. [300]

HUREWITZ, J. C., 'Recent books on the problem of Palestine'. *MEJ* **3**, 1949, pp. 86–91. [34]

'Merely a sampling of books in English published since 1937.'

GRASSMUCK, G., 'Selected material on Iraq and Jordan; the development of political documentation'. *Amer. pol. sci. rev.* **51**, 1957, pp. 1067–90. [172]

PATAI, R., *Jordan, Lebanon and Syria; an annotated bibliography.* New Haven, 1957. [1605]

CAIRO, DĀR AL-KUTUB, *A bibliographical list of works about Palestine and Jordan.* 2nd edn. (Bibliographical lists of the Arab world, 2.) Cairo, 1964. [1324]

ḤASAN, 'Abd al-Jalīl, 'List of Arabic books on the Palestine problem and Israel, 1940–1964'. *Hamizrah hehadash* (*The New East*) **15**, 1965, pp. 316–20. [200]

In Hebrew.

'ALĪ, 'Abd al-Raḥīm Muḥammad, *Thabt al-maṣādir 'an Filasṭīn.* Najaf, 1966. [781]

Sources on Palestine.

CAIRO. 'AYN SHAMS UNIVERSITY. MARKAZ BUḤŪTH AL-SHARQ AL-AWSAṬ, *Filasṭīn; qā'ima bibliyūjrāfiyya bi-al-kutub wa-al-marāji' al-'arabiyya.* Vol. **1**. Cairo, 1968. [766]

Bibliographical list of books and sources in Arabic on Palestine.

OFFICE OF RESEARCH AND PUBLICATIONS, UNIVERSITY CHRISTIAN CENTER, 'An annotated bibliography on the Palestine problem and Israel'. *Middle East Research Association* 1969–1970, ff. 86–93. [27]

OLIVER, C. E., 'A selected and annotated bibliography on the Palestine refugees'. *Middle East Research Association* 1969–1970, ff. 94–104. [36]

OLIVER, C. E. & KAPENGA, P., 'An annotated bibliography on the Palestine resistance movement'. *Middle East Research Association* 1969–1970, ff. 105–9. [11]

-AKHRAS, Mahmud, *Palestine-Jordan bibliography, 1900–1970.* Amman, 1972. [2740]

GEDDES, C. L., *The Arab-Israeli dispute; an annotated bibliography of bibliographies.* (American Inst. of Islamic St., Bibliographic ser., 7.) Denver, 1973. [26]

KHALIDI, Walid & KHADDURI, J. *eds., Palestine and the Arab-Israeli conflict; an annotated bibliography.* Beirut, &c., 1974. [4580]

HUSSAINI, Hatem I., *The Arab-Israeli conflict; an annotated bibliography.* (Assoc. of Arab American Univ. Graduates Inc.; Bibliographic ser., 1.) Detroit, 1975.

### (iii) SYRIA. LEBANON (*see also* PALESTINE. JORDAN)

MASSON, P., *Éléments d'une bibliographie français de la Syrie* (*géographie, ethnographie, histoire, archéologie, langues, littératures, religions*). Marseilles, 1919. [4534]

Includes Palestine and Jordan. Continued by J. A. Dagher, *L'Orient dans la littérature française d'après-guerre, 1919–1933*, Beirut, 1937.

NASSIF, A., 'Bibliographie juridique libanaise'. *Ann. Fac. Droit Beyrouth* 1958, pp. 57. [800]

CAIRO DĀR AL-KUTUB, *A bibliographical list of works about Syria.* 2nd edn. (Bibliographical lists of the Arab world, 3.) Cairo, 1965. [965]

DAGHER, J. A., *Les sources arabes de l'histoire du Liban. Manuel des études libanaises.* Beirut, 1972. [5157]

### (iv) Iraq

'AWWĀD, Gūrgīs, 'Bibliography of excavations in Iraq'.
1939–1946. *Sumer* **3**, 1947, pp. 30–5. [62]
1947–1951. *Ibid.* **8**, 1952, pp. 90–100. [166]
1952–1954. *Ibid.* **11**, 1955, pp. 61–70. [175]
1955–1959. *Ibid.* **16**, 1960, pp. 48–74. [650]

—— 'Mā ṭubi'a 'an buldān al-'Irāq bi-al-lugha al-'arabiyya'. *Sumer* **9**, 1953, Arabic section, pp. 63–97, 295–316; **10**, 1954, pp. 40–72. [1500]

Arabic publications on the historical geography of Iraq.

BOXER, R., *A bibliography of material on the development of modern Iraq.* Baghdad, 1953. [800]

ALLOUSE, Bashir, 'A bibliography of the invertebrate fauna of Iraq and the neighbouring countries'. *Publ. Iraq Nat. Hist. Museum* **8**, pp. 1–46. Also apparently in an Arabic version, Baghdad, 1956.

—— *A bibliography of the vertebrate fauna of Iraq and neighbouring countries.* 3v. Baghdad? 1954–55.

*See also* Palestine, Jordan: Grassmuck (1957).

KHAN, Rasheeduddin, 'Arabic source material for the political history of modern Iraq'. *Int. studies* **2**, 1961, pp. 298–316. [150]

Includes sections on important newspapers and journals and a list of libraries and private collections.

'AWWĀD, Gūrgīs & 'ALOUCHI, Abdul-Hameed, *A bibliography of Baghdad; Jamharat al-marāji' al-baghdādiyya.* Baghdad, 1962. [6425]

HĀDĪ (Muḥammad) al-Amīnī & 'ALĪ, 'Abd al-Raḥīm M., *Maṣādir al-dirāsa 'an al-Najaf wa-al-shaykh al-Ṭūsī.* Najaf, 1963.

Sources for the study of Najaf and Shaykh al-Ṭūsī.

CAIRO. DĀR AL-KUTUB, *A bibliographical list of works about Syria.* 2nd edn. (Bibliographical lists of the Arab world, 5.) Cairo, 1964. [649]

### (v) Egypt. U.A.R.

*General*

MAPLE, H. L., *A bibliography of Egypt consisting of works printed before A.D. 1801.* Pietermaritzburg, 1952. [750]

LIBRARY OF CONGRESS, *Select list of references on Egypt, 525 B.C. to the present time.* Washington, D.C., 1908. [36]

IBRAHIM HILMY, Prince, *The literature of Egypt and the Soudan from the earliest times to the year 1885 inclusive. A bibliography comprising printed books, periodical writings, and papers of learned societies; maps and charts; ancient papyri, manuscripts, drawings, etc. (with appendix of additional works to May, 1887).* 2v. London, 1886–87. [17,500]

LICHTENBERGER, M., *Écrivains français en Égypte contemporaine (de 1870 à nos jours)*. Paris, 1934.

CONOVER, H. F., *Egypt and the Anglo-Egyptian Sudan; a selective background reading*. Washington, D.C., 1952. [83]

GOBY, J. E., *Bibliographies de savants et d'érudits ayant publié sur les questions relatives à l'Égypte*. Ismailia, 1950. [200]

GEDDES, C. L., *An analytical guide to the bibliographies on modern Egypt and the Sudan*. (American Inst. of Islamic St., Bibliographic ser., 2.) Denver, 1972. [135]

ATIYAH, G. N., *Egypt from the Arab conquest to the present; a basic bibliography*. N.pl., n.d. [493]

*Geography. Topography*

GAUTHIER, H. (& MUNIER, H.), 'Bulletin bibliographique (from 1926: Bibliographie géographique de l'Égypte)'. *Bull. Soc. Géog. Égypte* **14–21**, 1926–43.

Covers the period 1925–42; it was preceded for 1919–20 onwards by a 'Bulletin bibliographique' of writings on the whole of Africa.

GAUTHIER, H., 'Bibliographie des études de géographie historique égyptienne'. *Bull. Soc. Géog. Égypte* **9**, 1920, pp. 209–81. [1931]

LORIN, H., *Bibliographie géographique de l'Égypte*. Publié sous la direction de H. Lorin. 2v. Cairo, 1938. [9049]

ZAKI, Abdel Rahman, *A bibliography of the literature of the city of Cairo*. Cairo, 1964. [1000]

*Travel*

KEIMER, L., 'Les voyageurs de langue allemande en Égypte entre 1800 et 1850 ainsi que leurs relations de voyage. Essai bibliographique'. *Cahiers hist. eg.* **5**, 1953, pp. 1–28. [40]

*Suez*

GOBY, J. E., 'Les bibliographies égyptiennes de l'Isthme de Suez'. *BSEHGIS* **1**, 1947, pp. 85–7.

—— 'Matériaux pour servir à l'établissement d'une bibliographie de l'Isthme de Suez'. *SEHG Note d'information* **12**, 1948, pp. 17–19; **13**, 1948, pp. 26–34; **14**, 1948, pp. 44–51.

—— 'Bibliographie méthodique de l'Isthme de Suez et des régions voisines pour les années 1939 a 1950'. *BSEHGIS* **4**, 1951–52, pp. 191–219. [227]

GOBY, J. E., 'Bibliographie critique du Canal de Suez'. *BSEHGIS* **5**, 1953–54, pp. 237–56.

FONTAINE, A. L., *Monographie cartographique de l'Isthme de Suez, de la péninsule du Sinaï, du nord de la Chaîne arabique, suivie d'un catalogue raisonné sur les cartes de ces regions*. (SEHGIS, Mémoires, 2.) Cairo, 1955. [300]

*People*

COULT, L. H. jnr. & DURZI, Karim, *An annotated research bibliography of studies in Arabic, English and French of the fellah of the Egyptian Nile, 1798–1955*. Coral Gables, Fla., 1958.

'Éléments de bibliographie sur la démographie égyptienne'. *Proche Orient, études économiques* (*Ann. Fac. Droit Beyrouth*) **51**, 1967, pp. 113–21. [150]

*History*

GUÉMARD, G., 'Histoire et bibliographie critique de la Commission des Sciences et Arts et de l'Institut d'Egypte'. Cairo, 1936. He had earlier written 'Essai de bibliographie critique . . .'. *BIE* **6**, 1923–24, pp. 135–57. [50]; 'Supplement'. *BIE* **8**, 1925–26, pp. 221–49. [50]

PRATT, I. M., *Modern Egypt; a list of references to material in the New York Public Library*. New York, 1929. [6000]

'Littérature et colonialisme; l'Égypte dans la littérature française'. *Cahiers contre-enseignement française* 6:20, March 1936.

MUNIER, H., *Tables de la Description de l'Egypte, suivies d'une bibliographie sur l'expédition française de Bonaparte*. Cairo, 1943. [631]

ḤASAN, Muḥammad 'Abd al-Ghanī, 'Bayn al-suṭūr (Ibrāhīm Bāshā)'. *Al-Kitāb* **3**, 1948, pp. 617–29. [30]

—— Muḥammad 'Alī fī 'ālam al-Kutub'. *Al-Kitāb* **4**, 1949, pp. 618–34. [100]

TAGHER, J., 'Bibliographie analytique et critique des publications françaises et anglaises relatives à l'histoire de la règne de Mohammad Ali'. *Cahiers hist. ég.* **2**, 1949, pp. 128–235. [850]

GOBY, J., 'De l'établissement d'une bibliographie de l'histoire de l'Égypte'. *Cahiers hist. ég.* **1**, 1949, pp. 283–94.

McCLANAHAN, G. V., 'Recent books on contemporary Egypt'. *MEJ* **5**, 1951, pp. 101–7. [**31**]

UNITED NATIONS. FOOD AND AGRICULTURE ORGANIZATION, *Select bibliography on modern Egypt*. (FAO/52/4/1285) [Washington, D.C., 1952?] [167]

Also issued as:

HEYWORTH-DUNNE, G., *Select bibliography on modern Egypt*. (The Muslim world ser., 2.) Cairo, 1952. [167]

TIGNOR, R. L., 'Some materials for a history of the 'Arābī revolution. A bibliographical survey'. *MEJ* **16**, 1962, pp. 239–48. [125]

HOPWOOD, D., 'Some Western views of the Egyptian revolution'. (In P. J. Vatikiotis *ed.*, *Egypt since the revolution*, London, 1968, pp. 181–95.)

GEDDES, C. L., *An analytical guide to the bibliographies on modern Egypt and the Sudan*. (American Inst. of Islamic St., Bibliographic ser., 2.) Denver, 1972. [135]

*Social sciences*

MAUNIER, R., *Bibliographie économique, juridique et sociale de l'Égypte moderne (1798–1916)*. (Trav. spéc. de la Soc. Sultanieh d'Écon. Pol., de Statistique et de Législation, 1.) Cairo, 1918. [6695]

—— 'Supplément (addenda et corrigenda), par G. Guémard'. *Égypte contemp.* **16**, 1925, pp. 240–60.

SALAMA, Ibrahim, *Bibliographie analytique et critique touchant la question de l'enseignement en Égypte depuis la période des Mameluks jusqu'à nos jours*. Cairo, 1938.

ZINK, H., 'Material for a comparative study of local government'. *Amer. pol. sci. rev.* **50**, 1956, pp. 1120–3. [40]

HASHAD, M. & AFIFI, M., *Guide to selected references on education and man-power planning and related subjects.* (Institute of National Planning Memo, 709.) Cairo, 1966.

EWIEDA, M., *Selected bibliography from foreign and Arabic periodicals dealing with agricultural development and related fields.* (Institute of National Planning Memo, 734.) Cairo, 1967.

—— *Classified index to articles of the periodicals for the years 1965 and 1966.* (Institute of National Planning Memo, 824.) Cairo, 1968.

*Science*

SHERBORN, C. D., *Bibliography of scientific and technical literature relating to Egypt, 1800–1900.* Compiled for the Survey Dept. Prelim. edn. Cairo, 1910. [3500]

KELDANI, Elias Habib, *A bibliography of geology and related sciences concerning Egypt, up to the end of 1939.* Cairo, 1941. [2939]

(vi) SUDAN (*see also* EGYPT)

*General*

HILL, R. L., *A bibliography of the Anglo-Egyptian Sudan from the earliest times to 1937.* London, 1939. [4500]

—— 'Recent Italian literature concerning the Sudan'. *SNR* **22**, 1939, pp. 167–9. [16]

McCLANAHAN, G. V., 'Postwar books on the Anglo-Egyptian Sudan'. *MEJ* **6**, 1952, pp. 341–6. [32]

INTERNATIONAL AFRICAN INSTITUTE, *Select annotated bibliography of tropical Africa,* compiled . . . under the direction of D. Forde. New York, 1956. [113]

UNIVERSITY OF KHARTOUM LIBRARY, *A bibliographical introduction to the Sudan. Part I: European languages,* comp. by Shaké Keshkekian. Khartoum, 1957.

JONES, R., *North-East Africa; general, ethnography, sociology, linguistics.* London, 1959. [900]

CAIRO. DĀR AL-KUTUB, *A bibliography of works about Sudan; Qā'ima bi-al-kutub wa-al-marāji' 'an al-Sūdān.* 2nd edn. (Arab world bibliographic ser., 6.) Cairo, 1961. [500]

-NASRI, Abdel Rahman, *A bibliography of the Sudan 1938–1958.* London, 1962. [2763]

Based on the bibliographies contained in *SNR* **29–36**, 1948–55.

'Sudan bibliography 1959–1963'. *SNR* **46**, 1965, pp. 130–66. [896]

*Theses on the Sudan and by Sudanese accepted for higher degrees,* comp. by Maymouna Mirghani Hamza, assisted by the library staff. Khartoum, 1966 [263]; 2nd edn. 1971.

*Theses accepted for higher degrees by the University of Khartoum to September, 1966.* (Univ. Khartoum Library Publs., 1.) Khartoum, 1966. [47]

DAGHER, J. A., *Al-uṣūl al-'arabiyya li-al-dirāsa al-sūdāniyya*. Beirut, 1968. Arabic sources for Sudanese studies.

UNIVERSITY OF KHARTOUM LIBRARY, *The classified catalogue of the Sudan collections in the University of Khartoum Library*. Khartoum, 1971. [5114]

GEDDES, C. L., *An analytical guide to the bibliographies on modern Egypt and the Sudan*. (American Inst. of Islamic St., bibliographic ser., 2.) Denver, 1972.

NŪR, Qāsim 'Uthmān, *Maṣādir al-dirāsāt al-sūdāniyya bi-al-majallāt wa-al-dawriyyāt al-sūdāniyya 1931–1967*. Khartoum, 1970. [8177]

*Subjects*

SCHÖTTER, H. von, 'Zur Bibliographie des Sudan'. (In W. Braumüller, *Tagebuchblätter einer Jagdreise weiland des Prinzen Georg Wilhelm . . . von Khartoum an den Oberen Nil*, Vienna, 1915, pp. 390–412.)

SUDAN GOVERNMENT SCIENTIFIC RESEARCH COMMITTEE, *Bibliography of scientific and technical literature relating to the Anglo-Egyptian Sudan published subsequently to 1900*. Khartoum, 1922. [500]

EVANS-PRITCHARD, E. E., 'Bibliographical note on the ethnology of the Southern Sudan'. *Africa* **13**, 1940, pp. 62–7. [17]

ANDREW, G., 'Sources of information on the geology of the Anglo-Egyptian Sudan'. *Bull. Geol. Survey Dept. Khartoum* **3**, 1945, 36 pp.

KNIGHT, R. L. & BOYNS, B. M., *Agricultural science in the Sudan; a bibliography with abstracts*. Arbroath, 1950. [969]

SMIRNOV, S. R., 'Obzor literatury po Sudanu, vyshedshey posle 1945 goda'. *Sov. etn.* 1952(2), pp. 194–200. [12]

HILL, R. L., 'The Gordon literature'. *Durham Univ. J.* **47**, 1955, pp. 97–103.

LEBON, J. H., 'Recent contributions to the geography of the Sudan'. *Geog. rev.* **46**, 1956, pp. 246–52. [33]

SUDAN SURVEY DEPT., *Catalogue of topographical maps*. Khartoum, 1956. [137]

HOLT, P. M., 'The source materials of the Sudanese Mahdia'. *St. Antony's papers* **4** (Middle Eastern affairs, 1), 1958, pp. 107–8.

TWINING, W. and others, 'Bibliography of Sudan law'. *SLJR* **5**, 1960, pp. 313–35. [341]

PETER McLOUGHLIN ASSOCIATES, *Research for agricultural development in Northern Sudan to 1967; a classified inventory and analysis*. New Brunswick, 1971. [1073]

GARSSE, Y. van, *Ethnological and anthropological literature on the three Southern Sudan provinces; Upper Nile, Bahr el Ghazal, Equatoria*. Sint Nicklaas Waas, 1972. [1072]

### (vii) North Africa

*General*

GUILBERT, A., *De la colonisation du Nord de l'Afrique. Nécessité d'une association nationale pour l'exploitation agricole et industrielle de l'Algérie*. Paris, 1839; 2nd edn. 1841.

Pp. 497–551: 'Liste bibliographique des auteurs qui ont écrit sur l'Afrique septentrionale depuis la conquête de cette contrée par les Arabes'.

JACQUETON, G., 'Chronique africaine. Histoire moderne contemporaine'. *RA* **37**, 1893, pp. 247–87. [250]

Publications of 1891–2.

DOUTTÉ, E., *Bulletin bibliographique de l'Islam maghrébin . . . i. 1897–1er semestre 1898.* (Bull. Soc. Géog. Oran 79, janvier–mars 1899.)

KAMPFFMEYER, G., 'Eine alte Liste arabischer Werke zur Geschichte Spaniens und Nordwestafrikas'. *MSOS* 2. Abt., **9**, 1906, pp. 74–110. [153]

ROUARD DE CARD, E., *Livres français des XVIIe et XVIIIe siècles concernant les états barbaresques. Régence d'Alger, de Tunis, de Tripoli et Empire du Maroc.* Paris, 1911. [60]; *Supplément.* 1917. [15]

—— *Bibliographie des ouvrages relatifs à la Barbarie aux XVIIe et XVIIIe siècles.* Paris, 1913.

MONCHICOURT, Ch., 'Essai bibliographique sur les plans imprimés de Tripoli, Djerba et Tunis-Goulette au XVIe siècle et note sur un plan d'Alger'. *RA* **66**, 1925, pp. 385–418. [50]

ALBERTINI, E., 'Bulletin des antiquités africaines (1925–1926)'. *RA* **68**, 1927, pp. 274–302. [250]

MINISTÈRE DE LA GUERRE. ÉTAT-MAJOR DE L'ARMÉE, SERVICE HISTORIQUE, *L'Afrique française du Nord. Bibliographie militaire des ouvrages français ou traduits en français des articles des principales revues françaises relatifs à l'Algérie, à la Tunisie et au Maroc de 1830 à 1926.* 4v. Paris, 1930–35 (repr. 1972). [9446]

SLADE, W. A., *France and Italy in North Africa; a bibliographical list.* Washington, D.C., 1930. [306]

BORDEAUX UNIV. INSTITUT D'ÉTUDES ET DE DOCUMENTATION ÉCONOMIQUES ET SOCIALES, *Afrique du Nord (1928–1930).* (Bulletin bibliographique, sér. C, no. 11.) Bordeaux, 1931.

CONOVER, H. F., *French North Africa (Algeria, Morocco, Tunis); a bibliographical list.* Washington, D.C., 1942. [725]

GRAY, R. A., *Annotated list of inexpensive publications on North Africa and the Middle and Near East.* Washington, D.C., 1943. [67]

COURTOIS, Chr., 'Bibliographie de l'histoire de l'Afrique du Nord des origines à la fin du Moyen Âge. (Ouvrages parus de 1939 a 1946 inclus.)'. *RA* **91**, 1947, pp. 278–300. [400]

Also published in *Rev. hist.* **198**, 1947, pp. 228–49 and in *Documents algériens* **33**, 1948.

—— '(Ouvrages parus de 1946 a 1951 inclus.)'. *RA* **96**, 1952, pp. 416–48. [600]

Also published as: *Documents algériens* 1953, pp. 142–63. Continued in the annual bibliography published in *Libyca.*

POTS, A., 'Étude critique des revues et périodiques de langue française traitant des questions nord-africaines et islamiques'. *Rev. tunisienne* 3e sér., 1948, pp. 191–200.

'Références', *IBLA* **11**, 1948–.

LEMAIRE, E. T., *Répertoire de documentation nord-africaine.* Constantine, 1954. [1300]; *Supplément,* par G. Quincy. 2v. 1956–57. [1300]

RIVLIN, B., 'A selective survey of the literature in the social sciences and related fields on modern North Africa'. *Amer. pol. sci. rev.* **48**, 1954, pp. 826–48. [218]

TILLET, M. L. and others, 'Éléments bibliographiques sur les problèmes d'enseignement et d'éducation en Afrique du Nord'. *IBLA* **17**, 1954, pp. 285–308. [300]

*Pour une bibliothèque 'nord-africaine'. Études sociales nord-africaines.* (Cahiers nord-africains, 47.) Paris, 1955. [300]

CONOVER, H. F., *North and Northeast Africa; a selected, annotated list of writings, 1951–1957.* Washington, D.C., 1957. [346]

ANAWATI, G. C., 'Textos árabes sobre España y el Magrib publicados en Egipto (1957)'. *And.* **23**, 1958, pp. 381–90. [8]

PICARD, G. C., *Archaeology (1945–1955)*: IV–V, *North Africa and Italy.* New York, 1958. [1782]

CAIRO. DĀR AL-KUTUB, *A bibliographical list of works about al-Maghrib; Qā'ima bi-al-kutub wa-al-marāji' 'an al-Maghrib.* (Bibliographical lists of the Arab world . . . 7.) Cairo, 1961. [550]

BRUNSCHVIG, H., 'Histoire de l'Afrique du Nord. (Bulletin historique.)' *Rev. hist.* **232**, 1964, pp. 191–208.

GANIAGE, J. & MARTEL, A., 'Chronique de l'histoire d'Outre-Mer; l'Afrique du Nord'. *Rev. franç. hist. Outre-Mer* **52**, 1965, pp. 127–33. [20]

ARNAUD, J. and others, *Bibliographie de la littérature nord-africaine d'expression française 1945–1962.* Publié sous la direction de A. Memmi. Paris, 1965. [527]

'Bibliographie Maghreb-Sahara. Anthropologie, préhistoire, ethnographie'. *Libyca* **9–10**, 1961–62, pp. 253–69; **11**, 1963, pp. 247–60; **12**, 1964, pp. 351–60. [109]

IBN SŪDA, 'Abd al-Salām b. 'Abd al-Qādir, *Dalīl mu'arrikh al-Maghrib al-Aqṣā.* 2nd edn. 2v. Casablanca, 1960. [2363]

'Bibliographie alphabétique. Bibliographie systématique'. *Annuaire Afr. Nord* 1962–.

MASSIGNON, G., 'Bibliographie des recueils de contes traditionnels du Maghreb (Maroc, Algérie, Tunisie)'. *Fabula* **4**, i–ii, 1961, pp. 111–29. [260]

ATTAL, R., 'A bibliography of publications concerning North African Jewry'. *Sefunot* **5**, 1961, pp. 467–508. [940]

In Hebrew.

JULIEN, Ch. A., *Histoire de l'Afrique du Nord.* 2nd edn. rev. Paris, 1951–52.
(i) Des origines à la conquête arabe (647 ap. J.-C.), ed. Chr. Courtois.
(ii) De la conquête arabe à la prise d'Alger par les Français (1830), ed. R. le Tourneau.
(iii) De la prise d'Alger à 1954.

An English translation of part ii, by John Petrie, ed. by C. C. Stewart, appeared in 1970; this continues the bibliography, by the editor, on pp. 351–421. [1500]

*Maghreb: documents Algérie, Maroc, Tunisie.* Paris, 1964–.

'Select bibliography on modern North Africa'. (In L. C. Brown *ed.*, *State and society in independent North Africa*, Washington, D.C., 1966, pp. 317–20.) [65]

MARTEL, A., 'État de recherches historiques françaises sur le Maghreb contemporain'. (In *Atti 3. Cong. studi arabi e islamici, 1966*, Naples, 1967, pp. 493–509.) [35]

MÖLLER, T. & WICHMANN, U., 'Ausgewählte neuere Literatur zur Strategie und Politik im Maghreb'. *Afrika Spectrum* 3/70, pp. 58–65. [192]

MARTEL, A., 'Le Maghreb, Méditerranée et Méditerranéens. Chronique bibliographique'. *Rev. franç. hist. Outre-Mer* **57**, 1970, pp. 91–132. [27]

AMAN, M. M., 'Bibliographical activities of the Arab countries of North Africa'. *Int. libr. rev.* **2**, 1970, pp. 263–73.

HOWARD, H. N. and others, *Middle East and North Africa; a bibliography for undergraduate libraries.* (Foreign Area Materials Center occasional publs., 14.) Williamsport, 1971. [1192]

TANGIER. CAFRAD, *Bibliography on Magheb.* Tangier, 1971. [119]

*Sahara*

FUNCK-BRENTANO, Chr., 'Bibliographie du Sahara occidental'. *Hespéris* **11**, 1930, pp. 203–96. [1034]

MONOD, Th., 'Notes bibliographiques sur le Sahara occidental'. *J. Soc. Afr.* **3**, 1933, pp. 129–96; **5**, 1935, pp. 117–24. [96]

Includes: *Supplément* to the bibliography of Funck-Brentano.

'Liste des travaux publiés sur le Sahara français au cours des années 1942 et 1943'. *Trav. Inst. Rech. Sahar.* **3**, 1945, pp. 193–98. [53]

BLAUDIN DE THÉ, B., *Essai de bibliographie du Sahara français et des régions avoisinantes.* 2nd edn. Paris, 1960. [9301]

Part I is a new edition in part of *Les territoires du Sud de l'Algérie*, 3e partie: *Essai de bibliographie* (Algiers, 1930 [2372]), but omitting the list of maps [800] compiled by M. Flotte de Roquevaire.

Part II is a new edition corrected, revised and augmented, of three bibliographies published officially:

(i) 'Essai de bibliographie', in *Exposé de la situation générale des territoires du Sud de l'Algérie de 1930 à 1946* (1947, pp. 485–536), by chef de bataillon Leneveu. [745]

(ii) 'Essai de bibliographie', in *Les territoires du Sud de l'Algérie. Compte rendu de l'oeuvre accomplie de 1947 à 1952* (1953, pp. 417–572), by Blaudin de Thé. [3104]

(iii) *Contribution à la bibliographie du Sahara* (*1953–57*). Algiers, 1958. [1141]

The bibliographies of Funck-Brentano and Monod were 'exploited' for this work, all titles therein being included with the exception of those on ichthyology and fishing.

*Berbers*

BEGUINOT, F., 'Gli studi berberi dal 1919 al maggio 1922'. *RSO* **9**, 1921–23, pp. 382–408. [127]

BOUSQUET, G. H. & MARCY, G., 'Bibliographie des droits berbères'. *Hespéris* **39**, 1952, pp. 508–13. [120]

APPLEGATE, J. R., 'Berber studies, I: Shilha'. *MEJ* **11**, 1957, pp. 324–7. [45]

GALAND, L., 'Les études de linguistique berbère de 1954 à 1956'. *Annuaire Afr. Nord* **4**, 1965, pp. 743–65. [310]
*Ibid.* **5**, 1966, pp. 813–32; **6**, 1967, pp. 1035–43; **7**, 1968, pp. 865–73; **8**, 1969, pp. 1073–81; **9**, 1970, pp. 907–19; **10**, 1971, pp. 927–42; **11**, 1972, pp. 857–70; **12**, 1973, pp. 1045–72.

WILLMS, A., 'Auswahlbibliographie des berberologischen Schrifttums, mit Besitznachweisen für drei hamburgische Bibliotheken'. *Afrika u. Übersee* **50**, 1967, pp. 64–128. [316]

*Spanish Africa*

FONTAN LOBÉ, J., *Bibliografía colonial; contribución a un índice de publicaciones africanas*. Madrid, 1946. [16,903]

RICARD, R., 'Bulletin de bibliographie hispano-africaine (– espagnole et portugaise). Publications parues en 1938, 1939 et 1940'. *Hespéris* **28**, 1941, pp. 101–8; **29**, 1942, pp. 91–4. [56]

HELLMAN, F. S., *A list of references on Spanish colonies in Africa*. Washington, D.C., 1942. [261]

RISHWORTH, S. K., *Spanish-speaking Africa; a guide to official publications*. Washington, D.C., 1973. [640]

ALTAMIRA, R., *Bibliographie d'histoire coloniale (1900–1930); Espagne*. Paris, 1932. [900]

GONZALEZ ECHEGARAY, C., 'XXV años de bibliografía africana'. *AIEA* **20**, no. 79, 1966, pp. 19–44. [100]

*Italian Africa*

VARLEY, D. H., *A bibliography of Italian colonization in Africa*. London, 1936 (repr. 1970). [2000]

ITALY. ISTITUTO FASCISTA, *Bibliografia dell'Istituto Fascista dell'Africa Italiana*. Rome, 1939. [2000]

FULLER, G. H., *A list of references on the Italian colonies in Africa (Libya, Eritrea, Italian Somaliland and Ethiopia)*. Washington, D.C., 1942. [454]
*Additional references (Cyrenaica, Tripolitania and Eritrea)*. 1947. [117]

ZANUTTO, S., *Pubblicazioni edite dall'amministrazione coloniale o sotto i suoi auspici, 1882–1937*. Rome, 1938. [1500]

### (viii) Libya

*Lists of biographies*

BONO, F., 'Bibliografie italiane della Libia'. *Libia* **51**, 1953, pp. 119–21. [32]
A more complete list was published in *L'Italia che scrive* **35**, nos. 2–3, 1952.

WARD, P., *A survey of Libyan bibliographical resources; Maṣādir al-kutub fī Lībiya*. 2nd edn. Tripoli, 1965.
Gives details of libraries, bibliographies and a Libyan press guide.

*General*

PLAYFAIR, Sir R. L., 'The bibliography of the Barbary States, part 1: Tripoli and the Cyrenaica'. *RGS supplementary papers* **2**, 1889, pp. 559–614 (repr. 1971). [641]

MINUTELLI, F., *Bibliografia della Libia. Catalogo alfabetico e metodico di tutte pubblicazioni . . . esistenti sino a tutto il 1902 sulla Tripolitania, la Cirenaica, il Fezzan e le confinanti regioni del Deserto.* Turin, 1903. [1269]

ITALY. MINISTERIO DI AGRICOLTURA, *Primo saggio di una bibliografia economica sulla Tripolitania e Cirenaica dal 1902 al 1912.* Rome, 1912. [750]

CECCHERINI, U., *Bibliografia della Libia (in continuazione alla 'Bibliografia della Libia' di F. Minutelli).* Rome, 1915. [3041]

SOCIETÀ ITALIANA PER LO STUDIO DELLA LIBIA E DELLE ALTRE COLONIE, *Archivio bibliografico coloniale (Libia).* Florence, 1915–21. [1600]

MORI, A., *L'esplorazione geografia della Libia. Rassegna storica e bibliografica.* (Rapporti e monografie coloniali, 2nd ser., 5.) Florence, 1927. [250]

ROMANELLI, P., 'Bibliografia archeologica ed artistica della Tripolitania'. *Boll. R. Inst. Archeol. e Storia dell'Arte* **1**, 1927, pp. 113–30. [450]

EVANS-PRITCHARD, E. E., 'A select bibliography of writings on Cyrenaica'. *Afr. st.* **4**, 1945, pp. 146–50; **5**, 1946, pp. 189–94; **8**, 1949, pp. 62–5. [414]

BONO, F., 'Bibliografia dell'archeologia tripolitana del dopo-guerra'. *L'Italia che scrive* **34**, iii–iv, 1951, p. 32. [24]

CRUDGINGTON, J. W., 'Literature on Arab Libya'. *MEJ* **6**, 1952, pp. 247–51.

FLORENCE. ISTITUTO AGRONOMICO, *Contributo ad una bibliografia italiana sulla Libia con particolare riferimento all'agricoltura ed argomenti affini.* Florence, 1953. [3500]

HILL, R. W., *A bibliography of Libya.* (Dept. of Geog., Research papers ser., 1.) Durham, 1959. [2000]

MURABET, Mohammed, *A bibliography of Libya. With particular reference to sources available in libraries and public archives in Tripoli.* Valetta, 1959. [710]

CAIRO. DĀR AL-KUTUB, *A bibliographical list of works about Libya; Qā'ima bi-al-kutub wa-al-marāji' 'an Lībiya.* (Bibliographical lists of the Arab world, 9.) Cairo, 1961.

WARD, P., *What to read on Libya.* Tripoli, 1963. [50]

PANETTA, E., *Studi italiani di etnografia e di folklore della Libia.* Rome, 1963. [450]

*The Libyan oil industry: a reader's guide.* Tripoli, 1967.

'ABBĀS, Iḥsān & NAJM, Muḥammad Yūsuf, *Lībiyā fī kutub al-ta'rīkh wa-al-siyar.* Benghazi, 1968.

ALLAN, J. A., *A select map and air-photo bibliography of Libya.* London, [1970]. [323]

TANGIER. CAFRAD, *Bibliography on Libya.* Tangier, 1971. [37]

SCHLUTER, H., *Index Libycus. Bibliography of Libya 1957–1969, with supplementary material 1915–1956.* Boston, 1972. [4418]

*National bibliography of the Libyan Arab Republic, current and retrospective.*

i. Periodicals. Current: Jan. 1972. Retrospective: 1827–1971. 1972. [354]
ii. [Books and treatises 1951–1971.] [1817]
[iii.] 1971. [249]

[iv.] The Arab bibliography of Libya. Including books, reports, researches and current periodicals published during 1972 in Libyan Arab Republic. Tripoli, 1973.

BAZAMA, M. M., 'Biblio-Libyca 1841–1968'. *J. Fac. Arts Malta* **5**, 1973, pp. 253–60.

### (ix) Tunisia

DEMARSY, A., *Essai de bibliographie tunisienne ou indication des principaux ouvrages publiés en France sur la Régence.* Paris, 1869. [200]

HOUDAS, O. & BASSET, R., 'Mission scientifique en Tunisie. 2e partie: bibliographie'. *Bull. corresp. afr.* 1884, fasc. 1–3.

ASHBEE, H. S., *A bibliography of Tunisia, from the earliest times to the end of 1888 (in two parts), including Utica and Carthage, the Punic Wars, the Roman Occupation, the Arab Conquest, the Expeditions of Louis IX and Charles V and the French Protectorate.* London, 1889. [2100]

BÉGOUËN, Comte, *Notes et documents pour servir à une bibliographie de l'histoire dz la Tunisie (sièges de Tunis 1535 et de Mahédia 1550).* Paris &c., 1901. [26]

CASTANY, G., *Bibliographie géologique de la Tunisie.* Tunis, 1954–56. [433]
No more published?

LEEUWEN, A. van, 'L'eau en Tunisie: essai de bibliographie'. *IBLA* **20**, 1957, pp. 173–7. [97]

ROMERIL, P. E. A., 'Tunisian nationalism: a bibliographical outline'. *MEJ* **14**, 1960, pp. 206–15. [120]

QUÉMÉNEUR, J., 'Essai bibliographique sur la Tunisie de 1956 à 1961'. *IBLA* **24**, 1961, pp. 415–31. [250]

CAIRO. DĀR AL-KUTUB, *A bibliographical list of works about Tunisia; Qā'ima bi-al-kutub wa-al-marāji' 'an Tūnis.* Cairo, 1961. [330]

GOBERT, E. G., 'Bibliographie critique de la préhistoire tunisienne'. *CT* **41–2**, i–ii, 1963, pp. 37–77. [129]

BORRMANS, M., 'Bibliographie succincte sur la famille tunisienne'. *IBLA* **30**, 1967, pp. 279–90. [100]

*Les unités de documentation en Tunisie. Essai de recensement, situation au 30 juin 1967.* Tunis, 1967.
List of 85 institutions in the social, natural and applied sciences which undertake documentation.

HORNWALL, M. & RUDEBECK, L., *Litteratur om Etiopen, Kenya, Tanzania, Tunesien.* Uppsala, 1967. [32]

'Références tunisiennes'. *IBLA* **31**, 1968, and in each subsequent volume.

BACCOUCHE, Taïeb, 'Bibliographie critique des études linguistiques concernant la Tunisie'. *Rev. tunis. sci. soc.* **7** (no. 20), pp. 239–86. [247]

TANGIER. CAFRAD, *Bibliography on Tunisia.* Tangier, 1971. [200]

### (x) Algeria

*General*

PLAYFAIR, Sir R. L., 'A bibliography of Algeria, from the Expedition of Charles V in 1541 to 1887'. *RGS supplementary papers* **2**, 1889, pp. 127–430. [4745]
*Supplement.* London, 1898. [3108]

TAILLART, Ch., *L'Algérie dans la littérature française; essai de bibliographie méthodique et raisonnée jusqu'à l'année 1924*. Paris, 1925. [3177]

CAIRO. DĀR AL-KUTUB, *A bibliographical list of works about Algeria; Qā'ima bi-al-kutub wa-al-marāji' 'an al-Jazā'ir*. 2nd edn. (Bibliographical lists of the Arab world, 1.) Cairo, 1963. [363]

TANGIER. CAFRAD, *Bibliography on Algeria*. Tangier, 1971. [237]

LAWLESS, R. I., *A bibliography of works on Algeria published in English since 1954*. (Centre for Middle Eastern and Islamic Studies, Occasional papers ser., 1.) Durham, 1972. [450]

'Recherches universitaires sur l'Algérie (en Algérie et à l'étranger)'. *Rev. hist. civ. Maghreb* **4**, 1968, pp. 113–18. [93]

*Regions*

MOTYLINSKI, A. de C., 'Bibliographie du Mzab. Les livres de la secte abadhite'. *Bull. corresp. afr.* **3**, 1885, pp. 43–6.

TRUILLOT, A., 'Bibliographie de la région de Tebessa'. *Recueil de la Soc. de Préhist. et d'Archéol. de Tebessa* **1**, 1936–37, pp. 321–53.

JANIER, E., 'Bibliographie des publications qui ont été faites sur Tlemcen et sa région'. *RA* **93**, 1949, pp. 314–34. [300]; 'Supplément'. *Ibid.* **95**, 1951, pp. 400–13. [200]

FONTAINE, H., 'Quelques ouvrages et articles en français sur le Mzab'. *Bull. liaison saharienne* **29**, 1958, pp. 68–71. [79]

PARRAIN, R., *Catalogue des ouvrages entrés à la bibliothèque jusqu'au 31 décembre 1960*. Tizi-Ouzou, 1961. [400]

LACOSTE, C., *Bibliographie ethnologique de la Grande Kabylie*. Paris, 1962. [732]

*Arabic studies*

MASSE, H., 'Les études arabes en Algérie (1830–1930)'. *RA* **74**, 1933, pp. 208–58, 458–505. [700]

*Archaeology*

SEMPRE, S. & WAROT, S., 'Libyca (archeologie-epigraphie); tables, tomes I à V'. *Libyca* **6**, 1958, pp. 267–325.

*Geography*

POINDRON, D., 'Bibliographie algérienne 1934. Géographie'. *RA* **77**, 1935, pp. 196–209. [120]

LARNAUDE, M., 'Bibliographie "possible" et relativement récent de l'Algérie'. *Ann. alg. géog.* **1**, 1966, pp. 75–7. [75]

BENCHETRIT, M., 'Publications récentes et travaux de recherche sur la géographie économique de l'Algérie'. *Ann. alg. géog.* **3**, 1968, pp. 116–17. [39]

*History*

*Histoire et historiens de l'Algérie*. Paris, 1931.

'Vingt-cinq ans d'histoire algérienne 1931–1956'. *RA* **100**, 1956, pp. 41–190.

I. La préhistoire (L. Balout). [126]

II. L'antiquité (J. Lassus). [118]
III. Le Moyen Âge et les temps modernes (R. Le Tourneau). [75]
IV. L'Algérie depuis 1830 (X. Yacono). [167]

Also published by Gouvernement Général de l'Algérie, Sous-Commission des Beaux-Arts, 1958.

DÉJEUX, J., *Essai de bibliographie algérienne, 1er janvier 1954–30 juin 1962.* (*Lecture d'une guerre.*) Paris, 1962.

HEGGOY, A. A., 'The sources for nineteenth-century Algerian history; a critical essay'. *MW* **54**, 1964, pp. 292–9.

VATIN, J. C., 'Éléments pour une bibliographie d'ensemble sur l'Algérie d'aujourd'hui, rassemblés et présentés'. *Rev. alg.* 1968, pp. 167–278. [397]

HEGGOY, A. A., 'Books on the Algerian revolution in English; translations and Anglo-American contributions'. *Afr. hist. studies* **3**, 1970, pp. 163–8. [65]

BURKE, E., 'Recent books on colonial Algerian history'. *MES* **7**, 1971, pp. 241–50. [25]

*Social sciences*

COLLOT, C., 'Éléments de bibliographie juridique et économique sur l'Algérie de 1945 à 1967'. *Rev. hist. civ. Maghreb* **4**, 1968, pp. 113–18. [93]

DEUTSCHES INSTITUT FÜR AFRIKA-FORSCHUNG, *Algerien, Wirtschaft und Entwicklungsplanung – ausgewählte neure Literatur.* (Dokumentationsdienst Afrika, 5.) Hamburg, 1972. [180]

## (xi) Morocco

*Surveys*

CENIVAL, P. de, 'Note sur la bibliographie générale du Maroc'. *Bull. IHEM* **1**. 1920, pp. 10–16. [22]

HARIKI, G., 'La Bibliographie nationale marocaine'. *Hespéris-Tamuda* **7**, 1966, pp. 97–100.

*General*

RENOU, É., *Description géographique de l'Empire de Maroc.* Paris, 1846, pp. 425–8. [264]

—— *Liste des ouvrages, cartes, plans, vues et dessins relatifs à l'empire du Maroc.* Paris, 1846. [500]

LA MARTINIÈRE, H. M. P. de, 'Bibliography of Morocco 1844–1885'. [Supplement to Renou, 1846] (In his: *Morocco. Journeys in the Kingdom of Fez and to the court of Mulai Hassan,* London, 1889, pp. 423–70.) [800]

—— 'Essai de bibliographie marocaine, 1844–1886'. *Rev. de géog.* (Drapeyron) **19**, 1886, pp. 96–107, 184–94.

PLAYFAIR, Sir R. L. & BROWN, R., *A bibliography of Morocco, from the earliest times to the end of 1891.* (*Bibliography of the Barbary States,* part IV.) *RGS supplementary papers* **3**, 1893, pp. 201–476. [2243]

KAMPFFMEYER, G., 'Studien und Mitteilungen der Deutschen Marokko-Bibliothek. I: Marokko-Literatur'. *MSOS* 2 Abt., **14**, 1911, pp. 1–85; **18**, 1915, pp. 131–86. [1000]

'Bibliographie marocaine: ouvrages parus en 1921 (–1953)'. *Hespéris* **1**, 1921–42, 1955; *Hespéris-Tamuda* **3**, 1962, pp. 157–591.

The issues for the years 1923–33 were reprinted and issued separately as: *Bibliographie marocaine 1923–1933*, by P. de Cenival and others, Paris, 1937.

RICARD, R., 'Les dernières publications portugaises sur l'histoire du Maroc, notes bibliographiques'. *Hespéris* **7**, 1927, pp. 33–51. [50]

—— 'Publications portugaises sur l'histoire du Maroc. Notes bibliographiques'. *Hespéris* **9**, 1929, pp. 295–301. [20]

—— 'Notes de bibliographie luso-marocaine'. *Hespéris* **17**, 1933, pp. 149–52. [22]

—— 'Publications récentes pour l'histoire des portugais au Maroc'. *Hespéris* **23**, 1936, pp. 55–66. [50]

'Ibrāz al-ghawāmiḍ al-laṭīfa *fī* bayān maṭbū'āt al-īyāla al-sharīfa; Liste des ouvrages arabes imprimés au Maroc ou relatifs à ce pays, édités en 1930 (–1932)'. *Hespéris* **12**, 1931. [19]; **14**, 1932, annexes en fin de fasc. 1. [17]

LIBRARY OF CONGRESS, *The Morocco question; a bibliographical list.* Washington, D.C., 1936. [134]

MIÈGE, J. L. & MICHEL, V., 'Le Maroc, 1959–1962; état des travaux'. *Rev. franç. sci. pol.* **15**, 1965, pp. 885–910.

Supplements an essay in the same journal for June 1959.

CAIRO. DĀR AL-KUTUB, *A bibliographical list of works about al-Maghrib; Qā'ima bi-al-kutub wa-al-marāji' 'an al-Maghrib.* (Bibliographical lists of the Arab world, 7.) Cairo, 1961.

*Anbā' al-bibliyūghrāfiyya al-maghribiyya; Informations bibliographiques marocaines.* Rabat, 1931–62.

*Bibliographie nationale marocaine; Al-bibliyūghrāfiyya al-waṭaniyya al-maghribiyya.* Rabat, 1962; nouvelle série, 1963–.

*Bulletin signalétique.* Rabat, 1962(?)–.

(i) La recherche scientifique universitaire au Maroc. Principaux périodiques paraissant au Maroc. [17]
Principaux articles de revue et études d'intérêt scientifique concernant le Maroc. [91]
Principaux ouvrages parus en 1961–1962. [46]
(ii) La Bibliothèque générale et archives. Bibliographie marocaine, 1963.
(iii) Thèses et mémoires de l'Université Mohammed V. 1970. [352]
(iv) Bibliographie historique marocaine 1954–1962. i: Préhistoire et antiquit
(iv) Bibliographie historique marocaine 1954–1962: i: Préhistoire et antiquité. [350]
(v) Période médiévale. 1972. [500]

TANGIER. CAFRAD, *Bibliography on Morocco. Books and articles of reviews classified in the library of CAFRAD.* Tangier, 1970.

—— *Bibliography on Maghreb.* Tangier, 1971.

GARCIA FIGUERAS, T., 'Notas de bibliografía marroquí'. *Africa* [Madrid] **25**, 1968, pp. 587–90; **26**, 1969, pp. 55–9.

(i) La bibliografía de Marruecos de Playfair y Brown (1892).
(ii) La bibliografía española sobre Marruecos hasta el año 1892.

*Spanish Morocco*

FERNÁNDEZ DURO, C., 'Apuntes para la bibliografía marroquí'. (In his 'El-Hach Mohammed el-Bagdady y sus andanzas en Marruecos', *Bol. Soc. Geog. Madrid* **3**, 1877, pp. 210–55.) 'Continuación'. *Ibid.* **5**, 1879, pp. 33–64.

BAUER Y LANDAUER, I., *Biblioteca hispano-marroquí. Apuntes para una bibliografía de Marruecos.* Madrid, [1922]. [3044]

BACAICOA ARNÁIZ, D., 'Bibliografía marroquí, 1953–58'. Supplements to *Tamuda* **1**, 1953–57, 1959, except 5.

HELLMAN, F. S., *A list of references on Ifni, Spanish Morocco.* New York, 1942. [33]

*Agriculture*

DEUTSCHES INSTITUT FÜR AFRIKA-FORSCHUNG, *Marokko; Landwirtschaft, Forsten, Fischerei – ausgewählte neuere Literatur.* (Dokumentationsdienst Afrika, 6.) Hamburg, 1972. [114]

*Archaeology*

MARION, J., 'Bibliographie d'archéologie marocaine 1958–1960'. *Bull. archéol. maroc.* **4**, 1960, pp. 583–600.

*Botany*

GATTEFOSSÉ, J & JAHANDIEZ, E., 'Essai de bibliographie botanique marocaine'. *Bull. Soc. Sci. Nat. Maroc* **1**, 1922, pp. 71–86.

*Economics. Sociology*

COMBE, Chr., 'Bibliographie marocaine 1939–1945'. *Bull. écon. soc. Maroc* **28**, 1946, pp. 296–302.

KHATIBI, Abdelkabir, *Bilan de la sociologie au Maroc.* Rabat, [1967]. [103]

HARIKI, G., 'Bibliographie économique du Maroc'. *Bull. écon. soc. Maroc* **29–32**, 1967–69.

*Geography*

CHARTON, A., 'Bibliographie marocaine'. *BRSGM* 1923, pp. 600–16; 1924, pp. 61–78, 220–42; 1925, pp. 159–71, 225–46; 1926, pp. 148–69, 268–85.
In progress?

*History*

IBN SŪDA, 'Abd al-Salām b. 'Abd al-Qādir, *Dalīl mu'arrikh al-Maghrib; Bibliographical guide to the historians of Morocco.* Tetuan, 1950; 2nd edn. Casablanca, 1960. [2263]

HARIKI, G., 'Bibliographie historique (1968–1969). Maroc-Espagne musulmane'. *Bull. Soc. Hist. Maroc* **2**, 1969, pp. 61–70. [138]

-MIKNĀSĪ, Aḥmad, *Ahamm maṣādir al-ta'rīkh wa-al-tarjama fī al-Maghrib.* Tetuan, 1963.

*Morocco in English literature*

GARNIER, Ch. M., 'L'entrée du Maroc dans la littérature anglaise'. *Bull. enseign. publ. Maroc* mars 1934, pp. 79–84.

*Morocco in French literature*

LEBEL, R., 'Le Maroc dans la littérature française (esquisse préliminaire)'. *Bull. enseign. publ. Maroc* déc. 1925, pp. 387–402.

*Law*

'Bibliographie juridique marocaine'. *Rev. maroc. droit* **14**, 1962, pp. 807–29. [400]

*Relations with Europe*

MIÈGE, J. L., *Le Maroc et l'Europe, 1830–1894. Tome I: Sources, bibliographie.* Paris, 1961. [2500]

*Earth sciences*

MORIN, P., *Bibliographie analytique des sciences de la terre; Maroc et régions limitrophes depuis le début des études géologiques à 1964.* Casablanca, 1965. [12,000]

BLONDEL, F., *Bibliographie géologique et minière de la France d'Outre-Mer.* Extrait de l'édition définitive, tome 1, *Maroc*, revu et mis au point par J. Marçais et V. Ortoli. Paris, &c., 1943, pp. 243–422. [3000]

*Topography*

CENIVAL, P. de, 'Bibliographie du nord marocaine (Rif et Jbala)'. (In *Rif & Jbala* (Éditions de Bull. enseign. publ. Maroc, 71), Paris, 1926.)

*Zoology*

ALLUAUD, Chr., 'Aperçu sur la zoologie du Maroc'. *Bull. IHEM* **1**, 1920, pp. 10–16. [65]

(xii) Muslim Spain

IMAMUDDIN, S. M., 'Sources of Muslim history in Spain'. *JPHS* **1**, 1953, pp. 357–79.

—— 'Sources of the economic history of Spain under the Banu Umayyah (711–1031 A.C.)'. *JPHS* **6**, 1958, pp. 104–23, 174–94.

MILLÁS VALLICROSA, J. M., 'Sobre bibliografía agronómica hispanoárabe'. *And.* **19**, 1954, pp. 129–42.

GARCÍA GÓMEZ, E., 'Sobre agricultura arábigoandaluza: cuestiones bibliográficas'. *And.* **10**, 1945, pp. 127–46.

—— 'Ediciones y reediciones de textos arábigoandaluces o relativos a al-Andalus en el Oriente árabe'. *And.* **19**, 1954, pp. 467–70. [20]

## IV. WRITINGS IN ARABIC. NATIONAL BIBLIOGRAPHY OF ARAB COUNTRIES

*The Fihrist*

IBN AL-NADĪM, *Kitab al-Fihrist,* mit Anmerkungen herausgegeben von Gustav Flügel. Nach dessem Tode besorgt von Johannes Roediger und August Mueller. 2v. Leipzig, 1871–72 (repr. Cairo, 1348/1929 with some eight pages missing from the Flügel edition; Beirut, 1964; Lahore, 1972).

New material on the *Fihrist* was published by J. Fück, who for many years had been working on a new edition to be published in the series 'Bibliotheca Islamica', in *ZDMG* **90** (N.F. 15), 1936, pp. 298–321, and by Arberry (on a Chester Beatty MS.) in *Islamic Research Association Miscellany* **1**, 1948, pp. 19.45.

—— *Translations*

*The Fihrist of al-Nadīm, a tenth-century survey of Muslim culture.* Bayard Dodge, ed. and trans. 2v. New York, 1970.

A Persian translation by R. Tajadod was published in Tehran, 1965.

*Earlier translations of parts of the Fihrist*

FLÜGEL, G. L., *Die Aufzählung der Schriften Kindi's bei welcher wir ganz der Reihe und Anordnung folgen, wie sie uns Ibn Abī Ja'kūb an Nadīm in seinen Fihrist überliefert hat.*

—— *Mani, seine Lehre und seine Schriften; ein Beitrag zur Geschichte des Manichäismus. Aus dem Fihrist . . . im Text nebst Uebersetzung, Commentar und Index* zum ersten Mal hrsg. Leipzig, 1862.

MÜLLER, A., *Die griechischen Philosophen in der arabischen Überlieferung.* Halle, 1873.

HOUDAS, O., 'Dixième section du Kitāb-al-Fihrist. Renseignement sur les alchimistes et sur ceux des philosophes anciens ou modernes qui ont pratiqué le grand oeuvre'. (In M. P. E. Berthelot, *Histoire des sciences*, Paris, 1893, vol. 3.)

FÜCK, J., 'The Arabic literature on alchemy according to An-Nadīm (A.D. 987). A translation of the tenth discourse of the Book of the Catalogue (Al-Fihrist) with introduction and commentary'. *Ambix* **4**, 1951, pp. 81–144.

SUTER, H., 'Das Mathematiker-Verzichniss im Fihrist . . . Zum ersten Mal vollständig ins Deutsche übersetzt und mit Anmerkungen versehen'. *Abh. z. Gesch. d. Math.* **6**, 1892, pp. 1–87; **10**, 1900, and **14**, 1902.

HAMMER-PURGSTALL, J. von, 'Extraits du Fihrist, sur la religion des Sabéens'. *JA* II série, **12**, 1841, pp. 246–72.

GRAY, L. H., 'Iranian material in the Fihrist'. *Le Muséon* III série, **1**, 1915, pp. 24–39.

*Fahāris*

IBN KHAYR, *Fahrasat mā rawāhu 'an shuyūkhihi min al-dawāwīn al-muṣannafa fī ḍurūb al-'ilm wa-anwā' al-ma'rifa; Index librorum de diversis scientiarum ordinibus quos a magistris didicit Abu Bequer ben Khair* . . . Arabice . . . ediderunt . . . Franciscus Codera et J. Ribera Tarrago. 2v. (Bibliotheca Arabico-Hispana, 9–10.) Saragossa, 1894–5. [900]

*Fahrasa* (plural, *Fahāris*) is the name given to a catalogue in which a scholar enumerated his teachers and the works studied under their direction. Three such works have been published and a study of extant manuscripts made by 'Abd al-'Azīz al-Ahwānī. See the article 'Fahrasa' in *EI*, 2nd edition, by Ch. Pellat.

*Ḥājjī Khalīfa*

ḤĀJĪ KHALĪFA, *Kashf al-ẓunūn 'an asāmī al-kutub wa-al-funūn; Lexicon bibliographicum et encyclopaedicum a Mustafa ben Abdallah, Katib Jelebi dicto et nomine Haji Khalfa celebrato compositum* . . . primum edidit, Latine vertit, et commentario indicibusque instruxit Gustavus Fluegel. 7v. Leipzig, &c., 1835–58. [14,501]

*Other editions:*

Bulaq, 1858. 2v. Ed. Muḥammad al-Sharīf al-Adkāwī.

Istanbul, 1893. 2v. Ed. Ḥasan Hilmī.

Istanbul, 1941–43. 2v. Ed. Şerefettin Yaltkaya and Kilisli Rifat Bilge.

A French translation by Fr. Pétis de la Croix is preserved in the Bibliothèque Nationale, Paris, at 'fonds arabe 4462/4'.

*Continuations by:*

Sheikh Vīshnezade Mahmet 'Izzeti (1629–81).

Ḥanīfzāde Aḥmed Ṭāhir (†1802): *Āthār-i nau*, publ. in vol. 6 of the Flügel edition, contains works numbered 14502–15007, mostly Persian and Turkish publ. up to 1758.

Sheikh al-Islām 'Ārif Ḥikmet (†1858).

Bağdatli Isma'īl Pasha (†1920): *Īḍāḥ al-maknūn fī al-dhayl 'alā Kashf al-ẓunūn*, ed. by Yaltkaya and Bilge. 2v. Istanbul, 1945–47. [*c.* 19,000]

Volume 6 contains also:

1. (pp. 525–646) *Āthār-i nau; Nova opera ab Ahmed Hanífzádeh ad continuandum Haji Khalfae Lexicon bibliographicum, collecta et ad ordinem literarum disposita.* Ad codicis Vindobonensis fidem primum edidit Gustavus Fluegel. [506]

2. (pp. 647–64) *Barnāmaj al-kutub allatī hiya mutadāwala fī bilād al-Maghrib; Catalogus librorum qui praeter ceteros in regionibus Africae Occidentalibus in usu sunt in ordinem doctrinarum digestus et e codicibus Vindobonensibus primum editus.* [641]

3. (pp. 665–79) *Fihrist mu'allafāt al-imâm Jalāl al-Dīn al-Suyûṭī; Catalogus librorum ab Imámo doctissimo Jelál-ed-Din el-Soyúti compositorum.* E codice Parisiensi, primum edidit. [504]

In volume 7 will be found:

4. (pp. 1–539) *Catalogus bibliothecarum Cahirensium Damascenae Halebensis Rhodiae et Constantinopolitarum continens.* Accedunt commentarius in six tomos priores et indices duo. [30,000]

5. (pp. 540–6) *Fihrist kutub wa-tawālīf; Catalogus librorum et scriptorum* ab Abu Bekr Mohammed Ben Khair Ben Khalifa el-Andalusi compositus.

Indexes:

(pp. 947–1000) Index librorum quorum tituli extra ordinem alphabeticum medio in orationis cursu ab Hāji Khalfa, Arabajibáshi et Hanífzadeh commemorantur. [1381]

(pp. 1001–1257) Index auctorum. [9513]

For a general account of the work and its sources, see Renaud, *Notice sur la dictionnaire bibliographique . . . de Hadji Khalfa.* Extrait no. 9 de l'année 1859 du *Journal Asiatique.*

BROCKELMANN, C., *Geschichte der arabischen Litteratur.* 2v. Weimar, 1898–1902.

1. Supplementband. Leiden, 1937.
2. Supplementband. 1938.
3. Supplementband. 1942.

Zweite den Supplementbänden angepasste Auflage. 2v. Leiden, 1943–49.

—— *Ta'rīkh al-adab al-'arabī*, naqalahu ilā al-'arabiyya 'Abd al-Ḥalīm al-Najjār. Cairo, [1960–]62.

Three volumes published, but not completed.

SEZGIN, F., *Geschichte des arabischen Schrifttums*. Leiden.

1. Qur'ānwissenschaften, Ḥadīt, Geschichte, Fiqh, Dogmatik, Mystik, bis ca 430h. 1967.
2. Poetik. 1975.
3. Medizin, Pharmazie, Zoologie, Tierheilkunde, bis ca. 430h. 1970.
4. Alchimie, Chemie, Botanik, Agricultur bis ca. 430h. 1971.
5. Mathematik bis ca. 430h. 1974.
6. Astronomie-Astrologie bis ca. 430h. [In the press]

—— *Ta'rīkh al-adab al-'arabī*. Arabic translation by F. Abū al-Faḍl. Vol. 1, pt. 1. Cairo, 1970.

*Books printed in Europe and the Orient*

SCHNURRER, C. F., *Bibliotheca Arabica*. Auctam nunc atque integram edidit . . . C. F. de S. Halle, 1811. [2000] (Repr. Amsterdam, 1966.)

An index was published by Chauvin (see below).

ZENKER, J. Th., *Bibliotheca Orientalis. Manuel de bibliographie orientale*. I. Contenant (1) Les livres arabes, persans et turcs imprimés depuis l'invention de l'imprimerie jusqu'à nos jours, tant en Europe qu'en Orient, disposés par ordre des matières; (2) table des auteurs, des titres orientaux et des éditeurs; (3) un aperçu de la littérature orientale. 2v. Leipzig, 1846–61 (repr. Amsterdam, 1966). [750] Supplement contained in vol. 2.

CHAUVIN, V., *Bibliographie des ouvrages arabes ou relatifs aux arabes publiés dans l'Europe chrétienne de 1810 à 1885*. 12 pts. Liège, 1892–1922.

I. Préface. Table de Schnurrer. Les proverbes. 1892. [175]
II. Kalilah. 1897. [1000]
III. Louqmâne et les fabulistes. Barlaam. Antar et les romans de chevalerie. 1898. [250]
IV–VII. Les Mille et une nuits. 1900–3. [350]
VIII. Syntipas. 1904. [100]
IX. Pierre Alphonse? Secundus. Recueils orientaux. Tables de Henning et de Mardrus. Contes occidentaux. Les maqâmes. 1905. [250]
X. Le Coran et la tradition. 1907. [400]
XI. Mahomet. 1909. [1000]
XII. Le Mahométisme. 1913–22. [1831]

VAN DYCK, E. A., *Kitāb iktifā' al-qunū' bimā huwa maṭbū' fī ashhar al-ta'ālīf al-'arabiyya fī al-maṭābi' al-sharqiyya wa-al-gharbiyya*. Cairo, 1896.

SARKIS, J. E., *Mu'jam al-maṭbū'āt al-'arabiyya wa-al-mu'arraba wa huwa shāmil li-asmā' al-kutub al-maṭbū'a fī al-aqṭār al-sharqiyya wa-al-gharbiyya . . .; Dictionnaire encyclopédique de bibliographie arabe*, comprenant: 1, le nom de tous les ouvrages imprimés jusqu'à 1919 inclusivement; 2, une biographie succincte de la plupart des auteurs; 3, les sources des notes biographiques. Cairo, 1246/1928–30.

—— *Jāmi' al-taṣānīf al-ḥadītha allatī ṭubi'at fi al-bilād al-sharqiyya wa-al-gharbiyya wa-al-amrīkiyya . . .*; Bulletin bibliographique 1920–1926. Cairo, 1927.

—— *Bulletin bibliographique*. Tome 2, 1927. Cairo, [1930?] [25,000]

*Books published in the Arab-Islamic world*

'Bibliographie ottomane, ou Notices des ouvrages publiés dans les imprimeries turques de Constantinople, et en partie dans celles de Bulac, en Égypte, depuis les derniers mois de 1856 (1273) jusqu'à ce moment (1279), par M. Bianchi'. *JA* 5e sér., **13**, 1859, pp. 519–55; **14**, 1859, pp. 287–98; **16**, 1860, pp. 323–46; 6e sér., **2**, 1863, pp. 217–71. [146]

'Notice des livres turcs imprimés à Constantinople durant les années 1281–1282 et 1283 (1284 et 1285, 1286 et 1287, 1288 et 1289, 1290–1293) de l'Hégire, par F. A. Belin'. *JA* 6e sér., **11**, 1868, pp. 465–91; **14**, 1869, pp. 65–95; **18**, 1871, pp. 125–57; 7e sér., **1**, 1873, pp. 522–63; **9**, 1877, pp. 122–46.

'Notices des livres turcs, arabes et persans imprimés à Constantinople durant la période 1294 (–1307) de l'Hégire (1877–90), par C. Huart'. *JA* 7e sér., **16**, 1880, pp. 411–39; **19**, 1882, pp. 164–207; 8e sér., **5**, 1885, pp. 229–68, 415–63; **9**, 1887, pp. 350–414; **13**, 1889, pp. 428–89; **17**, 1891, pp. 357–410. [1808]

BEN CHENEB, Mohammed, 'Revue des ouvrages arabes (édités ou publiés par les musulmanes en 1322 et 1323 du l'hégire (1904–1905)'. *RA* **50**, 1906, pp. 261–96. [49]

Works printed at Cairo and Boulaq, Beirut, Tunis, Algiers and Fez.

'Ittijāh al-ta'līf fī 'ām 1945 (–1950)'. *Al-Kitāb* **1**, 1945–46, pp. 92–414; **2**, 1947, pp. 463–89, 785–92; **5**, 1949, pp. 165–99; **7**, 1949, pp. 138–66; **8**, 1949, pp. 729–63; **10**, 1951, pp. 333–66.

Surveys of books printed in Egypt, Palestine, Lebanon, Syria and Iraq.

MOUHASSEB, Jamal, *Al maktabah. A selective Arabic bibliography for Iraq, Jordan, Lebanon and Syria*. Harissa, 1956–58. [400]

Books suitable for university, college and secondary school libraries.

MORENO, M. M., 'Rassegna di pubblicazioni arabe'. *Levante* **8**, iii, 1961, pp. 32–6. [30]

JAM'IYYAT AL-MAKTABĀT AL-MADRASIYYA, *Fihris al-muṣannafāt li-al-kutub al-mukhtāra li-al-maktabat al-madrasiyya* . . . Cairo, 1969. [2809]

Books for school libraries.

DAMASCUS. SYRIAN DOCUMENTATION PAPERS, *Bibliography of the Middle East; a complete and classified list of all the books published in about ten Middle Eastern countries*. 1969–.

*Majallat al-kitāb al-'arabī; Arabic book journal*. Cairo, 1969–.

ARAB LEAGUE DEPT. OF DOCUMENTATION AND INFORMATION, *The bulletin of Arab publications*, 1970–. Compiled in co-operation with the National Library and Archives in the Arab Republic of Egypt.

*Egypt*

-ANṢĀRĪ, 'Abd Allāh, *Kitāb jāmi' al-taṣnīfāt al-miṣriyya al-ḥadītha min sana 1301 ilā sana 1310 hijriyya*. Bulaq, 1312/1893.

New books printed in Egypt 1881–91.

*Liste des ouvrages imprimés en Égypte de 1936 à 1942*. Cairo, n.d.

ANAWATI, G. C. & KUENTZ, Ch., *Bibliographie des ouvrages arabes imprimés en Égypte en 1942, 1943 et 1944*. Cairo, 1949. [854]

ANAWATI, G. C., 'Index bibliographique des livres arabes publiés en Égypte en 1954'. *MIDEO* **2**, 1955, pp. 321–40. [319]
—— 1955. *Ibid.* **3**, 1956, pp. 397–418. [341]
Also published in *Revue du Caire*, vols. 35–6.

ANAWATI, G. C., 'Textes arabes anciens édités en Égypte au cours de l'année . . .'
1953. *MIDEO* **1**, 1954, pp. 103–40. [32]
1954. *MIDEO* **2**, 1955, pp. 257–306. [60]
1955–56. *MIDEO* **3**, 1956, pp. 259–348. [74]
1957. *MIDEO* **4**, 1957, pp. 203–46. [30]
1958. *MIDEO* **5**, 1958, pp. 387–416. [43]
1959–60. *MIDEO* **6**, 1959–61, pp. 227–80. [33]
1961–62. *MIDEO* **7**, 1962–63, pp. 141–86. [46]
1963–65. *MIDEO* **8**, 1964–66, pp. 253–322. [66]
1966–67. *MIDEO* **9**, 1967, pp. 271–8. [56]
1966–69. *MIDEO* **10**, 1970, pp. 109–88. [72]
1969–71. *MIDEO* **11**, 1972, pp. 275–89. [81]
1969–73. *MIDEO* **12**, 1974, pp. 91–186. [77]

-*Sijill al-thaqāfī 1948–52*. 5v. Cairo.
'Cultural yearbook'.

*Al-nashra al-miṣriyya li-al-maṭbū'at . . . fī Dār al-Kutub min aghustus 1955–*. Cairo, 1956.

AFRO-ASIAN DISTRIBUTION CENTRE (ARABIC BOOK DIVISION), *Arabic publications; five years bibliography, 1956–1960; Al-nashra al-miṣriyya li-al-maṭbū'āt* . . . Cairo, 1962. [8048]
Cumulation of titles given in five years' issues of the four-monthly journal of the same title. Continued annually as:
*Egyptian publications bulletin*. 1955–56–.
Since 1969 with the added title: *The U.A.R. national bibliography*.

'The Arab book annual, 1960–'. *'Ālam al-maktabāt*, passim.

'The Arab bibliography, I: Publications of U.A.R. (Egypt), 1962'. *Majallat al-maktabat al-'arabiyya* **1**, i, 1963–.

ANAWATI, G. C., 'Livres arabes parus récemment en Égypte'. *MIDEO* **9**, 1967, pp. 279–86. [150]
Titles listed in *Majallat al-kitāb*, 1966–Aug. 1967.

CORM, Y., 'L'edition égyptienne en 1967'. *Travaux et jours* **27**, 1968, pp. 25–49.
Statistical survey of 1088 titles published during January to June 1967 from a list in *Majallat al-kitāb al-'arabī* no. 39.

CAIRO. DĀR AL-KUTUB, *Nashrat al-īdā' al-shahriyya; Legal deposit monthly bulletin*. Cairo, 1969–.

NUṢAYR, 'Ā'ida Ibrāhīm, *Al-kutub al-'arabiyya allatī nushirat fī al-Jumhūriyya al-'Arabiyya al-Muttaḥida baina 'āmay 1926/1940; Arabic books published in the U.A.R. 'Egypt' between 1926 and 1940: a study and a bibliography*. Cairo, 1969. [5000]
Has a most useful introduction on libraries and published bibliographies and catalogues.

LIBRARY OF CONGRESS AMERICAN LIBRARIES PROCUREMENT CENTER, *Accessions list, Middle East*. Cairo, 1962–.

In progress. Has always included a few books published in other Middle Eastern countries, but from 1974 will list books, wherever published, which have been acquired in Cairo for American libraries.

*Dalīl al-kitāb al-miṣrī; Egyptian books in print.* Cairo, 1972–. [15,000 in 1972]

*Egypt: single places*

BIANCHI, T. X., 'Catalogue général des livres arabes, persans et turcs, imprimés à Boulac en Égypte depuis l'introduction de l'imprimerie dans ce pays'. *JA* 4e sér., **2**, 1843, pp. 24–61. [243]

Books printed 1822–42.

*A catalogue of Arabic and Turkish books printed at the Government Press, and sold at the Government Book Depot, Cairo.* Issued by the Imprimerie Khédiviale at Bulaq in 1845, [1850?], [1972?] A.H. 1295 [1886? (title varies)] and 1890.

The history of this press from 1821 onwards is told in Abu'l-Futūḥ Riḍwān, *Ta'rīkh maṭba'at Būlāq* (Cairo, 1953).

*Government publications*

MINISTRY OF PUBLIC WORKS, *A list of publications, maps and plans.* 1901–. Various editions, that of 1952, on loose leaves, being entitled: *List of maps and publications for sale at the Survey of Egypt maprooms.* [1000]

MINISTRY OF FINANCE, *A list of publications.* 1906 [400] and 1908. [500]

CAIRO. NATIONAL RESEARCH CENTRE, *Classified list of Egyptian scientific papers published in 1951–53.* [500 in 1951]

No more published.

*Al-dalīl al-bībliyūjrāfī li-maṭbū'āt Wizārat al-Tarbiyya wa-al-Ta'līm al-Markaziyya wa Wizārat al-Tarbiyya wa-al-Ta'līm al-Tanfīdhī bi-al-iqlīm al-janūbī, 1950–1960.* Cairo, 1961. [506]

Publications of the Central Ministry of Education and of the Regional Ministry of the Southern Region 1950–1960.

A list of publications of the National Library is given in *MIDEO* **9**, 1967, pp. 308–9.

*Guide to U.A.R. government publications at the U.A.C. Library.* Cairo, 1965. [500]

HASHAD, Mahmoud A., *Subject guide to memos of the Institute of National Planning, Cairo, September 1960–December 1966.* (Inst. of National Planning memo. no. 724.) Cairo, 1967. [711]

*Institutes, Societies, etc.*

*Egypt*

KÜHNEL, E., 'Publicationen des Arabischen Museums in Cairo, 1929–1939'. (*AI* **6**, 1939, p. 175 f.)

ELLUL, J., *Index des communications et mémoires publiés par l'Institut d'Égypte (1859–1952).* Cairo, 1952. [2000]

'Table des matières des travaux imprimés de la Société d'Études Historiques et Géographiques de l'Isthme de Suez (1947–1956)'. *BSEHGIS* **6**, 1955–56, pp. 217–27.

RIZZITANO, U., 'Recenti pubblicazioni edite dall'Istituto di Studi Superiori Arabi del Cairo, dipendente dalla "Lega Araba" '. *OM* **36**, 1956, pp. 204–16. [35]

*India*

ʿĀDIL, Maulvi Muḥammad, 'The Dā'irat-ul-Maʿārif; with an introduction by Syed Hashimi (Faridabadi)'. *IC* **4**, 1930, pp. 625–65. [70]

*Iran*

MUSHĀR, Khānbābā, *Fihrist-i kitābhā-yi chāpī-yi Īrān*. Tehran, 1344/1966. [10,000]

Arabic books published in Iran since the beginning of printing and elsewhere after A.H. 1340.

*Iraq*

CORM, Youssef, 'L'édition irakienne en 1967'. *Travaux et jours* **28**, 1968, pp. 33–5.

Study based on the accessions list of the central library of the University of Baghdad, from an article in *Majallat al-kitāb al-ʿarabī* **42**, 1968.

*Classified catalog of government publications available in the Central Library, Baghdad University*. Baghdad, 1969. [750]

ʿAWWĀD, Gūrgīs, *Mushārak al-ʿIrāq fī nashr al-turāth al-ʿarabī*. Baghdad, 1969.

Iraq's share in the publication of the Arab cultural heritage.

MAHMOOD, E. M. & -LAWAND, A., *Maṭbūʿāt al-Mawṣil mundhu sana 1861–1970 m.; Mosul printed books from 1861–1970*. Mosul, 1971. [1500]

*Israel*

MOREH, S., 'Fihris al-kutub al-adabiyya wa-al-ṣuḥuf wa-al-majallāt allatī ṣudirat fī Isrā'īl bi-al-lugha al-ʿarabiyya mundhu 1948–1964'. *Hamizraḥ hehadash* (*The New East*) **14**, 1964, pp. 296–309. [229]

Arabic books and journals published in Israel 1948–1964.

MOREH, S. & SHAHIN, O., 'Catalogue of Arabic books and publications published in Israel since May, 1964'. *Ibid.* **21**, 1971, pp. 218–30. [180]

(In Hebrew and Arabic.)

MOREH, S. & KHAYAT, S., 'Catalogue of Arabic publications written and published by Jews'. *Ibid.* **21**, 1971, pp. 343–59. [250]

(In Hebrew and Arabic.)

*Lebanon. Syria*

MAOUAD, Ibrahim, *Bibliographie des auteurs libanais de langue française*. (Troisième Conférence Générale de l'UNESCO, nov.–déc. 1948, Beyrouth.) Beirut, 1948.

Works on all subjects published 1845–1945.

LAOUST, H. & DAHHAN, Sami, 'L'oeuvre de l'Académie Arabe de Damas, 1921–1950; notes bibliographiques'. *BEO* **13**, 1949–51, pp. 161–219.

*Bibliographie de l'Université Saint Joseph de Beyrouth, par les bibliothécaires de la Bibliothèque Orientale*. Beirut, 1951.

INSTITUT FRANÇAIS DE DAMAS, *Liste des publications 1929–1959*. [By H. Laoust.] Damascus, 1959.

DAGHER, J. A., 'Wissenschaftliche und literarische Veröffentlichungen im Libanon 1960 und 1961'. *ZDMG* **112** (N.F. 37), 1962, pp. 447–54. [200]

GROTZFELD, S., 'Wissenschaftliche und literarische Veröffentlichungen im Libanon 1962'. *ZDMG* **115**, 1965, pp. 3*–11*. [200]

DIRANI, Afifa and others, 'Wissenschaftliche und literarische Veröffentlichungen im Libanon und in Syrien 1963–66'. *ZDMG* **119**, 1969–70, pp. *13*–*44*. [650]

TAMIN, Suha, *A bibliography of A.U.B. faculty publications, 1866–1966*. Beirut 1967. [5000]

HEIN, H., 'Annotierte Bibliographie der im Jahre 1968 im Libanon und in Syrien erschienenen orientalischen Sekundarliteratur'. *ZDMG* **120**, 1970, pp. *14*–*28*. [83]

*A bulletin of books published in the Syrian Arab Republic; Al-nashra al-maktabiyya bi-al-kutub al-ṣādira fī al-Jumhūriyya al-ʿArabiyya al-Sūriyya*. Damascus, 1970, 1971.

KHOURY, R. G., *Bibliographie raisonnée des traductions publiées au Liban à partir des langues étrangères de 1840 jusqu'aux environs de 1905*. Paris, 1966. [542]

*North Africa*

*Libya*

*National bibliography of the Libyan Arab Republic, current and retrospective*. 1972.

(i) Periodicals. Current, Jan. 1972; retrospective, 1827–1971. 1972. [354]
(ii) Books and treatises, 1951–1971; supplement for non-Arabic publications. [1817]
(iii) 1971. [249]
(iv) The Arab bibliography of Libya. Including books, reports, researches and current periodicals published during 1972 in Libyan Arab Republic. Tripoli, 1973.

*Tunisia*

ZAWADOWSKI, G., 'Index de la presse indigène de Tunisie'. *REI* **11**, 1937, pp. 357–89. [247]

*Listes des publications disponibles*. Service botanique et agronomique de Tunisie. Ariana, 1951. [400]; *Supplément*. 1954. [50]

*Catalogue des publications*. Direction des travaux publiques. Service géologique. Tunis, 1954. [40]

*Liste des ouvrages publiés en Tunisie année 1963*. Tunis, 1963. [89]

*Algeria*

FIORI, H., *Bibliographie des ouvrages imprimés à Alger de 1830 à 1850*. Algiers, 1938. [253]

*Bibliographie de l'Algérie; Al-bibliyūghrāfiyya al-jazāʾiriyya*. 1964–.

DÉJEUX, J., 'Bibliographie de la littérature algérienne d'expression française'. *Cahiers alg.* **2**, 1967, pp. 121–94. [1000]
For the period 1 July 1962 to 30 June 1967.

*Morocco*

BEN CHENEB, M. & LÉVI-PROVENCAL, E., 'Essai de répertoire chronologique des éditions de Fès'. *RA* 1921, pp. 158–73, 275–90; 1922, pp. 171–85, 333–47. [356]

PÉRÈS, H. & SEMPÉRÉ, A., 'Répertoire alphabétique des auteurs publiés à Fès de 1126H. [1714] à 1337H. [1919]'. *BEA* **7**, 1947, pp. 63–70.

RABAT. INSTITUT DE HAUTES ÉTUDES MAROCAINES, *Publications de l'Institut des Hautes Études Marocaines, 1915–1935. Tables et index.* Supplément à *Hespéris*, 1936. Rochefort-sur-Mer, 1936; *1936–1954. Tables et répertoires* (établis par M. Hosotte-Reynaud). Limoges, 1956. [2750]

*Publications de l'Institut des Hautes Études Marocaines et de la Section Historique du Maroc.* Rabat, 1943. [100]

*Liste des publications déposées à la Bibliothèque Générale et Archives au titre du dépôt légal au cours de l'année . . .; Qā'ima bi-al-maṭbū'āt wa-al-nashrāt al-mūdā'a bi-qism al-īdā' al-qānūnī khilāla sana . . . 1962–*. Rabat, [1963–8]

Continued as:

*Bibliographie nationale marocaine. Dépôt légal; Al-fahrasa (bibliyūghrāfiyya) al-waṭaniyya al-maghribiyya. Al-īdā' al-qānūnī.* 1968–.

HARIKI, G., 'La Bibliographie nationale marocaine'. *Hespéris Tamuda* **7**, 1966, pp. 97–100.

## V. WRITINGS OF SCHOLARS AND PERSONS INTERESTED IN THE ARAB NEAR AND MIDDLE EAST

Lists of the works of Islamic scholars (*islamisants*) are customarily appended to obituary notices and in *Festschriften*. Those which have appeared in dependent works are listed in *Index Islamicus*, section I, v. Others may be found in I, iii where articles devoted to individual scholars are listed. They are not repeated here.

The list which follows gives only those titles which have appeared as separate publications.

COZZO, G. S., *Le opere a stampa di Michele AMARI.* Palermo, 1909. [302]

ASHKENAZI, Touvia, *A bibliographical list of [his own] writings, 1922–1954, with published biographical notes.* Washington, D.C., 1954. [176]

'AWWĀD, Gūrgīs, *Arabic philologist: ANASTASE-MARIE the Carmelite (1866–1947), his life and writings.* Baghdad, 1966. [1399]

DONKIN, W. C., *Catalogue of the Gertrude BELL collection in the library of King's College.* Newcastle upon Tyne, 1960. [750]

SPIES, O., *Verzeichnis der Schriften von Carl BROCKELMANN.* Leipzig, 1938. [600]

PENZER, N. M., *An annotated bibliography of Sir Richard BURTON.* London, 1923. [500]

[DAGHER, J. A.], *L'oeuvre scientifique et littéraire de M. Joseph A. DAGHER.* Harissa, 1951. [26]

—— *Joseph A. DAGHER, curriculum vitae.* Beirut, *c.* 1960. [180]

*Notice sur les travaux de M. Henri DÉHÉRAIN.* 1898. [30]

BEIDELMAN, T. O., *A bibliography of the writings of E. E. EVANS-PRITCHARD*. 1974.

FIELD, H., *Bibliography, 1926–66*. Ann Arbor, 1966. [631]
*Bibliography, 1964–71*. [104]
*Bibliography, 1972–73*.

HELLER, B., *Bibliographie des oeuvres de Ignace GOLDZIHER ... avec une introduction bibliographique de Louis Massignon*. Paris, 1927. [692]; supplemented by A. Schreiber in the *Goldziher memorial volume* (Budapest, 1948), vol. 1, pp. 419–30.

*Résumé des travaux et publications de M. Octave HOUDAS*. [c. 1900.] [33]

*Notice des travaux et publications de Cl. HUART*. Chalon-sur-Saône, *c*. 1900. [50]

SAMOYLOVICH, A. N., *Bibliografiya pechatnykh rabot akademika Ignatiya Yulianovicha KRACHKOVSKOGO*. Moscow, &c., 1936. [392]; Addenda were published in *Palestinskii sbornik* **1** (63), 1954, pp. 125–9.

*Titres et publications de Henri LAOUST*. Macon, 1955. [25]

DUVAL, E. W., *T. E. Lawrence. A bibliography*. New York, 1938. [159]

LAWRENCE, T. E., *A list of references by and on Col. T. E. LAWRENCE in the Imperial War Museum Library*. London, 1952. [30]

DISBURY, D. G., *T. E. LAWRENCE (of Arabia); a collector's book-list*. Egham, 1972. [396]

CLEMENTS, F., *T. E. LAWRENCE; a reader's guide*. Newton Abbot, 1972.

MEYERS, J., *T. E. LAWRENCE; a bibliography*. New York, 1975.

HÖFNER, M., *Verzeichnis der Schriften von Enno LITTMAN, zum 16. September 1945*. Tübingen, 1945. [451]

MOUBARAC, Y., *Bibliographie de Louis MASSIGNON*. Damascus, 1956. [613]

*The works of Max MEYERHOF; a bibliography*. Jerusalem, 1944. [400]

*Bibliographie der Schriften des Universitätsprofessors Dr. Hans von MZIK*. Vienna, 1936. [70]

KUHN, E., *Übersicht der Schriften Theodor NÖLDEKE's*. Giessen, 1907. [628]

LITTMAN, E., *Der wissenschaftliche Nachlass von Th. NÖLDEKE*. Leipzig, 1933. [246]

SECRET, Fr., *Bibliographie des manuscrits de Guillaume POSTEL*. Geneva, 1970. [250]

*Exposé des titres et travaux scientifiques de M. Éduard RONDOT*. Bordeaux, 1888. [52]

SCHMIDT, J. H., *Friedrich SARRE, Schriften. Zum 22 Juni 1935*. Berlin, 1935. [207]

His writings after 1935 are listed in *Kunst des Orients* **6**, 1969, p. 184.

SOURDEL-THOMINE, J. & SOURDEL, D., *Index analytique de l'oeuvre de Jean SAUVAGET*. Damascus, 1961. [5000]

*Publications du R. P. Paul SBATH*. Cairo, 1939. [18]

# Encyclopaedias and reference works

DIANA GRIMWOOD-JONES

If Gabrieli had few published sources at his disposal when he compiled his *Manuale*, he also had few rivals. In recent years, however, the proliferation of literature on all aspects of Islam and the Arab countries plus the greater sophistication of modern bibliographical methods have encouraged the production of numerous and generally reliable reference guides. Several of these are listed below in the section 'Guides to the literature', and vary considerably in their form and content, depending not only on the type of readership envisaged (scholars, undergraduates, librarians, general readers, etc.) but also on the country of production: the European and American guides tend to rely mainly on works produced by Westerners; the Arabs, not unnaturally, base their reference guides firmly on material written in, or translated into, Arabic. One of the main aims of this chapter, then, is to try to effect some sort of balance between European-language material and that in Arabic. Also, with such a volume of literature available, the accent has been on supplementation rather than duplication, although a certain amount of this is inevitable. The major sources have been the published catalogues of the libraries of the British Museum and School of Oriental and African Studies, London (including the latter's Monthly accessions lists) and the holdings of the Oriental Section of Durham University Library. Other sources include the *Abstracta Islamica* and, of course, *Index Islamicus*.

## I. ENCYCLOPAEDIAS

Gabrieli, in his section 'Dizionari o repertorii enciclopedici' mentions none of the classical Arabic 'encyclopaedias', and certainly the ordinary student of Islam can have few calls to consult them. Readers interested in this aspect of Arabic literary development should see the article

PELLAT, C., 'Les encyclopédies dans le monde arabe'. *JWH* **9**, 1966, pp. 631–58.
Gives an excellent survey of Arabic encyclopaedias, with details of contents, from Jāḥiẓ's *Kitāb al-ḥayawān* in the ninth century to Tâshköprüzâde's *Miftāḥ al-sa'āda* in the sixteenth century. Encyclopaedias listed below are, therefore, all 'modern'.

AMĪN, Ḥasan, *Islamic Shi'ite encyclopaedia*. Beirut, 1968–.
At least eight volumes have so far been published.

'AṬIYYAT ALLĀH, Aḥmad, *Al-qāmūs al-islāmī*. 3v. Cairo, 1966.
Deals with all aspects of Islamic thought and civilization, and includes biographies of eminent Western scholars, e.g. Derenbourg, De Sacy.

-BUSTĀNĪ, Buṭrus, *Dā'irat al-ma'ārif; Encyclopédie arabe.* 11v. Beirut, 1876–1900.

The first attempt at an Arabic encyclopaedia along modern lines. At present being revised and greatly enlarged by

-BUSTĀNĪ, Fu'ād Afrām, *Dā'irat al-ma'ārif: qāmūs 'āmm li-kull fann wa maṭlab.* Beirut, 1956–.

An illustrated encyclopaedia, with a French index of principal articles. 30v. are proposed, of which at least ten have appeared to date.

DĀ'IRAT AL-MA'ĀRIF AL-ISLĀMIYYA FĪ TARJAMA 'ARABIYYA, tr. Aḥmad Thābit al-Fandī and others. Vols. 1–14 (all publ.). Cairo, 1933 (repr. Baghdad, 1970).

Arabic partial translation of the *Encyclopaedia of Islām*, ending with the letter *ṣād*.

ENCYCLOPAEDIA OF ISLĀM. 4v. and Suppl. Leiden, &c., 1913–38.

—— New edn. Leiden, &c., 1954–.

ENCYCLOPÉDIE DE L'ISLĀM. Nouvelle édn. Tome 1–. Leiden, &c., 1960–.

The new edition has reached (1975) the letter 'K', so it will still take several years to complete. An index to both the English and French editions has been prepared.

İSLÂM ANSİKLOPEDİSİ; İSLÂM ÂLEMİ TARİH, ĞOGRAFYA, ETNOGRAFYA VE BIOGRAFYA LUGATİ. 11v. in 12. Istanbul, 1943–70.

Unfortunately never completed: the last issue ends with *tarika*.

In addition to the above-mentioned *Encyclopaedias of Islām*, there are also

GIBB, H. A. R. & KRAMERS, J. H., *Shorter encyclopaedia of Islam*, ed. on behalf of the Royal Netherlands Academy . . . Leiden, &c., 1953 (repr. 1969).

and

WENSINCK, A. J. & KRAMERS, J. H., *Handwörterbuch des Islam* . . . Leiden, 1941,

which consist of articles, primarily on religion and law, taken from the larger work. The bibliography of the English version is more up to date, but the German edition is rather fuller – 829 pp. as against 661 pp.

HERAVI, M. *ed.*, *Concise encyclopedia of the Middle East.* Washington, D.C., 1973.

A good general encyclopaedia devoted almost exclusively to the modern Middle East, which includes a number of useful biographies.

HUGHES, T. P., *A dictionary of Islam, being a cyclopedia of the doctrines, rites, ceremonies and customs . . . of the Muhammadan religion.* London, 1896 (repr. Karachi, 1964).

-KAYYĀLĪ, 'Abd al-Wahhāb & ZUHAYRĪ, Kāmil, *Al-mawsū'a al-siyāsiyya.* Beirut, 1974.

Not confined to Middle Eastern politics.

KREISER, K. and others *eds.*, *Lexikon der islamischen Welt.* 3v. Stuttgart, 1974.

A paperback edition containing about 600 articles on a great diversity of topics, both classical and modern.

-MAWSŪ'A AL-'ARABIYYA AL-MUYASSARA. Cairo, 1965.

A general, non-illustrated one-volume encyclopaedia based in part on the *Columbia Viking desk encyclopaedia.*

MUFARRIJ, Ṭūnī Bishāra, *Al-mawsū'a al-lubnāniyya al-muṣawwara*. 2v. Beirut, 1969–70.

RONART, S. & N., *Lexikon der arabischen Welt* . . . ed. by F. Hofer. Zurich, 1972.

A revised German translation of their *Concise encyclopaedia of Arabic civilization*, 2v., Amsterdam, 1966.

SHEIKH, M. S., *A dictionary of Muslim philosophy*. Lahore, 1970.

SHIMONI, Y. & LEVINE, E. *eds.*, *Political dictionary of the Middle East in the twentieth century*. London, 1972.

Includes material on the history and politics, social and military aspects of the countries of the region, with a good deal of biographical information.

ZAKĪ, 'Abd al-Raḥmān, *Mawsū'a madīnat al-Qāhira fī alf 'ām*. Cairo, 1969.

## II. GUIDES TO THE LITERATURE AND REFERENCE HISTORIES

These two sections are sufficiently similar in character to allow them to be placed next to each other, though not similar enough to allow them to be combined. The 'Guides to the literature' is the more obviously bibliographical, but could not be left out of any paper claiming to be of reference books; the 'Reference histories' section is intended to list those works which are regarded primarily as storehouses of facts rather than of bibliographical information, though a good deal of this may be obtained also therefrom.

### (a) Guides to the Literature

ABBOUD, P. F., 'Spoken Arabic'. (In T. A. Sebeok *ed.*, *Current trends in linguistics, v.6 : Linguistics in South West Asia and North Africa*, The Hague, 1970, pp. 439–66.)

A critical account of the significant linguistic studies made on Arabic dialects[1] in the period following World War II, with a sketch of the history of dialect studies in Europe and the major scholarly works prior to World War II.

'ABD AL-RAḤMĀN, 'Abd al-Jabbār, *Dalīl al-marāji' al-'arabiyya wa al-mu'arraba; Guide to Arabic reference books: an annotated bibliography*. Basra, 1970.

Intended primarily to serve as an aid to the reference librarian and those relying on Arabic sources for their research, therefore stress has been laid on the latest editions to facilitate its use as a buying list. The author plans to issue periodic supplements.

-AMĪN, 'Abd al-Karīm & IBRĀHĪM, Zāhida, *Dalīl al-marāji' al-'arabiyya; Guide to Arabic reference books*. Baghdad, 1970–.

A fully annotated guide to reference works in Arabic.

BIRNBAUM, E., *Books on Asia from the Near East to the Far East; a guide for the general reader*. Toronto, 1971.

The section entitled 'The Islamic world' (pp. 17–131), which includes North Africa, covers such topics as history, religion, the social sciences, arts and literature in translation.

[1] Other surveys of Arabic dialect studies will be found under Section VI(c) '*Dialect dictionaries*' below.

BLANC, H., 'Semitic languages'. (In T. A. Sebeok *ed.*, *Current trends in linguistics, v. 1 : Soviet and East European linguistics*, The Hague, 1970.)

The part of this dealing with Arabic, though only a few pages long (pp. 377–83) is an extremely useful guide to Arabic philological studies in Russian on syntax, morphology, lexicography, &c., incorporated in a history of the study of Arabic philology in Russia. It includes material on the Central Asian Arabic dialects.

BROCKELMANN, C., *Geschichte der arabischen Litteratur.* Zweite den Supplementbänden angepasste Auflage. 2v. Leiden, 1943–49.

—— Supplementbände I–III. Leiden, 1937–42.

—— *Ta'rīkh al-adab al-'arabī*, tr. 'Abd al-Ḥalīm al-Najjār. Cairo, 1960–.

DE BARY, W. T. & EMBREE, A. T. *eds.*, *A guide to Oriental classics* . . . New York, &c., 1964.

'Classics of the Islamic tradition' covers pp. 9–35. A small section on general works is followed by seven 'classics' – The *Mu'allaqāt*; *Qur'ān*; *Maqāmāt al-Ḥarīrī*; *The Arabian Nights*; Ghazālī's *Munqidh min al-ḍalāl*; Ibn Rushd's *Faṣl al-maqāl*; Ibn Khaldūn's *Muqaddima*. No editions of texts are listed, just translations and secondary readings.

-HAJRASĪ, Sa'd M., *Bibliographical guide to reference works in the Arab world; Al-dalīl al-bibliyūjrāfī li-al-marāji' bi-al-'ālam al-'arabī.* Cairo, 1965.

Nearly all the works treated are in Arabic, but with comments in English and French.

ḤIMĀDA, Muḥammad Māhir, *Al-maṣādir al-'arabiyya wa-al-mu'arraba.* (Beirut?) 1972.

KILLEAN, C. G., 'Classical Arabic'. (In T. A. Sebeok *ed.*, *Current trends in linguistics, v.6 : Linguistics in South West Asia and North Africa.* The Hague, 1970, pp. 413–38.)

Divided into three sections: Descriptive studies; Diachronic studies (both subdivided into phonological studies, morphological studies, historical dialectology, &c.); Arabic linguistics in the modern Arab world – a survey of modern linguistic analyses of classical Arabic.

LATHAM, J. D., 'Arabic literature'. (In D. M. Lang *ed.*, *A guide to Eastern literatures*, London, 1971, pp. 1–50.)

The volume as a whole is designed for a wide public, especially school and university students. This particular section gives a brief historical background, a survey of the main trends in literature, and short biographies of 37 classical writers, followed by a basic bibliography.

LENINGRAD. AKADEMIYA NAUK S.S.S.R., *Spravochnaya literatura po stranom Azii i Afriki; svody katalog inostrannykh fondov biblioteki Akademii Nauk S.S.S.R. i Gosudarstvennoi Publichnoi Biblioteki, 1945–1968*; pod red. T. A. Vaganovoi i S. S. Bulatova. Leningrad, 1972.

MEISELES, G., *A bibliography of reference books and basic works on Arab language, literature, history, civilization and Islam.* (In Hebrew.) Tel-Aviv, 1970.

MIDDLE EAST LIBRARIES COMMITTEE, *Middle East and Islam; a bibliographical introduction*, ed. D. Hopwood and D. Grimwood-Jones. (Bibliotheca Asiatica, 9.) Zug, 1972.

A guide to the basic books in a wide variety of subjects.

PAREJA CASAÑAS, F. M., *Islamologie.* Par F. M. Pareja . . . en collaboration avec L. Hertling . . . A. Bausani . . . (et) Th. Bois . . . Beirut, 1957–63.

Short chapters covering the history of the entire Muslim world in all its aspects are followed by substantial bibliographies.

PEARSON, J. D. *comp., Index Islamicus, 1906–1955; a catalogue of articles on Islamic subjects in periodicals and other collective publications.* Cambridge, 1958, with Supplements for 1956–60 (1962); 1961–65 (1967); 1966–70 (London, 1972); 1971–72 (London, 1973); 1972–73 (London, 1973); in progress.

Apart from its indexes to articles from about 500 periodicals, it is a useful guide to collective volumes – Festschriften, &c. – concerned with the Middle East.

SAUVAGET, J., *Introduction à l'histoire de l'Orient musulman; éléments de bibliographie.* Édn. refondue et complétée par Cl. Cahen. (Initiation à l'Islam, 1.) Paris, 1961.

—— *Introduction to the history of the Muslim East; a bibliographical guide, based on the second edition* . . . by Cl. Cahen, Berkeley, 1965.

The French edition is a more 'scholarly' production – the revised edition is aimed primarily at the undergraduate, and has additions designed specifically for the English-speaking student.

-ṢĀWĪ, ʿAbd Allāh Ismāʿīl, *Al-marājiʿ al-ʿarabiyya.* Cairo, *c.* 1956.

An introduction to such classical Arabic reference texts as Ibn al-Nadīm's *Fihrist*, Thaʿlabī's *Yatīmat al-dahr* and Ibn Manẓūr's *Lisān al-ʿArab.*

SEZGIN, F., *Geschichte des arabischen Schrifttums.* Vol. **1**–. Leiden, 1967–.

For the main entry see p. 43.

SPULER, B. & FORRER, L., *Der vordere Orient in islamischer Zeit.* (Wissenschaftliche Forschungsberichte; Geisteswissenschaftliche Reihe . . . Bd. 21 . . . Orientalistik, III. Teil.) Bern, 1954.

## (b) Reference Histories

ARBERRY, A. J. *ed., Religion in the Middle East; three religions in concord and conflict. Vol.* **2**: *Islam.* Cambridge, 1969.

A collection of articles by leading authorities.

BLACHÈRE, R., *Histoire de la littérature arabe des origines à la fin du XVe siècle de J.C.* Vols. **1–3**. Paris, 1952–66.

Vol. 1, in the nature of an introduction, examines the Arab mode of life, historical factors, the adoption of Arabic as a literary language, up to A.D. 725. Vol. 2 deals with the period before 670, including the Qur'ān, pre-Islamic and early Islamic poetry and poetic themes. Vol. 3 continues as far as A.D. 725.

CAETANI, L., *Annali dell'Islam.* 10v. Milan, &c., 1905–26 (repr. Hildesheim, 1972–73).

Minutely detailed treatment of the early years of Islam from the Flight to 40 A.H., with critical analyses of the Arabic sources.

—— *Chronographia islamica, ossia riassunto cronologico della storia di tutti i populi musulmani dall'anno I all'anno 922 della Higrah.* 5 fasc. Paris, 1912–1923.

Regrettably only five fascicles of this work (to 132 A.H.) appeared. It provides a list of the main events, year by year and in topographical order, with detailed references to sources.

CAMBRIDGE HISTORY OF ARABIC LITERATURE. Cambridge (in preparation).

CAMBRIDGE HISTORY OF ISLAM, ed. P. M. Holt, A. K. S. Lambton and B. Lewis. 2v. Cambridge, 1970.

Despite the editors' remarks that it is not intended primarily for reference, it may be used very successfully as such.

GABRIELI, F., *Storia della letteratura araba*. Milan, 1951.

HAMMER, J. von, *Literaturgeschichte der Araber von ihrem Beginne bis zu Ende des XII. Jhr. der H.* 7v. Vienna, 1951–56.

A full description of the contents of this is to be found in Gabrieli's *Manuale*, pp. 164–6.

LEWIS, B. & HOLT, P. M. *eds.*, *Historians of the Middle East*. London, 1962.

An important source for Islamic historiography.

NICHOLSON, R. A., *A literary history of the Arabs*. London, 1907 (repr. Cambridge, 1953).

Still useful for the classical period.

MANSOOR, M., *Political and diplomatic history of the Arab world, 1900–1967: a chronological study*. 7v. Washington, D.C., 1972.

A detailed chronological account of all major political events in the Arab world; the work is entirely factual, with no attempt at critical evaluation.

MIDDLE EAST RECORD, London, later Jerusalem, 1960–.

A survey of politics and international relations. The latest volume is 1967 (published 1971) with extracts from major world newspapers as well as policy statements, reports of summit conferences, &c.

PITCHER, D. E., *An historical geography of the Ottoman Empire, from the earliest times to the end of the sixteenth century*. Leiden, 1972.

RECUEIL DES HISTORIENS DES CROISADES. 16v. Paris, 1841–1906 (repr. Farnborough, 1966–67).

A monumental collection of texts and translations, comprising five sections: Historiens occidentaux (5v. in 6); Lois (2v.); Historiens grecs (2v.); Documents arméniens (2v.); Historiens orientaux (5v. in 4).

SOURDEL, D. and J., *La civilisation de l'Islam classique*. Paris, 1968.

In addition, useful reference can be made to the relevant volumes of the *Handbücher der Orientalistik* published in Leiden, a series which has produced some excellent handbooks on such topics as Islamic music, medicine and law.

## III. THE MUSLIM CALENDAR: CONVERSION TABLES

CAMPANI, R., *Calendario arabo*. Modena, 1914.

CATTENOZ, H., *Tables de concordance des ères chrétiennes et hégiriennes*. 2nd edn. Rabat, 1954.

DELPECH, A., 'Tables chronologiques'. *Bulletin de la Société Géographique d'Alger*, 5/6, 1903, pp. 497–522.

FREEMAN-GRENVILLE, G. S. P., *The Muslim and Christian calendars, being tables for the conversion of Muslim and Christian dates from the Hijra to the year A.D. 2000*. London, 1963.

Probably the easiest to use.

HAIG, Sir Wolseley, *Comparative tables of Muhammadan and Christian dates . . .* London, 1932.

Useful for quick year-to-year conversions.

JIMÉNEZ, M. O., *Tablas de conversión de datas islámicas a cristianas y viceversa.* Madrid, 1946.

JUSUÉ, E., *Tablas de reducción del cómputo musulmán al cristiano y viceversa, precedidas de una explicación en castellano y en latín.* Madrid, 1903.

KIKANO, A. B., *Table de concordance des années hégiriennes et chrétiennes; Jadwal al-sinīn al-hijriyya wa mā yuwāfiquhā min al-sinīn al-mīlādiyya.* Beirut, 1966.

LACOINE, E., *Table de concordance des dates des calendriers arabe, copte, grégorien, israélite . . .* Paris, 1891.

ORBELI, I., *Sinkhronistischeskie tablitsy khidzhry i evropeiskogo letoschisleniya.* Moscow, 1961.

TSYBUL'SKII, V. V., *Sovremennye kalendari stran Blizhnego i Srednego Vostoka; sinkhronisticheskie tablitsy i poyasneniya.* Moscow, 1964.

WÜSTENFELD, F., *Wüstenfeld-Mahler'sche Vergleichungs-Tabellen zur muslimischen und iranischen Zeitrechnung mit Tafeln zum Umrechnung orient-christlicher Ären.* 3. . . . Auflage unter Mitarbeit von J. Mayr; neu bearb. von B. Spuler. Wiesbaden, 1961.

Tables for the conversion of Muslim dates are also found on pp. 41–8 of L. Caetani and G. Gabrieli's *Onomasticon Arabicum,* vol. 1, Rome, 1915; pp. 358–80 of Gabrieli's *Manuale,* entitled 'Tabella comparativa dell'era musulmana e della cristiana'; p. 37 of A. Grohmann's *Arabische Chronologie . . .* (Handbuch der Orientalistik, Abt. 1, Ergsbd. 2, Halbbd. 1), Leiden, 1966; and opposite p. 116 of M. Guboglu's *Palaeografia si diplomatica Turco-Osmana,* Bucharest, 1958.

## IV. DIRECTORIES AND GENERAL GUIDES TO THE AREA

For guides to individual countries, a series of Area Handbooks, which includes all the countries of the Middle East, has been published by Foreign Area Studies Division, The American University, Washington, D.C.

ADAMS, M. *ed., The Middle East; a handbook.* London, 1971.

Begins with comparative statistics and country-by-country facts and figures, followed by six sections: General background; The countries of the Middle East (including the Maghreb); Political affairs; Economic affairs; Social patterns; The arts and mass media. Numerous maps.

AFRICAN BOOK TRADE DIRECTORY, 1971, ed. S. Taubert. Munich, 1971.

Includes Egypt and the Maghreb.

ANNUAIRE DES PROFESSIONS AU LIBAN; LEBANESE INDUSTRIAL AND COMMERCIAL DIRECTORY. Beirut, 1953–.

Published every two years, the directory is divided into two sections: Renseignements généraux (géographie, histoire, informations générales, aperçu économique) and Toutes les professions au Liban.

ANNUAIRE DES SOCIÉTÉS LIBANAISES PAR ACTIONS; YEARBOOK OF THE LEBANESE JOINT-STOCK COMPANIES. Beirut, 1964–.

ANNUAIRE DU MONDE MUSULMAN; STATISTIQUE, HISTORIQUE, SOCIAL ET ÉCONOMIQUE, réd. par L. Massignon. 4e édn. rev. de V. Monteil. Paris, 1955.

Divided broadly into three sections: Asia; Africa; Europe, subdivided according to individual countries. It gives details of geographical situation, principal towns, population, religion, government and administration, industry, &c., followed by short bibliographies which include newspaper articles. Unfortunately, not continued after 1955, but still of historical importance.

ANON, 'Language tapes, records and correspondence courses in Middle Eastern languages'. *MESA bull.* **7**, ii, 1973, pp. 32–9.

For the United States only. Covers Modern Standard Arabic, Algerian, Egyptian, Iraqi, Moroccan, Syrian and Tunisian.

ARAB DIRECTORY FOR COMMERCE, INDUSTRY AND LIBERAL PROFESSIONS IN THE ARAB COUNTRIES. New York, 1947–. (Also Beirut?)

BACHARACH, J. L., *A Near East studies handbook 570–1974.* Seattle, &c., 1974.

A most useful handbook for the student; it includes dynastic and genealogical tables, a historical atlas and calendars.

BAHRAIN TRADE DIRECTORY. 7th edn., ed. A. E. Ashir. Bahrain, 1967.

DIRECTORY OF THE REPUBLIC OF THE SUDAN, (later:) TRADE DIRECTORY OF THE REPUBLIC OF THE SUDAN, (later:) SUDAN TRADE DIRECTORY. London, 1957–.

HACHETTE, *Hachette world guides; the Middle East-Lebanon-Syria-Jordan-Iraq, Iran.* Paris, 1966.

IRAQ INTERNATIONAL TRADE DIRECTORY, 1970–71, (later:) THE ARAB TRADE DIRECTORY; DALĪL AL-IQTIṢĀD AL-ʿARABĪ. Baghdad, 1971–.

ISTIPHAN, I., *Directory of social agencies in Cairo.* Cairo, 1956.

Covers 652 agencies in Cairo.

LJUNGGREN, F. & GEDDES, C. L., *An international directory of institutes and societies interested in the Middle East.* Amsterdam, 1962.

Arranged according to country, and covers the ancient as well as the modern Middle East. Gives the addresses, history, purpose and fields of interest of 351 institutions.

MATTISON, F. C. *ed.*, *A survey of American interests in the Middle East.* Washington, D.C., 1953.

THE MIDDLE EAST, 1948–, (later:) THE MIDDLE EAST AND NORTH AFRICA, 1964/65–, A SURVEY AND DIRECTORY. London, 1948–.

Published annually, is undoubtedly the best directory on the Middle East. Divided into four sections: General survey; Regional organizations; Country surveys; Other reference material – Who's who, bibliography, research institutions (mostly outside the Middle East).

MIDDLE EAST TRADE DIRECTORY: COMMERCIAL- INDUSTRIAL, TOURISTIC AND AGRICULTURAL, 1961/62–. Beirut, 1961–.

MOTAMAR AL-ALAM AL-ISLAMI; WORLD MUSLIM GAZETTEER. Karachi, 1965.

Divided into three sections: Independent Muslim countries; Semi-independent countries and areas under non-Muslim control (e.g. Ethiopia, some of the Central Asian republics); The Muslim world in facts and figures.

MOUTSATSOS, B., 'Directory of films on the Middle East'. *MESA bull.* **5**, i, 1971, pp. 39–55; **6**, ii, 1972, pp. 44–50.

Gives names and addresses of U.S. organizations renting or selling films on the Middle East, with details of films available.

ROYAL INSTITUTE OF INTERNATIONAL AFFAIRS, *The Middle East; a political and economic survey*, 4th edn., ed. P. Mansfield. London, 1973.

A revised and updated version of Sir R. Bullard's 1958 edition.

UNESCO, *Directory of archives, libraries, documentation centres and bibliographical institutions in Arabic speaking states*; prep. by A. Badr. Cairo, 1965.

## V. THESES AND GUIDES TO RESEARCH

AMERICAN UNIVERSITY OF BEIRUT JAFET MEMORIAL LIBRARY, *Masters' theses, 1909–1970*; comp. by N. Mikdashi. Beirut, 1971.

BAGHDAD UNIVERSITY CENTRAL LIBRARY, *Fihris bi-uṭrūḥāt al-'irāqiy-yīn al-mūda'a fī al-Maktaba al-Markaziyya li-Jāmi'at Baghdād*. Baghdad, 1967; First suppl., Baghdad, 1969.

BLOOMFIELD, B. C. [and others], *Theses on Africa accepted by universities in the United Kingdom and Ireland*. (Standing Conference on Library Materials on Africa.) Cambridge, 1964.

Covers the period *c.* 1920–62, and includes the whole of North Africa.

—— *Theses on Asia accepted by universities in the United Kingdom and Ireland, 1877–1964*. London, 1967.

The work is divided into large general areas, of which Islam is one: of the 2571 items listed, 405 are concerned either with some aspect of Islamic culture or a Muslim country. It is continued in the *Bulletin of the Association of British Orientalists* N.S. **4**, 1968, pp. 56–65; N.S. **5**, 1970, pp. 19–40.

CAIRO. JĀMI'AT AL-AZHAR, *Qā'ima ... li-al-rasā'il al-jāmi'iyya allatī ujīzat li-nayl darajāt al-dirāsāt al-'ulyā li-kulliyyat uṣūl al-dīn, al-Sharī'a, al-lugha al-'arabiyya*. Cairo, 1968.

CAIRO. JĀMI'AT 'AYN SHAMS, *Al-taqrīr al-'ilmī, 1956–1960*. Cairo, 1961.

Summaries of theses presented at Ain Shams.

CAIRO. JĀMI'AT AL-QĀHIRA, *Al-rasā'il al-'ilmiyya li-darajatay al-mājistīr wa-al-duktūrāh*. Cairo, 1958.

—— *Dalīl 'anāwīn rasā'il al-mājistīr wa-al-duktūrāh bi-Kulliyyāt Jāmi'at al-Qāhira li-al-'ām 1969–70*. Cairo, *c.* 1971.

DINSTEL, M. *comp.*, *List of French doctoral dissertations on Africa, 1884–1961*. Boston, Mass., 1966.

Out of 2918 titles, 1740 are directly concerned with what is now known as the Arab Middle East (including Sudan), although no distinction is made between, say, Pharaonic and present-day Egypt.

DURHAM UNIVERSITY CENTRE FOR MIDDLE EASTERN AND ISLAMIC STUDIES, *Register of current British research in Middle Eastern and Islamic studies*. Durham, 1969; rev. edn. 1971.

FINKE, D. and others, *Deutsche Hochschulschriften über den modernen islamischen Orient; German theses on the Islamic Middle East*. (Deutsches Orient-Institut, Dokumentationsdienst Moderner Orient, Reihe A, 1.) Hamburg, 1973.

HAMZA, M. M. *comp.*, *Theses on the Sudan and by Sudanese accepted for higher degrees*. Khartoum, 1966.

KAPPERT, P. and others *comps.*, 'Dissertationen zu Geschichte und Kultur des Osmanischen Reiches, angenommen an deutschen, österreichischen und schweizerischen Universitäten seit 1945'. *Der Islam* **49**, 1972, pp. 110–19.

Only of fringe interest for the Arab Middle East, but contains a few relevant items.

KÖHLER, J., *Deutsche Dissertationen über Afrika; ein Verzeichnis für die Jahre 1918–1959*. Bonn, 1962.

MIDDLE EAST STUDIES ASSOCIATION, 'Directory of graduate and undergraduate programs and courses in Middle East studies in the United States, Canada and abroad'. *MESA bull.* **6** (Special issue), 1972.

MOSCOW. INST. VOSTOKOVEDENIYA, *Doktorskie i kandidatskie dissertatsii, zashchishchennye v Institute Vostokovedeniya A.N.S.S.R. s 1950 po 1970*. Moscow, 1970.

RABAT. UNIV. MOHAMMED V. CENTRE UNIVERSITAIRE DE LA RECHERCHE SCIENTIFIQUE, 'Thèses et mémoires de l'Université Mohammed V'. *Bull. signalétique* **3** (Special issue), 1970.

SCHWARZ, K., *Verzeichnis deutschsprachiger Hochschulschriften zum islamischen Orient (1885–1970). Deutschland-Österreich-Schweiz*. (Islamkündliche Materialen, 2.) Freiburg im Breisgau, 1971.

SELIM, G. D., *American doctoral dissertations on the Arab world, 1883–1968*. Washington, D.C., 1970.

Covers all Arabic-speaking countries of the Near East and North Africa, and all communities where Arabic is spoken. Its main source was *Dissertation Abstracts*, but unpublished sources, e.g. university lists, were used. If the dissertation has been published, this is indicated.

SHULMAN, F. J., *American and British doctoral dissertations on Israel and Palestine in modern times*. Ann Arbor, 1973.

Lists 530 theses, classified according to subject: Palestine before 1948; Zionism and related Jewish nationalism; the State of Israel; the Palestine Arabs and minority groups; the Arab-Israeli conflict.

STANDING CONFERENCE ON LIBRARY MATERIALS ON AFRICA, *United Kingdom publications and theses on Africa, 1963–*. Cambridge, 1966–.

Has a sizeable section on North Africa.

Research facilities in various Middle Eastern countries have been surveyed periodically in the *MESA bull.*, and details of these will be found on pp. 190–193 (Hopwood: 'Archives'). The *Bulletin* also includes a section on current research in progress.

## VI. DICTIONARIES

This area of Arabic studies is extraordinarily well covered bibliographically. The major reference work is:

GHĀLĪ, Wajdī Rizq, *Al-mu'jamāt al-'arabiyya: bibliyūjrāfiya shāmila mashrūḥa; Arabic dictionaries: an annotated comprehensive bibliography*. Cairo, 1971.

This lists 707 dictionaries divided into monoglot, bilingual and polyglot, and special (subdivided according to subject). It is copiously annotated in Arabic and includes most of the dictionaries published during 1971. A shorter version is the author's 'Arabic dictionaries: an annotated comprehensive bibliography', *MIDEO* **10**, 1970, pp. 341–66, which is limited to bilingual and polyglot dictionaries. Another guide to Arabic dictionaries, but with a North African emphasis, is

IBN AL-'ARABĪ, al-Ṣādiq, 'Mu'jam al-ma'ājim al-'arabiyya al-mu'allafa khilāl mi'ah 'ām 1869–1969'. *Al-Lisān al-'Arabī* **7**, ii, 1970, pp. 160–84,

containing about 300 entries.

It would be pointless to attempt to rival these. However, in addition to dictionaries, there are several useful glossaries and vocabularies – outside the terms of reference of the bibliographies mentioned above – which are worthy of note. A fruitful source for these is the periodical *Al-Lisān al-'Arabī*, and selected glossaries from this and other periodicals appear below together with the odd item that has slipped through Ghālī's net, those dictionaries which have been published since his work appeared, and any new editions or reprints which update his entries. Of the (unannotated) items in the list of dictionaries on pp. 7–9 of J. H. Hospers *ed.*, *A basic bibliography for the study of the Semitic languages* vol. **2**, Leiden, 1974, Ibn Manẓūr's *Lisān al-'Arab* and Salmoné's dictionary are also included here for the sake of the notes.

### (a) Monoglot Dictionaries

(i) classical authors (pre-1800)

IBN MANẒŪR, Muḥ. b. Mukarram Jamāl al-Dīn, *Lisān al-'arab*. New edn. 15v. Beirut, 1968.

Ghālī mentions only the 1881–90 edition of Ibn Manẓūr's famous lexicon. This new edition is a good deal clearer and easier to use.

—— *Lisān al-'arab al-muḥīṭ*; ed. Yūsuf Khayyāṭ and Nadīm Mir'ashlī. 3v. Beirut, 1970.

A modernized and shortened version commissioned by the Academies in Cairo, Damascus and Baghdad, and the universities in Syria and Rabat.

(ii) modern authors (1800–)

-BUSTĀNĪ, 'Abd Allāh, *Al-bustān, mu'jam lughawī muṭawwal*. 2v. Beirut, 1927–30 (repr. Beirut, 1973?).

MUNJID AL-ṬULLĀB; rev. by Fu'ād Afrām al-Bustānī. 12th edn. Beirut, 1971.

-QĀMŪS AL-KABĪR. Beirut, 1974.

About 80,000 entries, including archaic as well as modern terms.

TAYMŪR, Aḥmad, *Mu'jam Taymūr al-kabīr fī al-alfāẓ al-'āmmiyya*. Cairo, 1971.

(b) Bilingual Dictionaries

ʻABD AL-NŪR, Jabbūr and IDRĪS, Suhayl, *Al-manhal al-wasīṭ; dictionnaire usuel français-arabe.* Beirut, 1972.

ABŪ AL-FAḌL, Fahmī, 'Neue arabische Ausdrücke'. (In *Festgabe für Hans Wehr* . . . hrsg. W. Fischer, Wiesbaden, 1969, pp. 112–29.)

About 500 Arabic neologisms, with German translations.

-BAʻLBAKKĪ, Munīr, *Al-mawrid al-wasīṭ.* Beirut, 1971?

BARANOV, K. K., *Arabsko-Russkii slovar'.* Moscow, 1958.

BELKIN, V. S., *Karmannyi Arabsko-Russkii slovar'.* Moscow, 1970.

BELOT, J.-B., *Belot classique français-arabe.* 12e édn. Beirut, 1971.

—— *Dictionnaire français-arabe.* Nouvelle édn. entièrement refondue sous la direction du R. P. R. Nakhla. 3e édn. Beirut, 1970.

—— *Al-farā'id al-durriyya li-al-ṭullāb, ʻarabī-faransī.* 21e édn. Beirut, 1968.

CHERBONNEAU, A., *Dictionnaire arabe-français* (*langue écrite*). 2v. Paris, 1876 (repr. Beirut, 1972).

CORRIENTE, F., *Diccionario español-arabe.* Madrid, 1970.

DALL'ARCHE, G., *Corso d'arabo per le scuole secondarie.* 2v. Rome, 1963.

Vol. 2 contains a *Vocabolario italiano-arabo, arabo-italiano, libico-italiano.*

-FARĀ'ID AL-DURRIYYA LI-AL-ṬULLĀB, ʻARABĪ-INKLIZĪ. 3rd edn. Beirut, 1970.

GASSELIN, M. E., *Dictionnaire français-arabe* (*arabe parlé-arabe grammatical*). 2v. Beirut, 1974.

GOTTSTEIN, M. H., *Millon ʻaravi-ʻivri ḥadash.* Tel-Aviv, 1972–.

ILYĀS, Mitrī, *Al-qāmūs al-ḥadīth, faransī-ʻarabī.* Cairo, n.d.

JANNOTTA, E., *Dizionario italiano-arabo moderno.* (A cura del Ministero degli Affari Esteri, Direzione Generale delle Relazioni Culturali con l'Estero.) 2v. Rome, 1964.

KAZIMIRSKI, A. de Biberstein, *Dictionnaire arabe-français* . . . 2v. Paris, 1860 (repr. Beirut, 1971).

KOJMAN, Y., *Millon ʻivri-ʻaravi; qāmūs ʻibrī-ʻarabī.* Tel-Aviv, 1970.

MADINA, Maan Z., *Arabic–English dictionary of the modern literary language.* New York, 1973.

MUʻJAM INKLĪZĪ-ʻARABĪ LI-AL-ṬULLĀB. 4th edn. Beirut, 1968.

NASR, R. T., *An English-colloquial Arabic dictionary.* Beirut, 1972.

Has over 9000 entries in transliterated Arabic.

PEDRO DE ALCALÁ, *Petri Hispani De lingua Arabica libri 2* (Pedro de Alcala, arte para ligeramente saber la lengua Araviga, eiusdem Vocabulista araviga con letra castellana, Granada, 1505); ed. P. de Lagarde. Göttingen, 1883.

ROME. ISTITUTO PER L'ORIENTE, *Vocabulario arabo-italiano.* 3v. Rome, 1966–73.

SABEK, Jerwan, *Al-wasit trilingual dictionary, English–French–Arabic.* Beirut, 1974.

SALMONÉ, H. A., *An advanced learner's Arabic–English dictionary.* Beirut, 1972.

A reprint of his *Arabic–English dictionary on a new system* of 1890.

SCHREGLE, G. and others, *Deutsch-arabisches Wörterbuch*. Wiesbaden, 1974.

TEZA, E., *Un piccolo glossario italiano e arabico del Quattrocento*. Rome, 1893.

### (c) Dialect Dictionaries

In addition to the general bibliographies mentioned above, Arabic dialect studies are further served by two which list not only dictionaries but important vocabularies and glossaries as well. These are:

SOBELMAN, H. *ed.*, *Arabic dialect studies; a selected bibliography*. Washington, D.C., 1962.

PÉRÈS, H., *L'arabe dialectale algérien et saharien; bibliographie analytique avec un index méthodique*. (Bibl. Inst. Ét. Sup. Isl. Alger, 14.) Algiers, 1958.

A good survey of Arabic dialect studies is also given on pp. 257–78 of J. Cantineau's *Études de linguistique arabe*, Paris, 1960. The section 'Modern Arabic dialects' compiled by F. Leemhuis on pp. 88–107 of Hospers, *op. cit.*, vol. 2, should also be consulted.

The following list is an attempt to supplement these four while avoiding the duplication of items already in Ghālī.

*Sudan and Central Africa*

DICTIONNAIRE FRANÇAIS-ARABE (DIALECTE DU TCHAD), publ. par les Assemblées chrétiennes du Tchad. Selsey, n.d.

FAURE, P., *Introduction au parler arabe de l'est du Tchad. 2: Vocabulaire*. Lyon, &c., *c*. 1969.

QĀSIM, ʿAwn al-Sharīf, *Qāmūs al-lahja al-ʿāmmiyya fī al-Sūdān*. Khartoum, 1972.

ROTH-LALY, A., *Lexique des parlers arabes tchado-soudanais; an Arabic-English-French lexicon of the dialects spoken in the Chad-Sudan area*. 4v. Paris, 1969–72.

Compiled from G. Trenga's *Le bura-mabang du Ouadaï*, Paris, 1947; H. Carbou's *Méthode pratique pour l'étude de l'arabe parlé au Ouaday et à l'est du Tchad*, Paris, 1913; G. L. Lethem's *Colloquial Arabic; Shuwa dialect of Bornu, Nigeria and of the region of Lake Tchad*, London, 1920, and S. Hillelson's *Sudan Arabic; English-Arabic vocabulary*, 2nd edn. London, 1930.

*Egypt*

ʿABD AL-ʿĀL, ʿAbd al-Munʿim Sayyid, *Muʿjam al-alfāẓ al-ʿāmmiyya al-miṣriyya dhāt al-uṣūl al-ʿarabiyya*. Cairo, 1971.

*Arabian Peninsula*

LEACH, H. R., *A short vocabulary of Omani Arabic*. Nizwa, 1961.

Has about 300 words in Arabic script with English translation, and about the same number in transliterated Arabic. In addition, has quite a large section on salutations and greetings, polite phrases, etc.

*Iraq*

THOMPSON, R. C., *A list of words and phrases in the Basrah dialect of Arabic . . .* Simla, 1915.

*Lebanon*

FURAIḤA, Anīs, *Mu'jam al-alfāẓ al-'āmmiyya fī al-lahja al-lubnāniyya; a dictionary of non-classical vocables in the spoken Arabic of Lebanon.* (A.U.B. publs., Or. ser., 19.) Beirut, 1947 (repr. Beirut, 1973).

*Palestine*

ELIHAI, Y., *Dictionnaire de l'arabe parlé palestinien. Français-arabe.* ? 1974.

### (d) Special and Technical Dictionaries

Though largely superseded by Ghālī, the following is still quite a useful bibliography of Arabic technical dictionaries:

GHALEB, É., *Al-mawsū'a fī 'ulūm al-ṭabī'a ... Dictionnaire des sciences de la nature ...* vol. 1, Beirut, 1966, pp. 13–15.

In addition to the items listed below, the Bureau Permanent d'Arabisation in Rabat has produced a series of dictionaries on a variety of subjects. At least 15 have so far been produced in this *Série Lexicographique.*

#### (i) language and literature

-'ADNĀNĪ, Muḥammad, *Mu'jam al-akhṭā' al-shā'i'a.* Beirut, 1973.

A dictionary of common language errors and their corrections.

BAILEY, E. M., *A list of modern Arabic words as used in daily and weekly newspapers of Cairo.* Cairo, *c.* 1948.

CACHIA, P., *The monitor, al-'arīf; a dictionary of Arabic grammatical terms.* Beirut, 1973.

FĀKHŪRĪ, Riyād, *Mu'jam shawārid al-naḥw.* Homs, 1971.

A dictionary of anomalies in Arabic grammar.

GHĀLIB, H., *Kanz al-lugha al-'arabiyya.* Beirut, 1973.

A thesaurus rather than a dictionary, its layout is based on Roget.

ISKANDAR, Najīb, *Mu'jam al-ma'ānī li-al-mutarādif wa-al-mutawārid wa-al-naqīd min asmā' wa af'āl wa adawāt wa ta'ābīr.* Baghdad, 1971.

A dictionary of synonyms and contradictory terms.

JĀR ALLĀH, Zuhdī Ḥasan, *Al-kitāba al-ṣaḥīḥa.* Beirut, 1968.

Deviations from standard Arabic usage, with corrections.

MALKA, É., *Pour rediger et traduire; lexique moderne français-arabe des termes, expressions, formules.* Rabat, 1961.

-TŪNISĪ, Zayn al-'Ābidīn, *Al-mu'jam fī al-naḥw wa-al-ṣarf.* Damascus, 1971.

-TŪNJĪ, Muḥammad, *Mu'jam al-adawāt al-naḥwiyya.* 4th edn. Damascus, 1968.

WAHBA, Majdī, *A dictionary of literary terms, English-French-Arabic, with an index of French words and an index of Arabic words.* Beirut, 1974.

-YĀZIJĪ, Ibrāhīm, *Nuj'at al-rā'id wa shir'at al-wārid fī al-mutarādif wa-al-mutawārid.* 2nd edn. 2v. in 1. Beirut, 1970.

#### (ii) the arts

BEN 'ABD ALLĀH, 'Abd al-'Azīz, 'Mu'jam al-alwān'. *Al-Lisān al-'Arabī* **6**, 1969, pp. 381–99.

384 terms, Arabic–French.

HIMĀDA, Ibrāhīm, *Mu'jam al-muṣṭalaḥāt al-drāmiyya wa-al-masraḥiyya*. Cairo, 1971.

MURSĪ, Aḥmad Kāmil and WAHBA, Majdī, *Dictionnaire du cinéma (anglais–français–arabe)*. Cairo, 1973.

STRIKA, V., 'Note sulla terminologia araba dell'arte'. *OM* **43**, 1963, pp. 799–814.
Italian–Arabic glossary of 79 technical terms.

(iii) ARMS AND ARMOUR; WARFARE

BOUDOT-LAMOTTE, A., 'Lexique de la poésie guerrière dans le Dīwān de 'Antara b. Šaddād al-'Absī'. *Arabida* **11**, 1964, pp. 19–56.
Contains the most representative elements recurring in all Arabic epic literature.

ZAKĪ, 'Abd al-Raḥmān, *Al-silāḥ fī al-Islām; vocabulary relating to arms and armour in Islam*. (Maktabat adāwāt al-baḥth al-ta'rīkhī wa-al-wathā'iq wa-al-nuṣūṣ, 1.) Cairo, 1951.

(iv) LAW

ABDESSELAM, Abou-Bekr, *Dictionnaire arabe–français des termes juridiques et dogmatiques*. Beirut, 1935.

BEN 'ABD ALLĀH, 'Abd al-'Azīz, 'Al-mu'jam al-fiqhī al-mālikī'. *Al-Lisān al-'Arabī* **4**, 1966, pp. 215–37.

FARŪQĪ, Ḥārith Sulaymān, *Faruqi's law dictionary, Arabic–English*. Beirut, 1972.

—— *Faruqi's law dictionary, English–Arabic*. 2nd rev. edn. Beirut, 1970.

ḤAQQĪ, Mamdūḥ, *Dictionnaire juridique et commercial; termes et expressions*. 2v. Beirut, 1972.
French–Arabic and Arabic–French, covering the fields of Sharī'a, Roman Jurisprudence and modern International Law.

-MAHDI, Saeed M. A., *Definitions of common legal words and phrases*. Khartoum, 1969.
Based on the definitions of Farūqī's law dictionary and Sudanese legal practice.

MALKA, É., *Nouveau dictionnaire pratique français–arabe des termes juridiques*. Rabat, 1954.

-WAHAB, Ibrahim, *Law dictionary ... English–Arabic*. Baghdad, 1963 (repr. Beirut, 1972).

YAMMINE, A., *Al-qāmūs al-qaḍā'ī ... Dictionnaire judiciaire, politique, commercial*. Beirut, 1938.

(v) COMMERCE AND ECONOMICS

HENNI, M., *Dictionnaire des termes économiques et commerciaux, français–anglais–arabe, avec index des mots-clés anglais et arabe*. Beirut, 1972.
A French–Arabic edition was published in 1973.

JOHANNSEN, H. & ROBERTSON, A., *Management glossary, English–Arabic*, ed. by E. F. L. Brech, tr. by N. D. Ghattas. Beirut, 1972.

MÜLLER-LUTZ, H. L., *Mu'jam al-ḍamān; insurance dictionary* ... Karlsruhe, &c., 1971.

-SĀBIQ, Jirwān, *Trilingual dictionary; economics, laws . . . sociology, statistics . . . political and diplomatic sciences. Arabic–French–English, French–English–Arabic, English–French–Arabic.* Beirut, 1971.

(vi) ARCHERY/FALCONRY

LATHAM, J. D. & PATERSON, W. F., *Saracen archery; an English version and exposition of a Mameluke work on archery* . . . London, 1970, pp. 178–94.

About 400 technical archery terms, Arabic–English.

PHILLOTT, D. C., 'Vocabulary of technical falconry terms in Urdu, Persian and Arabic'. *JPASB* N.S. **6**, 1910, pp. 315–80.

English into Urdu, Persian or Arabic – mainly Persian and Urdu. Sometimes no equivalent is given: 'it is left to some future falconer to fill in the gaps'. In the case of Arabic, some of these gaps are filled by

VIRÉ, F., 'Falconaria Arabica: glanures philologiques'. *Arabica* **8**, 1961, pp. 273–93; **9**, 1962, pp. 37–60, 152–92.

Contains about 400 Arabic roots, with derivations and French translations.

(vii) DIPLOMACY AND GOVERNMENT

'AṬIYYAT ALLĀH, Aḥmad, *Al-qāmūs al-siyāsī*. 3rd edn. Cairo, 1968.

FAWQ EL 'ADAH, Samouhi, *A dictionary of diplomacy and international affairs, English–French–Arabic.* Beirut, 1974.

KEEN, M. F. A. & BESHIR, M. A., *A vocabulary of modern government for the Sudan.* Khartoum, 1950.

LEWIS, B., *A handbook of diplomatic and political Arabic.* London, 1956.

English–Arabic and Arabic–English, with appendices on Arabic honorifics, civil ranks and titles.

MEZZI, A., 'Le lexique politique de l'arabe de presse'. *GLECS* **12–13**, 1967–69, pp. 182–8.

(viii) PHILOSOPHY AND ETHICS; SUFISM

ARKOUN, M., 'Contribution à l'étude du lexique de l'éthique musulmane'. *BEO* **22**, 1969, pp. 205–37.

Derives from the author's translation of Miskawayh's *Tahdhīb al-akhlāq*. About 1000 terms are listed (Arabic–French) giving the page numbers of the translation where the term occurs.

BEN 'ABD ALLĀH, 'Abd al-'Azīz, 'Al-mu'jam al-ṣūfī'. *Al-Lisān al-'Arabī* **4**, 1966, pp. 176–208.

Arabic–French.

GOICHON, A.-M., *Lexique de la langue philosophique d'Ibn Sīnā (Avicenne).* Paris, 1938.

—— *Vocabulaires comparés d'Aristote et d'Ibn Sīnā; supplément au Lexique* . . . Paris, 1939.

-JURJĀNĪ, 'Alī b. Muḥammad, *Ta'rīfāt . . . Definitiones viri meritissimi Sejjid Scherif Ali ben Mohammed Dschordschâni, accedunt definitiones theosophi Mohji-ed-Dîn Mohammed ben Ali vulgo Ibn Arabi dicti*; ed. G. Flügel. Lipsiae, 1845.

WAHBA, Majdī [and others], *Al-mu'jam al-falsafī 'arabī-inklīzī-faransī; vocabulaire philosophique arabe avec tables françaises et anglaises*. 2nd rev. edn. Cairo, 1971.

(ix) LIBRARIANSHIP

BASYŪNĪ, Kamāl, *Qā'ima mu'jiza bi-ahamm al-muṣṭalaḥāt al-musta'mila fī 'ilmiyyat al-fahrasa ma'a ta'rīfāt lahā*. Cairo, 1964.

DĀGHIR, Yūsuf As'ad, *Dalīl al-a'ārib ilā 'ilm al-kutub wa fann al-makātib; Manuel pratique de bibliographie*. Beirut, 1947, pp. 252–325.

Subject headings of the Dewey Decimal Classification translated from Arabic into English.

KHALĪFA, Sha'bān 'Abd al-'Azīz, 'Mu'jam muṣṭalaḥāt 'ilm al-maktaba, inglīzī–'arabī'. *'Ā. al-M.* 1966, i; 1967, iii.

(x) ARMY

TAYMŪR, Aḥmad, *Al-rutab al-alqāb al-miṣriyya li-rijāl al-jaysh wa-al-hay'a al-'ilmiyya wa-al-qalamiyya*. Cairo, 1950.

(xi) SEAFARING

BRUNOT, L., *Notes lexicologiques sur le vocabulaire maritime de Rabat et Salé*. Paris, 1920.

Derived from the author's *Traditions et industries de la mer*.

GATEAU, A., *Atlas et glossaire nautiques tunisiens. Vol. 2 : Glossaire*. (Recherches publ. sous la direction de l'Inst. de Lettres Orientales de Beyrouth. Série 2: Langue et Littérature Arabes, t. 33.) Beirut, 1966.

Entirely in transliteration, thus for example the 'G' section covers the letters *ghayn*, *qāf* and *kāf*.

(xii) MEDICINE

FIḤĀM, Shākir, 'Mu'jam ṭibbī jadīd: muṣṭalaḥāt fī amrāḍ al-udhun wa-al-anf wa-al-ḥanjara'. *Al-Lisān al-'Arabī* 7, ii, 1970, pp. 110–22.

-KAWĀKIBĪ, Ṣalāḥ al-Dīn, *Naẓra 'ayyān wa tibyān fī maqālāt asmā' a'ḍā' al-insān*. Damascus, 1967–71.

Arabic–English–French.

KHĀṬIR, Murshid & KHAYYĀṬ, Aḥmad, *Mu'jam al-'ulūm al-ṭibbiyya*. Damascus, 1974.

French–English–Arabic.

SHARAF, Mohammad, *An English–Arabic dictionary of medicine, biology and allied sciences*. 3rd edn. rev. Baghdad, &c., n.d.

(xiii) SCIENCE AND TECHNOLOGY

AYYŪB B. MŪSĀ, Abū al-Baqā, *Al-kulliyyāt*. 2nd edn. Bulaq, 1281/1864.

An encyclopaedia of technical terms.

ĀL NĀṢIR AL-DĪN, Amīn, *Al-rāfid*. Beirut, 1971.

Arabic–Arabic dictionary containing the names of parts of the human body, diseases, animals, plants, minerals, &c.

ARAB LEAGUE. IDĀRA SHU'ŪN AL-BATRŪL, 'Tawḥīd al-muṣṭalaḥāt al-batrūliyya'. *Al-Lisān al-'Arabī* **7**, ii, 1970, pp. 98–103.

The English term is followed by its equivalent in the Arabic of Libya, Kuwait, U.A.R., Iraq, Lebanon and Saudi Arabia.

ARAB LEAGUE. AL-MAKTAB AL-DĀ'IM, 'Mu'jam al-muṣṭalaḥāt al-tiqniyya al-ikhrāṭiyya . . .'. *Al-Lisān al-'Arabī* **7**, ii, 1970, pp. 123–55.

A multilingual cartographic glossary.

BEIRUT. PETROLEUM TRANSLATION AND PUBLISHING SERVICES, *Dictionary of petroleum terms, English–French–Arabic.* Beirut, 1972.

-DĪNAWARĪ, Aḥmad b. Da'ūd, Abū Ḥanīfa, *The book of plants . . . Part of the alphabetical section alif-zāi*; ed. . . . with . . . notes . . . and a vocabulary of selected words by B. Lewin. (Uppsala Univ. Årsskrift 1953:10.) Uppsala, 1953.

—— *Le dictionnaire botanique* (*Kitāb an-nabāt, de sīn à yā'*). *Reconstitué d'après les citations des ouvrages postérieurs* par Muḥammad Ḥamīd Allāh. (Textes et traductions d'auteurs orientaux, 5.) Cairo, 1973.

FANOUS, W., *Deutsch-arabisches technisches Wörterbuch*, rev. von F. S. Atiya. Cairo, 1960.

-KHAṬĪB, Aḥmad S., *A dictionary of petroleum* (*technology and geology*), *English–Arabic.* Beirut, 1974.

—— *A new dictionary of scientific and technical terms, English–Arabic.* 2nd edn. Beirut, 1974.

LECOMTE, G., 'Lexique français–arabe de l'automobile'. *Orient* **17**, 1961, pp. 195–213.

French–Arabic vocabulary taken from nine works including Pellat's *L'arabe vivant* and the *Code de la route marocain.*

MUṢLIḤ, 'Umar, *Glossary of petroleum terms; mu'jam al-muṣṭalaḥāt al-nafṭiyya.* Beirut, 1970.

English–Arabic.

SALMON, G., 'Sur quelques noms de plantes en arabe et en berbère'. *Archives Marocaines* **8**, 1906, pp. 1–98.

Arabic–French, in fact a French translation of an anonymous Arabic manuscript entitled *Tuḥfat al-aḥbāb fi nihāyat al-nabāt wa-al-a'shāb.*

SHUBĀṬ, Anīs, 'Al-qāmūs al-tiqnī li-al-ṭuruq, faransī-inklīzī–'arabī'. *Al-Lisān al-'Arabī* **7**, ii, 1970, pp. 68–97.

A trilingual list of road terms.

SINAWĪ, Sahl and ANṢĀRĪ, Naḍīr, *Glossary of earth science terms.* Baghdad, 1970.

SOUISSI, M., *La langue des mathématiques en arabe.* Tunis, 1969.

WAHBA, Majdī, *An English–Arabic vocabulary of scientific, technical and cultural terms.* Cairo, 1971.

-ẒĀHIR, Muḥammad Wāṣil, 'Al-muṣṭalaḥāt al-riyāḍiyya fī al-lugha al-'arabiyya'. *Al-Lisān al-'Arabī* **7**, ii, 1970, pp. 5–9.

(xiv) POLICE

'IṢMAT, Shafīq, *Qāmūs al-shurṭa.* Cairo, 1970.

(xv) SOCIAL SCIENCES

BADAWĪ, A. Zakī, *Dictionary of the social sciences, English–Arabic*. Beirut, 1973.

### (e) Qur'ānic Dictionaries and Concordances

'ABD AL-BĀQĪ, Muḥammad Fu'ād, *Mu'jam gharīb al-Qur'ān, mustakhraj min Ṣaḥīḥ al-Bukhārī*. Cairo, 1950.

—— *Al-mu'jam al-mufahras li-alfāẓ al-Qur'ān al-karīm*. Cairo, 1945.

BARAKĀT, Muḥammad Fāris, *Al-murshid ilā āyāt al-Qur'ān al-karīm wa kalimātihi*. 2nd edn. Damascus, 1957.

DIETERICI, F., *Arabisch-Deutsches Handwörterbuch zum Koran und Thier und Mensch vor dem König der Genien*. Leipzig, 1894 (repr. 1973).

FLÜGEL, G., *Concordantiae Corani arabicae* . . . Leipzig, 1842.

-HARAWĪ, Aḥmad b. Muḥammad, *Kitāb al-gharībayn; gharībay al-Qur'ān wa-al-Ḥadīth*. Cairo, 1970–.

-ḤASANĪ, 'Ilmīzāda Faiḍ Allāh, *Fatḥ al-raḥmān li-ṭālib āyāt al-Qur'ān*. Beirut, 1323/1905.

JEFFERY, A., *The foreign vocabulary of the Qur'ān*. (Gaekwad's Or. ser., 79.) Baroda, 1938.

NAṢṢĀR, Ḥusain, *Mu'jam āyāt al-Qur'ān al-karīm* . . . 2nd edn. Cairo, 1965.

PARET, R., *Der Koran, Kommentar und Konkordanz*. Stuttgart, 1971.

PENRICE, J., *A dictionary and glossary of the Ḳor-ân* . . . London, 1873 (repr. New York, 1971; Beirut, 1973).

Based on Flügel's edition of 1834, he also makes frequent reference to the 2nd edition of De Sacy's grammar.

RAHBAR, D., *Indices to the verses of the Qur'ān in the commentaries of al-Ṭabarī and al-Rāzī*. Hartford, 1962.

Indices to the verses in the *Jāmi' al-bayān fī tafsīr al-Qur'ān* of Ṭabarī in the Bulaq edition of 1323–29 and the Maymāniyya Press edition of 1321, and the *Mafātiḥ al-ghayb* (the *Tafsīr al-kabīr*) of Rāzī in the Khayriyya Press edition of 1307–8 and the Sharafiyya Press edition of 1308.

TORREY, C. C., *The commercial-theological terms in the Koran*. Leiden, 1892.

### (f) Ḥadīth

The most important Arabic concordances are to be found on pp. 55–78 of Amīn and Ibrāhīm, *Dalīl al-marāji' al-'arabiyya*, Baghdad, 1970.

RESCHER, O., *Vocabulaire du recueil de Bokhârî*. Stuttgart, 1922.

—— *Sachindex zu Bokhârî, nach der Ausgabe Krehl-Juynboll und der Übersetzung von Houdas-Marçais*. Stuttgart, 1923.

A supplement to the above.

WENSINCK, A. J. and others, *Concordance et indices de la tradition musulmane; les six livres, le Musnad d'al-Dārimī, le Muwaṭṭa' de Malik, le Musnad de Aḥmad ibn Ḥanbal*. 7v. Leiden, 1936–69.

# Arabic grammars

J. P. C. AUCHTERLONIE

## I. GUIDES

No convenient Western bibliography exists for the study of Arab grammarians. The best conspectus still remains Brockelmann's *Geschichte der arabischen Litteratur*, 2. Aufl., Leiden, 1937–49, 2 vols. and 3 supplements, where the chapters on Philologie deal also with grammar. Especially useful are the bibliographical notes to be found on p. 96 (new edn.) or p. 98 (old edn.) of Band I, and on pp. 157–8 of Supplementband I. These notes will presumably be updated in the forthcoming volume of Sezgin's *Geschichte des arabischen Schrifttums*, Leiden, 1967–, which will deal *inter alia* with philology and grammar up to A.D. 1040/A.H. 430. Other works which deal with grammar to a greater or less extent are:

FLEISCH, H., 'Esquisse d'un historique de la grammaire arabe'. *Arabica* **4**, 1957, pp. 1–22.

FLÜGEL, G. L., *Die grammatischen Schulen der Araber. 1. Abt.: Die Schulen von Basra und Kufa und die gemischten Schulen.* Leipzig, 1862 (repr. Liechtenstein, 1973).

FÜCK, J. W., *Arabiya; Untersuchungen zur arabischen Sprach- und Stilgeschichte.* Berlin, 1950.

A revised edition was later published in French:

—— *'Arabiya: recherches sur l'histoire de la langue et du style arabe*; trad. par C. Denizeau. Paris, 1955.

HAYWOOD, J. A., *Arabic lexicography; its history and its place in the general history of lexicography.* 2nd edn. Leiden, 1959 (repr. Leiden, 1965).

KAḤḤĀLA, 'Umar Riḍā, *Al-lugha al-'arabiyya wa 'ulūmuhā.* Damascus, 1971.

## II. ARABIC GRAMMARS IN ARABIC

The selection of Arab grammatical works presented below is entirely arbitrary and mentions only a few of the most representative authors. The editions noted make no claim to be either the best or the most recent, but should be available in major orientalist libraries. The exceptions may prove to be those works much used for teaching Arabic in South and South-East Asia, such as Jurjānī's *'Awāmil* and Ibn al-Ḥājib's *Al-kāfiyya.* These were printed many times during the nineteenth century, but are relatively rare today. Nevertheless, they remain an important part of the Arabic grammatical tradition.

IBN ĀJURRŪM, Muḥammad b. Muḥammad, *Al-Ājurrūmiyya*; ed. Muḥammad Muḥyī al-Dīn 'Abd al-Ḥamīd. 7th edn. Cairo, 1950.

IBN AL-ḤĀJIB, ʿUthmān b. ʿUmar, *Al-shāfiyya*; commentary by ʿAbd al-Qādir al-Baghdādī. 4v. Cairo, 1939.
—— *Al-kāfiyya*; commentary by Raḍī al-Dīn al-Astarābādhī, gloss by al-Jurjānī. Istanbul, 1275/1858.
IBN HISHĀM, ʿAbd Allāh b. Yūsuf, *Qaṭr al-nadā wa ball al-ṣadā*; ed. Muḥammad Muḥyī al-Dīn ʿAbd al-Ḥamīd. 11th edn. Cairo, 1963.
—— *Shudhūr al-dhahab fī maʿrifat kalām al-ʿArab*; ed. Muḥammad Muḥyi al-Dīn ʿAbd al-Ḥamīd. 5th edn. Cairo, 1951.
—— *Mughnī al-labīb ʿan kutub al-aʿārīb*; ed. Muḥammad Muḥyī al-Dīn ʿAbd al-Ḥamīd. 2nd edn. Cairo, 1965.
IBN JINNĪ, Abū ʾl-Fatḥ ʿUthmān, *Sirr al-ṣināʿa*; ed. Muṣṭafā al-Saqqāʾ and others. Cairo, 1954–.
—— *Al-khaṣāʾiṣ fī al-naḥw (fī ʿilm uṣūl al-ʿarabiyya)*; ed. Muḥammad ʿAlī al-Najjār. 3v. Cairo, 1952–56; 2nd edn. 3v. Beirut, n.d.
IBN MĀLIK, Muḥammad b. ʿAbd Allāh, *Al-alfiyya*; ed. Muḥammad Muḥyī al-Dīn ʿAbd al-Ḥamīd. 6th edn. Cairo, 1951.
-JURJĀNĪ, ʿAbd al-Qāhir b. ʿAbd al-Raḥmān, *Al-ʿawāmil al-miʾa* (*Miʾat ʿāmil*); commentary *Kashf al-manẓūm*. Cawnpore, 1324/1926.
-MUBARRAD, Muḥammad b. Yazīd, *Al-kāmil*; ed. Muḥammad Abū ʾl-Faḍl Ibrāhīm and al-Sayyid Shaḥāṭa. 4v. Cairo, 1956.
An alternative edition is: *The Kāmil of el-Mubarrad*; ed. . . . by W. Wright, critical notes ed. by M. J. de Goeje. 12 pts. Leipzig, 1874–92 (repr. Osnabrück, 1971).
SIBAWAIHĪ, ʿAmr b. ʿUthmān, *Kitāb Sibawaihī*. With extracts from the commentaries of al-Sīrafī and al-Shantamarī. Bulaq, 1316/1898 (repr. Baghdad, *c.* 1968).
-ZAMAKHSHARĪ, Maḥmūd b. ʿUmar, *Al-mufaṣṣal*; commentary by Abū Fāris al-Ḥalabī. Cairo, 1324/1906 (repr. Beirut, 1973).
An earlier European edition is: *Al-mufaṣṣal*; ed. J. P. Broch. Editio altera . . . adnotationibus criticis aliisque aucta. Christiania, 1879 (repr. Beirut, n.d.).
An interesting if outdated anthology is:
SILVESTRE DE SACY, A. I., Baron, *Anthologie grammaticale arabe, ou morceaux choisis de divers grammariens et scholiastes arabes avec une traduction française et des notes*. Paris, 1829 (repr. New York, 1973).

## III. GRAMMARS IN WESTERN LANGUAGES

Despite the efforts of a few early pioneers such as Pedro de Alcalà, European interest in Arabic grammar only began in earnest around the beginning of the seventeenth century when, for example, translations of the *Ājurrūmiyya* were published by J. Casaubon in Rome in 1592, by T. Erpenius in Leiden in 1617 and by T. Obicini in Rome in 1631.

Nevertheless, works on Arabic grammar remained relatively unusual till the nineteenth century, which saw a dramatic expansion of interest in all fields of oriental studies. This period fostered not only works of major scholarship, but also a large quantity of popular guides to the language for the use of European officials and travellers. These guides have continued to be produced in the twentieth century, but they are being increasingly replaced by teaching manuals designed for university use. Correspondingly, the Victorian interest in comparative studies has now mostly given way to linguistic analysis. Both these two recent developments, student grammars and linguistic studies, have become more pronounced during the last few years, and it is likely that they will continue to dominate the field of Arabic grammar for some time to come.

The main criterion on which this selective bibliography is based is modernity, though exceptions have been made in the case of reference grammars. It also seemed desirable to limit references to works in the more common European languages. In almost all cases, only those works with a clear grammatical basis have been included; conversation manuals, phrase books, readers, basic non-grammatical courses and phonological and linguistic studies have been almost entirely excluded. For a useful study of all types of teaching material for Arabic in English, see, however:

ABBOUD, P. F., 'Arabic language instruction'. *MESA bull.* **5**, ii, 1971, pp. 1–23.

### (a) General

BAKALLA, Muhammad H., *A bibliography of Arabic linguistics*. London, 1975.
Over 2000 entries. Will presumably cover grammar and grammatical studies.

HOSPERS, J. H. *ed.*, *A basic bibliography for the study of the Semitic languages*. 2v. Leiden, 1973–74.
Vol. 1 includes Epigraphic South Arabian by A. J. Drewes. Vol. 2 is devoted entirely to Arabic and contains a useful section on Arabic dialects by F. Leemhuis; this chapter is a competent supplement to Sobelmann (see section (d), below). The section on classical and modern standard Arabic by Hospers is, however, less satisfactory; a strange amalgam of linguistic, historical and religious material, it is marred by poor organization, arbitrary selection, and a lack of critical comment. Neither volume has an index.

RABIN, C. and others, 'ʿArabiyya'. $EI^2$ **1**, pp. 561–603.
Good bibliographical references.

### (b) Reference Grammars

*English*

CANTARINO, V., *Syntax of modern Arabic prose*. Bloomington, 1974–.
To be completed in three volumes.

FORBES, D., *A grammar of the Arabic language*. 2nd edn. London, 1874.

HOWELL, M. S., *A grammar of the classical Arabic language*. 4v. Allahabad, 1894–1911 (repr. Amsterdam, 1973; also Beirut, 1975, in 7 vols.).

THORNTON, F. du P., *Elementary Arabic; a grammar . . . being an abridgement of Wright's Arabic grammar*; ed. R. A. Nicholson. Cambridge, 1905.

WRIGHT, W., *A grammar of the Arabic language translated from the German of Caspari and edited with numerous additions and corrections*. 3rd edn. rev. by W. Robertson Smith and M. J. de Goeje (reissued with corrections by A. A. Bevan). 2v. Cambridge, 1933 (repr. 1967, and issued as one volume the same year; repr. with preface, addenda et corrigenda by P. Cachia, Beirut, 1974).

The standard reference grammar with comprehensive indexes. Leans heavily on Latin terminology.

*French*

CANTINEAU, J., *Cours de phonétique arabe.* Paris, 1960.

FLEISCH, H., *L'arabe classique; esquisse d'une structure linguistique.* Nouvelle édn. Beirut, 1968.

GAUDEFROY-DEMOMBYNES, M. & BLACHÈRE, R., *Grammaire de l'arabe classique.* 2nd rev. edn. Paris, 1970.

MOINFAR, M., *Grammaire comparée de l'arabe et du persan.* Paris, 1973–.
Fascicule 1 deals with Arabic grammar.

PÉRIER, J. B., *Nouvelle grammaire arabe.* Paris, 1901.

SILVESTRE DE SACY, A. I., Baron, *Grammaire arabe.* 3rd edn. rev. by L. Machuel. 2v. Tunis, 1904–5.

VERNIER, D., *Grammaire arabe, composée d'après les sources primitives.* 2v. Beirut, 1891–92.

*German*

BROCKELMANN, C., *Arabische Grammatik.* 14th edn. Leipzig, 1958 (repr. Leipzig, 1969).
Based on Socin's *Arabische Grammatik*, this work includes a glossary, reading exercises and a useful general bibliography. Has no index of grammatical terms.

CASPARI, C. P., *Arabische Grammatik.* 5th edn. ed. August Müller. Halle, 1887 (reprint promised).
Originally published in Latin as *Grammatica arabica* in 1844–48, this work forms the basis of Wright's monumental *Grammar of the Arabic language.* It was also translated into French as:
—— *Grammaire arabe* . . . trad. E. Uricoechea. Brussels, 1881.

HARDER, E., *Arabische Grammatik.* 4th edn. Heidelberg, 1931.
A previous edition entitled *Arabische Konversations-Grammatik mit besonderer Berücksichtigung der Schriftsprache* (1898), forms the basis of Thatcher's *Arabic grammar of the written language*, for which see section (c), below.

NÖLDEKE, T., *Zur Grammatik des classischen Arabisch.* Vienna, 1896 (repr. with *die handschriftlichen Ergänzungen im Handexemplar T. Nöldekes*, bearb. und mit Zusätzen von A. Spitaler, Darmstadt, 1963).

RECKENDORF, F., *Arabische Syntax.* Heidelberg, 1921.
Still a standard authority on the subject.

SOCIN, A., *Arabische Grammatik, Paradigmen, Litteratur, Chrestomathie und Glossar.* Karlsruhe & Leipzig, 1885.
Translated into English as: *Arabic grammar, paradigms, literature, chrestomathy and glossary*; tr. T. Stenhouse and R. Brünnow. Karlsruhe & Leipzig, 1885.

*Russian*

GRANDE, B. M., *Kurs arabskoi grammatiki v sravnitel'no-istoricheskom osveshchenii.* Moscow, 1963.

### (c) Teaching Grammars

*English*

ABBOUD, P. F., *Elementary modern standard Arabic.* 3 pts. Ann Arbor, 1968.

ABDO, D. A., *A course in modern standard Arabic; Manhaj fī taʿlīm al-lugha al-ʿarabiyya.* 2v. Beirut, 1962–64.

BEESTON, A. F. L., *Written Arabic; an approach to the basic structures.* Cambridge, 1968.

BISHAI, W. B., *Concise grammar of literary Arabic; a new approach; with vocabulary lists, exercises, reading selections and a cumulative glossary.* Dubuque, Iowa, 1971.

COWAN, D., *An introduction to modern literary Arabic.* Cambridge, 1958.

ELDER, E. E., *Arabic grammar; inductive method.* 2nd edn. Cairo, 1950.

FERGUSON, C. A. & ANI, M., *Lessons in contemporary Arabic. Lessons 1–8.* Washington, 1964.

Grammar coverage limited. Further lessons were planned but have not yet been published.

HANNA, S. A., *An elementary manual of contemporary literary Arabic.* Salt Lake City, Utah, 1962, and Boulder, Colo., 1964.

Concentrates on morphology.

HANNA, S. A. & GREIS, N., *Introducing literary Arabic.* Salt Lake City, Utah, 1971.

To be used in sequence after *Beginning Arabic* and *Writing Arabic*, for which see section (d) – Egyptian, below.

HAYWOOD, J. A. & NAHMAD, H. M., *A new Arabic grammar of the written language.* 2nd edn. London, 1965. Key publ. in 1964.

A lineal descendant of Harder's *Arabische Grammatik* (section (b), above) out of Thatcher's *Arabic grammar.* Intended to replace the 6th edn. of the latter.

KAPLIWATSKY, J., *Arabic language and grammar.* 4v. and Key. Jerusalem, 1940–47.

Long exercises but little grammar.

MIDDLE EAST CENTRE FOR ARAB STUDIES (MECAS), *The MECAS grammar of modern literary Arabic.* Beirut, 1965.

SCOTT, G. C., *Practical Arabic.* Beirut, 1962.

THATCHER, G. W., *Arabic grammar of the written language*; rev. and corr. by A. S. Tritton. 6th edn. London, 1956? Key publ. in 1942.

Based on Harder's *Arabische Grammatik* (section (b), above) and now used as a basis for Haywood and Nahmad's *New Arabic grammar*, this work has the longest tradition of use in the English-speaking world; it has not yet been entirely superseded. It has also been translated into Spanish as:

—— *Gramática árabe del lenguaje escrito.* Buenos Aires, 1958.

TRITTON, A. S., *Teach yourself Arabic.* London, 1943.

TUBBS, E. J., *Visual Arabic grammar lexicon.* London, 1973.

YOUNG, E. J., *Arabic for beginners.* Grand Rapids, Mich., 1949.

ZIADEH, F. J. & WINDER, R. B., *An introduction to modern Arabic.* Princeton, 1957.

*French*

D'ALVERNY, A., *Cours de langue arabe; vocabulaire commenté et sur textes.* 3ème éd., revue et corrigée par R. Lavenant and L. Pouzet. Beirut, 1969.

BLACHÈRE, R., *Éléments de l'arabe classique.* 4th rev. edn. Paris, 1970.

BLACHÈRE, R. & CECCALDI, M., *Exercices d'arabe classique.* 2nd rev. edn. Paris, 1970.

These two works are to be used in conjunction.

KHAWAM, R. R., *Initiation rapide à l'arabe classique.* Paris, 1972.

LECOMTE, G., *Grammaire de l'arabe.* (Que sais-je? 1275.) Paris, 1968.

Contains no exercises.

LECOMTE, G. & GHEDIRA, A., *Méthode d'arabe littéral.* 2v. Paris, 1960–61. (Vol. 2 is the 2nd edn.)

School grammar.

PELLAT, C., *Introduction à l'arabe moderne.* Paris, 1956.

*German*

AMBROS, A. A., *Einführung in die moderne arabische Schriftsprache.* Munich, 1969.

FISCHER, W., *Grammatik des klassischen Arabisch.* (Porta Linguarum Orientalium, N.S. 11.) Wiesbaden, 1972.

KLOPFER, H., *Modernes Arabisch; eine Einführung ins heutige Zeitungs-Schriftsprache.* 2nd edn. Heidelberg, 1970.

KRAHL, G. & REUSCHEL, W., *Lehrbuch des modernen Arabsich.* Leipzig, 1974.

*Italian*

VECCIA VAGLIERI, L., *Grammatica elementare di arabo.* Rome, 1951.

—— *Grammatica teorico-pratica della lingua araba.* 2v. Rome, 1941–61.

The latter work also serves as a reference grammar for Italian arabists.

*Russian*

FROLOVA, O. B., *My govorim po-arabski; uchebnoe posobie dlya I i II kursov.* Moscow, 1969.

KOVALEV, A. A. & SHARBATOV, G. S., *Uchebnik arabskogo yazyka.* 2nd edn. Moscow, 1969.

SEGAL', V. S., *Nachal'nyiy kurs arabskogo yazyka*; ed. K. K. Baranov. Moscow, 1962.

SHARBATOV, G. S., *Samouchitel' arabskogo yazyka.* (Supplements to *Aziya i Afrika segodnya* nos. 7–12, 1965 and nos. 1–4, 6, 1966.) Moscow, 1965–66.

YUSHMANOV, N. V., *Kratkaya grammatika arabskogo yazyka.* Leningrad, 1964.

*Spanish*

ABBUD, M., *Gramática árabe.* Madrid, 1955.

## (d) Dialect Grammars

Arabic dialect studies are fortunate in possessing a fully-fledged and relatively recent bibliography, namely:

SOBELMAN, H., *Arabic dialect studies; a selected bibliography*. Washington, D.C., 1962.

This is a comprehensive guide to readers, grammars and linguistic studies of all the Arabic vernaculars, excluding Sudanese and Central Asian. Comments are detailed and perceptive and articles are included. The work replaces individual studies of Arabic dialects by C. A. Ferguson, R. S. Harrell, R. A. C. Goodison and H. Blanc, all to be found in the *Middle East Journal* (respectively, **9**, 1955, pp. 187–94; **10**, 1956, pp. 307–12; **12**, 1958, pp. 205–13; and **13**, 1959, pp. 449–53) and also:

BROCKELMANN, C., 'Das Arabische und sein Mundarten'. (In *Handbuch der Orientalistik* **1**, iii, Semitistik, Leiden and Cologne, 1953–54, pp. 207–45; repr. Leiden, 1964.)

In his turn, Sobelman is supplemented by:

JOHNSTONE, T. M., 'Arabic dialect studies'. (In D. Hopwood and D. Grimwood-Jones *eds.*, *Middle East and Islam; a bibliographical introduction*, Zug, 1972, pp. 339–45.)

and F. Leemhuis, 'Modern Arabic dialects' on pp. 88–108 of Hospers, *op. cit.*

The list below attempts to fill in a few of the gaps in the bibliographies mentioned above, and no titles to be found in either Sobelman or Johnstone have been duplicated here. The criteria in force in earlier sections of Part 2 apply here as well.

*Ancient dialects*

BLAU, J., *A grammar of Christian Arabic based mainly on South Palestinian texts from the first millennium*. 3 fascs. Louvain, 1966–67.

*Arabian*

ABBOUD, P. F., *Syntax of Najdi Arabic*. Ph.D. thesis, Austin, Texas, 1964.

JONES, W. I., *The Aden dialect of Arabic; a study of its grammatical peculiarities as compared with the classical language*. M.A. thesis, Univ. of Wales, 1940.

SCHREIBER, G., *Der arabische Dialekt von Mekka; Abriss der Grammatik mit Texten und Glossar*. (Islamkündliche Untersuchungen, 9.) Freiburg, 1971.

SHARAF AL-DĪN, Aḥmad Ḥusayn, *Lahjat al-Yaman, qadīman wa ḥadīthan*. Cairo, 1970.

*Egyptian*

HANNA, S. A. & GREIS, N., *Beginning Arabic; a linguistic approach; from sound to script*. 2nd edn. Leiden, 1972.

—— *Writing Arabic; a linguistic approach; from cultivated Cairene to formal literary Arabic*. 2nd edn. Leiden, 1972.

Originally published in Salt Lake City, Utah, in 1965. To be followed by the same authors' *Introducing literary Arabic*, for which see section (c), above.

HARRELL, R. S., *Lessons in colloquial Egyptian Arabic*. Georgetown, 1963.

JOMIER, J. & KHOUZAM, J., *Manuel d'arabe égyptien* (*parler du Caire*). 2ème ed. Paris, 1973.

TOMICHE, N., *Le parler arabe du Caire*. The Hague, 1964.

A descriptive analysis.

*Iraqi*

MALAIKA, N., *Grundzüge der Grammatik des arabischen Dialekts von Bagdad.* Wiesbaden, 1963.

McCARTHY, R. J. & RAFFOULI, F., *Spoken Arabic of Baghdad.* 2v. Beirut, 1964.

Vol. 1 deals with the grammar and related exercises; vol. 2 is devoted to texts.

*Levantine* (Syrian, Lebanese, Palestinian)

ABU-HAIDAR, F., *A study of the spoken Arabic of Baskinta.* Ph.D. thesis, London, 1970.

D'ALVERNY, A., *Petite introduction au parler libanais.* 2nd edn. 3 fasc. Beirut, 1970.

Fascicule 2 covers grammar.

BISHR, Kamāl Muḥammad 'Alī, *A grammatical study of Lebanese Arabic.* Ph.D. thesis, London, 1956.

COWELL, M. W., *A reference grammar of Syrian Arabic, based on the dialect of Damascus.* Georgetown, 1964.

GROTZFELD, H., *Syrisch-Arabische Grammatik, Dialekt von Damaskus.* (Porta Linguarum Orientalium, N.S. 8.) Wiesbaden, 1965.

KAPLIWATSKY, J., *Colloquial Arabic.* Jerusalem, 1968.

On Palestinian Arabic.

KASSAB, J., *Manuel du parler arabe moderne en Moyen-Orient.* Vol. 1. Paris, 1970–.

On Lebanese Arabic.

SHAWKAT, Maḥmūd Ḥamīd, *A descriptive grammar of educated Damascene Arabic.* Ph.D. thesis, Cornell, 1962.

*North African*

'ABD AL-ĀL, 'Abd al-Mun'im Sayyid, *Lahjat shimāl al-Maghrib; Tiṭwān wa mā ḥawlahā.* Cairo, 1968.

COHEN, D., *Le parler arabe des Juifs de Tunis; étude descriptive et historique.* (Janua Linguarum, seria practica, 161.) The Hague, 1974.

HARRELL, R. S., *A short reference grammar of Moroccan Arabic.* Georgetown, 1962.

KYAMILEV, S. K., *Marokkanski dialekt arabskogo yazyka.* Moscow, 1968.

*Sudanese and Saharan*

FAURE, P., *Introduction au parler arabe de l'est du Tchad.* 3 pts. Lyon and Fort Lamy, 1969.

Part 3 deals with grammar.

# Genealogy, Biographical dictionaries and Who's Whos

DIANA GRIMWOOD-JONES

## I. GENEALOGY

Though providing a vital and copious source for Islamic history, the science of genealogy has been something of a wallflower as far as Western scholars are concerned, and the majority of those Arabic genealogical texts which *have* been published, have been edited by Arabs. The West, however, has shone in the production of genealogical/chronological lists, which are in the main dynastic rather than tribal and not based on one specific source only. As these latter are the most frequently used and easily accessible, they have been listed first, in chronological order of appearance.

WÜSTENFELD, F., *Genealogische Tabellen der arabischen Stämme und Familien* . . . 2v. Göttingen, 1852–53.

The sources for this were Ibn Qutayba, Abū al-Fiḍā, Nuwayrī, Ibn Khallikān, al-Nawāwī, Ibn Durayd and Maqdisī. One volume consists of genealogical tables, the other is a register of personal names, with biographical details.

LANE-POOLE, S., *The Mohammadan dynasties; chronological and genealogical tables with historical introductions*. London, 1893 (repr. Beirut, 1966).

A brief survey with lists of rulers and genealogical tables, which at the time of its compilation fulfilled a great need. It inspired some excellent translations and revisions:

—— *Musul'manskie dinastii: khronologicheskiya i genealogicheskiya tablitsy s istoricheskimi vvedeniyami*; perevod V. Bartol'd. St. Petersburg, 1899.

Russian translation with additions.

—— *Duval-i islāmiyyah*; trans. H. Edhem. Istanbul, 1927.

Revised Turkish edition.

ZAMBAUR, E. DE, *Manuel de généalogie et de chronologie pour l'histoire de l'Islam*. Hanover, 1927 (repr. Bad Pyrmont, 1955).

The standard work. Originally conceived as a revision of Lane-Poole, it far surpasses it. Using as a major source the *Kāmil* of Ibn al-Athīr, the work begins with chapters on the Caliphate and the Amṣār, followed by divisions according to area – Spain, the Caucasus, Arabia, etc. – listing ruling families, governors and so forth. It has been translated into Arabic:

—— *Mu'jam al-ansāb wa-al-usrat al-ḥakīma fī al-ta'rīkh al-islāmī*, tr. M. Ḥasan and others. Cairo, 1951 (repr. Baghdad, 1971).

BOSWORTH, C. E., *The Islamic dynasties; a chronological and genealogical handbook*. Edinburgh, 1967.

Intended for orientalists not requiring the detail of Zambaur's work, and for students starting Islamic history, it includes material either not found (or only sketched out) in Lane-Poole and Zambaur. Brief introductions are given for each dynasty, followed by a table of rulers, and each section has a short bibliography.

—— *Musulmanskie dinastii* . . . perevod . . . i primechaniya P. A. Gryaznevicha, Moscow, 1971.

Russian translation/revision with additions to the bibliography, mainly of Russian works.

—— *Silsilah-hāyi islāmī*, tr. Farīdūn Badrahayi. (Manābiʿ-i taʾrīkh va jughrāfyā-yi Īrān, 27.) Tehran, 1349/1970.

Persian translation from the English.

GOMAA, Ibrahim, *An historical chart of the Muslim world*. Leiden, 1972.

As for the original texts, the following section is based on K. W. Zettersteen's introduction to the *Ṭurfat al-aṣḥāb fī maʿrifat al-ansāb* of Ibn Rasūl, published in Damascus in 1949. Apart from his admirable survey of the historical development of the *ansāb* literature and the reasons for its importance in Arab eyes, Zettersteen lists 100 genealogical treatises, including a number which are only known through their inclusion in such works as the *Kashf al-ẓunūn* and the *Fihrist*, and giving publication details of such others as have appeared in print. The works listed below, therefore, are of post-1949 editions of texts listed by Zettersteen, with the addition of a few items which do not appear in the original list.

-BAKRĪ AL-ṢIDDĪQĪ, Muḥammad Tawfīq, *Bayt al-Ṣiddīq*. Cairo, 1323/1905.

Genealogies and biographies of persons belonging to the house of Abū Bakr al-Siddīq.

-BALĀDHURĪ, Aḥmad b. Yaḥyā, *Kitāb ansāb al-ashrāf; nukhba min al-ʿulamāʾ*; ed. Ṭaha Ḥusayn; vol. 1 ed. M. Ḥamid Allāh. (Dhakhāʾir al-ʿArab, 27.) Cairo, 1959.

—— *Kitab ansāb al-ashrāf*; ed. M. Schloessinger, rev. et annoté par M. J. Kister. Jerusalem, 1971.

-DAʾŪDĪ, Aḥmad b. ʿAlī, *ʿUmdat al-ṭālib fī ansāb āl Abī Ṭālib*; ed. Nizār Riḍā. Beirut, n.d.

-GHULAMĪ, ʿAbd al-Munʿim, *Al-ansāb wa-al-usar*. Baghdad, 1965–.

-HAMDĀNĪ, al-Ḥasan b. Aḥmad, *Al-iklīl*. Vols. 1 and 2 ed. Muḥammad b. ʿAlī al-Akwaʿ al-Hawālī. Cairo, 1963–66.

—— *Al-iklīl*. Vol. 1, fasc. i and ii, vol. 2, fasc. ii ed. O. Löfgren. Uppsala, 1954–65.

-HANBALĪ, Rashīd b. ʿAlī, *Muthīr al-wajd fī maʿrifat ansāb mulūk Najd*; ed. Muḥibb al-Dīn al-Khaṭīb. Cairo, 1959.

IBN ʿABD AL-BARR, Yūsuf b. ʿAbd Allāh, 'Al-qaçd wa'l-'amam fî't-taʿrîf bi-'uçûl ansâb al-ʿArab wa'l-ʿAjam . . . trad. française . . . par A. R. Mahdjoub'. *RA* **99**, 1955, pp. 71–112; **101**, 1957, pp. 45–84.

IBN BAKKĀR, al-Zubayr, *Jamharat nasab Quraysh wa akhbārihā*; ed. Maḥmūd Muḥammad Shākir. Vol. 1. Cairo, 1961.

IBN DURAYD, Muḥammad b. al-Ḥasan, *Al-ishtiqāq*; ed. ʿAbd al-Salām Muḥammad Hārūn. Cairo, 1958.

IBN QUDĀMA AL-MAQDISĪ, ʿAbd Allāh b. Aḥmad, *Al-istibsār fī nasab al-ṣaḥāba min al-anṣār*; ed. ʿAlī Yūsuf Nuwayhiḍ. Beirut, 1971.

IBN AL-ṢĀBŪNĪ, *Takmilat Kamāl al-ikmāl fī al-ansāb wa-al-asmāʾ wa-al-alqāb;* ed. Muḥammad Jawād. Baghdad, 1957.

IBN SHADQAM, ʿAlī b. al-Ḥasan, *Zahrat al-maqūl fī nasab thānī farʿay al-rasūl*, followed by *Nukhbat al-zahra al-thamīna fī nasab ashrāf al-Madīna*. Najaf, 1961.

KAḤḤĀLA, ʿUmar Riḍā, *Muʿjam qabāʾil al-ʿArab al-qadīma wa-al-ḥadītha*. 3v. Damascus, 1949 (repr. Beirut, 1968).

KALBĪ, Hishām b. Muḥammad, *Ǧamharat an-nasab, das genealogische Werk des Hišam ibn Muḥammad al-Kalbī*, von W. Caskel. Bd. 1: *Einleitung; Tafeln*. Bd. 2: *Erläuterungen zu den Tafeln; Das Register*. 2v. Leiden, 1966.

MILES, G. C., 'A provisional reconstruction of the genealogy of the Arab amirs of Crete'. *Kretika khronika* **15**, 1963, pp. 59–73.

-MUNAJJID, Ṣalāḥ al-Dīn, *Muʿjam Banī Umayya*. Beirut, 1970.
Extracted from Ibn ʿAsākir's *Taʾrīkh Dimashq*.

-QĀDIRĪ, Ibn ʿAbd al-Ṭayyib, 'La "Lamḥat al-bahǵat al-ʿaliyyah fī baʿḍ ahl an-nisbat aṣ-ṣiqilliyyah" . . . Un trattatello di storia dinastica sui "Siciliani" di illustra discendenza nel Marocco; ed. U. Rizzitano'. *Mélanges Islamologiques* (IFAO) **3**, 1956, pp. 85–127.

-QALQASHANDĪ, Aḥmad b. ʿAbd Allāh, *Nihāyat al-arab fī maʿrifat ansāb al-ʿArab*; ed. Ibrāhīm al-Abyārī. Cairo, 1959.

—— *Nihāyat al-arab* . . . ed. ʿAlī Khāqānī. Baghdad, 1958.

—— *Qalāʾid al-jumān fī al-taʿrīf bi-qabāʾil ʿĀrab al-zamān*; ed. Ibrāhīm al-Abyārī. Cairo, 1963.

-SADŪSĪ, Muʿarrij, *Kitāb ḥadf min nasab Quraysh*; ed. Ṣalāḥ al-Dīn al-Munajjid. Cairo, 1960.

-SAMʿĀNĪ, ʿAbd al-Karīm b. Muḥammad, *Al-ansāb*; ed. ʿAbdur Raḥmān b. Yaḥyā al-Muʿallimī al-Yamānī. (Dairatu'l-Maʿarif-il-Osmaniya publs., N.S. XIX/i–.) Hyderabad, 1962–.

-ṬĀHIR, ʿAbd al-Jalīl, *Al-ʿashāʾir al-ʿirāqiyya*. Beirut, 1972–.

-ZABĪDĪ, Muḥammad al-Murtaḍā b. Muḥammad, *Tarwīḥ al-qulūb fī dhikr al-mulūk banī Ayyūb*. Damascus, 1969.

-ZUBAYRĪ, Musʿab b. ʿAbd Allāh, *Kitāb nasab Quraysh* . . . publ. E. Lévi-Provençal. (Dhakhāʾir al-ʿArab, 11.) Cairo, 1953.

## II. BIOGRAPHICAL DICTIONARIES AND WHO'S WHOS

Much of the groundwork for a complete list of classical biographies was carried out by Caetani and Gabrieli as a basis for their *Onomasticon Arabicum*, and pp. 1–40 of the first volume of this[1] lists the principal biographical dictionaries

[1] CAETANI, L. & GABRIELI, G. *comps.*, *Onomasticon Arabicum, ossia repertorio alfabetico dei nomi di persona e di luogo contenuti nelle principali opera storiche, biografiche e geografiche, stampate e manoscritte, relative all'Islam*. Vol. 1: *Fonti-introduzione*. Rome, 1915.

from which they intended to work. This great project regrettably came to an end with vol. 2. In recent years, however, it has been revived by a team of researchers at the Centre National de la Recherche Scientifique in Paris, which is gathering together all available biographical information on persons who lived prior to the eleventh/seventeenth century, with the aim of providing, in the first instance, indexes to enable the researcher to use Arabic biographical works more easily, and in the second instance to help one to identify quickly individuals cited in the various sources. To date, five fascicles have appeared of this *Série Onomasticon Arabicum*:

1. *Documents sur la mise en ordinateur des données biographiques*. 1971.
2. *Index schématique du Ta'rīh Baġdād*, par J.-P. Pascual. 1971.
3. *Index du Nūr as-sāfir*, par A. Doux. 1971.
4. *Nouveaux documents sur la mise en ordinateur des données biographiques*, par P. Bichard-Bréaud . . . 1973.
5. *Traitement automatique des données biographiques*, par P. Bichard-Bréaud. 1973.

In addition to these, the oriental section of the Institut de Recherche et d'Histoire des Textes, one of the institutions participating in the scheme, has produced the first fascicle of a new series:

*Traitement par ordinateur des données biographiques du Šaḏarāt al-ḏahab années 1–200, lettre a*. Paris, 1973.

An interesting study of Arabic biographical dictionaries which considers their motive, method, selectivity and factual information and subjective evaluation is

KHALIDI, T., 'Islamic biographical dictionaries: a preliminary assessment'. *MW* **63**, 1973, pp. 53–65.

A selection of the vast amount of additional biographical material available, both classical and modern, appears below. Individual biographies have been omitted, and a subject arrangement has been preferred to a division between 'classical' and 'modern' – a false division in some ways, as biographies in the 'classical' disciplines are still being produced. However, to facilitate the chronological placing of works by classical authors, the date of the author's death has been added for all pre-twentieth century works. Items marked with an asterisk are those of which earlier editions (or original editions in the case of reprints) appear in Caetani and Gabrieli.

The scheme of the list is as follows:

1. *General*
2. *By subject*
(i) Companions and descendants of the Prophet; (ii) Traditionists; (iii) Qur'ānic reciters and *ḥuffāẓ*; (iv) Shī'ites; (v) Members of other sects; (vi) Jurists; (vii) Ṣūfīs and other holy men; (viii) Rulers: princes and governors; (ix) Men of letters; (x) Poets and musicians; (xi) Artists; (xii) Journalists; (xiii) Reformers; (xiv) Philosophers; (xv) Physicians; (xvi) Mathematicians and astronomers; (xvii) Geographers; (xviii) Orientalists; (xix) Women; (xx) Government ministers.
3. *By region*. (N.B. – Place takes precedence over subject)
(i) Spain; (ii) Morocco; (iii) Algeria; (iv) Tunisia; (v) Libya; (vi) Egypt; (vii) Sudan; (viii) Arabia; (ix) Yemen; (x) Kuwait; (xi) Iraq; (xii) Syria; (xiii) Lebanon.

## 1. General

-ʿABBĀDĪ, ʿAbd al-Ḥamīd, *Figures d'histoire musulmane, empire arabe; ṣuwar min al-taʾrīkh al-islāmī*. Alexandria, 1948.

ABŪ ḤADĪD, Muḥammad Farīd, *ʿIṣāmiyyūn ʿuẓamāʾ min al-sharq wa-al-gharb*. Cairo, 1958.

ABŪ AL-NAṢR, ʿUmar, *Al-ʿuẓamāʾ*. Beirut, 1971.
Twentieth century personalities.

-ĀLŪSĪ, ʿAlāʾ al-Dīn Aḥmad b. Nuʿmān, *Al-durr al-muntathir fī rijāl al-qarn al-thānī ʿashar wa-al-thālith ʿashar*; ed. Jamāl al-Dīn al-Ālūsī and ʿAbd Allāh al-Jubūrī. Baghdad, 1967.

-ʿAQQĀD, ʿAbbās Maḥmūd, *Rijāl ʿaraftuhum*. (Kitāb al-Hilāl, 151.) Cairo, 1963.
Short biographies.

-ʿAZM, Jamīl Bek, *ʿUqūd al-jawhar* . . . Beirut, 1326/1908.
Biographies of 40 classical authors.

-BAGHDĀDĪ, Ismāʿīl b. Muḥammad Amīn, *Hadiyyat al-ʿārifīn, asmāʾ al-muʾallifīn wa āthār al-muṣannifīn*; ed. R. Bilge and I. M. K. Inal. Istanbul, 1951–.

-BAʿTHĪ, Ibrāhīm, *Shakhṣiyyāt islāmiyya muʿāṣira*. Cairo, 1970.

-BAYHAQĪ, ʿAlī b. Zayd (d. 565/1169), *Taʾrīkh ḥukamāʾ al-Islām*; ed. Muḥammad Kurd ʿAlī. Damascus, 1946.
A supplement to the *Ṣiwān al-ḥikma* of Muḥammad b. Ṭāhir b. Bahrām al-Sijāzī (fourth/tenth century).

-BAYṬĀR, ʿAbd al-Razzāq b. Ḥasan, *Ḥilyat al-bashar fī taʾrīkh al-qarn al-thālith ʿashar*; ed. Muḥammad Bahjat al-Bayṭār. 3v. Damascus, 1961–63.
Biographies of Muslims from Egypt, Palestine, Lebanon and Syria from 1785–1882.

-BŪRĪNĪ, Ḥasan b. Muḥammad (d. 1024/1615), *Tarājim al-aʿyān min abnāʾ al-zamān*; ed. Ṣalāḥ al-Dīn al-Munajjid. 2v. Damascus, 1959.

-DHAHABĪ, Muḥammad b. Aḥmad (d. 748/1348), *Siyar aʿlām al-nubalāʾ*. Vol. 1 ed. Ṣalāḥ al-Dīn al-Munajjid; vol. 2 ed. Ibrāhīm al-Abyārī. 2v. (Dhakhāʾir al-ʿArab, 19.) Cairo, 1957.

—— *Taʾrīkh al-islām wa ṭabaqāt al-mashāhīr wa-al-aʿlām*; ed. Ḥusām al-Dīn al-Qudsī. 4v. Cairo, 1367–69/1948–50.

-DUJAYLĪ, ʿAbd al-Ṣāḥib, *Aʿlām al-ʿArab fī al-ʿulūm wa-al-funūn*. 2nd edn. 3v. Najaf, 1966.

-GHAZZĪ, Muḥammad b. Muḥammad, Najm al-Dīn (d. 1061/1651), *Al-kawākib al-sāʾira bi-aʿyān al-miʾa al-ʿāshira*; ed. Jibraʾīl S. Jabbūr. 3v. (A.U.B. Publs. of the Fac. of Arts and Sciences; Or. ser. 18, 20, 29.) Beirut, 1945–58.

*ḤĀJJĪ KHALĪFA (KÂTIB ÇELEBÎ), *Keşf-el-zunun*. 2v. Istanbul, 1941–43, and supplement *Keşf-el-zunun zeyli*, by Bağdatlī İsmail Paşa. 2v. Istanbul, 1945–47.

ḤASAN, Muḥammad ʿAbd al-Ghanī, *Aʿlām min al-sharq wa-al-gharb*. Cairo, 1949.

—— *Tarājim ʿarabiyya*. Cairo, 1968.

—— *Al-tarājim wa-al-siyar.* (Funūn al-adab al-ʿarabī; al-fann al-qiṣaṣī, 2.) 2nd rev. edn. Cairo, 1969.

The major classical biographical dictionaries are discussed according to subject.

ḤIRZ AL-DĪN, Muḥammad, *Maʿārif al-rijāl fī tarājim al-ʿulamāʾ wa-al-udabāʾ*; ed. Muḥammad Ḥusayn Ḥirz al-Dīn. 3v. Najaf, 1964–65.

ḤUSAIN, Muḥammad al-Khiḍr, *Tarājim al-rijāl*; ed. ʿAlī al-Riḍā al-Tūnisī. Damascus, 1972.

Famous historical figures.

IBN ḤAJAR AL-ʿASQALĀNĪ, Aḥmad b. ʿAlī (d. 852/1449), *Al-durar al-kāmina fī aʿyān al-miʾa al-thāmina.* 4v. Hyderabad, 1348–50/1929–32.

—— *Al-durar al-kāmina* ... ed. Muḥammad Sayyid Jād al-Ḥaqq. 5v. Cairo, 1966–67.

*IBN KHALLIKĀN, Aḥmad b. Muḥammad (d. 681/1282), *Wafayāt al-aʿyān wa anbāʾ abnāʾ al-zamān,* ed. Muḥammad Muḥyī al-Dīn ʿAbd al-Ḥamīd. 3rd edn. Cairo, 1964–.

*—— *Kitāb wafayāt al-aʿyān; Ibn Khallikān's biographical dictionary,* trans. from the Arabic by Bn MacGuckin de Slane. 4v. Paris, 1843–71 (repr. Beirut, 1970).

*—— *Ibn Khallikān's Wafayāt al-aʿyān wa anbāʾ abnāʾ al-zamān. M. de Slane's English translation* ... ed. S. Moinul Haq. (Pakistan Hist. Soc. publs., 28.) Karachi, 1961–.

and

*-KUTUBĪ, Muḥammad b. Shākir (d. 764/1362), *Fawāt al-Wafayāt,* ed. Muḥammad Muḥyī al-Dīn ʿAbd al-Ḥamīd. 2v. Cairo, 1951.

A correction and supplement to Ibn Khallikān.

and

IBN AL-QĀḌĪ, Aḥmad b. Muḥammad (d. 1025/1616), *Dhayl Wafayāt al-aʿyān, musamman Durrat al-ḥijāl fī asmāʾ al-rijāl,* ed. M. al-A. Abū al-Nūr. Cairo, 1970–.

and

IBN AL-ṢUQĀʿĪ, *Tālī Kitāb wafayāt al-aʿyān,* ed. and tr. J. Sublet. Damascus, 1974.

-JUNDĪ, Anwar, *Al-aʿlām al-alf.* Cairo, 1957.

KAḤḤĀLA, ʿUmar Riḍā, *Muʿjam al-muʾallifīn; tarājim muṣannifī al-kutub al-ʿarabiyya.* 15v. in 8. Damascus, 1957–61.

Authors are listed alphabetically under their first name. Brockelmann references are given where relevant, and also catalogues of mss. where their works appear.

KARĀMĪ, Nādiyā and Nawwāf, *Al-ʿālam al-ʿarabī; taʾrīkh wa rijāl.* 9 pts. in 1. Sidon, 1956.

-KHALĪLĪ, Jaʿfar, *Hākadhā ʿaraftuhum.* 2v. Baghdad, 1963–68.

MAʿLŪF, Yūsuf Nuʿmān, *Kitāb khizānat al-ayyām fī tarājim al-ʿiẓām.* New York, 1899.

Notable men of the nineteenth century, particularly Syrians in America.

MAN HUM FĪ AL-ʿĀLAM AL-ʿARABĪ. Damascus, 1957–.

MAʿRŪF, Nājī, *ʿUlamāʾ al-niẓāmiyyāt wa madāris al-mashriq al-islāmī.* Baghdad, 1393/1973.

-MARZUBĀNĪ, Muḥammad b. ʿImrān (d. 384/993), *Die Gelehrtenbiographien des Abū ʿUbaidallāh al-Marzubānī in der Rezension des Ḥāfiẓ al-Yagmūrī;* hrsg. von R. Sellheim. [The *Nūr al-qabas al-mukhtaṣar min al-Muqtabas fī akhbār al-nuḥā wa-al-udabāʾ wa-al-shuʿarāʾ wa-al-ʿulamāʾ*] (Bibliotheca Islamica, 23a–.) Wiesbaden, 1964–.

MUJĀHID, Zakī Muḥammad, *Al-aʿlām al-sharqiyya fī al-miʾa al-rābiʿa ʿashara al-hijriyya.* 3v. Cairo, 1949–55.

Divided according to subject: Kings and amirs, ministers and ambassadors, ulama, &c.

-QANNAWJĪ, Ḥasan b. ʿAlī (d. 1307/1890), *Al-tāj al-mukallal min jawāhir maʾāthir al-ṭirāz al-ākhir wa-al-awwal,* ed. ʿAbd al-Ḥakīm Sharaf al-Dīn. Bombay, 1963.

*-QIFTĪ, ʿAlī b. Yūsuf (d. 646/1248), *Taʾrīkh al-ḥukamāʾ*, hrsg. J. Lippert. Leipzig, 1903 (repr. Baghdad, n.d.).

RAFĪQ AL-ʿAZM, Bey, *Ashhar mashāhīr al-islām fī al-ḥarb wa-al-siyāsa.* Vol. 1, pts. 1–4. Cairo, 1921–22.

-RAYḤĀNĪ, Amīn, *Wujūh sharqiyya gharbiyya.* Beirut, 1957.

RIḌWĀN, Fatḥī and others, *ʿUẓamāʾ al-sharq.* Cairo, *c.* 1955.

*-ṢAFADĪ, Khalīl b. Aybak (d. 764/1362), *Kitāb al-wāfī bi-al-wafayāt; Das biographische Lexicon* . . . (Bibliotheca Islamica, 6a–.) Vol. 1–. Istanbul, &c., 1931–.

—— 'Indice alfabetico di tutte le biografie contenute nel Wafi . . . by G. Gabrieli'. *Rendiconti dell'Accad. Naz. dei Lincei; Classe di scienze morali, storiche e filologiche* **22**, 1913, pp. 547–77, 581–620; **23**, 1914, pp. 191–208, 217–65; **24**, 1915, pp. 551–615; **25**, 1916, pp. 341–98.

*-SAKHĀWĪ, Muḥammad b. ʿAbd al-Raḥmān (d. 902/1497), *Al-ḍawʾ al-lāmiʿ.* 12v. in 8. Cairo, 1353–55/1934–36.

Biographies of notable men and women of the ninth Hijra century.

SHABĀB AL-ʿUṢFURĪ, Khalīfa b. Khayyāṭ (d. 240/854), *Kitāb al-ṭabaqāt,* ed. Akram Ḍiyāʾ al-ʿUmarī. Baghdad, 1967.

—— *Kitāb al-ṭabaqāt,* ed. Suhayl Zakkār. (Iḥyāʾ al-turāth al-qadīm, 14.) Damascus, 1966–.

Divided according to town of origin.

-SHAWKĀNĪ, Muḥammad b. ʿAlī (d. 1250/1832), *Al-badr al-tāliʿ bi-maḥāsin man baʿd al-qarn al-sābiʿ.* 2v. Cairo, 1345/1926.

Nobles and learned men.

ṢIDDĪQĪ, Amīr Ḥasan, *Heroes of Islam.* 2v. Karachi, 1965–66.

-SIJISTĀNĪ, Abū Ḥātim Sahl b. Muḥammad (d. 250/864), *Das Kitâb al-mu-ʿammarîn des Abû Ḥâtim al-Siǵistânî,* bearb. von I. Goldziher. (Abhandlungen zur arabischen Philologie, 2.) Leiden, 1899.

People of exceptional longevity.

-SUYŪṬĪ, Jalāl al-Dīn (d. 911/1505), *As-Suyuti's Who's who in the fifteenth century, Nazm ul-iʾqyân fi aʿyân-il-aʿyân. Being a biographical dictionary of notable men and women in Egypt, Syria and the Muslim world* . . . ed. P. K. Hitti. New York, 1927.

TAYMŪR, Aḥmad, *Ḍabṭ al-aʿlām.* Cairo, 1366/1947.

—— *Tarājim aʿyān al-qarn al-thālith ʿashar wa awāʾil al-rābiʿ ʿashar.* Cairo, n.d.

TAYMŪR, Maḥmūd, *Malāmih wa ghudūn; ṣuwar khāṭifa li-shakhṣiyyāt lāmi'a.* n.p. 1950.

WHO'S WHO IN THE ARAB WORLD, 1965/66–. Beirut, 1966–.

Revised and published every two years, it is divided into two parts – a general survey of the Middle East, and a section of descriptions and biographical notices of the various Arab countries.

ZAYDĀN, Jurjī, *Tarājim mashāhīr al-sharq fī al-qarn al-tāsi' 'ashar.* 2v. Cairo, 1910–11.

Contains over 100 biographies.

ZIRIKLĪ, Khayr al-Dīn, *Al-a'lām; qāmūs tarājim li-ashhar al-rijāl wa-al-nisā' min al-'Arab wa-al-musta'ribīn wa-al-mustashriqīn.* 3rd rev. edn. 11v. in 12. Beirut, *c.* 1970.

Has about 10,000 short biographical notices.

ZIYĀDA, Niqūlā, *Shakhṣiyyāt 'arabiyya.* Jaffa, 1945.

## 2. By Subject

### (i) *Companions and descendants of the Prophet*

ABŪ AL-FARAJ AL-IṢBAHĀNĪ, 'Alī b. Ḥusayn (d. 356/967), *Maqātil al-ṭālibiyyīn.* Najaf, 1353/1934.

—— *Maqātil al-ṭālibiyyīn.* 2nd edn. intr. Kāẓim al-Muẓaffar. Najaf, 1965.

Biographies of the descendants of Abū Ṭālib who suffered martyrdom.

*IBN 'ABD AL-BARR, Yūsuf b. 'Abd Allāh (d. 463/1071), *Al-isti'āb fī ma'rifat al-aṣḥāb,* ed. 'Alī Muḥammad al-Bajāwī. 3v. Cairo, *c.* 1958.

*IBN SA'D, Muḥammad (d. 230/844), *Al-ṭabaqāt al-kubrā.* Cairo, 1358/1939–.

*—— vols. 1–9. Beirut, 1960–68.

*—— *Kitāb al-ṭabaqāt al-kabīr.* English translation by S. Moinul Haq and H. K. Ghazanfar. Karachi, 1967–.

KHĀLID, Khālid Muḥammad, *Rijāl ḥawla al-rasūl.* Vols. 1–5. Cairo, 1964.

-SAḤḤĀR, 'Abd al-Ḥamīd Jūdah, *Muḥammad rasūl Allāh wa alladhīna ma'hu.* 13v. Cairo, n.d.

-SHARABĀSĪ, Aḥmad, *Abṭāl 'aqīda wa jihād.* (Silsilat al-buḥūth al-islāmiyya, 58.) Cairo, 1972.

-SHUBRĀWĪ, 'Abd Allāh b. Muḥammad (d. 1172/1758), *Al-itḥāf bi-ḥubb al-ashrāf . . .* ed. Muḥammad al-Zuhrī al-Ghamrāwī. Cairo, 1316/1899.

### (ii) *Traditionists*

ABŪ SHAHBAH, Muḥammad b. Muḥammad, *A'lām al-muḥaddithīn.* Cairo, 1962.

IBN ḤAJAR AL-'ASQALĀNĪ, Aḥmad b. 'Alī (d. 852/1449), *Lisān al-mīzān.* 6v. in 3. Hyderabad, 1330–31/1912–13.

An abridgement of al-Dhahabī's *Mīzān al-i'tidāl.*

—— *Taqrīb al-tahdhīb,* followed by Muḥammad b. Ṭāhir al-Patnī's *Al-mughnī.* Delhi, 1320/1902.

IBN ḤIBBĀN AL-BUSTĪ, Muḥammad (d. 354/965), *Mashāhīr 'ulamā' al-amṣār; Die berühmten Traditionarier der islamischen Länder,* hrsg. M. Fleischhammer. (Bibliotheca Islamica, 22.) Wiesbaden, 1959.

-KHŪʾĪ, Abū al-Qāsim al-Mūsawī, *Muʿjam rijāl al-ḥadīth*. Najaf, 1970–. More than 20 vols. are proposed.

-MUNDHIRĪ, ʿAbd al-ʿAẓīm b. ʿAbd al-Qawī (d. 656/1258), *Al-takmila li-wafayāt al-naqala*, ed. Bashshār ʿAwaḍ Maʿrūf. 2v. Najaf, 1968–69.

(iii) *Qurʾānic reciters and ḥuffāẓ*

-DHAHABĪ, Muḥammad b. Aḥmad, Shams al-Dīn (d. 748/1347), *Maʿrifat al-qurrāʾ al-kibār ʿalā al-ṭabaqāt wa-al-aʿṣār*, ed. Muḥammad Sayyid Jād al-Ḥaqq. 2v. Cairo, 1969.

*—— *Kitab tadhkirat al-ḥuffāẓ*. 3rd edn. 4v. Hyderabad, 1375–77/1955–58.

Inspired numerous supplements:

-ḤUSAYNĪ, Muḥammad b. ʿAlī b. al-Ḥasan (d. 763/1362), *Dhayl Tadhkirat al-ḥuffāẓ li-al-Dhahabī* ... followed by *Laḥẓ al-alḥāẓ bi-Dhayl Ṭabaqāt al-ḥuffāẓ*, by ... al-Hāshimī, and *Dhayl Ṭabaqāt al-ḥuffāẓ*, ... by ... al-Suyūṭi, ed. Ḥusām al-Dīn al-Qudsī. Damascus, 1347/1928.

-TAḤTĀWĪ, Aḥmad Rāfiʿ al-Ḥusaynī, *Al-tanbīh wa-al-īqāẓ li-mā fī dhuyūl Tadhkirat al-ḥuffāẓ*. Damascus, 1348/1929.

IBN AL-JAZARĪ, Muḥammad b. Muḥammad (d. 833/1429), *Kitāb ghāyat al-nihāya fī ṭabaqāt al-qurrāʾ; Das biographische Lexicon der Koranlehrer*, hrsg. G. Bergsträsser und O. Pretzl. 2v. (Bibliotheca Islamica, 8.) Leipzig, &c., 1933–35.

*-SUYŪṬĪ, Jalāl al-Dīn (d. 911/1505), *Ṭabaqāt al-mufassirīn* ... ed. A. Meursinge. Leiden, 1839 (repr. Tehran, 1960).

Concerning those who made interpretations of the Qurʾān.

(iv) *Shīʿites*

ĀGHĀ BUZURG, Tihrānī, *Ṭabaqāt aʿlām al-shīʿa, al-qarn al-rābiʿ; Nawābigh al-ruwāt fi rābiʿat al-miʾāt*, ed. ʿA. N. Munzawī. Beirut, 1971.

-AMĪN, al-Ḥusayni al-ʿĀmilī, *Aʿyān al-shīʿa*. Beirut, &c., 1935–.

-BAḤRĀNĪ, Yūsuf b. Aḥmad (d. 1186/1773), *Luʾluʾat al-baḥrayn fī al-ijāzāt wa tarājim rijāl al-ḥadīth*, ed. Muḥammad Ṣādiq Baḥr al-ʿUlūm. Najaf, 1966.

-ḤĀʾIRĪ, Muḥammad b. Ismāʿīl, *Muntaha al-maqāl*, followed by *Amal al-āmil* ... by Muḥammad b. al-Ḥasan al-Ḥurr al-ʿĀmilī ... Tehran, 1302/1885.

Shīʿa traditionists.

-KHWĀNSĀRĪ, Muḥammad Bāqir b. Zayn al-ʿĀbidīn (d. 1315/1877), *Rawḍāt al-jannāt fī aḥwāl al-ʿulamāʾ wa-al-sādāt*. 4 pts. in 1. Tehran, 1305–6/1888.

—— *Rawḍāt al-jannāt*, ed. Muḥammad ʿAlī Rawḍātī. Tehran, 1341/1962–.

-KHWĀNSĀRĪ, Muḥammad Mahdī b. Muḥammad Ṣādiq, *Aḥsan al-wadīʿa fī tarājim ashhar mashāhīr mujtahdī al-shīʿa*. 2v. Baghdad, 1348/1929.

A continuation of the *Rawḍāt al-jannāt* by the original author's grand-nephew.

-MADANĪ, al-Sayyid ʿAlī Khān (d. 1104/1692), *Al-darajāt al-rafīʿa fī ṭabaqāt al-shīʿa*, intr. by Muḥammad Ṣādiq Baḥr al-ʿUlūm. Najaf, 1962.

-MĀMAQĀNĪ, ʿAbd Allāh, *Tanqīh al-maqāl fī aḥwāl al-rijāl* ... 3v. Najaf, 1349–52/1930–33.

-NAJASHĪ, Aḥmad b. ʿAlī (d. *c.* 450/1085), *Al-rijāl*. Bombay, 1317/1899.

Shīʿite narrators of Tradition.

NI'MA, 'Abd Allāh, *Falāsifat al-shī'a; ḥayātuhum wa arā'uhum.* Beirut, n.d.

-TAFRĪSHĪ, Muṣṭafā b. al-Ḥusaynī, *Naqd al-rijāl.* Tehran, 1318/1900.

-TŪNKĪ, Maḥmūd Ḥasan, *Mu'jam al-muṣannifīn.* 4v. Beirut, 1344/1925.

-ṬŪSĪ, Muḥammad b. al-Ḥasan (d. 459/1067), *Ikhtiyār ma'rifat al-rijāl al-ma'rūf bi-Rijāl Kāshshī,* ed. . . . Ḥasan al-Muṣṭafavī. Meshhed, 1348/1970.

—— *Rijāl al-Ṭūsī,* ed. Muḥammad Ṣādiq Baḥr al-'Ulūm. Najaf, 1381/1961.

-TUSTARĪ, Muḥammad Taqī, *Qāmūs al-rijāl.* Tehran, 1379/1959–.

(v) *Members of other sects*

-FĀSĪ, al-Ḥasan b. Muḥammad al-Kūhin, *Ṭabaqāt al-shādhiliyya al-kubrā.* Cairo, 1347/1928.

GHĀLIB, Muṣṭafā, *A'lām al-ismā'īliyya.* Beirut, 1964.

IBN AL-MURTAḌĀ, Aḥmad b. Yaḥyā (d. 840/1437), *Kitāb ṭabaqāt al-mu'tazila; Die Klassen der Mu'taziliten* . . . hrsg. S. Diwald-Wilzer. Wiesbaden, &c., 1961.

(vi) *Jurists*

-'ABBĀDĪ, Abū 'Āsim (d. 458/1066), *Ṭabaqāt al-fuqahā' aš-Šāfi'īya; Das Klassenbuch der gelehrten Šāfi'iten des Abū 'Āsim . . . al-'Abbādī,* mit Einl. und Kommentar hrsg. von G. Vitestam. (Veröff. der 'De-Goeje-Stiftung', 21.) Leiden, 1964 (repr. Baghdad, 1969).

-ASNAWĪ, 'Abd al-Raḥīm b. al-Ḥasan (d. 772/1370), *Ṭabaqāt al-shāfi'iyya,* ed. 'Abd Allāh al-Judūrī. Pts. 1, 2. Baghdad, 1970–71.

IBN ABĪ AL-WAFĀ, 'Abd al-Qādir (d. 775/1373), *Al-jawāhir al-muḍī'a fī ṭabaqāt al-ḥanafiyya.* 2 pts. in 1. Hyderabad, 1332/1914.

IBN ABĪ YA'LĀ AL-FARRĀ', Muḥammad b. Muḥammad (d. 526/1133), *Ṭabaqāt al-ḥanābila,* abridged by Muḥammad 'Abd al-Qādir al-Nābulusī, ed. Aḥmad 'Ubayd. Damascus, 1350/1931.

*IBN QUṬLŪBUGHA, Qāsim (d. 879/1474), *Die Krone der Lebensbeschreibungen enthaltend die Classen der Hanafiten . . .* [*Tāj al-tarājim*]; hrsg. G. Flügel. (Abh. der Deutschen Morgenländischen Gesellschaft, Bd. 2, no. 3.) Leipzig, 1862 (repr. 1966).

IBN RAJAB, 'Abd al-Raḥmān b. Aḥmad (d. 795/1392), *Kitāb al-dhayl 'alā ṭabaqāt al-ḥanābila,* ed. H. Laoust and Sāmī al-Dahhān. Vol. 1 (460 H.–540 H.). Damascus, 1370/1951.

-LAKNAWĪ, Abū al-Ḥasanāt Muḥammad (d. 1304/1886), *Kitāb al-fawā'id al-bahiyya fī tarājim al-ḥanafiyya,* ed. Muḥammad Badr al-Dīn Abū Firās al-Na'sānī. Cairo, 1324/1906.

MAKHLŪF, Muḥammad b. Muḥammad, *Shajarat al-nūr al-zakiyya fī ṭabaqāt al-mālikiyya.* 2v. Cairo, 1349/1930.

-SHAṬṬĪ, Muḥammad Jamīl, *Mukhtaṣar ṭabaqāt al-ḥanābila.* Damascus, 1339/1920.

The earlier portions of the book are abridged from *Al-manhaj al-aḥmad fī tarājim aṣḥāb al-imām Aḥmad* by al-'Ulaymī and *Al-na't al-ikmāl li-aṣḥāb al-imām Aḥmad ibn Ḥanbal* by Kamāl al-Dīn al-Ghazzī.

-SHĪRĀZĪ, Ibrāhīm b. ʿAlī, Abū Isḥāq (d. 476/1083), *Ṭabaqāt al-fuqahāʾ*, followed by *Ṭabaqāt al-shāfiʿiyya* by Abū Bakr b. Hidāyat Allāh al-Ḥusaynī, intr. ʿAbbās al-ʿAzzawī. Baghdad, 1356/1937.

*-SUBKĪ, ʿAbd al-Wahhāb b. ʿAlī, Tāj al-Dīn (d. 771/1370), *Ṭabaqāt al-shāfiʿiyya al-kubrā*, ed. Maḥmūd Muḥammad al-Ṭanāḥī and ʿAbd al-Fattāḥ Muḥammad al-Ḥulw. Cairo, 1964–.

-TAMĪMĪ AL-DĀRĪ, Taqī al-Dīn ʿAbd al-Qādir (d. 1010/1601), *Al-ṭabaqāt al-saniyya fī tarājim al-ḥanafiyya*. Cairo, 1970–.

TÂŞKÖPRÜZÂDE, Muṣṭafā b. Khalīl (d. 935/1529), *Ṭabaqāt al-fuqahāʾ*, ed. Aḥmad Nīlah. 2nd edn. Mosul, 1961.

-YAḤṢŪBĪ, ʿIyāḍ b. Mūsā (d. 544/1149), *Tartīb al-madārik wa taqrīb al-masālik li-maʿrifat aʿlām madhhab Mālik*, ed. Aḥmad Bakīr Maḥmūd. 5v. Beirut, &c., 1967.

(vii) *Ṣūfīs and other holy men*

*ABŪ NUʿAYM AL-IṢBAHĀNĪ, Aḥmad b. ʿAbd Allāh (d. 430/1038), *Ḥilyat al-awliyāʾ*. 10v. Cairo, 1932–38.

*IBN AL-JAWZĪ, ʿAbd al-Raḥmān (d. 597/1201), *Ṣifat al-ṣafwa* . . . by Ibn al-Jawzī . . . 4 pts. in 2. Hyderabad, 1355–57/1936–38.

Ibn al-Jawzī's abridgement of Abū Nuʿaym's *Ḥilyat al-awliyāʾ*, further abridged by:

—— *Mukhtaṣar Kitāb ṣafwat al-ṣafwa*. Cairo, 1339/1921.

IBN QILIJ, Mughulṭāʾi (d. 762/1361), *Mughulṭai's biographical dictionary of the martyrs of love* [*Al-wāḍiḥ al-mubīn*], ed. O. Spies. Vol. 1. (Bonner Orientalistische Studien, 18.) Stuttgart, 1936.

IBN ṬŪLŪN, Muḥammad b. ʿAlī (d. 953/1546), *Al-aʾimma al-ithnā ʿashar*, ed. Ṣalāḥ al-Dīn al-Munajjid. (Nawādir al-makhṭūṭāt, 1.) Beirut, 1958.

-KISĀʾĪ, Muḥammad b. ʿAbd Allāh (d. fifth/eleventh century), *Vita prophetarum* . . . [*Qiṣaṣ al-anbiyāʾ*] ed. I. Eisenberg. 2 pts. in 1. Leiden, 1922–23.

-MUNAWĪ, ʿAbd al-Raʾūf b. Tāj al-Dīn (d. 1031/1621), *Al-kawākib al-durriyya fī tarājim al-sāda al-ṣūfiyya*. Vol. 1. Cairo, 1357/1938.

-NABHĀNĪ, Yūsuf (thirteenth/nineteenth century), *Jāmiʿ karamāt al-awliyāʾ*; followed by the author's *Asbāb al-taʾlīf* . . . 2v. in 1. Cairo, 1329/1911.

*-SHAʿRĀNĪ, ʿAbd al-Wahhāb b. Aḥmad (d. 973/1566), *Al-ṭabaqāt al-kubrā* . . . *Lawāqiḥ al-anwār fi ṭabaqāt al-akhyār*; and *Al-anwār al-qudsiyya* . . . Cairo, n.d.

Ṣūfīs of the first half of the tenth Hijra century.

-SULAMĪ, Muḥammad b. al-Ḥusayn (d. 412/1021), *Kitāb ṭabaqāt al-ṣūfiyya*. Texte arabe, avec intr. . . . par J. Pedersen. Leiden, 1960.

—— *Kitāb ṭabaqāt al-ṣūfiyya*, ed. Nūr al-Dīn Shurayba. 2nd edn. Cairo, 1969.

-THAʿLABĪ, Aḥmad b. Muḥammad (d. 427/1035), *Qiṣaṣ al-anbiyāʾ al-musamma ʿArāʾis al-majālis*. 4th edn. Singapore, 1382/1962.

(viii) *Rulers: princes and governors*

GHARĪṬ, Muḥammad b. Muḥammad al-Mufaḍḍal, *Fawāṣil al-jumān fī anbāʾ wuzarāʾ wa kuttāb al-zamān*. Fez, 1346/1927.

MAJĪD, Ṣalāḥ al-Dīn, *Aqbās min akhbār al-khulafā' al-rāshidīn*. Baghdad, n.d.

-MAQRĪZĪ, Aḥmad b. ʿAlī (d. 845/1442), *Al-dhahab al-masbūk fī dhikr man ḥajja min al-khulafā' wa-al-mulūk*, with notes by Jamāl al-Dīn al-Shayyāl. (Maktabat al-Maqrīzī al-Ṣaghīra, 3.) Cairo, 1955.

-RAYḤĀNĪ, Amīn, *Mulūk al-ʿArab*. 2v. in 1. Beirut, 1924–25.

SAʿĪD, Amīn Muḥammad, *Mulūk al-muslimīn al-muʿāṣirūn wa duwaluhum*. Cairo, 1933.

-ṢŪLĪ, Muḥammad b. Yaḥyā (d. 243/857), *Ashʿār awlād al-khulafā' wa akhbāruhum from the Kitāb al-awrāk* . . . ed. J. Heyworth-Dunne. London, 1936.

-YAḤṢŪBĪ, ʿIyāḍ b. Mūsā (d. 544/1149), *Tarājim aghlabiyya; Biographies aghlabides extraites des Madārik du Cadi ʿIyāḍ*. Édn. critique avec intr. et index par M. Talbi. Thèse complémentaire pour le doctorat ès-lettres . . . de l'Univ. de Paris. Tunis, 1968.

(ix) *Men of letters*

ʿABD AL-FATTĀḤ, Muḥammad Muḥammad, *Ashhar mashāhīr udabā' al-sharq*. 2v. in 1. Cairo, *c*. 1950.

ĀL JUNDĪ, Adham, *Aʿlām al-adab wa-al-fann*. Damascus, 1954–.

*-ANBĀRĪ, ʿAbd al-Raḥmān b. Muḥammad (d. 577/1181), *Nuzhat al-alibbā' fī ṭabaqāt al-udabā'*, ed. Ibrāhīm al-Sāmarrā'i. Baghdad, 1959.

*—— *Nuzhat al-alibbā' fī ṭabaqāt al-udabā'*, ed. ʿAṭiyya Āmir. (Stockholm Or. ser., 2.) Stockholm, 1962.

*—— *Nuzhat al-alibbā' fī ṭabaqāt al-udabā'*, ed. Muḥammad Abū 'l-Faḍl Ibrāhīm. Cairo, 1967.

*—— *Ta'rīkh al-udabā' al-nuḥā al-musammā Nuzhat al-alibbā' fī ṭabaqāt al-udabā'*; preceded by a life of the author by ʿAlī Yūsuf. n.p., n.d.

-BUSTĀNĪ, Buṭrus, *Udabā' al-ʿArab fī al-ʿaṣr al-ʿabbāsiyya*. 6th rev. edn. Beirut, 1968.

—— *Udabā' al-ʿArab fī al-Andalus wa ʿasr al-inbiʿāth*. 6th rev. edn. Beirut, 1968.

—— *Udabā' al-ʿArab fī al-Jāhiliyya wa ṣadr al-Islām*. 10th edn. Beirut, 1968.

DĀGHIR, Yūsuf Asʿad, *Maṣādir al-dirāsa al-adabiyya wafqan li-manāhij al-taʿlīm al-rasmiyya; Éléments de biobibliographie de la littérature arabe, conforme aux programmes officiels de l'enseignement*. 2v. Sidon, 1950–56.

Vol. 1 covers the period from the Jāhiliyya to the time of the Nahḍa; vol. 2 is devoted to famous modern authors.

DAMASCUS. MUʿTAMAR AL-UDABĀ' AL-ʿARAB, *Udabā' al-muʿtamar*, comp. by ʿAbd al-Razzāq al-Hilālī. (Silsilat al-kutub al-ḥadītha, 13.) Baghdad, 1966.

Notes on the delegates to the conference of Arab writers held in Baghdad, 1965.

FARRŪKH, ʿUmar, *Arbaʿat udabā' muʿāṣirūn; Ibrāhīm al-Yāzijī, Walī al-Dīn Yakan, Muṣṭafā Luṭfī al-Manfalūṭī, Sulaymān al-Bustānī*. 2nd edn. Beirut, 1952.

—— *Ta'rīkh al-adab al-ʿarabī*. 2v. Beirut, 1965.

A well-documented general survey is followed by individual biographies.

GHALLĀB, Muḥammad, *Adab al-thawra*. Cairo, *c*. 1950.

Includes writers from all over the world.

IBN AL-ABBĀR, Muḥammad b. ʻAbd Allāh (d. 658/1260), *Iʻtāb al-kuttāb*, ed. Ṣāliḥ al-Ashtar. Damascus, 1961.

-JUNDĪ, Anwar, *Aḍwāʼ ʻalā ḥayāt al-udabāʼ al-muʻāṣirīn*. Cairo, 1956.

KHEMIRI, T. & KAMPFFMEYER, G., 'Leaders in contemporary Arabic literature; a book of reference. Pt. 1'. *WI* **9**, Hefte 2–4, 1930.

Contains 13 biographies of such writers as Ilyā Abū Māḍī, al-ʻAqqād, Jibrān, Nuʻayma and Ṭaha Ḥusayn.

MAKDISĪ, Anīs, *Al-funūn al-adabiyya wa aʻlāmuhā*. Beirut, 1963.

About two-thirds of the volume consists of biographies of modern Arab writers with a brief survey of the times they lived in.

MASʻŪD, Jubrān, *Al-muḥīṭ fī adab al-Bakalūriyā*. 2v. Beirut, 1959.

-NAQQĀSH, Rajāʼ, *Udabāʼ muʻāṣirūn*. Cairo, 1968.

-RAMĀDĪ, Jamāl al-Dīn, *Min aʻlām al-adab al-muʻāṣir*. Cairo, *c*. 1960.

ṢAYDAḤ, Jurj, *Adabunā wa udabāʼunā fī al-Mahājir al-Amīrikiyya*. 2nd edn. Beirut, 1957.

Lists over 100 writers.

*-SUYŪṬĪ, Jalāl al-Dīn (d. 911/1505), *Bughyat al-wuʻa fī ṭabaqāt al-lughawiyyīn wa-al-nuḥā*, ed. Muḥammad Abū al-Faḍl Ibrāhīm. 2v. Cairo, 1964–65.

-WAHHĀBĪ, Khaldūn, *Marājiʻ tarājim al-udabāʼ al-ʻarab*. Baghdad, 1956–.

Arranged alphabetically according to author. Author's name is followed by a list of Arabic works in which he is mentioned, with page references, then articles about him in periodicals and newspapers.

*YĀQŪT b. ʻAbd Allāh al-Ḥamawī (d. 626/1229), *Muʻjam al-udabāʼ*, rev. by the Ministry of Education; ed. Aḥmad Farīd al-Rifāʻī. 20v. in 10. Cairo, 1936–38.

(x) *Poets and musicians*

ʻABBŪD, Mārūn, *ʻAlā al-miḥakk*. Beirut, 1946.

Concerning poetry and poets.

*ABŪ AL-FARAJ AL-IṢBAHĀNĪ, ʻAlī b. Ḥusayn (d. 356/967), *Kitāb al-aghānī* . . . Cairo, 1927–.

*—— *Kitāb al-aghānī* . . . Beirut, 1955–.

—— *Muhadhdhib al-Aghānī*, ed. Muḥammad al-Khuḍarī. 7v. Cairo, 1925.

A rearranged version of the *Aghānī*, with the *isnāds* omitted.

GHĀNIM, Jurj, *Shuʻarāʼ wa arāʼ*. Pt. 1. Beirut, 1971.

IBN AL-AḤMAR, Ismāʻīl b. Yūsuf (eighth/fourteenth century), *Nathīr farāʼid al-jumān fi naẓm fuḥūl al-zamān*. Beirut, 1967.

Eighth-century poets, mainly from Spain and North Africa.

IBN AL-MUʻTAZZ, ʻAbd Allāh, al-Hāshimī (d. *c*. 296/998), *The Ṭabaqāt al-shuʻarāʼ al-muḥdathīn of Ibn al-Muʻtazz*. Reproduced in facsimile . . . with an intr., notes . . . by A. Eghbal. ('E. J. W. Gibb Memorial' ser., N.S. 13.) London, 1939.

—— *Ṭabaqāt al-shuʻarāʼ*, ed. ʻAbd al-Sattār Aḥmad Farrāj. (Dhakhāʼir al-ʻArab, 20.) Cairo, 1956.

IBRĀHĪM, Muḥammad ʿAbd al-Fattāḥ, *Shuʿarāʾunā al-ḍubbāṭ*. Cairo? 1935.
Officer poets who flourished in the last decades of the nineteenth century and the first couple of the twentieth. Includes such figures as al-Bārūdī and Ḥāfiẓ Ibrāhīm.

-JUBŪRĪ, ʿAbd Allāh, *Min shuʿarāʾinā al-mansiyyīn*. (Silsilat al-kutub al-ḥadītha, 11.) Baghdad, 1966.
Minor poets who died during the first half of this century.

-JUBŪRĪ, Jamīl, *Maʿ al-aʿlām*. Baghdad, 1968.
Poets and writers.

-JUMAHĪ, Muḥammad b. Sallām (d. 231/845), *Ṭabaqāt al-shuʿarāʾ; Die Klassen der Dichter*, hrsg. von J. Hell. Leiden, 1916.

—— *Ṭabaqāt fuḥūl al-shuʿarāʾ*, ed. Maḥmūd Muḥammad Shākir. (Dhakhāʾir al-ʿArab, 7.) Cairo, 1952.

-JUNDĪ, Anwar, *Al-shiʿr al-ʿarabī al-muʿāṣir, taṭawwuruhu wa aʿlāmuhu 1875–1940*. N.p., n.d.

*-KĀTIB AL-IṢFAHĀNĪ, Muḥammad b. Muḥammad (d. 597/1201), *Kharīdat al-qaṣr wa jarīdat al-ʿaṣr. Al-qism al-ʿirāqī*, juzʾ 1, ed. Muḥammad Bahja al-Atharī and Jamīl Saʿīd. Baghdad, 1375/1955.

—— *Al-qism al-rābiʿ*, juzʾ 2 [Shuʿarāʾ al-Andalus], ed. ʿUmar al-Dasūqī and others. Cairo, 1969.

—— *Qism shuʿarāʾ al-Maghrib*, vol. 1, ed. Muḥammad al-Marzūqī and others. Tunis, 1966.

—— *Qism shuʿarāʾ Miṣr*, ed. Aḥmad Amīn and others. 2v. Cairo, 1370/1951.

—— *Qism shuʿarāʾ al-Shām*, vols. 1–3, ed. Shukrī Fayṣal. Damascus, 1375–83/1955–64.

MARDUM BEY, Khalīl, *Jamharat al-mughannīn*, ed. ʿAdnān Mardum Bey and Aḥmad al-Jundī. Damascus, 1964.

-MARZUBĀNĪ, Muḥammad b. ʿImrān (d. 384/993), *Muʿjam al-shuʿarāʾ* (letters ʿayn to ya) preceded by *Al-muʾtalif wa-al-mukhtalif*, by Ḥasan b. Bishr al-Āmidī, ed. F. Krenkow. Cairo, 1354/1935.

-QIFTĪ, ʿAlī b. Yūsuf (d. 646/1248), *Al-muḥammadūn min al-shuʿarāʾ wa ashʿāruhum*, ed. Ḥasan Maʾmarī. Riyad, 1970.

-SHINQĪṬĪ, Aḥmad b. al-Amīn, *Tarājim aṣḥāb al-Muʿallaqāt al-ʿashar wa akhbāruhum*. Cairo, 1329/1911.

-ṢŪLĪ, Muḥammad b. Yaḥyā (d. 243/857), *Kitāb al-awrāḳ (section on contemporary poets)*, ed. J. Heyworth-Dunne. London, 1934.

(xi) *Artists*

MAYER, L. A., *Islamic architects and their works*. Geneva, 1956.

—— *Islamic armourers and their works*. Geneva, 1962.
Has a roll of swordsmiths and a roll of cannonmakers.

—— *Islamic astrolabists and their works*. Geneva, 1956.

—— *Islamic metalworkers and their works*. Geneva, 1959.

—— *Islamic woodcarvers and their works*. Geneva, 1958.

(xii) *Journalists*

ʿABDUH, Ibrāhīm, *Aʿlām al-ṣiḥāfa al-ʿarabiyya*. 2nd edn. Cairo, 1948.

ṬARRĀZĪ, Viscount P. de, *Ta'rīkh al-ṣiḥāfa al-'arabiyya*. 4v. Beirut, 1913–33 (repr. in 2v. Baghdad, 1969?).

(xiii) *Reformers*
AMĪN, Aḥmad, *Zu'amā' al-iṣlāḥ fī al-'aṣr al-ḥadīth*. Cairo, 1948.
Muslim reformers of the eighteenth–nineteenth centuries.

(xiv) *Philosophers*
JUM'A, Muḥammad Luṭfī, *Ta'rīkh falāsifat al-Islām fī al-mashriq wa-al-maghrib*. Cairo, 1927.

-YĀZIJĪ, Kamāl & KARAM, Anṭūn Ghaṭṭās, *A'lām al-falsafa al-'arabiyya*. Beirut, 1968.

(xv) *Physicians*
*IBN ABĪ 'USAYBI'A, Aḥmad b. al-Qāsim (d. 668/1270), *'Uyūn al-anbā' fī ṭabaqāt al-aṭibbā'*, hrsg. A. Müller. 2v. Cairo, &c., 1882–84 (repr. 1972).
Is supplemented by:

AḤMAD 'ĪSĀ, Bey, *Mu'jam al-aṭibbā'*. (Jāmi'at Fu'ād al-Awwal, Kulliyyat al-Ṭibb, 18.) Cairo, 1361/1942.

IBN JULJUL, Sulaymān b. Ḥassān (fourth/tenth century), *Les générations des médecins et des sages. Ṭabaqāt al-aṭibbā' wa'l-ḥukamā' . . . par . . . Ibn Ǧulǧul al-Andalusī*, édn. crit. par Fu'ād Sayyid. (Publs. de l'I.F.A.O., Textes et traductions d'auteurs orientaux, 10.) Cairo, 1955.

(xvi) *Mathematicians and astronomers*
*SUTER, H., *Die Mathematiker und Astronomen der Araber und ihrer Werke*. (Abh. z. Geschichte der mathemat. Wissensch., x Heft. Zugleich Suppl. 3, 45 Jhg. d. Z. f. Math. u. Physik.) Leipzig 1900 (repr. 1972). *Nachträge und Berichtungen*. *Ibid*. 1902 (XIV Heft. pp. 155–85).

(xvii) *Geographers*
ḤAMĪDA, 'Abd al-Raḥmān, *A'lām al-jughrāfiyyīn al-'Arab*. Damascus, 1970.

ḤASAN, Ṣabrī Muḥammad, *Al-jughrāfiyyūn al-'arab*. Najaf, 1958–.

(xviii) *Orientalists*
-'AQĪQĪ, Najīb, *Al-mustashriqūn*. 3rd rev. edn. 3v. Cairo, 1964–65.
See also the chapter on 'Orientalists' in this Guide.

(xix) *Women*
'ABD ALLĀH, Ṣūfī & LŪQĀ, Naẓmī, *Nawābigh al-nisā'*. (Kitāb al-Hilāl, 159.) Cairo, 1964.

FAWWĀZ, Zaynab bint 'Alī, *Al-durr al-manthūr fī ṭabaqāt rabbāt al-khudūr*. N.p., 1313/1895.

IBN AL-SĀ'Ī AL-KHĀZIN, 'Alī b. Anjab (d. 674/1275), *Nisā' al-khulafā', al-musamma Jihāt al-a'imma al-khulafā' min al-ḥarā'ir wa-al-imā'*, ed. Muṣṭafā Jawād. (Dhakhā'ir al-'Arab, 28.) Cairo, *c*. 1960.
Wives and concubines of the imams.

IBRĀHĪM, Mubārak, *Nisā' shahīrāt*. (Iqrā', 119.) Cairo, 1952.

KAḤḤĀLA, ʿUmar Riḍā, *Aʿlām al-nisāʾ fī ʿālamay al-ʿarab wa-al-Islām.* 2nd edn. 5v. Damascus, 1959.

-KHAṬĪB AL-ʿUMARĪ, Yāsīn b. Khayr Allāh (early thirteenth/nineteenth century), *Muhadhdhab al-rawḍha al-fayḥāʾ fī tawārīkh al-nisāʾ*, ed. Rajāʾ Maḥmūd al-Sāmarrāʾī. Baghdad, 1966.

QADRIYYAT ḤUSAYN, Princess, *Shahīrāt al-nisāʾ fī al-ʿālam al-iṣlāmī*, tr. into Arabic by ʿAbd al-ʿAzīz Amīn al-Khānjī. 2 pts. in 1. Cairo, 1924.

SAKĀKĪNĪ, Widād, *Ummahāt al-muʾminīn wa banāt al-rasūl.* Cairo, 1969.

—— & TAWFĪQ, Tamāḍir, *Nisāʾ shahīrāt min al-sharq wa-al-gharb.* Cairo, 1959.

-SUYŪṬĪ, Jalāl al-Dīn (d. 911/1505), *Al-mustaẓraf min akhbār al-jawārī*, ed. Ṣalāḥ al-Dīn al-Munajjid. (Rasāʾil wa nuṣūṣ, 2.) Beirut, 1963.

ZAYDĀN, Jurjī, *Banāt al-nahḍa al-ʿarabiyya.* Rev. edn. Cairo, 1958.

(xx) *Government ministers*

BIDWELL, R., *Bidwell's guide to government ministers. Vol. 2: the Arab world.* London, 1973.

## 3. By Region

(i) *Spain*

-ḤUMAYDĪ, Muḥammad b. ʿAbd Allāh (d. 488/1095), *Jadhwat al-muqtabis fī dhikr wulāt al-Andalus.* (Al-Maktaba al-Andalusiyya, 3.) Cairo, 1966.

*IBN AL-ABBĀR, Muḥammad b. ʿAbd Allāh (d. 658/1260), *Al-ḥulla al-siyarāʾ*, ed. ʿAbd Allāh Anīs al-Ṭabbāʾ. Beirut, 1962.

*—— *Al-ḥulla al-siyarāʾ*, ed. Ḥusayn Muʾnis. 2v. Cairo, 1963.

IBN AL-ʿARABĪ, Muḥyī al-Dīn (d. 638/1240), *Sufis of Andalusia; the Rūḥ al-quds and Al-durrat al-fākhira of Ibn ʿArabī*, trans. . . . R. W. J. Austin. London, &c., 1971.

—— *Vidas de santones andaluces. La 'Epistola de la santidad' de Ibn ʿArabi de Murcia*, trans. M. Asin Palacios. Madrid, 1933.

A translation of the third part of the *Risālat al-quds*, with a partial translation of parts 1, 2 and 4.

*IBN AL-FARAḌĪ, ʿAbd Allāh b. Muḥammad (d. 403/1012), *Taʾrīkh al-ʿulamāʾ wa-al-ruwā li-al-ʿilm bi-al-Andalus*, ed. ʿIzzat al-ʿAṭṭār al-Ḥusaynī. 2v. (Min turāth al-Andalus, 3.) Cairo, 1954.

*—— *Taʾrīkh ʿulamāʾ al-Andalus.* 2v. in 1. (Al-Maktaba al-Andalusiyya, 2.) Cairo, 1966.

Supplemented by:

*IBN BASHKUWĀL, Khalaf b. ʿAbd al-Mālik (d. 578/1183), *Kitāb al-ṣila fī taʾrīkh aʾimmat al-Andalus*, ed. ʿIzzat al-ʿAṭṭār al-Ḥusaynī. 2v. (Min turāth al-Andalus, 4.) Cairo, 1955.

This in turn was supplemented by:

*IBN AL-ABBĀR, Muḥammad b. ʿAbd Allāh (d. 658/1260), *Al-takmila li-Kitāb al-ṣila*, ed. ʿIzzat al-ʿAṭṭār al-Ḥusaynī. 2v. Cairo, 1956.

and

IBN AL-ZUBAYR, Aḥmad (d. 708/1308), *Ṣilat al-ṣila; Répertoire biographique andalou du XIIIme siècle.* Dernière partie, publ. . . . E. Lévi-Provençal. Rabat, 1938.

Ibn al-Faraḍī and Ibn Bashkuwāl combined were supplemented by:

-MARRĀKUSHĪ, Muḥammad b. Muḥammad (d. 702/1303), *Al-dhayl wa-al-takmila li-kitābay Al-mawṣūl wa-Al-ṣila*, ed. Iḥsān ʿAbbās. (Al-Maktaba al-Andalusiyya, 10–.) Beirut, 1965–.

*IBN KHĀQĀN, Fatḥ b. Muḥammad (d. 535/1140), *Qalā'id al-iqyān fī maḥāsin al-aʿyān*, ed. Muḥammad al-ʿInābī. (Min turāthinā al-islāmī, 1.) Tunis, 1966.

—— *Maṭmaḥ al-anfus*. Istanbul, 1302/1884.

A supplement to the previous work, which deals with Andalusian poets.

*IBN AL-KHAṬĪB, Muḥammad b. ʿAbd Allāh, Lisān al-Dīn (d. 776/1374), *Al-iḥāṭa fī akhbār Gharnāṭa*, ed. Muḥammad ʿAbd Allāh ʿInān. Vol. 1. Cairo, 1955–.

—— *Islamische Geschichte Spaniens; Übersetzung der Aʿmāl al-aʿlām und ergänzender Texte*, von. W. Hoenerbach. Zurich, &c., 1970.

*IBN SAʿĪD AL-MAGHRIBĪ, ʿAlī b. Mūsā (d. *c.* 685/1286), *Al-mughrib fī ḥulā al-maghrib*, ed. Shawqī Ḍaif. 2nd edn. 2v. (Dhakhā'ir al-ʿArab, 10.) Cairo, 1964.

-KHUSHANĪ, Muḥammad b. Ḥārith (d. 371/981), *Quḍāt Qurṭuba wa ʿulamā' Ifrīqiyya*. (Min turāth al-Andalus, 2.) Cairo, 1372/1952.

—— *Quḍāt Qurṭuba*. (Al-Maktaba al-Andalusiyya, 1.) Cairo, 1966.

*-MAQQARĪ, Aḥmad b. Muḥammad (d. 1041/1632), *Nafḥ al-ṭīb min ghuṣn al-Andalus al-raṭīb*, ed. Muḥammad Muḥyī al-Dīn ʿAbd al-Ḥamīd. 10v. Cairo, 1949.

-NUBAHĪ, Ibn al-Ḥasan (d. *c.* 792/1390), *Histoire des juges d'Andalousie, intitulée; Kitāb al-markaba al-ʿulyā*, édn. critique par E. Lévi-Provençal. Cairo, 1948.

*PONS BOIGUES, F., *Ensayo bio-bibliográfico sobre los historiadores y geógrafos arábigo-españoles*. Madrid, 1898 (repr. 1972).

-SILAFĪ, Aḥmad b. Muḥammad (d. 576/1180), *Akhbār wa tarājim andalusiyya*, selected and ed. Iḥsān ʿAbbās. (Al-Maktaba al-Andalusiyya, 7.) Beirut, 1963.

(ii) *Morocco*

GANNŪN, ʿAbd Allāh, *Dhikrayāt mashāhīr rijāl al-Maghrib*. Vol. 1–. Tetuan, 1950s.

Biographies of notable Moroccan men. At least 25 were published.

IBN AL-QĀḌĪ, Aḥmad b. Muḥammad (d. 1025/1616), *Jadhwat al-iqtibās*. Fez, 1309/1891.

Eminent men of Fez.

IBN ZAYDĀN, ʿAbd al-Raḥmān, *Al-durar al-fākhira bi-ma'āthir al-mulūk al-ʿalawiyyīn bi-Fās al-zāhira*. Rabat, 1356/1937.

The Sultans of Morocco.

-MAQQARĪ, Aḥmad b. Muḥammad (d. 1041/1632), *Rawḍat al-ās al-ʿāṭira al-anfās fī dhikr man laqaituhu min aʿlām al-ḥaḍratayn Marrākush wa Fās*. Rabat, 1964.

-MARRĀKUSHĪ, ʿAbbās b. Ibrāhīm (thirteenth/nineteenth century), *Al-iʿlām bi-man ḥalla Marrākush wa Aghmāt min al-aʿlām*. Vol. 1–. Fez, 1936–.

—— *Iẓhār al-kamāl fī tatmīm manāqib awliyā' Marrākush*. 2v. N.p., n.d.

-SHINQĪṬĪ, Aḥmad b. al-Amīn, *Al-wasīṭ fī tarājim udabā' Shinqīṭ*. Cairo, 1911.
—— *Al-wasīṭ fī tarājim udabā' Shinqīṭ*, ed. Fu'ād Sayyid. 3rd edn. Casablanca, 1961.

(iii) *Algeria*

*-GHUBRĪNĪ, Aḥmad b. Aḥmad (d. 714/1315), *'Unwān al-dirāya fī man 'urifa min 'ulamā' al-mi'a al-sābi'a fī Bijāya*, ed. 'A. Nuwayhiḍ. Beirut, 1969.
Savants of Bougie of the seventh Hijra century.

-HAFNAWĪ, Abū al-Qāsim Muḥammad, *Ta'rif el-khalef bi-ridjal es-salef; ou, Biographies des savants musulmans de l'Algérie du IVe siècle de l'Hégire à nos jours*. 2v. Algiers, 1906–9.

IBN MARYAM, Muḥammad b. Muḥammad (d. *c.* 1011/1602), *El-Bostan, ou jardin des biographies des saints et savants de Tlemcen*, tr. et annoté par F. Provenzali. Algiers, 1910.
French translation of a work listed by Caetani and Gabrieli.

NUWAYHIḌ, 'Ādil, *Mu'jam a'lām al-Jazā'ir min ṣadr al-Islām ḥattā muntaṣaf al-qarn al-'ishrīn*. Beirut, 1971.

(iv) *Tunisia*

'ABD AL-WAHHĀB, Ḥasan Ḥusnī, *Shahīrāt al-tūnisiyyāt*. 2nd edn. Tunis, 1966.

ḤUSAYN, Abū 'Abd Allāh Khwāja (d. 1164/1755), *Al-dhayl li-kitāb Bashā'ir ahl al-īmān*. Tunis, 1908.
Biographies of eminent men, mainly from Tunis.

IBN 'ĀSHŪR, Muḥammad al-Fāḍil, *Tarājim al-a'lām fī Tūnis*. Tunis, 1970.

-KINĀNĪ AL-QAYRAWĀNĪ, Muḥ. b. Ṣāliḥ (d. ?), *Takmīl al-ṣulaḥā' wa-al-a'yān li-ma'ālim al-īmān fī awliyā' al-Qayrawān*, ed. Muḥ. al-'Ināni. Tunis, 1970.

-MĀLIKĪ, Abū Bakr 'Abd Allāh (d. late fourth/tenth century), *Kitāb riyāḍ al-nufūs; Répertoire biographique des savants de Kairouan et de l'Ifrikia de la conquête arabe à l'an 356 de l'Hégire*. Édn. critique par H. Monès. Vol. 1. Cairo, 1951.

NĪFAR, Muḥammad, *'Unwān al-arīb 'amma nusha' bi-al-mamlaka al-tūnisiyya min 'ālim adīb*. 2v. Tunis, 1351/1932.

-SŪSĪ, Muḥammad al-Mukhtār, *Al-ma'sūl*. 20v. Casablanca, 1960–62.
Famous people of Sūs.

*-TAMĪMĪ, Abū al-'Arab Muḥammad b. Aḥmad (d. 333/944), *Kitāb ṭabaqāt 'ulamā' Ifrīqiyya . . . wa Kitāb ṭabaqāt 'ulamā' Ifrīqiyya, ta'līf Muḥammad b. al-Ḥārith b. Asad al-Khushanī . . . Classes des savants de l'Ifrīqīya . . .* Texte arabe publié avec une traduction française . . . de M. Ben Cheneb. Vol. 1 [Text]. (Publs. de la Fac. des Lettres d'Alger, Bulletin de Correspondance Africaine, 51.) Algiers, 1915.
*—— *Ṭabaqāt 'ulamā' Ifrīqiyya wa Tūnis*, ed. 'Alī al-Shābbī and Na'īm Ḥasan al-Yāfī. Tunis, 1968.

-TANŪKHĪ, Muḥammad b. al-Nājī (d. 837/1433), *Maʿālim al-īmān* . . . 4 pts. in 2. Tunis, 1320–25/1902–7.

Derived from ʿAbd al-Raḥmān b. Muḥammad al-Dabbāgh's *Maʿālim al-īmān*, concerning the famous men of Qairawan.

(v) *Libya*

ʿAFĪFĪ, Muḥammad al-Ṣādiq, *Al-shiʿr wa-al-shuʿarāʾ fi Lībiyā*. Cairo, 1957.

About half the work is devoted to biographies, mainly of twentieth-century poets.

-ANṢĀRĪ, Aḥmad al-Nāʾib, *Nafaḥāt al-nasrīn wa-al-rayḥān fī man kāna bi-Ṭarāblus min al-aʿyān*, ed. ʿAlī Muṣṭafā al-Miṣurātī. Beirut, 1963.

LEWICKI, T., *Études ibāḍites nord-africaines, partie 1: Tasmiya šuyūḫ ǧabal Nafūsa wa-qurāhum; liste anonyme des šayḫs ibāḍites et des localités du Ǧabal Nafūsa contenu dans le ʿSiyar al-mašāʾiḫʾ* (*VIe = XIIe s.*). Warsaw, 1955.

ZĀWĪ, Ṭāhir Aḥmad, *Aʿlām Lībiyā*. 2nd edn. Tripoli, 1971.

—— *Wulāt Ṭarāblus min bidāyat al-fatḥ al-ʿarabī ilā nihāyat al-ʿahd al-turkī*. Tripoli, 1970.

(vi) *Egypt*

ABKĀRIYŪS, Iskandar, *Al-manāqib al-ibrāhīmiyya wa-al-maʾāthir al-khidīwiyya*. Cairo, 1299/1882.

The Khedives of Egypt.

-ADFUWĪ, Jaʿfar b. Thaʿlab (d. 748/1347), *Al-ṭāliʿ al-saʿīd al-jāmiʿ asmāʾ nujabā al-ṣaʿīd*. Cairo, 1914.

—— *Al-ṭāliʿ al-saʿīd al-jāmiʿ asmāʾ nujabā al-ṣaʿīd*, ed. Saʿd Muḥammad Ḥasan and Ṭāha al-Ḥājirī. Cairo, 1966.

Famous men of Upper Egypt.

ĀṢĀF, Yūsuf, *Ashhūr rijāl al-ʿaṣr*. Cairo, *c.* 1890.

Important men of Cairo.

DALĪL AL-AFRĀD AL-ʿILMIYYĪN BI-AL-WIZĀRĀT WA-AL-JĀMIʿĀT . . . BI-AL-JUMHŪRIYYA AL-ʿARABIYYA AL-MUTTAḤIDA (earlier: BI-AL-JUMHŪRIYYA AL-MIṢRIYYA). Cairo, 1957–.

Directory of scientists and technicians in ministries, universities, government organizations and public establishments.

FAHMĪ, Zakī, *Ṣafwat al-ʿaṣr fī taʾrīkh wa rusūm rijāl Miṣr*. Pt. 1 (all publ.). Cairo, 1926.

FUʾĀD, Faraj Sulaymān, *Al-kanz al-thamīn li-ʿuẓamāʾ al-miṣriyyīn*. Cairo, 1917.

Notable nineteenth-century Egyptians.

HAYKAL, Muḥammad Ḥusayn, *Tarājim miṣriyya wa gharbiyya*. Cairo, 1929.

IBN SAʿĪD, ʿAlī b. Mūsā (d. 685/1286), *Al-nujūm al-zāhira fi ḥulā ḥaḍrat al-Qāhira* . . . Cairo, 1970.

Derived in part from the 3rd book of *Al-mughrib fī ḥulā al-Maghrib*.

ʿISĀ, Maḥmūd, *Shuʿarāʾ wa udabāʾ fī ʾaṣr Fārūq*. Cairo, *c.* 1947.

Biographies of nine literary men, including ʿAbd al-Raḥmān Zakī, Maḥmud Muḥammad al-Shādhilī and Yūsuf al-Sibāʿī.

-KINDĪ, Muḥammad b. Yūsuf (d. 350/961), *Wulāt Miṣr*, ed. Ḥusayn Naṣṣār. Beirut, 1959.

LE MONDAIN ÉGYPTIEN; THE EGYPTIAN WHO'S WHO (later:) WHO'S WHO IN EGYPT AND THE MIDDLE EAST (later:) WHO'S WHO IN EGYPT AND THE NEAR EAST (later:) LE MONDAIN ÉGYPTIEN ET DU PROCHE ORIENT. Cairo, 1935–.

RASHĀD, ʿAzīza, *Dalīl al-mushtaghilīn bi-al-ʿulūm al-ijtimāʿiyya bi-al-iqlīm al-miṣrī; Directory of social scientists in Egypt, United Arab Republic*. Cairo, 1961.

-SHAYYĀL, Jamāl al-Dīn Muḥammad, *Aʿlām al-iskandariyya fī al-ʿaṣr al-islāmī*. Cairo, 1965.

ZĀKHŪRA, Ilyās, *Kitāb mirʾāt al-ʿaṣr fī taʾrīkh wa rusūm kabīr al-rijāl bi-Miṣr*. 2v. Cairo, 1897–1917.
Contains almost 400 biographies.
—— *Al-Sūriyūn fī Miṣr*. Cairo, 1927.

ZAKĪ, ʿAbd al-Raḥmān, *Aʿlām al-jaysh wa-al-baḥriyya fī Miṣr ithnāʾ al-qarn al-tāsiʿ ʿashar*. Cairo, 1947.

(vii) *Sudan*

ABŪ SAʿD, Aḥmad, *Al-shiʿr wa-al-shuʿarāʾ fī al-Sūdān, 1900–1958*. Beirut, 1959.
Basically an anthology of poetry, but it does give single-page biographical descriptions of the 15 poets whose works are quoted.

HILL, R., *A biographical dictionary of the Sudan*. 2nd edn. London, 1967.
The standard work.

IBN ḌAYF ALLĀH, Muḥammad al-Nūr (d. 1225/1810), *Kitāb al-ṭabaqāt fī khuṣūṣ al-awliyāʾ wa-al-ṣāliḥīn wa-al-ʿulamāʾ wa-al-shuʿarāʾ fī al-Sūdān*, ed. Yūsuf Faḍl Ḥasan. Khartoum, 1971.

(viii) *Arabia*

-FILĀLĪ, Ibrāhīm Hāshim, *Rijālāt al-Ḥijāz*. Vol. 1. Cairo? 1946.

-RĀFIʿĪ, ʿAbd Allāh b. al-ʿAlawī, *ʿUnwān al-najāba fī maʿrifat man māta bi-al-Madīna al-munawwara min al-ṣaḥāba*. Cairo, *c*. 1953.

-SAQQĀF, ʿAbd Allāh b. Muḥammad, *Taʾrīkh al-shuʿarāʾ al-ḥaḍramiyyīn*. 5v. Cairo, 1353–63/1934–44.

ẒĀFIR AL-AZHARĪ, Muḥammad al-Bashīr, *Al-yawāqīt al-thamīna fī aʿyān madhhab ʿālim al-Madīna*. Pt. 1. N.p., 1324/1906.

(ix) *Yemen*

-SHARJĪ AL-ZABĪDĪ, Aḥmad b. Aḥmad (d. 893/1488), *Ṭabaqāt al-khawāṣṣ*, ed. Muḥammad al-Zuhrī al-Ghamrāwī. Cairo, 1321/1903.
Sufis and holy men of Yemen.

ZABĀRA, Muḥammad b. Muḥammad, *Aʾimmat al-Yaman bi-al-qarn al-rābiʿ ʿashar li-al-hijra*. Cairo, n.d.

—— *Nayl al-waṭar min tarājim rijāl al-Yaman fī al-qarn al-thālith ʿashar*. 2v. Cairo, 1348–50/1929–31.

550 biographies covering the eighteenth and nineteenth centuries.

(x) *Kuwait*

-ZAYD, Khālid Saʿūd, *Udabāʾ al-Kuwayt fī qarnayn*. 2nd edn. Vol. 1. Kuwait, 1964.

A brief historical essay on intellectual life in Kuwait is followed by biographies of and selections from 20 authors.

(xi) *Iraq*

ABŪ SAʿD, Aḥmad, *Al-shiʿr wa-al-shuʿarāʾ fī al-ʿIrāq, 1900–1958*. Beirut, 1959.

An anthology, with brief biographies of 31 authors.

ʿAWWĀD, Gūrgīs, *Muʿjam al-muʾallifīn al-ʿirāqiyyīn ... A dictionary of Iraqi authors during the nineteenth and twentieth centuries*. 3v. Baghdad, 1969.

Covers the period 1800–1969. Authors are listed under *ism*, with details of both their published and unpublished work.

-ʿAZZĀWĪ, ʿAbbās, *Al-taʿrīf bi-al-muʾarrikhīn*. Vol. 1. Baghdad, 1957.

Famous Iraqi historians.

-DARŪBĪ, Ibrāhīm, *Al-Baghdādiyyūn, akhbāruhum wa majālisuhum*. Baghdad, 1958.

Eminent men of Baghdad.

IBN RĀFIʿ, Muḥammad Abū al-Maʿālī (d. 774/1372), *Taʾrīkh ʿulamāʾ Baghdād, al-musammā Muntakhab al-mukhtār*, ed. ʿAbbās al-ʿAzzāwī. Baghdad, 1357/1938.

A continuation of Muḥammad b. Maḥmūd Ibn al-Najjār's supplement (never published?) to al-Khaṭīb al-Baghdādī's *Taʾrīkh Baghdād*:

*-KHAṬĪB AL-BAGHDĀDĪ, Aḥmad b. ʿAlī (d. 463/1071), *Taʾrīkh Baghdād*. 14v. Cairo, &c., 1349/1931.

MAʿRŪF, Nājī, *Taʾrīkh ʿulamāʾ al-Mustanṣiriyya*. 2nd edn. 2v. Baghdad, 1965.

-SĀMARRĀʾĪ, Yūnus Ibrāhīm, *Taʾrīkh shuʿarāʾ Sāmarrāʾ min taʾsīsihā ḥattā al-yawm*. Baghdad, 1970.

—— *Taʾrīkh ʿulamāʾ Sāmarrāʾ*. Baghdad, 1966.

-SHAHRĀBĀNĪ, ʿAbd al-Qādir, al-Khaṭībī (thirteenth/nineteenth century), *Shuʿarâuʾ Bagdad wa kuttâbuhâ; les poètes de Bagdad ... de l'an 1780 à l'an 1830 de l'ère chrétienne* ... ed. A.-M. de St. Élie. Baghdad, 1936.

-SĪRĀFĪ, Ḥasan b. ʿAbd Allāh (d. 368/979), *Biographies des grammairiens de l'école de Basra* ... publié et annoté par F. Krenkow. (Bibliotheca Arabica ... 9.) Paris, &c., 1936 (repr. 1970).

-SUHRAWARDĪ, Muḥammad Ṣāliḥ, *Lubb al-albāb; kitāb taʾrīkh wa adab yaḍaʿu tarājim ṭāʾifa kabīra min al-ʿulamāʾ wa-al-udabāʾ wa-al-siyāsiyyīn wa-al-shuyūkh wa dhawī al-buyūtāt fī al-ʿIrāq*. 2v. Baghdad, 1933.

UNESCO. CENTRE DE CO-OPÉRATION SCIENTIFIQUE DU MOYEN-ORIENT, *List of scientists in Iraq*. Cairo, 1954.

(xii) *Syria*

ĀL TAQĪ AL-DĪN, Muḥammad Adīb, al-Ḥiṣnī, *Muntakhabāt al-tawārīkh li-Dimashq*. 3v. Damascus, 1927–34.
Includes 200 pages of biographies.

-DAHHĀN, Sāmī, *Al-shiʿr al-ḥadīth fī al-iqlīm al-sūrī*. Cairo, 1960.
Biographies of five modern poets.
—— *Al-shuʿarāʾ al-aʿlām fī Sūriyā*. 2nd edn. Beirut, 1968.

-DARĪNĪ, ʿAbd al-Jabbār b. ʿAbd Allāh al-Khawlānī (d. *c.* 370/975), *Taʾrīkh Darayyā*, ed. Saʿīd al-Afghānī. Damascus, 1369/1950.
Companions of the prophet who settled in Darayya.

ḤUMṢĪ, Qusṭākī, *Udabāʾ Ḥalab fī al-qarn al-tāsiʿ ʿashar*. Aleppo, 1968.

IBN ʿASĀKIR, ʿAlī b. al-Ḥasan (d. 571/1176), *Muʿjam Banī Umayya, istakhrajahu min Taʾrīkh Dimashq wa zāda fīhi*. Beirut, 1970.
—— *Taʾrīkh madīnat Dimashq*, ed. Ṣalāḥ al-Dīn al-Munajjid. Damascus, 1951–.

IBN ṬŪLŪN, Muḥammad b. ʿAlī (d. 953/1546), *Aʿlām al-warā bi-man wuliya nāʾiban min al-atrāk bi-Dimashq* ... ed. Muḥammad Aḥmad Duhmān. (Maṭbūʿāt Mudīriyya Iḥyāʾ al-Turāth al-Qadīm, 8.) Damascus, 1383/1964.
—— *Les gouverneurs de Damas sous les Mamlouks et les premiers Ottomans (658–1156/1260–1744)*, trad. des Annales d'Ibn Ṭūlūn et d'Ibn Ǧumʿa, de H. Laoust. Damascus, 1952.
—— *Quḍāt Dimashq; al-thaghr al-bassām fī dhikr man wuliya qaḍāʾ al-Shām*, ed. Ṣalāḥ al-Dīn al-Munajjid. Damascus, 1956.

QUDĀMA, Aḥmad, *Maʿālim al-aʿlām fī bilād al-ʿArab. Vol. 1: Al-qaṭr al-sūrī* (*ʾ-kh*). Damascus, 1965.

-ṢAFADĪ, Khalīl b. Aybak (d. 764/1363), *Umarāʾ Dimashq fī al-islām*, ed. Ṣalāḥ al-Dīn al-Munajjid. Damascus, 1955.

-SHAṬṬĪ, Muḥammad Jamīl, *Rawḍ al-bashar fī aʿyān Dimashq fī al-qarn al-thālith ʿashar, 1200–1300*. Damascus, 1946.
—— *Tarājim aʿyān Dimashq fī nuṣf al-qarn al-rābiʿ ʿashar al-hijrī, 1301–1350*. Damascus, 1948.

-ṬABBĀKH, Muḥammad Rāghib, *Aʿlām al-nubalāʾ*. 7v. in 3. Aleppo, 1342–45/1923–26.
Eminent men of Aleppo.

(xiii) *Lebanon*

GHURAYYIB, Jurj, *Aʿlām min Lubnān wa-al-mashriq*. Beirut, 1968.

-ḤURR AL-ʿĀMILĪ, Muḥammad b. al-Ḥasan (d. *c.* 1099/1688), *Amal al-āmil (fī ʿulamāʾ Jabal ʿĀmil)*, ed. Aḥmad al-Ḥusaynī. 2v. Baghdad, 1385/1965.
Deals with the Shīʿites of ʿĀmil.

IBRĀHĪM, Amilī Fāris, *Adībāt lubnāniyyāt*. Beirut, n.d.

KHĀZIN, Wilyām & ILYĀN, Nabīh, *Kutub wa udabāʾ; tarājim wa muqaddimāt wa aḥādīth li-udabāʾ min Lubnān wa-al-ʿālam al-ʿarabī*. Beirut, 1970.
Contains short biographies and interviews with 39 modern Arabic authors.

LIST OF SCIENTISTS IN LEBANON; LISTE DES HOMMES DE SCIENCE DU LIBAN. Cairo, 1952.

NAMAL, ʿAbd Allāh Ḥabīb, *Kitāb tarājim ʿulamāʾ Ṭarāblus al-fayḥāʾ wa udabāʾihi*. Tripoli, 1929.

-SHIDYĀQ, Ṭannūs (thirteenth/nineteenth century), *Akhbār al-aʿyān fī jabal Lubnān*. 2nd edn. 2v. in 1. Beirut, 1954.

WHO'S WHO IN LEBANON . . . Beirut, 1964–.

Published every two years, it has two biographical sections, one for the Lebanese in the Lebanon, the other for the Lebanese overseas. The 1973–74 edition had 2800 biographies.

# The press and periodicals

DEREK HOPWOOD

The Arabic periodical press is in many ways the single most rewarding source for the study of modern Arab society in its many aspects, but it is also the most difficult to handle. Its growth covers more than a century and a half through several thousand titles; collections are scattered and incomplete and their whereabouts often unknown. Their titles range from the daily newspaper to the most esoteric journals – *Al-Jarīda* to the *Journal of the Egyptian Association of Tax Officers*; from *Al-Fūnūghrāf* in 1904 to *Arab roads* in 1971. Their role has been of basic importance in the revival of Arab learning (the *nahḍa*), in politics and the growth of nationalism, in the development of modern Arabic literature and of a language more fitted to contemporary expression.

A good survey article may be found in *EI*², under the title 'Djarīda'.

An essential reference work for the early history of the Arabic press is:

ṬARRĀZĪ, P. de, *Ta'rīkh al-ṣiḥāfa al-ʿarabiyya.* 4 parts. Beirut, 1913–33 (repr. Beirut, 1969?).

Philippe ibn Naṣr Allāh de Ṭarrāzī (1865–1956) was born in Beirut and studied in St Joseph University. He participated in the founding of the National Library in Beirut and was appointed its director. His best known work is his history of the Arabic press which is useful in several ways. It is a history of literature and its authors as well as of the press. Unfortunately it deals only with the period up to 1892, although lists of journals continue until 1929. Nothing similar has been produced since and Ṭarrāzī claims that it is exhaustive up to his cut-off dates. The two volumes are arranged as follows:

*Part 1*

*Part II* The second period: 1869–92

| | |
|---|---|
| Chapter 1 | Newspapers (*jarā'id*) and periodicals (*majallāt*) – Beirut |
| Section 1 | Newspapers in Beirut 1870 (under title) |
| Section 2 | Newspapers in Beirut 1871–76 |
| Section 3 | Newspapers in Beirut 1877–85 |
| Section 4 | Newspapers in Beirut 1886–92 |
| Section 5 | Periodicals in Beirut 1870–75 |
| Section 6 | Periodicals in Beirut 1876–85 |
| Section 7 | Periodicals in Beirut 1886–92 |
| Chapter 2 | Biographies of journalists in Beirut (under name) |
| Chapter 3 | Journals in other Ottoman countries 1870–92 |
| Section 1 | Papers and periodicals in Constantinople |
| Section 2 | Papers and periodicals in Damascus |
| Section 3 | Papers and periodicals in Aleppo |
| Section 4 | Papers and periodicals in Lebanon |
| Section 5 | Papers and periodicals in North Africa and Arabia |
| Chapter 4 | Biographies of journalists in other Ottoman countries |

*Journalism in Europe*

| | |
|---|---|
| Chapter 1 | Journals 1870–92 |
| Section 1 | Condition of press in Europe |
| Section 2 | Papers and periodicals in London |
| Section 3 | Papers and periodicals in Paris |
| Section 4 | Papers and periodicals outside Paris |
| Section 5 | Papers and periodicals in Italy |
| Section 6 | Papers and periodicals in Malta |
| Chapter 2 | Biographies |

p. 311 Index of journals and personal names

*Part III* Egyptian Journalism 1869–92

Conditions of Journalism

| | |
|---|---|
| Chapter 1 | All journals in Cairo |
| Section 1 | Papers in Cairo 1869–77 (under title) |
| Section 2 | Papers in Cairo 1878–82 |
| Section 3 | Papers in Cairo 1883–86 |
| Section 4 | Papers in Cairo 1887–89 |
| Section 5 | Papers in Cairo 1890–92 |
| Chapter 2 | Papers in Alexandria |
| Section 1 | Papers in Alexandria 1869–76 |
| Section 2 | Papers in Alexandria 1877–80 |
| Section 3 | Papers in Alexandria 1881–86 |
| Section 4 | Papers in Alexandria 1887–92 |
| Chapter 3 | Periodicals in Cairo |
| Section 1 | Periodicals in Cairo 1848–79 |
| Section 2 | Periodicals in Cairo 1880–86 |
| Section 3 | Periodicals in Cairo 1887–89 |
| Section 4 | Periodicals in Cairo 1890–91 |
| Section 5 | Periodicals in Cairo to end of second period |
| Chapter 4 | Periodicals outside Cairo |

Section 1 Periodicals in Alexandra 1881–88
Section 2 Periodicals in Alexandria to end of second period

*Part IV* Lists of newspapers and periodicals from beginning to 1929 (in Arabic and English)

Division 1 Asia
Part 1 Newspapers arranged geographically and chronologically
Part 2 Periodicals arranged geographically and chronologically
Division 2 Africa
Part 1 Newspapers
Part 2 Periodicals
Division 3 Europe
Part 1 Newspapers
Part 2 Periodicals
Division 4 North America and Central America
Part 1 Newspapers
Part 2 Periodicals
Division 5 South America
Part 1 Newspapers
Part 2 Periodicals

*Appendix*

p. 483 Total number of journals from beginning to 1929: 3023
Statistical lists 1: Number of journals by Country
2: Number of journals by Continent
3: Order of magnitude by Country
4: Order of magnitude by City
5: Classification of founders by religion

No other work I have been able to discover covers the ground in quite the same way as does Ṭarrāzī. There are histories of the press in specific areas or countries, bare lists of titles which try to be exhaustive in restricted fields, limited annotated lists – but nothing which combines all the elements of Ṭarrāzī. Such a work would be a major undertaking and would establish itself as an essential reference work for Arabic and Islamic studies. Until that happy day the researcher must perforce use a variety of bibliographical and historical aids which I have tried to list hereunder.

## I. LISTS OF NEWSPAPERS AND JOURNALS

AHMED-BIOUD, Abdelghani, *3200 revues et journaux arabes.* Paris, 1969.
This is the latest full list based on the holdings of the National Library in Cairo and of 19 other libraries and contains 3,258 entries plus 230 additional items from Tunisia. The entries are in Arabic giving place of publication, date of foundation, transliterated title, some locations and the general field of interest of the journal. There is also an index of transliterated titles. It cannot be exhaustive as in 1929 Ṭarrāzī listed 3,023 titles and the growth of the press in the following 40 years has been enormous. It is an important work, however, and is being brought up to date.

ʿABD ALLĀH, Maḥmūd, *Fihrist al-dawriyyāt al-ʿarabiyya allatī taqtanīhā al-Dār.* (Dār al-Kutub) 2 v. Cairo, 1961, 63.

The fullest list of Arabic periodicals held by a Middle Eastern library. Its usefulness is enhanced by several indices. Volume one lists titles, dates and the holdings of the Dār al-Kutub, and founders/editors; volume two, places of publication, frequency, chronological list of dates of foundation under country, and subject headings.

*The Middle East and North Africa; a survey.* (Europa Publications.) New edn. each year. London.

Lists under each country heading names of leading newspapers and journals. It is not always consistent or accurate and is far from complete, but is useful for addresses.

LIBRARY OF CONGRESS PUBLIC LAW 480 PROJECT, *Accessions list. Middle East. Annual list of serials.* Cairo.

Each year the American book procurement centre in Cairo issues an annual list of serials, a valuable and up-to-date index of journals chiefly from Egypt. Especially noteworthy is the listing of government publications.

MAHDI, M. el, *Répertoire des périodiques en cours publiés au monde arabe.* (UNESCO.) Cairo, 1965.

'Social science periodicals published in the Middle East.' *Int. soc. sci. bull.* **5**, 1953, pp. 752–62.

Lists 70 titles.

EGYPT, *Union catalogue of scientific periodicals in Egypt up to the end of 1949.* (Fouad I National Research Council.) Cairo, 1951.

HOPWOOD, D., 'Arabic periodicals and newspapers.' (In D. Hopwood and D. Grimwood-Jones, *eds. Middle East and Islam: a bibliographical introduction.* Zug, 1972.)

This is a listing of the more important journals recommended for a library wishing to acquire a basic collection of such material.

SYRIAN DOCUMENTATION PAPERS, *The general directory of the press and periodicals in the Arab world.* Damascus, 1973.

Lists 403 titles in Arabic and other languages. Useful for addresses etc.

Many libraries issue lists of their holdings and a selection is given here. Such lists often include, of course, non-Arabic and non-Middle Eastern journals.

LONDON UNIVERSITY SCHOOL OF ORIENTAL AND AFRICAN STUDIES. *Library catalogue: catalogue of periodicals and series.* Boston, Mass., 1963.

DURHAM UNIVERSITY, *A union list of periodicals in the learned libraries of Durham.* Durham, 1962. (and) *Periodicals published in the Middle East (North Africa excepted) currently received* (in the Oriental Section). July, 1966.

BRITISH MUSEUM, Catalogue(s) of Arabic books . . . Vol. 1. London, 1894– , cf. entries under 'periodical publications'.

OXFORD UNIVERSITY, *Arabic periodicals in Oxford*: a union list, comp. by D. Hopwood. Oxford, 1968.

GREAT BRITAIN, *Trial checklist of current periodicals published in the Middle East located in British libraries* (and) *Supplement, December 1968*, ed. by D. E. Hall. London.

These list the holdings of 57 libraries. North Africa is excluded, Egypt included only in the supplement.

AUCHTERLONIE, P. *ed.*, *A union list of Arabic periodicals in British libraries.* (To be published.)

EL-HADI, Mohamed, *Union list of Arabic serials in the United States.* (Univ. of Illinois, Grad. School of Library Science, Occasional Papers, 75.) April, 1965.

The Arabic holdings of 17 libraries, but much out of date now after the influx of PL 480 material.

McGILL UNIVERSITY, *Periodica Islamica; a checklist of serials*, comp. by Muzaffar Ali. 1973.

The following institutions in the Middle East have issued lists of their holdings.

BAGHDAD. NATIONAL LIBRARY, *Fihris al-majallāt wa-al-jarā'id al-ʿiraqiyya wa-al-ʿarabiyya.* Baghdad, n.d.

BAGHDAD UNIVERSITY CENTRAL LIBRARY, *Fihris al-dawriyyāt wa-al-majallāt.* Baghdad, n.d.

BEIRUT. AMERICAN UNIVERSITY LIBRARY, *Qā'imat al-nasharāt al-dawriyya al-ʿarabiyya.* Beirut, 1967.

CAIRO. AMERICAN UNIVERSITY, *Qā'imat al-dawriyyāt al-ʿarabiyya.* March, 1965.

CAIRO. AIN SHAMS UNIVERSITY, *List of periodicals.* Cairo, 1966.

CAIRO. NATIONAL PLANNING INSTITUTE, *Dalīl al-dawriyyāt bi-markaz al-wathā'iq bi-Maʿhad* . . . Cairo, 1965.

CAIRO. LEAGUE OF ARAB STATES, *Fihris majmūʿat al-majallāt.* (Institute of Higher Studies. The Library.) Cairo, 1964.

TETUAN. PUBLIC LIBRARY, *Fihris khizānat al-ṣuḥuf al-ʿarabiyya li-manṭiqat al-ḥimāya.* Tetuan, 1953.

## II. GENERAL SURVEYS

There are a number of studies of the Arabic press and a large number of articles on the subject scattered throughout European and Arabic language periodicals. When the *Index Arabicus* is published many of the Arabic articles will become more accessible; at present the periodicals indexes cited later may be consulted under the appropriate key-word. For example there are a number of entries under *ṣiḥāfa* in the index to *Al-Muqtaṭaf.* The indispensable *Index Islamicus* has entries under 'The Press. Newspapers'.

*Index Islamicus.* Entries 10991–11065
Supplement 1: 2911–2931
Supplement 2: 2806–2813
Supplement 3: p. 133
and annual supplements.

A valuable survey of 'La presse musulmane' runs through many numbers of the

*Revue du Monde Musulman*, Paris, 1906–26.

These and many other such articles are listed in the 'Index général des années 1906–26' under *mots typiques: presse*, pp. 287–8. For example in 1912 Louis

Massignon published an article entitled 'La presse arabe'. In addition there were reports on and extracts from the press in articles which continued through most of the life of the journal.

ṢĀLIḤA, Muḥammad & ABŪ MUGHLĀ, Samīḥ, *Ta'rīkh al-ṣiḥāfa al-'arabiyya.* Amman, n.d.

A short survey with a section on journalism in general. The history of the Arabic press is given with a chapter devoted to each country.

McFADDEN, T. J., *Daily journalism in the Arab world.* Columbus, Ohio, 1953.

MURUWWA, Adīb, *Al-ṣiḥāfa al-'arabiyya; nash'atuhā wa-taṭawwuruhā.* Beirut, 1961.

A detailed study of the growth of the press. There is an irrelevant introduction on classical Arabic literature, followed by a section on the early Arabic press. There are then sections according to country with entries under journal titles. Together with Ṭarrāzī it provides the best survey up to 1960.

HUART, C., *A history of Arabic literature.* London, 1903.

Contains a chapter 'Periodical press'.

The Area Handbooks published under the auspices of the Foreign Area Studies of the American University contains sections on the press. These have been issued for Algeria, Iraq, Jordan, Lebanon, Libya, Morocco, Saudi Arabia, Sudan, Syria, Tunisia and the U.A.R.

-RAMĀDĪ, Jamāl al-Dīn, *Ṣiḥāfat al-fukahā.* Cairo, n.d.

This is the one work on the satirical press which developed largely in Egypt and will be referred to later.

'ABDUH, Ibrāhīm, *A'lām al-ṣiḥāfa al-'arabiyya.* 2nd edn. Cairo, 1948.

No biographical dictionary of journalists has appeared recently. Ṭarrāzī has many entries under individual names and other biographical works contain scattered information on those journalists who were also literary men or politicians. The work by 'Abduh is a slim volume indeed containing entries under a dozen or so names.

To the above general surveys of the press there can be added a considerable number of other works dealing with more theoretical aspects. The titles are mostly self explanatory – *The press and society; The revolutionary journalist; Freedom of the press in a developing society.* They are largely works arising from the present social and political situation in the Middle East, tackling such problems as the role of the journalist in society and how far he can exercise his freedom of opinion and how far it is his duty to support a 'revolution' or a new political order. The most prolific of Arab writers on the press, 'Abd al-Laṭīf Ḥamza, contributes a work striking to the root of the problem – *The crisis of the journalist's conscience.* In so far as the following works present case studies they are contributions to the history of the Arabic press, otherwise they are probably of greater value as works of sociology.

'ABD AL-QĀDIR, Ḥusayn, *Al-ra'y al-'āmm wa-al-di'āya wa-ḥurriyyat al-ṣiḥāfa.* Cairo, 1957.

—— *Al-ṣiḥāfa ka-maṣdar li-al-ta'rīkh.* 2nd edn. Cairo, 1962.

'ABDUH, Ibrāhīm, *Al-ṣuḥufī al-thā'ir.* N.pl., n.d.

-ABYĀRĪ, Fatḥī, *Al-ṣiḥāfa al-iqlīmiyya wa-al-tanẓīm al-siyāsī.* Alexandria, 1969.

'AZĪZ, Sāmī, *Thawrat al-ṣiḥāfa*. Cairo, 1956.
'AZMĪ, Muḥammad, *Mabādi' al-ṣiḥāfa*. Cairo, 1931.
-BAḤRĪ, Hishām, *Ṣiḥāfat al-ghad*. Cairo, 1968.
-DASŪQĪ, Yūsuf & KĀMIL, Muḥammad, *Fī al-ṣiḥāfa*. Cairo, n.d.
FAYṢAL, Shukrī, *Al-ṣiḥāfa al-adabiyya*. Cairo, 1960.
-ḤAMĀMṢĪ, Jalāl al-Dīn, *Al-ṣaḥīfa al-mithāliyya*. Cairo, 1972.
ḤAMZA, 'Abd al-Laṭīf, *Azmat al-ḍamīr al-ṣuḥufī*. Cairo, 1960.
—— *Al-madkhal fī al-taḥrīr al-ṣuḥufī*. Cairo, 1968.
—— *Mustaqbal al-ṣiḥāfa*. Pt. 1. Cairo, 1961.
—— *Al-ṣiḥāfa wa-al-mujtama'*. Cairo, 1963.
-HILĀL, Muḥammad, *Al-ṣiḥāfa al-ḥadītha*. Cairo, 1930.
IMĀM, Ibrāhīm, *The language of journalism*. Cairo, 1969.
-JAWHARĪ, Maḥmūd, *Al-ṣiḥāfa wa-al-ḥarb*. Cairo, 1966.
-MAQDISĪ, Rafīq, *Fī al-ṣiḥāfa*. Damascus, 1964.
MŪSĀ, Salāma, *Al-ṣiḥāfa – ḥirfa wa-risāla*. Cairo, 1951.
NASĪM, Māhir, *Al-ṣiḥāfa wa-al-sha'b*. Cairo, 1957.
SĀBĀT, Khalīl, *Al-ṣiḥāfa – risāla, isti'dād, fann, 'ilm*. Cairo, 1959.
ṢĀ'IGH, Anīs, *Min al-ṣiḥāfa*. Beirut, 1958.
SAMḤĀN, Maḥmūd, *Al-ṣiḥāfa*. Cairo, 1939.
ṢARRŪF, Maḥmūd, *Al-ṣiḥāfa*. Cairo, 1939.
ṢARRŪF, Fu'ād, *Al-ṣiḥāfa wa-al-'umrān*. Cairo, 1929.
SHĀHĪN, Mayy, *Shāri' al-ṣiḥāfa*. Cairo, 1957.
SHŪSHA, Muḥammad, *Asrār al-ṣiḥāfa*. Cairo, 1959.
TUENI, Ghassan, *Freedom of the press in a developing society*. Beirut, 1971.
-WAKĪL, Mukhtār, *Bayn al-adab wa-al-ṣiḥāfa*. Cairo, 1954.

## III. HISTORY OF THE PRESS

### Egypt

Journalism in Egypt began with Napoleon's invasion in 1798. Two French journals were published during this period – *La Décade Égyptienne* and *Courier de l'Égypte*. A project for an Arabic newspaper to be called *Al-Tanbīh* was mooted but never realized. One or two wallsheets appeared in Arabic and in Arabic and French, one of which had the heading *Al-Tanbīh*. Ṭarrāzī was mistaken in referring to a daily newspaper of this time called *Al-Ḥawādīth al-yawmiyya* as these were only the records of the Diwan meetings.

The first Arabic journal in Egypt was *Al-Waqā'i' al-miṣriyya* founded by Muḥammad 'Alī as his government's official gazette. It was printed in Bulaq, irregularly at first, in Turkish, then Turkish and Arabic and finally in Arabic. In the 1830s it was edited by Rifā'a Rāfi' al-Ṭahṭāwī, a pioneer of Arabic journalism, who helped to change it from an official gazette into more of a newspaper. Later it was edited by Muḥammad 'Abduh.

Egypt had no non-official newspaper until Abū al-Sa'ūd's *Wādī al-Nīl* appeared in 1866. The earliest newspapers in the Middle East due to private enterprise seem to have been a number of ephemeral journals in Syria in 1855–60. The first regular non-official paper was *Al-Jawā'ib* edited by Aḥmad Fāris al-Shidyāq in Constantinople from 1860. It was the first important newspaper to circulate in countries where Arabic was read and dealt with world politics, social problems, European life and so on. Charles Doughty discovered it being read in Bombay in the houses of merchants from Najd.

The great impetus to the development of the press in Egypt came with the emigration there of Syro-Lebanese escaping the press censorship of the Abdülhamid régime to the relatively freer atmosphere of Egypt. The growth in the numbers of printing presses, of Arabic writers, and of the reading public made possible the creation of private newspapers and journals mostly at the hands of Lebanese Christians. Together with the spread of journalism went the slower development of a form of Arabic suitable for newspaper writing. In fact, journalism imposed on the Arabic language the necessity of breaking out of its classical mould. Much modern literature was published for the first time in the pages of journals.

Newspapers of opinion emerged to play an important role in political life with articles written by one of the key figures of the modern world – the political journalist. The press also began to influence taste, opinion, business and the reading of newspapers became a prestige symbol.

European style newspapers began with the (still-existing) *Al-Ahrām* in 1876. Between 1866 and 1882 some 33 Arabic papers appeared in Egypt but only *Al-Ahrām* was worthy of the name, run in a professional manner by Syrians and Egyptians. Hard on its heels, edited by Adīb Isḥāq, one of the most celebrated Syrian Christian journalists, followed *Miṣr*, important as a vehicle through which certain new ideas were transmitted, for example that of *waṭan* – a homeland for one political community. Later, Isḥāq suffered the not unusual fate of banishment and went to live in Paris.

The angry young men of journalism sought reform of Khedive Ismail's corrupt Egypt. There was a growth of political opposition culminating in the ʿUrābī revolt and the British occupation. A leading agitator was a Jewish Egyptian Yaʿqūb Ṣanūʿ, known by the nickname of Abū Naḍḍāra, and his most serious contribution to the nationalist cause was his publication of a journal under that name.

The British occupation meant that journalists had to take up a position towards the occupying power. *Al-Ahrām* favoured the French and was not known to criticize French policy in the Maghrib. Its rival became *Al-Muqaṭṭam* founded in 1889 by two Syrians, Yaʿqūb Ṣarrūf and Fāris Nimr. Cromer, commenting on journalists, wrote that the press originally supported French and Turkish interests, but that by 1891 several papers, especially *Al-Muqaṭṭam*, were defending the British point of view. (Cromer also opined that newspapers in Egypt were lower than the press dare be anywhere else but in Ireland.)

Also in 1889 was founded *Al-Mu'ayyad* by ʿAlī Yūsuf as an opposition newspaper against the Khedive and the British. Of importance because Yūsuf was an Egyptian and his paper marked the beginning of an indigenous press and of the growth of nationalism. Later, in 1900, the leading Egyptian nationalist, Muṣṭafā Kāmil, founded *Al-Liwā'* which by 1907 had a circulation of 10,000. He was active in mobilizing public opinion against a permanent British presence in the country. His paper was the organ of the National Party, forming the left wing of the nationalist movement while *Al-Mu'ayyad* was on the right. A third group of journalists under Luṭfī al-Sayyid, editor of *Al-Jarīda*, in addition to political activity was concerned with the social and literary reform movements of the day.

There were of course many other newspapers in Egypt then and later, important because of their editor, because of the part they played in a particular political or intellectual struggle or because of the period during which they appeared. In 1892 approximately 40 journals were published in Egypt: by 1909 this number had risen to 144. The following list contains works chiefly on the Egyptian daily press but also a considerable number which deal with the whole range of periodical literature.

'ABDUH, Ibrāhīm, *Abū Naẓẓāra imām al-ṣiḥāfa al-fukāhiyya*. N.pl., 1953.
—— *Ḥawl al-ṣiḥāfa fī aṣr Ismā'īl*. Cairo, 1947.

'ABDUH, Ibrāhīm, *Jarīdat al-Ahrām: ta'rīkh wa-fann*. Cairo, 1964.
A history of the newspaper 1975–1964.
—— *Ta'rīkh al-ṭibā'a wa-al-ṣiḥāfa khilāl al-ḥamla al-firansiyya*. 2nd edn. Cairo, 1950.
—— *Ta'rīkh "al-Waqā'i' al-miṣriyya"*. 2nd edn. Bulaq, 1946.
—— *Taṭawwur al-ṣiḥāfa al-miṣriyya 1798–1951*. 3rd edn. Cairo, 1951.

ABU-L-LEL, Nayib, *Al-ṣiḥāfa al-firansiyya fī Miṣr mundh nash'atihā ḥattā sana 1914*. Cairo, 1953. (Thèse dact.)

ARTIN, Y., 'Etude statistique sur la presse égyptienne'. *BIE* 1904, Sér. 4, v. 6, pp. 89–98.

'AṬĪFĪ, Jamāl al-Dīn, *Ḥurriyyat al-ṣiḥāfa waqfa tashrī'āt al-Jumhūriyya al-'Arabiyya al-Muttaḥida*. Cairo, 1971.

'AZĪZ, Sāmī, *Al-ṣiḥāfa al-miṣriyya wa-mawqifuhā min al-iḥtilāl al-injilīzī*. Cairo, 1968.
pp. 344–5: list of newspapers and editors for 10 years before the invasion.
pp. 346–7: list of newspapers and editors for 10 years after the invasion.

-BUSTĀNĪ, Ṣalāḥ al-Dīn *ed.*, *The journals of Bonaparte in Egypt 1798–1801*. 10v. Cairo, 1971–.
A study of the press together with photocopies and translations of the journals. To date nine volumes have appeared.
1, 2, 3. *La Décade Égyptienne.*
4. *Courier de l'Égypte.*
5. Arabic translation of *Courier de l'Égypte.*
6. Arabic translation of *La Décade.* (3v. in 1.)
7. Index to *La Decade Égyptienne* and *Courier de l'Égypte.* (In French.)
8. Bonaparte's proclamations as recorded by 'Abd al-Raḥmān al-Jabartī. (In English and Arabic.)
9. Recueil des arrêtés et proclamations de l'autorité française en Égypte pendant l'occupation (reprints of the original French proclamations).

FAKKAR, Rouchdi, *L'influence française sur la formation de la presse littéraire en Égypte au XIX$^{e}$ siècle; aux origines des relations culturelles contemporaines entre la France et le monde arabe.* Paris, 1972.
Useful bibliography; pp. 156–60 'Liste des journaux et périodiques en français (et) en arabe sujets de cette étude'.

FOUAD, Mahmoud, *Le régime de la presse en Egypte*. Paris, 1912. (Thèse droit.)

GALAL, Kamal al-Din, *Entstehung und Entwicklung der Tagespresse in Ägypten*. Limburg, 1939. (Phil. Diss.)

GHAḌBĀN, ʿĀdil, ʿAl-ṣiḥāfa al-miṣriyya fī niṣf qarn'. *Al-Kitāb* **9**, 1950, pp. 676–81, 771–5.

ḤALABĪ, Ilyās Q., *Takwīn al-ṣuḥuf fī al-ʿālam; taʾrīkh takwīn al-ṣuḥuf al-miṣriyya*. Cairo, 1928.

ḤAMĀMṢĪ, Jalāl al-Dīn, *Hādhihi hiya ṣiḥāfatunā*. Cairo, 1957.

ḤAMZA, ʿAbd al-Laṭīf, *Adab al-maqāla al-ṣuḥufiyya fī Miṣr*. 7v. Cairo, 1950–59.

—— *Mustaqbal al-ṣiḥāfa fī Miṣr*. Cairo, 1957.

—— *Qiṣṣat al-ṣiḥāfa al-ʿarabiyya fī Miṣr*. Baghdad, 1967.

—— *Al-ṣiḥāfa wa-al-adab fī Miṣr*. Cairo, 1955.

—— *Al-ṣiḥāfa al-miṣriyya fī miʾat ʿām*. Cairo, 1960.

HARTMANN, M., *The Arabic press of Egypt*. London, 1899.

ḤUSAYN, ʿAbd Allāh, *Al-ṣiḥāfa wa-al-ṣuḥuf*. Cairo? 1948.

-JINDĪ, Anwar, *Taṭawwur al-ṣiḥāfa al-ʿarabiyya*.
Vol. 1. *Al-ṣiḥāfa al-siyāsiyya fī Miṣr mundh nashʾatiha ilā al-ḥarb al-ʿālamiyya al-thāniyya*. Cairo, n.d. (1963?).
Vol. 2. *Taṭawwur al-ṣihāfa al-ʿarabiyya fī Miṣr*. Cairo, 1967.

KHIḌR, ʿAbbās, *Ṣuḥufiyyūn muʿāṣirūn*. Cairo, 1964?

MORSY, Hassan R., *Die ägyptische Presse; Struktur und Entwicklung der ägyptischen Presse der Gegenwart*. Hanover, 1963.

MUNIER, J., *La presse en Egypte 1799–1900; notes et souvenirs*. Cairo, 1930.

MUṢṬAFĀ, Kāmil, *Al-ṣiḥāfa wa-al-adab fī miʾat yawm*. Cairo, n.d.

MUṬRĀN, Khalīl, *Taʾrīkh Bishāra Taqlā*. Cairo, 1902.

NAṢR, Muḥammad, *Dinshaway wa-al-ṣiḥāfa*. Cairo? n.d.

QABBĀNĪ, ʿAbd al-ʿAlīm, *Nashʾat al-ṣiḥāfa al-ʿarabiyya bi-al-Iskandariyya 1873–82*. Cairo, 1973.

RAMADAN, A. M. S., *Évolution de la législation sur la presse en Égypte*. Paris, 1938.

REINAUD, 'De la gazette arabe turque imprimé en Égypte'. *JA*, 2e sér., **8**, 1831.

SAʿĪD, Rifʿat, *Al-ṣiḥāfa al-yasāriyya fī Miṣr 1925–48*. Beirut, 1974.

-ṢĀWĪ, Aḥmad H., *Muḥammad ʿAbduh and Al-Waqāʾiʿ al-Miṣrīyah*. McGill Univ. 1954. (M.A. Thesis.)

—— *Al-ṣiḥāfa al-miṣriyya*.
To be published in Cairo.

WASSEF, Amin S., *L'information et la presse officielle en Égypte jusqu'à la fin de l'occupation française*. (Thèse doc.) Paris, 1952.

ZOLONDEK, L., 'Al-Ahrām and westernization, socio-political thought of Bishārah Taqlā (1853–1901)'. *WI* **12**, 1969, pp. 182–95.

PERIODICALS IN EGYPT

In conjunction with daily and weekly newspapers there grew up in Egypt another type of journal – the literary and scientific periodical destined to play an important role in the development of the modern culture and literature of the

Arab world and in the transmission of knowledge of the West. This type of periodical first appeared in Lebanon but flourished most notably in Egypt. Some journals had a political role, e.g. *Abu Naḍḍāra, Rūz al-Yūsuf* and the most famous, *Al-ʿUrwa al-wuthqā*, edited by Jamāl al-Dīn al-Afghānī and Muḥammad ʿAbduh in Paris in 1884. Published under the auspices of a secret society pledged to work for the unity and reform of Islam, it became the most influential journal of its time with a wide circulation.

The best known non-political journal was *Al-Muqtaṭaf* founded in Beirut in 1876 by the Ṣarrūf and Nimr who edited the newspaper *Al-Muqaṭṭam*. It soon moved to Egypt and continued until 1952. During this period it became the main channel by which knowledge of the technical aspects of scientific civilization was passed to the Arab reading public, but it was encyclopedic in its approach and covered a wide range of topics.

Of equal influence was *Al-Hilāl* founded in 1892 by Jurjī Zaydān, another Syrian, who had studied at the Beirut Protestant College. He had a different type of mind from that of Ṣarrūf and Nimr. He was a prolific author of literary histories and historical novels, but his major achievement was *Al-Hilāl*, a mainly literary periodical which contributed more to the growth of literary sensibility then any other similar journal. It is still current.

The third of the trio of long-run and influential periodicals was *Al-Manār* (1898–1940) founded by a disciple of ʿAbduh, Rashīd Riḍā. In it he expressed his ideas on nationalism, Islamic law and the problems of Muslim society. The course of the development of nationalism between 1908 and 1922 can nowhere be better studied than in the pages of *Al-Manār*.

It is impossible to mention the several scores of other journals, many short-lived but influential, dealing with poetry, literature, language, economics and religion. They are all listed in the various publications noted in this chapter.

ʿABDUH, Ibrāhīm, *Abū Naẓẓāra*. Cairo, 1953.

—— *Rūz al-Yūsuf; sīra wa-ṣaḥīfa*. Cairo, 1962.

FAKKAR, Rouchdi, *Al-Hilāl et la pensée progressiste en Europe*. Cairo, 1959.

FARAG, Nadia, *Al-Muqtataf; a study of the influence of Victorian thought on modern Arabic thought*. Oxford, 1969. (D.Phil. thesis.)

GENDZIER, I. L., *The practical visions of Yaʿqūb Sanūʿ*. Cambridge, Mass., 1966.

LOUCEL, H., 'Deux articles de la revue "al-Manār" (1885–1935)'. *Orient* **37**, 1966, pp. 129–40.

MASSIGNON, L., 'Liste des principaux articles de la politique sociale et religieuse publiés dans Al-Manar du Caire de 1916 à 1920, suivie de quelques notes'. *RMM* **38**, 1920.

MALYUKOVSKII, M. V., 'Zhurnal "al-Manar" kak istochnik dlya izucheniya musulmanskoi reformatsii v Egipete'. *KSIV* **19**, 1956, pp. 94–9.

SMITH, W. C., *The Azhar Journal – survey and critique*. Princeton, 1948. (Thesis.)

## Lebanon

The development of the press in Lebanon has obviously been different from that of Egypt, both because of the different cultural and religious background and of the political situation. The press developed early but, as has been noted, many leading journalists felt impelled to move to Egypt. The early flowering of journalism was followed by a period of stagnation to be succeeded by a period of growth until now Lebanon has by far the largest number of Arabic daily newspapers (25 compared to 7 in Egypt).

The first journal in the Levant was *Ḥadīqat al-akhbār* (1858–68) edited by Khalīl al-Khūrī, a Lebanese Christian. It provided general information. The first important journal was *Al-Jinna* (later *Al-Jinān*), 1870–85, which appeared under the name of Buṭrus al-Bustānī but was written largely by his son Salīm. It was a journal, literary and scientific, giving expression to political ideas and to nationalism. It ceased because of Abdülhamid's censorship and Buṭrus's disciples moved to Cairo.

The longest running daily in Beirut was *Lisān al-ḥāl* (1877–1959) founded by the brother-in-law of Buṭrus, Khalīl Sarkīs. To remain alive it had to tailor its editorial policy to the demands of the Ottoman government, and it did not support one sect more than another. Other current dailies usually are the organ of a particular sect or a political point of view.

In 1898 the University of Saint Joseph founded its own journal, *Al-Mashriq*, edited by Louis Cheikho, which appeared until 1972. It was devoted to a wide range of problems and to Oriental studies. A leading Muslim journal was *Thamarāt al-funūn*, 1875–1909, which represented the conservative attitude among Muslims. In the post Second World War period a plethora of journals has appeared, literary and other.

DAJJANI, N., 'The press in Lebanon'. *Gazette* **17**, 1971.

GEORGE, L., 'Une presse prolifique (Liban)'. *Le Monde* 5.5.65.

GHORAYEB, M., 'La presse quotidienne libanaise'. *Travaux et tours* **37**, 1970, pp. 5–26.

SA'ĀDA, Jurj A., *Al-nahḍa al-ṣuḥufiyya fī Lubnān*. Beirut, 1960.
—— *Al-ṣiḥāfa fī Lubnān*. Beirut, 1965.

SYRIAN DOCUMENTATION PAPERS, *The general directory of the press and periodicals in Lebanon*. Damascus, 1971.

YARED, M., 'Aperçus sur la presse libanaise'. *Travaux et jours* **21**, 1966, pp. 103–6.

## Other Countries

The other Arab countries do not on the whole have such a long or deeply ingrained tradition of journalism as Egypt and Lebanon. Several had early official newspapers, often in Turkish and Arabic.

| | | |
|---|---|---|
| Damascus | *Sūriyya* | 1865 |
| Aleppo | *Al-Furāt* | 1866 |
| Tunis | *Al-Rā'id al-Tūnisī* | 1860 |
| Baghdad | *Al-Zawrā'* | 1868 |
| Tripoli | *Ṭarābulus al-Gharb* | 1871 |
| Mosul | *Al-Mawṣil* | 1875 |
| Sana | *Al-Ṣan'ā'* | 1877 |

Most countries now have a developed press – some 85 Arabic dailies appearing and almost 300 weeklies.

### Syria

FARÈS, L., *Répertoire des publications périodiques de la République Arabe Syrienne*. 2nd edn. Damascus, 1968.

KHAIRALLAH, K. T., 'La Syrie'; chapter 'La presse'. *RMM* **19**, 1912.

-RIFĀ'Ī, Shams al-Dīn, *Ta'rīkh al-ṣiḥāfa al-sūriyya*. Cairo, 1909.
Pt. 1. *Al-ṣiḥāfa al-sūriyya fī al-'ahd al-'uthmānī 1800–1918*.
Pt. 2. *Al-intidāb al-firansī ḥattā al-istiqlāl 1918–47*.

### Jordan and Kuwait

SYRIAN DOCUMENTATION PAPERS, *The 1970 General directory of the press and periodicals in Jordan and Kuwait*. Damscus, 1970.

### Iraq

AL-QAYSI, Abdul Wahab, 'The beginning of printing press and journalism in Iraq'. *Maj. al-Jam'iyya al-'Irāqiyya li-al-Ta'rikh* **1**, 1970.

-'ABBĀS, Khiḍr, *Ḥadīth al-ṣiḥāfa*. Baghdad, 1945.

BAKR, Munīr, *Al-ittijāhāt al-siyāsiyya wa-al-thaqāfiyya wa-al-ijtimā'iyya fī al-ṣiḥāfa al-'irāqiyya*. Baghdad, 1969.

-BUSTĀNĪ, 'Abd Allāh, *Ḥurriyyat al-ṣiḥāfa fī al-'Irāq*. Baghdad, 1951.

BUṬṬĪ, Fā'iq, *A'lām fī ṣiḥāfat al-'Iraq*. Baghdad, 1971.
—— *Mūjaz li-ta'rīkh al-ṣiḥāfa fī al-'Iraq*. Baghdad, 1972.
—— *Qaḍāyā ṣuḥufiyya*. Baghdad, 1962.
—— *Al-ṣiḥāfa al-'irāqiyya; mīlāduhā wa-taṭawwuruhā*. Baghdad, 1961.
—— *Ṣiḥāfat al-aḥzāb wa-ta'rīkh al-ḥaraka al-waṭaniyya*. Baghdad, 1969.
—— *Ṣiḥāfat Tammūz wa-taṭawwur al-'Irāq al-siyāsī*. Baghdad, 1970.
—— *Ṣuḥuf Baghdād fī dhikrā ta'sīsihā*. Baghdad, 1962.

BUṬṬĪ, Rufā'īl, *Al-ṣiḥāfa fī al-'Irāq*. Cairo, 1955.

ENDE, W., 'Bibliographie zur Geschichte der Presse im Irak'. *Mitt., Dokumentations-Dienst Moderner Orient, Deutsches Or.-Inst.*, 1–74, pp. 23–30.
Lists 50 works, including a number of pamphlets and articles.

-ḤASANĪ, 'Abd al-Razzāq, *Ta'rīkh al-ṣiḥāfa al-'irāqiyya*. Rev. edn. Baghdad, 1957.

IRAQ MINISTRY OF INFORMATION, *Dalīl al-ṣiḥāfa al-'irāqiyya*. Baghdad, 1972.
311 titles with editors, frequency, dates, &c.
—— *Dirāsāt fī al-ṣiḥāfa al-'irāqiyya*. Baghdad, 1972.
—— *Fī al-'īd al-mi'awī li-al-ṣiḥāfa*. Baghdad, 1969.

'ĪSĀ, Razzūq, 'Fihris majallāt Baghdād min sanat 1905–24'. *Nashrat al-Aḥad* **3**, 1924, pp. 911–14.
—— 'Al-jarā'id wa-al-majallāt (fī Baghdād)'. *Nashrat al-Aḥad* **12**, 1934, pp. 590 ff.

-KARMILĪ, Anasṭās, 'Al-ṣiḥāfa fī Baghdād'. *Al-Masarra* **1**, 1911, pp. 519 ff.

-KUBAYSĪ, 'Inād I., *Al-adab fī ṣiḥāfat al-'Irāq*. Najaf, 1972.

KŪRIYYA, Ya'qūb Y., *Ḥikāyāt 'an al-ṣiḥāfa fī al-'Irāq*. Vol. 1. Baghdad, 1969.

TAKRĪTĪ, Munīr B., *Al-ṣiḥāfa al-ʿirāqiyya wa-ittijāhātuhā al-siyāsiyya wa-al-ijtimāʿiyya wa-al-thaqāfiyya min 1869 ilā 1921*. Baghdad, 1969.

—— *Al-Zawrāʾ, nushūʾuhā wa-taṭawwuruhā*. Baghdad, 1969.

### Arabia

MUKHLIṢ, Rushdī, 'Al-ṣiḥāfa wa-al-maṭābiʿ fī al-Ḥijāz'. *Umm al-Qurā*, Rajab 1347, nos. 207 and 211.

-SHĀMIKH, M. ʿAbd al-Raḥmān, *Al-ṣiḥāfa fī al-Ḥijāz 1908–1941*. Beirut, 1971.

### Yemen

LUQMAN, Ali M., 'Education and the press in South Arabia'. (In D. Hopwood *ed.*, *The Arabian Peninsula*, London, 1972, pp. 258–68.)

ROSSI, E., 'La stampa nel Yemen'. *OM* **18**, 1938.

### Palestine/Israel

MOREH, S., *Fihris al-kutub al-adabiyya wa-al-ṣuḥuf wa-al-majallāt fī Isrāʾīl*. Tel Aviv, n.d.

ʿUTHMĀN, Badr, 'Al-ṣiḥāfa al-ʿarabiyya fī Isrāʾīl'. *Ikhwāʾ* **1**, ii, 1969.

YEHOSHUAʿ, Y., *Taʾrīkh al-ṣiḥāfa al-ʿarabiyya fī Filasṭīn fī al-ahd al-ʿuthmānī, 1908–1918*. Jerusalem, 1974.

### Sudan

ʿABD AL-QĀDIR, Ḥasanayn, *Taʾrīkh al-ṣiḥāfa fī al-Sūdān*. Cairo, 1967. Pt. 1. 1899–1919.

ṢĀLIḤ, Maḥjūb M., *Al-ṣiḥāfa al-sūdāniyya fī nuṣf qarn*. Khartoum, n.d. Pt. 1. 1903–53.

SUDAN NOTES AND RECORDS, 'A list of academic periodicals published in the Sudan'. *SNR* **43**, 1962.

### North Africa

ALMAN, M. & TRAVIS, C., *Periodicals from Africa – a union list*. To be published. (SCOLMA.)

7500 titles.

ANNUAIRE DE L'AFRIQUE DU NORD, 1962–, Paris, 1964–.

This very useful year book contains numerous references to the press. The latest numbers under 'Bibliographie arabe' have a section 'Politique intérieure, presse, radio, télévision'.

MUDDATHIR, Ahmed, *Die arabische Presse in den Maghreb-Staaten*. (Deutsches Institut für Afrika-Forschung). Hamburg, 1966.

Contains a list of periodicals in the Maghrib with addresses, &c.

SOURIAU, C., 'Mutations culturelles et presse maghrébine'. (In C. Debbasch and others, *Mutations culturelles et coopération*. Paris, 1969.)

SOURIAU-HOEBRECHTS, C., *La presse Maghrébine; Libye – Tunisie – Maroc – Algérie*. Paris, 1969.

A most useful study.

### Libya

*National bibliography of the Libyan Arab Republic.* (i) Periodicals current January 1972; retrospective 1827–1971. Tripoli, 1972.

-MIṢURĀTĪ, ʻAlī M., *Kifāḥ ṣuḥufī Abī Qishsha wa-jarīdatuhu fī Tarāblus al-Gharb.* Beirut, 1961.

—— *Ṣiḥāfat Lībiyā fī nuṣf qarn.* Beirut, 1960.

### Tunisia

CANAL, A., *La littérature et la presse tunisiennes de l'occupation à 1900.* Paris, 1924.

pp. 119–204 'La revue, la presse'.

CHENOUFI, Monsef, *La presse tunisienne des origines.* Tunis, 1970s.

DABBAB, Mohamed, *Index des revues et journaux tunisiens de langue française, de 1907 à l'indépendence (1956).* (CERES, sér. doc. et bibliog. ,1.) Tunis, 1973.

DURAN-ANGLIVIEL, O., *La législation de la presse et les libertés publiques en Tunisie.* Paris, 1936.

LELONG, M., 'A travers les revues tunisiennes de langue arabe'. *IBLA* **19**, 1956; **21**, 1959 and other entries.

LIAUZU, C., 'La presse ouvrière européenne en Tunisie'. *Ann. Afr. Nord* 1970, pp. 933–56.

-MAHĪDĪ, Muḥammad Ṣ., *Ta'rīkh al-ṣiḥāfa al-ʻarabiyya wa-taṭawwuruhā bi-bilād al-tūnisiyya.* Tunis, 1965.

-SANŪSĪ, Muḥammad Ṭ., *Qānūn al-ṣiḥāfa wa-al-nashr.* Tunis, 1956.

TUNISIA, *Index de la presse et des publications de Tunisie de 1838 à nos jours.* (Sécretariat aux Affaires Culturelles.) Tunis, 1964.

VAN LEEUWEN, A., 'Index des publications périodiques parus en Tunisie 1874–1954'. *IBLA* **18**, 1955, pp. 153–67.

ZAWADOWSKI, G., 'Index de la press indigène de Tunisie'. *REI* **11**, 1937, pp. 357–89.

### Algeria

COLLOT, C., 'Le régime juridique de la presse musulmane algérienne'. *Rev. alg.* **6**, 1969, pp. 343–405.

GILBERT, F., 'La presse algérienne; bilan d'une année d'indépendance'. *Confluent* **32–3**, 1963.

MERAD, Ali, 'La formation de la presse musulmane en Algérie (1919–1939)'. *IBLA* **105**, 1964.

PÉRÈS, H., 'Le mouvement réformiste en Algérie et l'influence de l'Orient, d'après la presse arabe d'Algérie'. (In *Entretiens sur l'évolution des pays de civilisation arabe*, Paris, 1936.)

SAYF AL-ISLĀM, al-Zubayr, *Ta'rīkh al-ṣiḥāfa fī al-Jazā'ir.* Algiers, 1971.

SERS-GAL, G., 'La presse algérienne de 1830 à 1852'. *Documents algériens*, sér. politique, 21.

### Morocco

KATTĀNĪ, Zayn al-ʿĀbidīn, *Al-ṣiḥāfa al-maghribiyya*. Pt. 1. Muhammadiyyah, 1970?

MIÈGE, J.-L., 'Journaux et journalistes à Tanger au XIXe siècle'. *Hespéris* 1954, pp. 191–228.

MOLLARD, P. J., *Le régime juridique de la presse*. Rabat, 1963.

## IV. ARABIC PERIODICAL INDEXES

### General

*Al-kashshāf al-taḥlīli li-al-ṣuḥuf wa-al-majallāt al-ʿarabiyya*. Cairo, 1960s.
A short-lived journal indexing Egyptian periodicals.

HOPKINS, J. F. P. *ed.*, *Arabic periodical literature 1961*. Cambridge, 1966.
An ambitious attempt to produce an annual index to 23 Arabic journals. Only one number has appeared.

*Index Arabicus*.
As yet unpublished, this is modelled after *Index Islamicus* and lists articles in some 50 Arabic periodicals. In all there are over 50,000 entries.

ANNUAIRE DE L'AFRIQUE DU NORD, 'Bibliographie arabe' lists articles on North Africa.

### Individual Periods

-ABḤĀTH, Index 1948–57 in vol. 10, 1957; *Fihris al-Abḥāth 1958–67*, by Nawāl Mikdāshī. Beirut, 1970.

-ADĪB, *Fihrist majallat al-Adīb*, by Miryam F. Hāshim. 2v. Beirut, 1968.

-ISHTIRĀKĪ, *Fihris taḥlīlī bi-mawdūʿāt majāllat al-Ishtirākī*, by Sulaymān Jirjis. Cairo, 1967.

MAJALLAT AL-MAJMAʿ AL-ʿILMĪ AL-ʿARABĪ, *Fihris*, 4v. 1921–65 by ʿUmar R. Kaḥḥāla. Damascus, 1956–71.

MAJALLAT AL-MAJMAʿ AL-ʿILMĪ AL-ʿIRĀQĪ, *Fahāris 1950–67* by Ḥikmat Tūmāshī. Supplement to v. 16. Baghdad, 1968.

-MUQTAṬAF, *Fihris al-Muqtaṭaf*, by Fuad Sarrūf and Linda Sadaka. 3v. Beirut, 1967, 68.

## V. PERIODICALS FOR ISLAMIC AND MIDDLE EASTERN STUDIES

Strictly speaking, this guide is concerned with Islam in the Arab world. Many general orientalist periodicals contain material on Arab Islam, and journals devoted to the study of Islam cover a much wider area than the Arab countries. Consequently the journals in the following lists often contain articles on Arab Islam but most cover a wider field. Excluded are journals which deal with the Middle East before the rise of Islam, as are also exclusively economic journals and records of current affairs.

The list has been drawn up with the help of other published works (listed below), e.g. Pearson's *Index Islamicus*, Ljunggren and Hamdy, and Sauvaget/Cahen.

### Lists of Periodicals

PEARSON, J. D., *Index Islamicus*. Cambridge, 1958.

List of sources pp. x–xxii; brought up to date in the supplements. The net is spread very wide and some 650 periodicals are cited. However, many of the titles may contain only one article of Islamic interest in five or more years. See also the sections entitled 'Periodicals and their indexes' in

PEARSON, J. D., *Oriental and Asian bibliography*. London, 1966.

Pp. 110–11 'Orientalist periodicals'; 35 titles are given. A more selective list is given in pp. 51–2 of

MIDDLE EAST LIBRARIES COMMITTEE, *Middle East and Islam; a bibliographical introduction*, ed. D. Hopwood and D. Grimwood-Jones. Zug, 1972.

Pp. 22–6 contain a list of the most significant Islamic and Middle Eastern periodicals.

LJUNGGREN, F., and HAMDY, M., *Annotated guide to journals dealing with the Middle East and North Africa*. Cairo, 1965.

A useful guide with occasional mistakes, which lists 281 items, plus 73 in Arabic and 6 addenda.

CAHEN, C., *Jean Sauvaget's Introduction to the history of the Muslim East*. Berkeley, Calif., 1965.

Pp. 71–4 list periodicals important for the study of Islamic history.

LANDAU, J. M., 'Russian journals dealing with the Middle East'. *MES* **7**, ii, 1971.

'Social science periodicals dealing with the Middle East'. *Int. soc. sci. bull.* **5**, 1953, pp. 762–5.

Lists 18 titles.

### Library Lists

BEIRUT AMERICAN UNIVERSITY, *Checklist of serial publications dealing with the Middle East*. Beirut, 1968.

Some 350 titles are listed, including government publications.

LONDON UNIVERSITY SCHOOL OF ORIENTAL AND AFRICAN STUDIES, *Library catalogue. Catalogue of periodicals and serials*. Boston, Mass., 1963.

Other libraries list their periodicals in general and one has to seek orientalist titles among these; e.g. the Bodleian Library's lists of current foreign and commonwealth periodicals.

### Indexes of Articles

PEARSON, J. D., *Index Islamicus*, supra.

LJUNGGREN, F., *Arab world index 1960–64*. Cairo, 1967.

'An international guide to periodical literature in the social sciences and humanities in the contemporary Arab world'. Indexes some 70 European language periodicals.

HEBREW UNIVERSITY, *Selected bibliography of articles dealing with the Middle East 1939–58*. 3v. (Economic Research Inst.) Jerusalem, 1954–59.

Indexes some 50 journals covering most topics.

DOTAN, U. & LEVY, A., *A bibliography of articles on the Middle East 1959–67.* (Shiloah Center.) Tel Aviv, 1970.

Continuation of the previous item.

MIDDLE EAST JOURNAL, 'Bibliography of periodical literature' in each issue.

MOROCCO, *Bibliographie nationale marocaine* (Bibliothèque Générale). Rabat.

Appears monthly and includes periodical articles on Morocco.

ANNUAIRE DE L'AFRIQUE DU NORD, 'Bibliographie systématique'.

Lists articles on North Africa.

### Orientalist Periodicals

*Abr Nahrain* (Dept. of Middle Eastern Studies, Univ. of Melbourne). Leiden, 1961–.

*Acta Orientalia* (Societates Orientales Batava Danica Norvegica *now* Danica Norvegica Svecica). Copenhagen, 1923–.

*Acta Orientalia Academiae Scientiarum Hungaricae.* Budapest, 1950–.

*Annali* (R. Istituto Orientale di Napoli, *now* Istituto Universitario Orientale di Napoli). Naples, 1928–.

*Annuaire de l'Institut de Philologie et d'Histoire Orientales et Slaves* (Univ. Libre de Bruxelles). Brussels, 1932–.

*Archiv Orientalni* (Orientalni Ustav). Prague, 1929–.

*Asian affairs* (Royal Central Asian Society). London, 1914–.

Formerly *Royal Central Asian Journal*; includes the Middle East in its ambit. 1914–48 reprinted, London.

*Asian and African studies* (Israel Oriental Society). Jerusalem, 1965–.

Social, cultural and political development of Middle Eastern (and other Asian and African) countries.

*Asian and African studies.* Bratislava (Slovak Academy of Sciences), 1965–.

*Bibliotheca Orientalis.* Leiden, 1943–.

Reviewing journal.

*Bulletin of the School of Oriental (and African) Studies.* London, 1917–.

Partial reprint.

*Folia Orientalia* (Académie Polonaise des Sciences, Section de Cracovie, Commission Orientaliste). Krakow, 1959–.

*Journal of the American Oriental Society.* New Haven, 1843–.

Partial reprint; indexes for 1843–1940.

*Journal asiatique* (Société Asiatique). Paris, 1822–.

Indexes 1829–52.

*Journal of the economic and social history of the Orient.* Leiden, 1957–.

*Journal of the Royal Asiatic Society of Great Britain and Ireland.* London, 1834–. (Preceded by: *Transactions* 1827–34.)

Indexes for 1827–1950.

*Journal of Semitic studies* (Manchester University). Manchester, 1956–.

*Kratkie soobshcheniya Instituta Narodov Azii* (formerly Institut Vostokovedeniya). Moscow, 1951–.

*Mitteilungen des Instituts für Orientforschung*. Berlin, 1953–.
Later called *Asien, Afrika, Latein-Amerika*.

*Le monde oriental; archives pour l'histoire et l'ethnographie, les langues et littératures, religions et traditions de l'Europe orientale et de l'Asie*. Uppsala, 1906–41.

*Le Muséon; revue d'études orientales*. Louvain, 1882–.
Reprinted.

*Narody Azii i Afriki; istoriya, ekonomika, kul'tura* (Akad. Nauk SSSR, Inst. Narodov Azii i Afriki). Moscow, 1964–.
Formerly *Problemy vostokovedeniya* 1959–61 and *Sovetskoe vostokovedeniya* 1940–58.

*Oriens; Milletlerarasĭ Şark Tetkikleri Cemiyeti Mecmuasĭ* (International Society for Oriental Research). Leiden, 1948–.
Index for vols. I–X, publ. 1967.

*Orientalistische Literaturzeitung* (Deutsche Akademie der Wissenschaften). Berlin, 1898–.
Reprint, 1968. Reviewing journal.

*Rivista degli studi orientali* (Univ. di Roma, Scuola Orientale, *now* Istituto di Studi Orientali). Rome, 1907–.
1907–67, reprinted in 1971.

*Rocznik Orientalistyczny; Polish archives of Oriental research*. (Polska Akademia Nauk, Komitet Orientalistyczny). Warsaw, 1914–.

*Ucheniye zapiski Instituta Vostokovedeniya* (Akad. Nauk SSSR, Inst. Vostokovedeniya). Moscow, 1950–60.

*Wiener Zeitschrift für die Kunde des Morgenlandes* (formerly *Vienna Oriental Journal*). (Or. Inst. der Univ. Wien.) Vienna, 1887–.
Vols. 1–25, 1887–1911, reprinted New York, 1966.

*Zeitschrift der Deutschen Morgenländischen Gesellschaft*. Leipzig, 1847–.
Vols. 1–98, 1847–1944, with register for vols. 1–100 reprinted 1967–69.

### Islamic and Middle Eastern Periodicals

*Abstracta Islamica* (Extrait de la Revue des études islamiques). Series 1–. 1927– Paris, 1928– (quarterly).
A bibliographical bulletin. See also *Revue des études islamiques*.

*L'Afrique et l'Asie; revue politique, sociale et économique*. Paris, 1948– (quarterly).
Includes a 'chronologie trimestrielle' and a section 'documentation'; index for 1948–55.

*American Journal of Arabic studies*. Leiden, 1973–.

*Al-Andalus; revista de las escuelas de estudios arabes de Madrid y Granada*. (Instituto Miguel Asin). Madrid, 1933– (bi-annual).
Islamic Spain and Islamic studies more generally. Index 1933–55, published in 1958.

*Annales de l'Institut d'Études Orientales* (Inst., Fac. des Lettres et Sciences Humaines d'Alger). Algiers, 1934– (bi-annual).
Algerian studies; tables 1934–62 in *AIEO*, n.s. 1964.

*Annales* (earlier: *Mélanges*) *islamologiques* (Inst. Fr. d'Archéologie Orientale du Caire). Cairo, 1954– (irregular).
Islamic studies.

*Annales marocaines de sociologie* (Inst. de Sociologie de Rabat). Rabat, 1968– (annual).
Trilingual sociological review.

*Arabica; revue des études arabes* (Centre National de la Recherche Scientifique). Leiden, 1954– (3 per year).

*Ars Orientalis; the arts of Islam and the East* (Smithsonian Institute, Washington and University of Michigan). Washington, &c., 1954– (irregular).
A continuation of *Ars Islamica*, **1–16**, 1934–49, which was reprinted 1969.

*Bulletin des études arabes*. Algiers, 1941–52.
Reprinted in 1967.

*Bulletin d'études orientales* (Inst. Français de Damas). Damascus, 1931– (3 per year).
Islamic and Arabic studies.

*Cahiers de Tunisie; revue de sciences humaines* (Fac. des Lettres . . ., Univ. de Tunis). Tunis, 1953– (quarterly).
Tunisian and North African studies. Reprinted in New York, 1968.

*Cahiers de l'Orient contemporain* (Inst. d'Études Islamiques, Univ. de Paris, Centre d'Études de l'Orient Contemporain). Paris, 1944– (5 per year).
Documents and chronology.

*Correspondance d'Orient; études; bulletin d'information* (Centre pour l'Étude des Problèmes du Monde Contemporain). Brussels, 1957– (quarterly).
Includes bibliographies on modern Islam.

*Eastern churches review*. London, 1966– (bi-annual).
Successor to *Eastern churches quarterly* 1936–64. News of the Eastern churches.

*Edebiyat; journal of Middle Eastern literatures*. Philadelphia, 1976– (bi-annual).

*Gazelle*. London, 1975– (3 per year).
Translations of Arabic literature, classical and modern.

*Hespéris-Tamuda* (Univ. Mohammed V, Fac. des Lettres et des Sciences Hum.). Rabat, 1960– (quarterly).
Originally published separately, *Hespéris* (1921–59) in French by the Institut des Hautes-Études Marocaines, and *Tamuda* (1953–59) in Spanish as *Revista de Investigaciones Marroquies* in Tetuan.

*Hespéris* vols. 1–46 (1921–59), reprinted, with a general index to vols. 1–41; 'Répertoire analytique' to *Hespéris* 1921–35, 1936–54, published in Publications de l'I.H.E. Marocaines 1915–35 and 1936–54.

*Tamuda* 'indice general 1953–59' in vol. 7, 1959. Also: *Table générale des matières contenues depuis un demi-siècle dans* Hespéris, 1921–59, Tamuda, 1953–59, Hespéris Tamuda 1960–71 *avec classement des articles par noms d'auteurs et par matières* (Supplément au volume XIII).
History of Islamic countries in general and Morocco in particular.

*IBLA* (Inst. des Belles Lettres Arabes). Tunis, 1938– (quarterly).
General cultural problems in Tunisia; 'index des auteurs et des matières' in vol. 25, 1962.

*International Journal of Middle East studies*. Cambridge, 1970– (quarterly).
Studies of the Middle East from the birth of Islam to modern times.

*Der Islam; Zeitschrift für Geschichte and Kultur des islamischen Orients.* Berlin 1910– (1–4 fascicles per year).

*Islamic culture* (Islamic Culture Board). Hyderabad, 1927– (quarterly).
Islamic studies. Volumes for 1927–63 reprinted 1967–71.

*The Islamic quarterly* (Islamic Cultural Centre). London, 1954– (quarterly).
Islamic studies.

*Islamic review* (Shah Jehan Mosque). Woking, 1913– (monthly).
Vols. 1–35 reprinted 1971.

*Islamic studies* (Journal of the Central Inst. of Islamic Research). Karachi, 1962– (quarterly).

*Islamica; Zeitschrift für die Erforschung der Sprachen, der Geschichte und der Kulturen der islamischen Völker.* Leipzig, 1924–35.
Reprinted 1969.

*Journal of Arabic literature.* Leiden, 1970– (annual).
Covers both classical and modern literature.

*Journal of Near Eastern studies* (Dept. of Or. Lang. and Lit., Univ. of Chicago). Chicago, 1942– (quarterly).
The successor to the *American Journal of Semitic Languages*. Field ranges from Biblical to modern Arabic studies.

*Journal of Palestine studies.* Beirut, 1971– (quarterly).

*Levante* (Centro per le Relazione Italo-Arabe). Rome, 1953– (quarterly).
In Italian and Arabic. A general periodical devoted to Italo-Arab affairs.

*Maghreb* (later) *Maghreb-Machrek.* Paris, 1964–.
North African studies primarily. Index 1964–72 in vol. 57.

*Mélanges de l'Institut Dominicain d'Études Orientales* (MIDEO). Cairo, 1954– (annual).
Islamic studies; bibliographies of books printed and Arabic MSS edited in Egypt.

*Middle East forum* (American University of Beirut). Beirut, 1925–73 (quarterly).
Originally entitled *Al-Kulliyah*. Modern Middle East.

*Middle East international.* London, 1971– (monthly).
Modern Middle East.

*Middle East journal* (Middle East Inst.). Washington, D.C., 1947– (quarterly).
Modern Middle East. Twenty-year cumulative index for 1947–66 published in 1972.

*Middle Eastern affairs* (Council for Middle Eastern Affairs). New York, 1950–63.
Modern Middle East; index, 1968.

*Middle Eastern studies.* London, 1964– (3 per year).
Study of Arabic-speaking countries, Israel, Persia and Turkey, since the end of the eighteenth century.

*The Muslim world* (Hartford Seminary Foundation). Hartford, Conn., 1911– (quarterly).
Islamic studies. Index for 1911–35, vols. 1–25. Vols. 1–54, 1911–64, reprinted 1966–68 in New York.

*New Middle East.* London, 1968–73.
Contemporary reporting and background articles.

*La nouvelle revue du Caire; littérature et sciences humaines.* Cairo, 1975(?)– (annual).
Articles by Egyptian writers on Egypt and French culture, as well as studies by French orientalists on the Arab world.

*Orient* (Assoc. pour l'Étude de l'Orient Moderne et Contemporain). Paris, 1954– (quarterly).
Study of the evolution of the states of the Middle East; table des années 1957–62, in *Orient* 1962.

*Oriente moderno; rivista mensile d'informazione et di studi* (Istituto per l'Oriente). Rome, 1921– (monthly).
Modern Middle East. Useful chronologies and press summaries, 1921–66, reprinted 1968–72, Rome; 'indice generale 1921–55', 1960.

*Proche-Orient chrétien; revue d'études et d'informations* (Pères Blancs de Sainte-Anne de Jérusalem). Jerusalem, 1951– (quarterly).
Christian Near East.

*Revista del Instituto de Estudios Islamicos.* Madrid, 1953– (irregular).
Islamic studies, especially Muslim Spain.

*Revue africaine* (Société Historique Algérienne). Algiers, 1856– (quarterly).
Algerian and North African studies. Index for 1856–81, vols. 1–25; 1882–1921, vols. 26–62; 1922–50, vols. 63–94. Vols. 1–70 reprinted Nendeln, 1968.

*Revue des études islamiques* (Centre National de la Recherche Scientifique).
Islamic studies.

*Revue du monde musulman.* Paris, 1906–26.
This valuable journal was the predecessor of the previous item. Reprinted in 1973. Index for 1906–26; index for vols. 1–16 in vol. 17, and for years 1906–26 in vols. 65–6.

*Revue de l'occident musulman et de la Méditerranée* (Assoc. pour l'Étude des Sciences Hum. en Afrique du Nord). Aix-en-Provence, 1966– (irregular).
Successor to *Revue de la Méditerranée.* 'Une revue consacrée aux sciences humaines dans les limites géographiques de l'Occident musulman'.

*Studi magrebini* (Istituto Univ. Or. di Napoli, Centro di Studi Magrebini). Naples, 1966– (irregular).
Studies of North Africa in general.

*Studia Islamica.* Paris, 1953– (irregular).
Islamic studies.

*Sudan notes and records.* Khartoum, 1918– (bi-annual).
Volumes for 1918–65 (lacking three numbers) available on microfiche.

*TR.* London, 1974– (3 per year).
Arabic/English. Intended to introduce English writing to Arab readers and vice versa.

*Travaux et jours* (Centre Cultural, Univ. St. Joseph). Beirut, 1961– (3 per year).
General studies of Lebanon and Near East.

*Die Welt des Islams; internationale Zeitschrift für die Entwicklungsgeschichte des Islams, besonders in der Gegenwart.* New series, Leiden, 1951– (quarterly).
Originally published in Germany 1913–43; 'Register zu Band 1–17' in vol. 18, 1936. Vols. for 1913–43 available on microfiche.

# Maps and atlases of the Arab world

HELEN MEDLOCK

The two major sources of information about maps and atlases of the world, including the Middle East and North Africa, are

ALEXANDER, G. L., *Guide to atlases; world, regional, national, thematic; an international listing of atlases published since 1950*. Metuchen, N.J., 1971.

and

LOCK, C. B. M., *Modern maps and atlases; an outline guide to twentieth century production*. London, 1969.

## I. MAPS

This section has been divided into two parts:

(i) General maps.
(ii) Thematic maps.

### (i) General Maps

Included here are topographic maps showing major physical features, roads, railways, political boundaries, towns and other important settlements. These maps have been subdivided into two types:

A. Single sheet maps covering the area at scales of about 1:4,000,000 to 1:11,000,000 (approx. 60 miles = 1 inch to 175 miles = 1 inch)

B. Multi-sheet maps of the world or large regions which cover the Middle East in a number of sheets at a scale larger than A

A third subdivision, multi-sheet maps of an individual country at scales of 1:100,000 and larger, has not been discussed here as this material is adequately described in

HALE, G. A., 'Maps and atlases of the Middle East'. *MESA bull.* **3**, iii, 1969, pp. 17–39

together with general world maps and atlases, and maps of Africa as a whole. Wall maps, raised relief map models and map transparencies are also touched on.

#### A. Single sheet maps of the whole area

Maps covered here are those showing relief (by layer colouring or contours), political boundaries, major communications – roads, railways, airports, &c., names of major regions, towns and physical features.

ARAB INFORMATION CENTER, *The strategic Arab world*. Scale 1:8,000,000. New York, 1960.

Coloured to indicate members of the League of Arab States. Shows military bases, important holy places, historical sites, major mineral deposits, oil pipelines, major roads and railways.

BLÍZKY VÝCHOD. Scale 1:6,000,000. Prague, 1962.

General map of the Middle East, including North-East Africa. With insets: economic (minerals, &c.); oil pipelines; town plans; population distribution; air routes; climate; vegetation.

GEOGRAPHIA LTD., *The Daily Telegraph map of the Middle East, India and Pakistan*. Scale 1:7,000,000. London, 1970.

With insets: population; economic; religion; distances; Israel and neighbours.

GEORGE PHILIP & SON LTD., *Stanford's general map of the Middle East*. Scale 1:5,000,000. London, 1966.

GERMANY, AIR FORCE, *Orientierungsmappe Mittlerer Osten*. 9v. Berlin 1941–42.

Each volume contains several folded maps, including general topographic maps, maps showing communications, airports, &c.

—— ARMY, GENERALSTAB DES HEERES, *Militärgeographische Angaben*. Berlin, 1940s.

Volumes include Ägypten (1942); Algerien (1942); Irak (1943); Libyen (1941); Marokko (1942); Nordost-Afrika (1940); Palästina und Transjordanien (1941); Syrien (1941); Tunis (1941); Vorderer Orient (1941). Each publication is a portfolio containing a volume of text and photographs, and a number of folded maps (e.g. general map of the area, communications, location of industries, some town plans).

GREAT BRITAIN, ADMIRALTY, NAVAL INTELLIGENCE DIVISION, (Geographical handbook series.) London, 1941–45.

Each volume covers a different country and includes many maps in the text and in the end-pockets at various scales, some thematic, some topographic. They are mostly reprints of maps already published by the War Office, or French official sources, or locally published maps. Volumes covering the area include: No. 505 – Algeria, 2v. (1943–44); No. 506 – Morocco, 2v. (1941–42); No. 513 – Syria (1943); No. 514 – Palestine and Transjordan (1943); No. 523 – Tunisia (1945); No. 524 – Iraq and the Persian Gulf (1944); No. 527 – Western Arabia and the Red Sea (1946).

INTERNATIONAL ASSOCIATION OF FRIENDS OF THE ARAB WORLD, *The Arab world*. Scale 1:11,000,000. Lausanne [1959?].

Covers the whole of North Africa and the Middle East. Pictorial relief, with only a few places marked and no political boundaries.

ISRAEL, MAḤLEKET HA-MEDIDOTH, *Mi-yam ʿad yam*. [From sea to sea.] Scale 1:4,650,000. Ed. by H. Bar-Deroma. Jerusalem, 1957.

Extends from the Mediterranean and Black Seas to the Persian Gulf.

JOHN BARTHOLOMEW & SON LTD., *The Middle East*. Scale 1:4,000,000. (Bartholomew World Travel Series.) Edinburgh [1975].

Other useful maps in the same series include *Africa, North East*. Scale 1:5,000,000 (1968); and *Africa, North West*. Scale 1:5,000,000 (1966).

KÜMMERLY & FREY, *Naher Osten; politische Übersichtskarte mit Strassennetz und Eisenbahnen; Near East: political map with roads and railways*. Scale 1:5,000,000. Bern [*c*. 1960].

MICHELIN, *Afrique* (*nord-est*); *Africa* (*North East*). Scale 1:4,000,000. 5th edn. (Map 154.) Paris, 1972.

Road map showing political boundaries, settlements, forest, motoring and tourist features. Includes the south-western part of Saudi Arabia.

—— *Afrique (nord et ouest); Africa (North and West)*. Scale 1:4,000,000. 7th edn. (Map 153.) Paris, 1971.

B. MULTI-SHEET WORLD AND REGIONAL SERIES

AMERICAN GEOGRAPHICAL SOCIETY, *The world*. Scale 1:5,000,000. New York, 1958–.

Also published as A.M.S. series 1106. Sheet 3: *North Eastern Africa* includes the whole of the Middle East.

GREAT BRITAIN, MINISTRY OF DEFENCE, DIRECTORATE OF MILITARY SURVEY, *World 1:500,000*. (G.S.G.S. 1404.) London, 1956–.

Sheets so far published cover the whole of the Near and Middle East (with the exception of central Saudi Arabia), Egypt, the north-east coast of Libya, Tunisia and the northern half of Algeria.

INTERNATIONAL MAP OF THE WORLD, 1:1,000,000. Various eds. [v.p.] 1911–.

This is a joint venture between national governments and their cartographic agencies, to cover the world in over 2,000 sheets. Coverage of the Middle East is complete. Also in progress is the *World aeronautical chart* at the same scale giving emphasis on features easily identifiable from the air.

UNITED STATES OF AMERICA ARMY MAP SERVICE, *Southwestern Asia 1:250,000*. (A.M.S. K502.) [Washington,] 1954–.

Sheets so far published cover parts of North Africa and the Arabian Peninsula and the whole of Turkey, Syria, Lebanon and Iraq.

## (ii) Thematic Maps

(a) ECONOMIC

B. ORCHARD LISLE, *Map of Near and Middle East oil*. Scale 1:4,500,000. 7th edn. Fort Worth, Texas, 1965.

Shows concession areas, location of oilfields, pipelines, refineries. With insets of special areas.

—— *Map of North and Middle African oil*. Scale 1:5,000,000. Forth Worth, Texas, 1961.

Companion map to *Near and Middle East oil*.

BRITISH PETROLEUM CO. LTD., *Middle East concessions*. Scale 1:2,000,000. [London?] 1969.

Covers only the area around the Persian Gulf. Shows oil concessions, pipelines, wells, &c.

FRANCE, PRÉSIDENCE DU CONSEIL, DIRECTION DE LA DOCUMENTATION, *Moyen-Orient; essai de carte économique*. Scale 1:5,000,000. (Carte No. 77.) Paris, 1958.

Shows methods of cultivation, land use, minerals, industries. With inset maps of Middle East oil, Syria and the Lebanese coast. Other maps of interest in the same series include No. 62 – *Algérie et Tunisie: carte économique*; No. 80 – *Carte agricole de l'Afrique*.

INSTITUT GÉOGRAPHIQUE NATIONAL, *Les concessions pétrolières du Moyen Orient*. Scale 1:4,000,000. Paris, 1950.

In black and white, using shading to show individual concessions areas.

STANDARD OIL CO., *The Middle East; oil industry map*. Scale 1:2,000,000. [New York, 1950.]

In black and white. Shows names of oil company concession areas, pipelines, gas fields, &c.

UNITED STATES OF AMERICA, CENTRAL INFORMATION AGENCY, MAP BRANCH, *Arab states (excluding Egypt); agriculture, resources and transportation*. Scale 1:6,000,000. Washington, D.C., 1948.

(b) ETHNOGRAPHIC

AKADEMIYA NAUK SSSR, *Karta narodov Perednei Azii*. Scale 1:5,000,000. Moscow, 1960.

An ethnographic map of the Middle East. Shows distribution of major towns by size, and has accompanying text. A map of Africa: *Karta narodov Afriki*, Scale 1:8,000,000, was published in two sheets in 1970.

FRANCE, PRÉSIDENCE DU CONSEIL, DIRECTION DE LA DOCUMENTATION, *Les Musulmans dans le monde*. Scale 1:17,000,000. (Carte No. 55.) Paris, 1950?

Shows holy places and distribution of Moslems according to sects. With inset: Syrie-Leban.

UNITED STATES OF AMERICA, CENTRAL INFORMATION AGENCY, MAP BRANCH, *Arab states (excluding Egypt); tribes and administrative divisions*. Washington, 1948.

Also shows types of cultivation practices.

(c) PHYSICAL

ASHBEL, D., *Rainfall map of the Near East*. Scale 1:4,000,000. Jerusalem, 1940.

In English and Hebrew. Covers Iraq, Israel, Jordan, Syria and Turkey.

ASSOCIATION DES SERVICES GÉOLOGIQUES AFRICAINS & UNESCO, *Carte géologique de l'Afrique; Geological map of Africa*. Scale 1:5,000,000. 9 sheets. Paris, 1963.

Sheets 1–3 cover North Africa and the Middle East. In French and English with an explanatory text.

UNESCO & FAO, *Carte bioclimatique de la region méditerranéenne; bioclimatic map of the Mediterranean region*. Scale 1:5,000,000. 2 sheets. Paris, 1963.

Covers the Middle East and North Africa, and is coloured by climatic region (defined by temperature, length of dry season and frost free periods). In French and English, with explanatory text.

—— *Carte de la végétation de la région méditerranéenne; Vegetation map of the Mediterranean region*. Scale 1:5,000,000. 2 sheets. Paris, 1970.

Same geographic coverage as previous entry. In French and English, with explanatory text.

## II. ATLASES

ATLAS OF THE ARAB WORLD AND THE MIDDLE EAST, with an introduction by C. F. Beckingham. London, 1960.

Has an historical introduction, and includes sections on town plans, types of settlement, &c.

BRAWER, M. & KARMON, Y. *eds.*, *'Aṭlas ha-mizraḥ ha-tikhon . . . Atlas of the Middle East; physical, economic, political, with a geographical survey.* 2nd edn. Tel Aviv, 1967.

Hebrew text.

BOYD, A. & RENSBURG, P. VAN, *An atlas of African affairs.* London, 1965.

Included as a companion volume to Pounds and Kingsbury below because of its North African sections.

COLLINS-LONGMANS & LIBRAIRE DU LIBAN, [*The standard atlas of the Arab world.* Revised repr. Harlow and Beirut,] 1972.

In Arabic. Primarily intended as a school atlas.

ECONOMIST INTELLIGENCE UNIT, *Oxford regional economic atlas; the Middle East and North Africa.* Oxford, 1960 (repr. 1971).

Has climatic maps, distribution of crops, oil production and air communications, followed by notes and statistics on irrigation, agriculture, oil, transport, population, development schemes, foreign trade.

GILBERT, M., *The Arab-Israeli conflict; its history in maps.* London, 1974.

HAZARD, H. W., *Atlas of Islamic history.* 3rd edn. rev. and corr. Princeton, 1954.

Arranged in chronological order, with historical notes, important dates, &c., on the left-hand pages, maps on the right.

KAMAL, Y., *Monumenta cartographica Africae et Aegypti.* 5v. Cairo, 1926–51.

Facsimile maps relating to ancient and medieval Africa and Egypt.

KHANZADIAN, Z., *Atlas de géographie économique de Syrie et du Liban.* Paris, 1926.

Text with tables, plus maps.

KLEMP, E., *Africa on maps dating from the twelfth to the eighteenth century; 77 photocopies from European map collections.* Leipzig, 1968.

MILLER, K. *ed.*, *Mappae Arabicae. Arabische Welt-und Länderkarten des 9–13 Jahrhunderts in arabischer Urschrift, lateinischer Transkription und Übertragung in neuzeitliche Kartenskizzen.* Mit einleitenden Texten hrsg. von K. Miller. 6v. in 13. Stuttgart, 1926–31.

Contents: v.1. Die beiden Idrisi-Karten. v.2. Die arabischen Karten der Länder von Europa und Afrika. v.3. Asien I: Vorder- und Südasien. v.4. Asien II: Mittel-, Nord- und Ostasien. v.5. Weltkarten. v.6. Ergänzungsband.

MUNGER, A. H. & PLACIDI, E., *The Munger map book; petroleum developments and generalized geology of Africa and the Middle East.* Los Angeles, 1960.

Published by the Munger Oil Information Service. Provides separate treatment by country of the location of concessions, drilling areas, types of wells and pipelines, geology, &c.

POLLACCHI, P. and others, *Atlas de l'Afrique du Nord.* Paris, 1939.

POUNDS, N. J. & KINGSBURY, R. C., *An atlas of Middle Eastern affairs.* Rev. edn. London, 1966.

Divided into two main sections: 1 – The Middle East as a geographic region, including the history of the area, population, predominant languages and religions, and oil; 2 – Nations of the Middle East, divided according to country. There are small-scale maps facing each page.

REICHERT, R., *Atlas histórico regional do mundo árabe . . . a historical and regional atlas of the Arabic world.* Salvador, 1969.

ROOLVINK, R. *comp.*, *Historical atlas of the Muslim peoples*, comp. by R. Roolvink, with the collaboration of Saleh A. el Ali, Hussain Monés and Mohd. Salim. Amsterdam, 1957.

Consists entirely of maps, which although fully annotated are not always very clear. Covers the whole of the Muslim world, from Spain to Indonesia, showing different areas at different periods, e.g. Timurids, Middle Ages.

ṢABBĀGH, Saʿīd, *Al-aṭlas al-ʿarabī al-ʿāmm.* Beirut, 1973.

THE TIMES, *The Times atlas of the world*, ed. by J. Bartholomew. Mid-century edn. 5v. London, 1955–59.

Vol. 2 covers South West Asia and vol. 4 includes Africa.

TÜBINGER ATLAS DES VORDEREN ORIENTS. Tübingen, 1972–.

Although publication of the TAVO *Beihefte* began in 1972, the actual maps, in two volumes (Teil A: Geographie; Teil B: Geschichte) did not begin appearing until 1975. When complete the Atlas will cover an area geographically from Egypt to Afghanistan, Turkey to the Yemen, and historically from prehistoric times to the present.

U.A.R. WIZĀRAT AL-TARBIYYA, *Al-aṭlas al-ʿarabī.* Cairo, 1969.

# Arabic geographical names

P. J. M. GEELAN

The most convenient and detailed sources for the Arabic area as a whole are the gazetteers published by the United States Board on Geographic Names (= BGN).

*Egypt and the Gaza Strip*. (No. 45) 1959
*Arabian Peninsula*. (No. 54) 1961
*Iraq*. (No. 37) 1957
*Sudan*. (No. 68) 1962
*Libya*. (No. 41) 1958
*Tunisia* (No. 81) 1964
*Mauritania*. (No. 100) 1966
*Syria*. (No. 104) 1967
*Morocco*. (No. 112) 1970
*Lebanon*. (No. 115) 1970
*Jordan*. (No. 3.) 1st edn. 1955, 2nd edn. (unnumbered) 1971
*Algeria* (unnumbered) 1972

The main entries in all these gazetteers (except those for Morocco, Algeria and Mauritania) are spelled, as far as possible, in terms of the BGN/PCGN[1] system for the transliteration of Arabic. This system is characterized and immediately recognized by the use of *ay* and *aw* for the diphthongs and cedillas rather than dots under the pharyngalized consonants. The system is reversible for all practical purposes and the absence of Arabic script forms of names in these gazetteers is not therefore a serious disadvantage.

The main entries in the gazetteers for Algeria, Mauritania and Morocco follow the French-based spellings found on the latest available official romanized maps of the two countries.

It is unfortunately the case that the BGN gazetteers do not always reflect the romanized spellings that are found on available romanized maps of these countries. The position in the various areas is as follows:

*Arabian Peninsula*. All current maps (principally the Saudi Arabia 1:500,000 series produced by the U.S. Geological Survey; the Muscat/Oman/Trucial States 1:100,000 series produced by the Directorate of Military Survey; the South Arabia 1:100,000 series produced by the Directorate of Overseas Surveys; the 1:100,000 series of Kuwait produced by the Directorate of Military Survey) are in terms of the BGN/PCGN system. The BGN Gazetteer carries far fewer names than are found on the maps though in theory those that appear in both sources should be identically spelled. In practice there is considerable discrepancy in spelling due to differing material on names and/or differing interpretation of the same material.

*Iraq*. The BGN/PCGN system is gradually being introduced cartographically

[1] Permanent Committee on Geographical Names.

(as witness the Iraq plate of the current *Times Atlas*), but only sporadic and patchy mapping is so far available.

*Libya*. The BGN/PCGN system is supplanting the old Italian romanization, but again available mapping is at small scales only.

*Syria*. The BGN/PCGN system will now be introduced on maps of Syria (with French romanizations in brackets to aid identification), but it will probably be some years before general coverage of the country is available.

*Egypt, Sudan, Jordan*. Though there is some Arabic-script mapping produced by Egypt and, to a lesser extent, Jordan, the bulk of the available large-scale maps produced by the survey authorities of these three countries are in terms of an unsystematized romanization in which the diphthongs appear as ai/ei and au/o and the pharyngal consonants are marked with a subscript dot (in Egypt and Jordan) or undistinguished (Sudan). Though the BGN gazetteers give cross-references from these map spellings to the BGN/PCGN form, they do not supply cross-references the other way, and are in consequence difficult to use in conjunction with maps.

*Tunisia, Lebanon*. Available large-scale mapping is now, and will continue to be, solely in terms of French romanization. This being phonetic transcription rather than transliteration, the relationship with BGN/PCGN spellings in the BGN gazetteers (which again cross-reference only one way) is far from self-evident.

PCGN has produced very little in the way of material on Arabic names:

*List of names (New Series) No. 6: Bahrain*, 1962.

(This was in terms of the BGN/PCGN system though there were no maps in that system to go with it. However, it is hoped that a new map of Bahrain in the BGN/PCGN system will appear soon and that a revised list can be produced to accompany it.)

*List of names (New Series) No. 7: Kuwait*, 1962.

(Essentially a listing of the names on the 1:100,000 map.)

There exist a number of indexes to romanized map series, mostly old and somewhat out of date but still useful in the absence of anything later or more comprehensive:

*Egypt:* (a) *Index to place names appearing on the 1:500,000 scale map of Egypt. Survey of Egypt.* Cairo, 1945. (There seem to be both English and Arabic editions, though PCGN has only the former.)

(b) *Index to place names appearing on the normal 1:00,000 map series of Egypt. Survey of Egypt.* Cairo, 1932. (English only. Lists over 14,000 names.)

*Sudan:* *Index gazetteer of the Anglo-Egyptian Sudan showing place names* [on the 1:250,000 series]. Survey Department, Khartoum, 1931 (earlier edition 1921).

*Yemen:* Alphabetical index of all the names which appear on the map [of North-West Yemen in Arabic and romanized editions] according to the geographical positions in J. Werdecker, 'A contribution to the geography and cartography of North-West Yemen'. *Bull. Soc. Royale d'Égypte* **20**, February 1933, pp. 119–43.

There exist also a number of hastily produced wartime indexes to military map series. These are of little use today, being generally small-scale and giving only grid references to particular map sheets.

(a) *Index to place-names on T.C. maps* [of Mesopotamia]. Government Printing Office, Calcutta, 1918.

(b) *Iraq. Index gazetteer showing place-names on quarter-inch and 1 : 500,000 desert series maps*. GHQ Paiforce, Baghdad, 1943.

(c) *Syria. Index gazetteer showing place-names on map series 1 : 200,000 and quarter inch which cover the Lebanon and Syria*. GHQ Middle East, Fayid, 1947.

(d) *Transjordan. Index gazetteer showing place-names on all map series covering Transjordan*. GHQ Middle East, Fayid, 1947.

(e) *Index to place-names in North-Western Egypt, shown on 1 : 100,000 maps*. 2 NZEF, 1944.

## Sources of Names in Arabic Script

Apart from standard Arabic reference works (Yāqūt, &c.), there is not much material available in which the Arabic forms of the names appear.

(a) J. G. Lorimer's *Gazetteer of the Persian Gulf* (5v. and 1v. of tables and maps, Calcutta, 1908, repr. Farnborough, 1970) provides Arabic for virtually every name appearing in the text and tables, but there is unfortunately no overall index to the many thousands of names included.

(b) The Survey of Western Palestine, *Arabic and English name lists collected during the survey by Lieutenants Conder and Kitchener*. Palestine Exploration Fund, London, 1881. This list names alphetically (by romanization) within each sheet of the one-inch map series, though the Arabic script is shown alongside each name.

(c) *Syrie. Répertoire alphabétique des noms de lieux habités.* (Service Géographique des Forces Françaises du Levant.) 3rd edn., 1945. Arranged in alphabetical order of the French romanizations this provides Arabic script alongside in every case. Reference is by *caza*, 1:200,000 map sheet and kilometre co-ordinates.

(d) Lebanon. There exist separate Arabic and French typescript gazetteers of the Lebanon, apparently produced under the auspices of Point IV in 1955 or thereabouts. Reference is by map co-ordinates, district and subdistrict. Some 2700 names are listed. (This has been superseded by a bilingual gazetteer produced in 1970 by the Lebanese Survey authorities.)[1]

(e) The lists of names produced by PCGN during the 'twenties made a point of showing Arabic script, but they are at too small a scale and out of date to be of much use today:

(i) *First list of names in Arabia* (*NW and SW*), 1931
(ii) *Second list of names in Arabia* (*NE and SE*), 1937
(iii) *First list of names in Egypt* (*Upper*), 1929
(iv) *First list of names in Iraq* (*Mesopotamia*), 1932
(v) *Revised list of names in Palestine*, 1937
(vi) *First list of names in Syria*, 1927
(vii) *First list of names in the Anglo-Egyptian Sudan*, 1927
(viii) *First list of names in Transjordan*, 1927

[1] Liban. *Répertoire alphabétique des noms géographiques*. Direction des Affaires Géographiques [Beirut], 1970. Bilingual, French-Arabic.

Generally speaking, the further west one goes the more difficult it is to find sources for names in Arabic script. For Algeria we have nothing at all. For Morocco, only a sketch-map in the back of the all-French census results. For Tunisia a small-scale sketch map produced probably by a back-street printer. There are census tables in Arabic for both Libya and Egypt, but these are difficult to use as primary sources for names.

Little less difficult than determining the correct Arabic written form of a geographical name in the Arab world is deciding in what system to transliterate it. There are as many different views on this question as there are people concerned with it. No simple, single overall solution is possible or indeed desirable. Everything depends, or should depend, on the purpose for which and the context in which the name is to be used. It is important to distinguish what I have elsewhere called the reference and the information aspects. This can most easily be illustrated by taking an exaggerated case: if one is concerned with the second largest city in Tunisia it will be most useful in most circumstances to refer to it as Sfax, a reference form which if not immediately understood can quickly and easily be looked up and found in directories, atlases, maps, etc. There will much less frequently be circumstances in which the object is to give information on the Arabic form of the name. This can most efficiently be done by giving the Arabic script pointed, but where this is expensive or inconvenient transliteration may be necessary. The problem then is to decide which system of transliteration will be appropriate. Ṣafāqus will probably be generally comprehensible, but in a purely French context Çafâḳus would also no doubt be acceptable.

Naturally one wishes to avoid the necessity for a dual approach wherever possible. This is why we and our American counterparts have, over the last 20 years, encouraged the use of the BGN/PCGN system on maps and in gazetteers, so that both reference and information purposes may be served by a single, reversible transliteration. Within the limits imposed by the lack of knowledge as to what the true form of many names actually is, this finalized nomenclature has been more or less achieved in the Arabian Peninsula, and is well on its way in Iraq and Libya. But even so there will still be circumstances in which the most efficient and useful reference will be by means of the old Italian spellings in Libya or the old Government of India spellings in Aden and Mesopotamia.

One must be constantly on one's guard against obstinate belief that there is only one correct way of romanizing an Arabic name. Context is everything. It may be difficult to decide which of two possible forms is more useful in particular circumstances, but the use of brackets is in no way an admission of failure.

*Editorial Note*: For reasons beyond our control it has not been possible, as was originally hoped, to offer an additional section treating of sources of reference more familiar to the Arabist than to the geographer. It should be noted that there is no comprehensive gazetteer of the Arab world in the Arabic language and that scholars with a knowledge of written Arabic, whether they be concerned with the medieval period or the modern, have only too often to rely on book indexes (e.g. to Arabic texts and/or translations – on which useful information, in the sphere of geographical writings, may be derived from the new edition of *The Encyclopaedia of Islām* s.v. 'Djughrāfiyya' – handbooks published by Arab governments, monographs of one sort or another) and periodical articles.

For the heartlands of Islam one or two items considered as standard works of reference are worthy of mention. Of these, pride of place may be given to Guy Le Strange's *The lands of the Eastern Caliphate* (Cambridge, 1905; repr. 1930), a work in which the author has conveniently assembled data supplied by medieval geographers on Iraq, Iran and Central Asia from the Arab conquest until the fifteenth century. Although not without deficiencies, the book is an indispensable tool. The other similar works by the same author are *Palestine under the Moslems* (London, 1890) – meaning Syria–Palestine – and *Baghdâd during the Abbassid Caliphate* (Oxford, 1900; repr. London, 1924). Another work which must not pass unnoticed is René Dussaud's *Topographie historique de la Syrie antique et médiévale* (Paris, 1927). Other works of reference which immediately spring to mind are the following: M. Asín Palacios, *Contribución a la toponimia árabe de España* (2nd edn., Madrid–Granada, 1944) – which may to some extent be supplemented, complemented and corrected by reference to items listed by H. Rudolf-Singer in 'Die Verbreitung der Imāla im Spanisch-arabischen' in *Festgabe für Hans Wehr* (ed. W. Fischer, Wiesbaden, 1969), pp. 37 ff.; H. Lautensach, *Maurische Züge im geographischen Bild der Iberischen Halbinsel* (Bonn, 1960) – with excellent bibliography; idem, *Über die topographischen Namen arabischen Ursprungs in Spanien und Portugal* (Bonn, 1960); Anis Frayha, *Mu'jam asmā' al-mudun wa-al-qurā al-Lubnāniyya* (Dictionary of the names of towns and villages in the Lebanon) (Beirut, 1972); Muḥammad Ramzī, *Al-qāmūs al-jughrāfī li-al-bilād al-Miṣriyya min 'ahd qudamā' al-Miṣriyyīn ila sanat* 1945), (Geographical dictionary of Egyptian territory from the time of the ancient Egyptians up to 1945) (2 vols., Cairo, 1953–68; index, Cairo, 1968); U. Thilo, *Die Ortsnamen in der altarabischen Poesie: ein Beitrag zur vor- und frühislamischen Dichtung und zur historischen Topographie Nordarabiens* (Wiesbaden, 1958); S. Wild, *Libanesische Ortsnamen. Typologie und Deutung* (Beirut, 1973). Attention is also drawn to publications appearing in the series *Nuṣūṣ wa-abḥāth jughrāfiyya wa-ta'rīkhiyya 'an Jazīrat al-'Arab* (Geographical and historical texts on the Arabian Peninsula), published in Riyadh.

For North Africa the following are useful:

*Répertoire alphabétique des confédérations de tribus de la zone française de l'Empire Chérifien.* Casablanca, 1927.

*Répertoire alphabétique des agglomérations de la zone française de l'Empire Chérifien classé par tribus et fractions de tribus d'après des résultats du recensement quinquennial, 1936.* Rabat, 1941.

*Répertoire des tribus et des douars communs de l'Algérie.* Algiers, 1900.

# Festschrifts and commemorative volumes

J. D. LATHAM

Festschrifts and commemorative volumes constitute a well-known category of scholarly publication. Comprising a range of papers solicited from a select number of contributors, they aim at (i) honouring the life or memory of scholars who have established a reputation in their chosen fields of study; (ii) celebrating the anniversary of the foundation of some institution; (iii) commemorating some luminary of Islamic civilization; (iv) commemorating the anniversary of some momentous event in the history of the Muslim peoples. Nowadays there is, for obvious financial reasons, a growing tendency for special issues of periodicals to be devoted to the first of the four categories indicated.

Festschrifts and memorial volumes have both merits and defects. A common criticism is that not all contributions are of equal value or interest and that some are nothing less than trivialities lifted without too much thought from commonplace books or thrown together at the last minute without due care and attention. While such a stricture is not entirely without foundation, it should not be taken too seriously: most contributions are neither better nor worse than those appearing in many periodical publications. One advantage of the Festschrift or memorial volume is that it often carries a biography and/or bibliography of the scholar to whom it is dedicated.

As it would not be very practicable to include here every volume which contains just one or two items of interest to readers of the present *Guide*, the list which follows is by no means exhaustive. The *Index Islamicus* regularly lists and indexes Festschrifts.

ABEL, A., *Mélanges d'Islamologie; volume dédié à la mémoire de Armand Abel par ses collègues, ses élèves et ses amis*, ed. by P. Salmon. Leiden, 1974.

AMARI, M., *Centenario della nascita di Michele Amari; scritti di filologia e storia araba*. 2v. Palermo, 1910.

AMERICAN UNIVERSITY OF BEIRUT, *American University of Beirut 1866–1966. Kitāb al-ʿīd* (*Festschrift*), ed. by Jibrail S. Jabbur. Beirut, 1967.

—— *Festival book*, ed. by Fuad Sarruf and Suha Tamin. Beirut, 1967.

-ʿAQQĀD, ʿAbbās Maḥmūd, *Al-ʿAqqād; dirāsa wa-taḥiyya. A Festschrift for al-ʿAqqād's reaching 70*. Cairo, n.d.

AVICENNA (IBN SĪNĀ), *Avicenna commemoration volume*. Calcutta, 1956.

—— *Avicenna: scientist and philosopher; a millenary symposium*, ed. by G. M. Wickens. London, 1952.

—— *Mahrajān Ibn Sīnā; muʾallafāt Ibn Sīnā*, ed. by G. C. Anawati [Jurj Shaḥḥāta Qanawātī]. *Millénaire d'Avicenne*. Cairo, 1950.

BABINGER, F., *Serta Monacensia Franz Babinger zum 15. Januar 1951 als Festgruss dargebracht*, ed. by H. J. Kissling and A. Schmaus. Leiden, 1952.

BAGHDAD, *Volume spécial publié à l'occasion du 1,000ème anniversaire de la fondation de cette cité.* 1962.

BASSET, A., *Mémorial André Basset, 1895–1956.* Paris, [1957].

BASSET, H., *Mémorial Henri Basset; nouvelles études nord-africaines et orientales,* publiées par l'Institut des Hautes-Études Marocaines. (Publs., Inst. des Hautes-Études Marocaines, 17, 18.) Paris, 1928.

BASSET, R., *Études nord-africaines et orientales,* publiées par l'Institut des Hautes-Études Marocaines. 2v. (Publs., Inst. des Hautes-Études Marocaines, 10, 11.) Paris, 1923–25.

-BĪRŪNĪ, *Al-Biruni commemoration volume, A.H. 1362.* Calcutta, 1951.

—— *Sbornik statei,* ed. by S. P. Tolstov. Moscow, 1950.

BRAUDEL, F., *Mélanges en honneur de Fernand Braudel.* 2v. Toulouse, 1973.

BROCKELMANN, C., *Studia orientalia in memoriam Caroli Brockelmann.* Hrsg. im Auftrage der Martin-Luther-Universität Halle-Wittenberg. (Wissenschaftliche Z. der M.-L. Univ. Halle-Wittenberg, Gesellschafts- u. Sprachwissenschaftl. Reihe, Heft 2/5, Jahrg. 17.) Halle-Wittenberg, 1968.

BROWNE, E. G., *A volume of oriental studies presented to Edward G. Browne on his 60th birthday* (*7 February, 1922*), ed. by T. W. Arnold and R. A. Nicholson. Cambridge, 1922 (repr.).

CAIRO, *Colloque international sur l'histoire du Caire* [on the 1000th anniversary of its founding]. Cairo, 1972.

CASKEL, W., *Festschrift Werner Caskel zum siebzigsten Geburtstag, 5 März, 1966, gewidmet,* ed. by E. Gräf. Leiden, 1968.

CASTRO Y CASADA, A., *Collected studies in honor of Américo Castro's eightieth year,* ed. M. P. Hornik. Oxford, 1965.

COHEN, M., *Mélanges Marcel Cohen. Études de linguistique, ethnographie et sciences connexes offertes par ses amis et ses élèves à l'occasion de son 80ème anniversaire, avec des articles et études inédits de Marcel Cohen; réunis par David Cohen.* The Hague, &c., 1970.

CRESWELL, K. A. C., *Studies in Islamic art and architecture in honor of Professor K. A. C. Creswell.* Cairo, 1965.

DERENBOURG, H., *Mélanges Hartwig Derenbourg* (*1844–1908*), *recueil de travaux d'érudition dédiés à la mémoire d'Hartwig Derenbourg,* par ses amis et ses élèves. Paris, 1909.

DESPOIS, J., *Maghreb & Sahara: études géographiques offertes à J. Despois,* ed. by X. de Planhol. *Acta Geographica* (Special issue), 1973.

DIEZ, E., *Beiträge zur Kunstgeschichte Asiens; in memoriam Ernst Diez,* ed. by O. Aslanapa. Istanbul, 1963.

DÖLGER, F., *Polychordia. Festschrift Franz Dölger zum 75. Geburtstag,* ed. P. Wirth. (Byzantinische Forschungen, 1.) Amsterdam, 1966.

DUDA, H. W., *Festschrift Herbert W. Duda zum 60. Geburtstag gewidmet,* von seinen Freunden und Schülern. (Wiener Zeitschrift für die Kunde des Morgenlandes, 56.) Vienna, 1960.

EILERS, W., *Festschrift für Wilhelm Eilers: ein Dokument der internationalen Forschung zum 27. September 1966,* ed. by G. Wiessner. Wiesbaden, 1967.

ERDMANN, K., *Forschungen zur Kunst Asiens. In memoriam Kurt Erdmann, 9. Sept. 1901–30. Sept. 1964*, ed. by O. Aslanapa and R. Naumann. Istanbul, 1969.

ETTINGHAUSEN, R., *Studies in art and literature of the Near East in honor of Richard Ettinghausen*, ed. by P. J. Chelkowski. Salt Lake City, 1974.

EVANS-PRITCHARD, E. E., *Studies in social anthropology; essays in memory of E. E. Evans-Pritchard*, ed. by J. M. Beattie and R. G. Lienhardt. 1974.

—— *Essays in Sudan ethnography presented to Sir E. Evans-Pritchard*, ed. by I. Cunnison and W. James. London, 1972.

GABRIELI, F., *A Francesco Gabrieli. Studi orientalistici offerti nel sessantesimo compleanno dai suoi colleghi o discepoli.* (Univ. di Roma; Studi orientali pubblicati a cura della Suola Orientale, 5.) Rome, 1964.

—— *'Oriente moderno' 54, iv. Dedicato a Francesco Gabrieli nel 70° anno.* Rome, 1974.

GAUDEFROY-DEMOMBYNES, M., *Mélanges offerts à Gaudefroy-Demombynes, par ses amis et anciens élèves.* Cairo, 1935–45.

GERMANUS, J., *The Muslim East; studies in honour of Julius Germanus*, ed. by Gy. Káldy-Nagy. Leiden, 1974.

-GHAZZĀLĪ, *Abū Ḥāmid al-Ghazzālī fī al-dhikrā al-miʾawiyya li-mīlādihi.* [Articles delivered at the celebration . . . held in Damascus, March 1961.]

GIBB, H. A. R., *Arabic and Islamic studies in honor of Hamilton A. R. Gibb*, ed. by G. Makdisi. Leiden, 1965.

GOEJE, M. J. de, *Feestbundel aan M. J. de Goeje op den 6den October 1891 aangebode.* Leiden, 1891.

GOLDZIHER, I., 'Festschrift für Ignaz Goldziher hrsg. von Carl Bezold mit einem Bildnis Goldziher's'. *Zeits. f. Assyriologie* **26**, 1912.

—— *Ignace Goldziher memorial volume*, ed. by S. Löwinger and J. Somogyi. 2v. Budapest, &c., 1948–58.

HERZFELD, E., *Archaeologica orientalia in memoriam Ernst Herzfeld*, ed. G. C. Miles. Locust Valley, N.Y., 1952.

HEYD, U., *The 'Ulama' in modern history; studies in memory of Professor Uriel Heyd*, ed. by G. Baer. Jerusalem, 1971.

HITTI, P. K., *The world of Islam; studies in honor of P. K. Hitti*, ed. by J. Kritzeck and R. Bayly Winder. London, 1960.

ḤUNAYN B. ISḤAQ, *Collection d'articles publiée à l'occasion du onzième centenaire de sa mort.* Présentation . . . G. Troupeau. Leiden, 1975.

ḤUSAYN, Ṭāhā, *Omaggio degli arabisti italiani a Ṭāhā Husein in occasione del 75 compleanno.* Naples, 1964.

—— *Mélanges Taha Husain offerts par ses amis et ses disciples à l'occasion de son 70ème anniversaire*, ed. by Abdurrahman Badawi. Cairo, 1962.

HUSAIN, Z., *Zahir Husain presentation volume on his 71st birthday.* New Delhi, 1968.

IBN AL-ʿARABĪ, Muḥyī al-Dīn, *Al-kitāb al-tidhkārī; Muḥyī al-Dīn Ibn ʿArabī fi al-dhikrā al-miʾawiyya al-thāmina li-mīlādihi 1165–1240*, ed. by Ibrāhīm Bayūmī Madkūr. Cairo, 1969.

IBN SĪNĀ, see AVICENNA.

JÄSCHKE, G., 'Festschrift Gotthard Jäschke aus Anlass seines 80. Geburtstages, ed. by O. Spies'. *WI* **15** (Special issue), 1974.

JEJEEBHOY, J. J., *Sir J. J. Zarthoshti Madressa centenary volume.* Bombay, 1967.

JULIEN, Ch.-A., *Études maghrébines; mélanges Charles André Julien.* (Publs., Fac. des Lettres et Sciences Humaines, Sér. ét. et méthodes, 2.) Paris, 1964.

KAHLE, P., *Studien zur Geschichte und Kultur des Nahen und Fernen Ostens; Paul Kahle zum 60. Geburtstag überreicht von Freunden und Schülern*, ed. by W. Heffening and W. Kirfel. Leiden, 1935.

KISSLING, H. J., *Islamkundliche Abhandlungen. H. J. Kissling zum 60. Geburtstag gewidmet von seinen Schülern.* (Beiträge zur Kenntnis Südosteuropas und des Nahen Orients, 17.) Munich, 1974.

KÜHNEL, E., *Aus der Welt der islamischen Kunst; Festschrift für Ernst Kühnel zum 75. Geburtstag am 26.10.1957*, ed. by R. Ettinghausen. Berlin, 1959.

LE TOURNEAU, R., 'Mélanges Roger Le Tourneau'. *Revue de l'Occident Musulman et de la Méditerranée* **13–14**, 1973; **15–16**, 1974.

LEVI DELLA VIDA, G., *Studi orientalistici in onore di Giorgio Levi Della Vida.* 2v. Rome, 1956.

LÉVI-PROVENÇAL, E., *Études d'orientalisme dédiées à la mémoire de Lévi-Provençal.* 2v. Paris, 1962.

LITTMANN, E., *Ein Jahrhundert Orientalistik. Lebensbilder . . . und Verzeichnis seiner Schriften, zum 80. Geburtstag zusammengestellt* von R. Paret und A. Schall. Wiesbaden, 1955.

—— *Orientalische Studien Enno Littmann zu seinem 60. Geburtstag am 16. September 1935 überreicht von Schülern*, ed. by R. Paret. Leiden, 1935.

MACDONALD, D. B., *The Macdonald presentation volume; a tribute to Duncan Black Macdonald, consisting of articles by former students presented to him on his seventieth birthday, April 9, 1933.* Princeton, 1933.

MARÇAIS, G., *Mélanges d'histoire et d'archéologie de l'occident musulman.* 2v. (Vol. 1 contains articles and lectures by G.M.; Vol. 2 is the Festschrift.) Algiers, 1957.

MARÇAIS, W., *Mélanges offerts à William Marçais par l'Institut d'Études Islamiques de l'Université de Paris.* Paris, 1950.

MASPÉRO, G., *Mélanges Maspéro III; Orient islamique.* (Mémoires de l'I.F.A.O., 68.) Cairo, 1935–40.

MASSÉ, H., *Mélanges d'orientalisme offerts à Henri Massé à l'occasion de son 75ème anniversaire.* Tehran, 1963.

MASSIGNON, L., *Louis Massignon*, ed. by J.-F. Six. Paris, 1970.

—— *Mélanges Louis Massignon.* 3v. Damascus, 1956–57.

MAYER, L. A., *L. A. Mayer memorial volume 1895–1959*, ed. by M. Avi-Yonah and others. (Eretz-Israel, 7.) Jerusalem, 1964.

MEIER, F., *Islamwissenschaftliche Abhandlungen; Fritz Meier zum sechzigsten Geburtstag*, ed. by R. Grämlich. Wiesbaden, 1974.

MENÉNDEZ PIDAL, R., *Estudios dedicados a Menéndez Pidal*. 7v. Madrid, 1950–63.

—— *Homenaje ofrecido a Menéndez Pidal; miscelánea de estudios lingüísticos, literarios e históricos*. 3v. Madrid, 1925.

MILES, G. C., *Near Eastern numismatics, iconography, epigraphy, and history; studies in honor of George C. Miles*, ed. by D. K. Kouymjian. Beirut, 1974.

MILLÁS-VALLICROSA, J., *Homenaje a Millás-Vallicrosa*. 2v. Barcelona, 1954–56.

MINORSKY, V., *Iran and Islam. In memory of the late Vladimir Minorsky*, ed. by C. E. Bosworth. Edinburgh, 1971.

MUNRO, D. C., *The Crusades and other historical essays presented to D. C. Munro*, ed. by L. J. Paetow. N.Y., 1928 (repr. 1968).

MUSHKAT, M., *The changing international community; some problems of its law, structures, peace research and the Middle East conflict. Essays in honour of Marion Mushkat*, ed. by C. Boasson and M. Nurock. 1973.

-MUTANABBĪ, *Al-Mutanabbī; recueil publié à l'occasion de son millénaire*. Beirut, 1936.

NÖLDEKE, T., *Orientalische Studien Theodor Nöldeke zum siebzigsten Geburtstag (2 März 1906) gewidmet von Freunden und Schülern*, ed. by C. Bezold. 2v. Giessen, 1906.

PAREJA, F. M., *Orientalia Hispanica sive studia F. M. Pareja octogenaria dicata*, ed. by J. M. Barral. 2v. [in 3]. Leiden, 1974. (So far only I/i published.)

PEDERSEN, J., *Studia Orientalia Ioanni Pedersen septuagenario . . . dicata*. Copenhagen, 1953.

POPPER, W., *Semitic and oriental studies; a volume presented to William Popper on the occasion of his seventy-fifth birthday, October 29, 1949*, ed. by W. J. Fischel. Berkeley, 1951.

RICE, D. T., *Studies in memory of David Talbot Rice*, ed. by G. Robertson and G. Henderson. 1975.

SACHAU, E., *Festschrift Eduard Sachau zum siebzigsten Geburtstage gewidmet von Freunden und Schülern*, ed. by G. Weil. Berlin, 1915.

SAUVAGET, J., *Mémorial Jean Sauvaget*. Vol. 1. Damascus, 1954.

SCHACHT, J., 'Volumes dédiés à la mémoire de J. Schacht, ed. by R. Brunschvig'. *Studia Islamica* **31**, 1970; **32**, 1971.

SHAH, I., *Sufi studies, east and west. A symposium in honor of Idries Shah's services to Sufi studies . . . marking the 700th anniversary of the death of Jalaluddin Rumi (A.D. 1207–1273)*, ed. by L. F. R. Williams. New York, 1973.

SPIES, O., *Der Orient in der Forschung; Festschrift für Otto Spies zum 5. April 1966*, ed. by W. Hoenerbach. Wiesbaden, 1967.

STERN, S., *In memoriam Samuel Miklós Stern 1920–1969*. (Israel Oriental studies, 2.) Tel Aviv, 1972.

THATCHER, G. W., *Essays in honour of Griffiths Wheeler Thatcher 1863–1950*, ed. by E. C. B. Maclaurin. London, 1967.

TSCHUDI, R., *Westöstliche Abhandlungen Rudolf Tschudi zum siebzigsten Geburtstag überreicht von Freunden und Schülern*, ed. by F. Meier. Wiesbaden, 1954.

VECCIA VAGLIERI, L. V., *Scritti in onore di Laura Veccia Vaglieri*. 2v. Naples, 1964.

VINNIKOV, I. N., *Voprosy filologii stran Azii i Afriki, 1. Sbornik I. N. Vinnikova*. Moscow, 1971.

VON GRUNEBAUM, G. E., *Islam and its cultural divergence; studies in honour of G. E. von Grunebaum*, ed. by G. L. Tikku. Urbana, Ill., 1971.

WALZER, R. R., *Islamic philosophy and the classical tradition; essays presented to Richard Walzer on his seventieth birthday by his friends and pupils*, ed. by S. M. Stern, A. H. Hourani and V. Brown. Oxford, 1971.

WEHR, H., *Festgabe für Hans Wehr zum 60. Geburtstag am 5 Juli 1969 überreicht von seinen Schülern*, ed. by W. Fischer. Wiesbaden, 1969.

WELLHAUSEN, J., *Studien zur semitischen Philologie und Religionsgeschichte; Julius Wellhausen zum siebzigsten Geburtstag am 17. Mai 1914 gewidmet von Freunden und Schülern*, ed. by K. Marti. Giessen, 1914.

WHITEHEAD, R. B., 'Dr. Richard Bertram Whitehead commemoration volume'. *Journal of the Numismatic Society of India* **30**, 1968.

WIET, G., Volume dédié à la mémoire de Gaston Wiet. *Ann. islam.* **11**, 1972.

# Scientific expeditions

ANN WALSH

For the purposes of this chapter, the term expedition has been restricted to multidisciplinary expeditions made by several scholars, although a number of one-man expeditions which were truly multidisciplinary have perforce been included. Straightforward descriptions of exploration or travel, however eminent the traveller, have been omitted, as have military missions such as Napoleon's expedition to Egypt.

## I. GENERAL

The Royal Geographical Society's *Geographical Journal* contains each year (usually in parts 3 and 4) a list of expedition reports received by the Library, with a brief summary of each. Reports are mainly, but not exclusively, of British expeditions, including those which have not received funds from the Society. School and college expeditions figure prominently in these listings. For Cambridge colleges, *Cambridge Expeditions Journal* gives details of expeditions approved for the year, and those completed in the previous year.

*Archives des missions scientifiques et littéraires. Choix de rapports et instructions publié sous les auspices du ministère de l'Instruction Publique.*
1. sér. 6v. Paris, 1850–56.
2. sér. 6v. Paris, 1864–71.
3. sér. 15v. Paris, 1873–90.
Table général . . . comprenant les trois séries. Paris, 1890.

Continued as:
*Nouvelles archives des missions scientifiques* . . . Paris, 1891–1921.
A work of paramount importance, whose scope is defined by Gabrieli, p. 81.

## II. NORTH AFRICA

### Algeria

*Exploration scientifique de l'Algérie pendant les années 1840, 1841, 1842, publiée par ordre du Gouvernement et avec le concours d'une commission académique.* 40v. Paris, 1844–81 (repr. Amsterdam, 1968–).

[A] *Sciences historiques et géographiques*
I. CARETTE, E., *Étude des routes suivies par les Arabes dans la partie méridionale d'Algérie et de la Régence de Tunis.* 1844.
II. —— *Recherches sur la géographie et le commerce de l'Algérie méridionale. Notice géographique sur une partie de l'Afrique septentrionale,* par E. Renou. 1844.

III. —— *Recherches sur l'origine et les migrations des principales tribus de l'Afrique septentrionale.* 1853.

IV and V. —— *Études sur la Kabilie.* 2v. 1848.

VI. PELLISSIER, E., *Mémoires historiques et géographiques sur l'Algérie.* 1844.

VII. PELLISSIER, E. & RÉMUSAT, E. *trans., Histoire de l'Afrique de Mohammed-Ben-Abi El-K'aïrouâni.* 1845.

VIII. RENOU, E., *Description géographique de l'Empire de Maroc. Itinéraires et renseignements sur le pays* . . . par A. Berbrugger. 1846.

IX. BERBRUGGER, A., *Voyages dans le sud de l'Algérie . . . par El-'Aïachi.* 1846.

X–XV. PERRON, N. A., *Précis de jurisprudence musulmane . . . selon le rite mâlekite par Khalîl Ibn-Ishâ'k.* 6v. 1848–54.

XVI. PELLISSIER, E., *Description de la Régence de Tunis.* 1853.

[B] *Sciences médicales*

I and II. PÉRIER, J. A. N., *De l'hygiène en Algérie. Mémoire sur la peste en Algérie,* par A. Berbrugger. 2v. 1847.

[C] *Physique générale*

I. AIMÉ, G., *Recherches de physique générale sur la Méditerranée.* 1845.

II. —— *Observations sur le magnétisme terrestre.* 1846.

[D] *Sciences physiques*

RENOU, E., *Géologie de l'Algérie . . . Notice minéralogique* . . . par M. Ravergie . . . *Description des coquilles fossiles* par M. Deshayes. 1848.

*Sciences physiques: Zoologie*

I–III. LUCAS, H., *Histoire naturelle des animaux articulés.* 3v. 1849.

IV. —— *Histoire naturelle des animaux articulés; Atlas.* 1849.

V. GUICHENOT, A., *Histoire naturelle des reptiles et des poissons.* 1v. and *Atlas.* 1850.

LOCHE, Commandant, *Histoire naturelle des mammifères.* 1867.

—— *Histoire naturelle des mammifères; Atlas.* 1844–48.

—— *Histoire naturelle des oiseaux.* 2v. 1867.

—— *Histoire naturelle des oiseaux; Atlas.* 1844–48.

DESHAYES, *Histoire naturelle des mollusques.* 2v. and *Atlas.* 1845.

[E] *Sciences naturelles: Botanique*

I. MAISONNEUVE, D. DE, *Flore d'Algérie; cryptogamie.* 1846–49.

II. COSSON, E. & MAISONNEUVE, D. DE, *Flore d'Algérie; phanérogamie.* 1854–67.

Pages xv–xlviii contain a detailed list of botanists who have contributed to the knowledge of Algerian, Tunisian and Moroccan flora.

III. MAISONNEUVE, D. DE, *Atlas de la flore d'Algérie.* 1846–49.

[F] *Archéologie*

DELAMARE, Ad. H. Al., *Archéologie.* 2v. of plates. 1850.

RENIER, L., *Inscriptions romaines de l'Algérie.* 1855.

### Libya

French activity in Libya is documented in *Archives des missions* and *Nouvelles archives*. The Società Geografica Italiana organized considerable exploration and research, details of which are to be found in the *Bollettino della Reale Società Geografica Italiana*. One such programme was the Esplorazioni Scientifiche nel Fezzàn, begun in 1933, and recorded in *BRSG Italiana* ser. VI, vol. 10 for that year.

*Missione Franchetti*

FRANCHETTI, L. and others, *La missione Franchetti in Tripolitania*. Florence, 1914.

'An important publication, giving the results of studies of the geology, water supply, agriculture and economic resources' (*JRGS* 1914).

*Giarub Oasis*

DESIO, A. and others, *Resultati scientifichi della Missione alla Oasi Giarub (1926–1927)*. Rome, 1928–31.

1. La morfologia.
2. La geologia.
3. La paleontologia.
4. Notizie geografiche, fisiche e biologiche.

Further reports were intended, but do not appear to have been published. Additional brief reports are included in *Atti X. Congr. Geog. Ital., Milano* **1**, 1927, pp. 149–69.

### Morocco

In recent years, Morocco has attracted a whole host of school and college expeditions, presumably through its proximity to Europe. The early investigations were conducted by the French, whose activities may be traced in *Archives des missions*. The following expeditions were particularly important:

FOUCAULD, C. DE, *Reconnaissance au Maroc, 1883–1884*. 2v. Paris, 1888.

A description of his explorations, ethnological studies, astronomical and meteorological observations. Modern studies of de Foucauld have concentrated rather on his missionary activities, but

SIX, J. F., *Itinéraire spirituel de Charles de Foucauld*. Paris, 1958

contains a comprehensive bibliography.

SEGONZAC, Marquis de, *Voyages au Maroc (1899–1901) avec . . . des Appendices politique, astronomique, météorologique, botanique, entomologique, numismatique, géographique*. Par MM. de Vanssay, Hasse [and others]. Paris, 1903.

The second Segonzac expedition, with Louis Gentil and de Flotte-Roquevaire, droduced

*Au coeur de l'Atlas. Mission au Maroc, 1904–1905. Note de géologie et de géographie physique* par M. Louis Gentil. Paris, 1910.

FLOTTE-ROQUEVAIRE, DE, *Cinq mois de triangulation au Maroc*. Algiers, 1909.

SI SAÏD BOULIFA, *Textes berbères, en dialecte de l'Atlas marocain*. Paris, 1909.

The works of Louis Gentil relating to the 1904–5 expedition are listed in *Au coeur de l'Atlas*, pp. 771–3.

LEMOINE, P., *Mission dans le Maroc occidental. Rapport au Comité du Maroc.* Paris, 1905.

An expedition concerned mainly with geology and geography. Further reports are to be found in *Renseignements coloniaux* for 1905, pp. 65–95, 141–55, 157–82.

*Mission scientifique du Maroc*

The Mission, founded by A. Le Chatelier at Tangier in 1904, published *Archives marocaines* from 1904–20, and *Revue du Monde Musulman* from 1906. The series *Villes et tribus du Maroc* was begun by Le Chatelier, but vol. 8 was produced after his death by Lt.-Col. Julien. Further volumes were planned, but no more appear to have been issued. The Mission was transferred to Rabat, and became *Section Sociologique des Affaires Indigènes* after the First World War.

VILLES ET TRIBUS DU MAROC

I. *Casablanca et les Châouïa.* Tome 1. 1915.
II. *Casablanca et les Châouïa.* Tome 2. 1915.
III. *Rabat et sa région; les villes avant la conquête.* 1918.
IV. *Rabat et sa région; les villes après la conquête.* 1919.
V. *Rabat et sa région; les tribus.* 1920.
VI. *Rabat et sa région; le Gharb (Les Djebala).* 1918.
VII. *Tanger et sa zone.* 1921.
VIII. *Tribus berbères, 1 : Les Aït ba Amran.* 1930.

*Institut Scientifique Chérifien*

*Les Hamada sud-marocaines; résultat de la mission d'étude 1951.* Par F. Joly . . . (Travaux de l'Inst., Sér. gen., 2.) Tangier, 1954.

Studies in geology, geography, botany and zoology.

## SAHARA

Sahara expeditions are legion, but the majority, on closer investigation, turn out to be merely attempts to reach the other side. In addition, the French government sent out several military/geographical expeditions, including that of Arnaud and Cortier, and the Mission Augiéras-Draper of 1927–28. The following two expeditions collected data on a rather wider range of subject:

*Mission Foureau-Lamy, 1898–1900*

FOUREAU, F., *Mission Saharienne Foureau-Lamy. D'Alger au Congo par le Tchad.* 2v. Paris, 1902.

—— *Documents scientifiques de la Mission Saharienne, Mission Foureau-Lamy.* 2v. Paris, 1903–5.

GUILLEAUX, C., *Journal de route . . . de la Mission Saharienne.* Paris, 1904.

REIBEL, E., *Carnet de la route de la Mission Saharienne.* Paris, 1931.

KRYSZANOWSKI, L., 'La pénétration du Sahara par l'Algérie et la Mission Foureau-Lamy'. *Quest. dipl. et colon.* 7, 1899, pp. 129–45.

See also: *Index Islamicus* vol. 1, Nos. 12248, 12376, 12404.

*Mission Tilho, 1906–9*

TILHO, M. A. J., *Documents scientifiques de la Mission Tilho, 1906–9.* 2v. and a vol. of maps. Paris, 1910.

Studies of geography, geology, meteorology, astronomy and anthropology. The Mission's main object was a survey to establish the demarcation line between French and British possessions, according to a treaty signed in 1906.

MISSION TILHO, *Grammaire et contes haoussas*, par M. Landeroin et J. Tilho. Paris, 1909; *Dictionnaire haoussa*. Paris, 1910.

## III. MIDDLE EAST

### Syria and Iraq

GROTHE, H., *Meine Reise durch Vorderasien* (*Kleinasien, Mesopotamien, Persien*). Halle, 1908.

—— *Meine Vorderasienexpedition 1906 und 1907*. 2v. Leipzig, 1911–12.

A scientific expedition despatched in 1906 under Imperial auspices. A bibliography is found on pp. viii– of the second work.

*Field Museum Anthropological Expedition to the Near East, 1934*

FIELD, H., *The anthropology of Iraq*:

Part 1, No. 1: *Upper Euphrates*. (Field Museum of Natural History [FMNH] vol. 30, pt. 1, No. 1.) Chicago, 1940.

Part 1, No. 2: *Lower Euphrates-Tigris region*. (FMNH vol. 30, pt. 1, No. 2.) Chicago, 1949.

Part 2, No. 1: *Northern Jazira*. (Peabody Museum Papers 46, i.) Cambridge, Mass., 1951.

Part 2, No. 2: *Kurdistan*. (Peabody Museum Papers 46, ii.) Cambridge, Mass., 1952.

Part 2, No. 3: *Conclusions*. (Peabody Museum Papers 46, iii.) Cambridge, Mass., 1952.

Botanical, zoological and geological surveys were also carried out. All Field's works are listed in Field, H., *Bibliography; 1926–1966*, Coconut Grove, Fla., 1966. Particularly relevant to the expedition are Nos. 51, 55–7, 398.

*Danish Dokan Expedition, 1957*

HANSEN, H. H., *The Kurdish woman's life; field research in a Muslim society: Iraq*. (Nationalmuseets Skrifter, Etnografisk Raekke, 7.) Copenhagen, 1961.

An archaeological expedition on which a place was offered to a cultural anthropologist. *Allah's Døtre* (Copenhagen, 1958; English translation: *Daughters of Allah*, London, 1960) by the same author, is a rather more 'popular' description of the expedition.

### Israel, Jordan, Lebanon

The exploration of Israel and Jordan, and to some extent Syria and Lebanon has been carried out largely in the interests of Biblical studies. A good summary of early work is:

HILPRECHT, H. V. *ed*., *Explorations in Bible lands during the nineteenth century*. Edinburgh, 1933.

The Palestine Exploration Fund, established in 1865, financed many studies, details of which are to be found in the various reports of the Fund, and in the *Quarterly statement* [later: *Palestine Exploration Quarterly*].

### Arabia

*Danish Expedition of 1761–67*

NIEBUHR, C., *Beschreibung von Arabien.* Copenhagen, 1772.

—— *Reisebeschreibung nach Arabien und andern umliegenden Ländern.* 3v. Copenhagen, 1774–78 and Hamburg, 1837.

Translated as: *Voyage en Arabie.* 2v. Amsterdam, 1776–80.

*Travels through Arabia and other countries in the East.* 2v. Edinburgh, 1972 (repr. Beirut, 1970).

FORSSKÅL, P., *Flora aegiptiaco-arabica,* ed. C. Niebuhr. Copenhagen, 1775.

—— *Resa till Lycklige Arabien. Dagbok 1761–63.* Uppsala, 1950.

FORSSKÅL, P. & BAURENFEIND, G. W., *Icones rerum naturalium,* ed. C. Niebuhr. Copenhagen, 1775.

Modern description and bibliography:

HANSEN, T., *Det Lykkelige Arabien.* Copenhagen, 1962.

Translated as: *Arabia Felix.* London, 1964.

*Reise nach Arabien.* Hamburg, 1965.

See also:

HOPKINS, I. W. J., 'The maps of Carsten Niebuhr'. *Cartographic J.* **4**, 1967, pp. 115–18.

Discussion and bibliography.

*Eduard Glaser*

Glaser's many expeditions in Southern Arabia between 1882 and 1894 are described in two sources:

WEBER, O., *Eduard Glasers Forschungsreisen in Südarabien.* Leipzig, 1909.

WERDECKER, J., 'A contribution to the geography and cartography of North West Yemen (based on the results of the explorations by Eduard Glaser) . . .'. *Bull. Soc. Géog. Égypte* **20**, 1939–42, pp. 1–160.

The former has an accurate but incomplete list of Glaser's works; the bibliography in Werdecker is fuller, but inaccurate in detail. In particular:

No. 4 *should read* Sitz. der Kais. Akad der Wissensch. Math.-nat. Kl., XCI (1885).

No. 19 *insert date of publication*: 1899.

No. 21 *date of publication*: 1906, not 1910.

No. 22 *is* Sammlung Eduard Glaser I – *see below.*

The results of much of Glaser's work were published after his death:

HANN, J., *Ergebnisse aus Dr. E. Glaser's meteorologischen Beobachtungen in Ṣan'â (el-Jemen).* Vienna, 1914.

KRUMPHOLZ, H., *Eduard Glaser's astronomische Beobachtungen im Jemen im Jahre 1883.* Vienna, 1911.

*Sammlung Eduard Glaser* (Kaiserliche, *later* Österreichische, Akademie der Wissenschaften. Philosophisch-historische Klasse).

I. MÜLLER, D. H. & RHODOKANAKIS, N. *eds.*, *Eduard Glasers Reise nach Mârib.* 1913.

II. HÖFNER, M. & SOLÁ SOLÉ, J. M., *Inschriften aus dem Gebiet zwischen Mârib und dem Ǧōf.* (Sitzb. 238, Bd. 3.) 1961.

III. WISSMANN, H., *Zur Geschichte und Landeskunde von Alt-Südarabien.* (Sitzb. 246.) 1964.

IV. SOLÁ SOLÉ, J. M., *Inschriften aus Riyām.* (Sitzb. 243, Bd. 4.) 1964.

V. LUNDIN, A. G., *Die Eponymenliste von Saba, aus dem Stamme Halīl.* (Sitzb. 248, Bd. 1.) 1965.

VI. TSCHINKOWITZ, H., *Kleine Fragmente (1. Teil).* (Sitzb. 261, Bd. 4.) 1969.

*Kaiserliche Akademie der Wissenschaften. Südarabische Expedition, 1898–99*

*Linguistic studies*

I, II, V. REINISCH, S. L., *Die Somali-Sprache: Texte.* Vienna, 1900; *Wörterbuch.* Vienna, 1902; *Grammatik.* Vienna, 1903.

III. JAHN, A., *Die Mehri-Sprache in Südarabien. Texte und Wörterbuch.* Vienna, 1902.

IV, VI, VII. MÜLLER, D. H., *Die Mehri- und Soqoṭri-Sprache.* Vienna, 1902; 1905; 1907.

VIII, X. RHODOKANAKIS, N., *Der vulgärarabische Dialekt im Ḍofâr* [*i.e.*] *Zfâr.* Vienna, 1908; 1911.

IX. MÜLLER, D. H., *Mehri- und Ḥaḍrami-Texte, gesammelt im Jahre 1902 in Gischin von* . . . W. Hein. Vienna, 1909.

*Scientific studies*

Geological, zoological, botanical, entomological and mineralogical results were published in:

*Denkschriften der Kaiserliche Akademie der Wissenschaften, Mathematisch-naturwissenschaftliche Klasse*, Bd. 71. Vienna, 1907.

*Works about the Expedition*

LANDBERG, C., *Die Südarabischen Expedition . . . und das Vorgehen des Prof. D. H. Müller.* Munich, 1899.

—— *Die Expedition nach Süd Arabien. Bericht an die Kaiserliche Academie* . . . Vienna, 1899.

MÜLLER, D. H., *Die Südarabischen Expedition . . . und die Demission des Grafen Carlo Landberg.* Vienna, 1899.

—— *Zur Geschichte der Südarabischen Expedition.* Vienna, 1907.

VOLLERS, K., 'Die arabischen Teile der Wiener Südarabischen Expedition'. *Zeits f. Assyriologie* **23**, 1909.

*Expedition of the Liverpool and British Museum to Sokotra, 1898–99*

FORBES, H. O. *ed.*, *The natural history of Sokotra and Abd-el-Kuri.* Liverpool, 1903.

The volume contains the botanical and zoological and some geological results; a second volume of anthropological and ethnological studies was projected, but seems not to have been published.

WILSON, A., 'Summary of scientific research in the Persian Gulf'. *J. Bombay Nat. Hist. Soc.* **31**, iii, 1926.

A most useful historical survey of activities in the area.

*Expedition of Rathjens and Wissmann to the Yemen, 1927–28*

RATHJENS, C., 'Exploration au Yemen'. *JA* **215**, 1929.

—— *Rathjens-v. Wissmannsche Südarabien-Reise*. Bd. 1: *Sabäische Inschriften*, bearb. von J. H. Mordtmann und E. Mittwoch. (Hamburg Universität; Abh. Gebiet Auslandkunde Bd. 36, Reihe B, Bd. 17.) Hamburg, 1931.

*American Geographical Society. Oriental explorations and studies*

A series of explorations and studies undertaken by Alois Musil for the Society between 1926 and 1928, edited by J. K. Wright.

1. *The Northern Ḥeǧâz; a topographical itinerary*. New York, 1926.
2. *Arabia Deserta*. 1927.
3. *The Middle Euphrates*. 1927.
4. *Palmyrena*. 1928.
5. *Northern Neǧd*. 1928.
6. *The manners and customs of the Rwala Bedouins*. 1928.

WRIGHT, J. K. 'Northern Arabia: the explorations of Alois Musil'. *Geog. rev.* **17**, 1927, pp. 117–206.

A further, usually lone, explorer of Arabia was H. St. J. Philby. Details of his life and works are to be found in a memorial notice by Ryckmans:

RYCKMANS, G., *H. Saint John B. Philby, le 'Sheikh 'Abdallah', 3 avril 1885–30 septembre 1960*. Istanbul, 1961.

and more fully in:

MONROE, E., *Philby of Arabia*. London, 1973.

In 1951–52 Philby took part in a Belgian expedition to Saudi Arabia, with Ryckmans and Lippens. The results of this archaeological survey, and anthropological/sociological studies were published as:

LIPPENS, P., *Expédition en Arabie Centrale*. Paris, 1956.

*North Arabian Desert Archaeological Survey*

FIELD, H. and others, *North Arabian Desert Archaeological Survey, 1925–50*. (Peabody Museum Papers **45**, ii.) Cambridge, Mass., 1950.

Accounts and bibliographies of the Field Museum Expeditions of 1927, 1928 and 1934, and [very briefly] the Peabody Expedition of 1950. Studies of zoology, botany and geology were made, as well as archaeology.

Further to the Peabody Expedition, 1950:

FIELD, H., *An anthropological reconnaissance in the Near East, 1950*. (Peabody Museum Papers **48**, iii.) Cambridge, Mass., 1956.

See also: Field, H., *Bibliography: 1926–1966*, especially Nos. 321, 324, 353, 360, 366–7, 374.

*Socotra Expedition, 1967*

BOXHALL, P. G., *General report on the Expedition to Socotra Island, 1967*.

A mimeographed report by the Expedition leader. Detailed reports are awaited. The projects included:

Archaeology – survey for the British Academy and South Arabian government.

Geology – for Leeds University.

Botany and entomology – for Kew Gardens and British Museum.

Study of spoken Socotri – by Prof. T. Johnstone.

Arabic studies, including fishing, genealogy of the ruling family, constitution – by Prof. R. Serjeant.

# Orientalism and orientalists

C. E. BOSWORTH

The history of orientalism is, in its early phase, the history of the medieval Christian West's clash with the Muslim East on the religious and ideological plane. In the Dark Ages, Islam was regarded as little more than an abominable Christian heresy prevalent among the Saracens of the Syrian and Arabian Deserts. It was really the beginnings, in the course of the eleventh century, of the Christian Reconquista in Spain and Sicily, the two regions where the Muslim and Christian worlds enmeshed most intimately, which stimulated the first scholarly interest in Islam. This stimulus was heightened once the Crusades in the Levant got under way and it was clearly necessary to understand something of the beliefs and practices of the Muslims. The Latin warriors and settlers in the Crusading states must often have acquired considerable knowledge of the Muslims under their rule and those over the border in Syria and Egypt, though little of this was set down on record. It was the theological polemicists rather than the local Crusaders who built up the picture of Islam as an odious and malignant force, with its Prophet depicted either as an idol or tribal god and therefore false and spurious, or else equated with Satan or Antichrist. By no stretch of imagination were they concerned with objective truth. One of these polemicists, Guibert de Nogent, freely admitted that he used no written sources for his writings against Islam, but only hearsay, adding that 'It is safe to speak evil of one whose malignity exceeds whatever ill can be spoken'.

A more objective view of Islam appeared in the realm of philosophy, medicine and science, where it was early realized that the Arabs held the key to much of the heritage from the classical world. Latin translations appeared of Arabic texts, especially through the channel of intercommunication in Spain, above all after the fall to the Christians in 1085 of the intellectual centre of Toledo. Most notable here were the efforts of the group working in Spain and inspired by Peter the Venerable, Abbot of Cluny (d. 1157), who aimed at acquiring and transmitting to the West a more objective knowledge of Islamic religion, if only in order to combat the heresies of Judaism and Islam. Amongst the resulting 'Cluniac corpus' of Arabic texts and scholarly compositions was the Englishman Robert of Ketton's translation of the Qur'ān (1143). It was also in the twelfth century that western scholars began to utilize Arabic versions of what were originally Greek scientific and philosophical texts, so that Gerard of Cremona (d. 1187) was sent to Toledo to seek Arabic manuscripts of Greek texts which he could translate, and the works of Avicenna, including parts of his *Kitāb al-shifā'*, appeared towards the end of this century.

There thus appeared a dichotomy of aims and attitudes in these early stages of orientalism. The first set were theological and savagely polemical, and viewed Islam through a haze of popular legend and superstition; whereas the second set were more objective and scientific, and viewed the Islamic world (at that time, essentially the world of the Arabs, the only Muslim people with whom the westerners had contact) as the cradle of science, medicine and philosophy. Unfortunately, the crude and credulous popular view of Islam was kept alive down to the seventeenth century or later by the political and military clash of Christendom and Islam, in the first period by the above-mentioned Reconquista and the Crusades, then subsequently by the expansion of the Ottoman empire in the Balkans and Mediterranean basin. Only among a few enlightened souls like the Hohenstaufen Emperor Frederick II of Sicily did a less polemical view of Islam prevail.

Significant for the development of orientalism was the gradual realization that the Islamic languages would have to be learnt by Europeans if any progress towards the conversion of the Muslims was to be made. This realization is seen in the attitude of men like Roger Bacon and Raymond Lull and in the approval of the Council of Vienne in 1311 for the learning of eastern languages, and especially of Arabic.

Political and diplomatic contacts with the expanding Ottoman empire contributed to the progress of oriental studies in the later Middle Ages. Christian powers, such as some of the Italian states and Valois France, did not scruple to have loose ententes with Turkey at certain periods; but above all, it was commercial aspects across the Mediterranean basin, from Spain and Italy at one end to Turkey, the Black Sea region, Syria and Egypt at the other, which were the prime factor. At this period, it was Turkey and the Turks, rather than the Arabs, which became synonymous in the popular western Christian mind with Islam.

The humanism and cosmopolitanism of the Renaissance; the questing search for new frontiers in knowledge; the realization from the great discoveries that a Eurocentric conception of the universe was no longer valid; above all, the decline of religious passions as the Wars of Religion burnt themselves out, all contributed to a more dispassionate study of Islam. In the sixteenth century, the Roman Papacy encouraged the learning of oriental languages for missionary purposes, and specifically, in the interests of reunion with the Eastern Christian Churches which used Arabic or Syriac or Coptic as liturgical languages and with which Uniate Roman Catholic Churches were being formed. In this century can be found the first real orientalists, like Guillaume Postel (d. 1581), holder of the first chair of Arabic, established in 1539 at the Collège de France, and his pupil Joseph Scaliger (d. 1609); and in 1586 Arabic printing in Europe was facilitated by the use of the printing press set up by the Cardinal Grand Duke of Tuscany, Ferdinand de' Medici, from which emerged such works as Avicenna's books on medicine and philosophy and Arabic grammars.

In the seventeenth century, European princes and patrons and individual scholars began to collect Islamic manuscripts. Part of the Bodleian's Arabic and Hebrew holdings come from Archbishop Laud's donations of 1639–42; in 1634 he had procured a letter from Charles I to the Levant Company requiring that each of their ships returning from the Near East should bring back one Arabic or Persian manuscript. The first English chairs of Arabic were founded at Cambridge in 1632 by Sir Thomas Adams and at Oxford in 1634 by Laud. On the continent, Dutch scholars like Erpenius and Golius specialized in Arabic grammar and lexicography, and the Lorrainer Franz Meninski produced in 1680 a compendious Turkish dictionary which was published where one would expect interest in Turkish studies to be greatest, i.e. in Austria. General works on Islam as an institution and on Islamic culture and literature now appear, starting with the *Bibliothèque orientale* of Barthélemy d'Herbelot (d. 1695; his book was published for him posthumously by Antoine Galland in Paris in 1697), a pioneer effort at an *Encyclopaedia of Islām.* On the theological level, the view of Muḥammad as a devil and the Qur'ān as a farrago of nonsense was giving way to calmer views, encouraged by the growth of latitudinarianism and rationalism in England and philosophical attitudes in France, seen, for instance, in the article on Muḥammad in the philosopher Pierre Bayle's *Dictionnaire historique et critique* (2v. Rotterdam, 1697). Simon Ockley of Oxford, in his *History of the Saracens* (2v. London, 1708–18), following in Edward Pocock's footsteps, provided a historical account of remarkable dispassionateness, even though his description of Muḥammad as 'a very subtle and crafty man, who put on the appearance only of those good qualities; while the principles of his soul were ambition and lust' shows a reversion to earlier attitudes. However, in Germany and Holland, orientalism still remained more closely tied to Christian theological studies, the hope being here that the study of Arabic would elucidate the Old Testament text and throw light on the structure and vocabulary of Hebrew, still widely regarded as the language of God Himself.

Scientific orientalism may be said to have begun in France with Silvestre de Sacy and the establishment in Paris in 1795 of the École des Langues Orientales Vivantes, where there was laid stress not only on the study of oriental languages for historical and scientific purposes, but as the very name of the institution implied, on the pursuit of proficiency in the contemporary, spoken languages. The term 'orientalist' appeared in late eighteenth-century England and soon afterwards in France; the topic 'orientalisme' was treated in the *Dictionnaire de l'Académie Françiase* of 1838. Many orientalists, especially in Germany and Austria, began their careers as dragomans or consuls in the Near East. The Armenian Turk Mouradja d'Ohsson (1740–1807), author of the valuable *Tableau général de l'empire ottoman* (7v. Paris, 1788–1824), was in the early part of his life in the service of Sweden in Istanbul; Joseph von Hammer-Purgstall (1774–1856), founder of the first specialist orientalist journal in Europe, the *Fundgruben des Orients, bearbeitet durch eine Gesellschaft von Liebhabern* (6v. Vienna, 1809–18) and author of a long-standard history of the Ottomans, the *Geschichte des osmanischen Reiches* (10v. Pest, 1827–55), had been a dragoman in Istanbul and a consul in the Balkans for the Habsburg monarchy. Already in the late eighteenth century Sir William Jones (1746–94) had begun his series of *Asiatick researches* in Calcutta (1788).

Von Hammer's career brings us up to the period when there were enough scholars in Europe with general orientalist interests (embracing the fields of the ancient Near East and biblical studies, the Islamic world, Indian and Chinese studies) to justify the foundation of societies for the pursuit of oriental studies. First in the field was the Société Asiatique of Paris (1822), then the Royal Asiatic Society of Great Britain and Ireland (1823), the American Oriental Society (1842) and the Deutsche Morgenländische Gesellschaft (1845). All these societies very soon started journals of their own, the *Journal asiatique* in 1822, the *Journal of the Royal Asiatic Society* in 1834, the *Journal of the American Oriental Society* in 1843 and the *Zeitschrift der Deutschen Morgenländischen Gesellschaft* in 1847. The Indian counterparts of the Royal Asiatic Society in London, the Bengal and Bombay Asiatic Societies, also started their own journals in 1832 and 1841 respectively, replacing the earlier *Asiatick researches.*

It was not until the very end of the nineteenth century that Islamic studies were established as a separate discipline within general orientalism, and many of the giants of Arabic and Islamic studies of this time, such as Nöldeke, Goldziher and Wellhausen, were equally famed as general Semitists, Hebraists or biblical scholars. In 1895 there appeared at Paris the first journal devoted specifically to the Islamic world, the *Revue de l'Islam*, precursor of the *Revue du monde musulman* published by the Mission Scientifique du Maroc from 1906 onwards and now metamorphosed into the *Revue des études islamiques*. In Germany, *Der Islam* appeared from Strassbourg in 1910; in Russia, the short-lived *Mir Islama* from St. Petersburg in 1912; in Britain, *The Moslem world* from London in 1911. Noteworthy here is an intellectual link with the imperial policies of the European powers, who by the end of the nineteenth century had acquired amongst their colonial possessions vast expanses of Muslim territory. The founder of *Der Islam*, the scholar-statesman C. H. Becker (1876–1933) and the Hamburg University Seminar für Geschichte und Kultur des Orients were especially concerned with questions connected with Germany's African colonies and the alliance with Ottoman Turkey. The *Mitteilungen* of the University of Berlin's Orientalisches Seminar published much work on the contemporary languages and cultures of the German African territories and of the Arab and Turkish lands. W. Barthold (1869–1930), founder of *Mir Islama*, was much employed by the Imperial Russian and then Soviet governments for research into questions connected with Russian rule in Central Asia. The Dutch Islamist C. Snouck Hurgronje (1857–1936) had an important voice in the shaping of colonial and educational policy in the Dutch East Indies. British interest in the Islamic world had, of course, long been stimulated by the extension of British power in India; Indian civilians and soldiers in Muslim areas had to acquire some familiarity with Persian and Urdu-Hindi, and a knowledge of classical *Sharī'a* law was a necessary concomitant of the application of Anglo-Muhammadan law. A subordinate factor in the development of Islamic studies, exemplified in the founding of *The Moslem world* by S. M. Zwemer and in much German publishing, was the missionary one. But by the opening of the twentieth century, after much experience of missions in places like Muslim India, it was generally realized that direct Christian proselytism in the Muslim world was an uphill and largely unprodcutive work. Christian missionary literature concerning Islam is therefore now more concerned with achieving a sympathetic understanding of the Muslim religious spirit and genius, and the oecumenical and eirenical approach has found its apotheosis in the work of Louis Massignon (1883–1962) and his disciples.

In our own century, Islamic studies have inevitably become more and more specialized, and one discerns the beginnings of compartmentalization. New disciplines like political science, anthropology, sociology, comparative religion, &c., have increasingly become part of the tools of trade of an appreciable proportion of orientalists. A need for specialist journals has consequently arisen in recent years. Earlier efforts at this were usually premature, seen for instance in the ephemeral *Mitteilungen zur osmanischen Geschichte* (Vienna, 1922–26); it has really only been since the Second World War that we have seen the successful launching of journals like *Journal of the economic and social history of the Orient* (1958), *Turcica; revue d'études turques* (1969) and *Journal of Arabic literature* (1970).

A corollary of the foundation of orientalist societies and the publication of journals has been the holding of international congresses of the specialists concerned. Local orientalists' gatherings were held at an early date, e.g. in Germany at Dresden in 1849, and until the present, the Deutsche Orientalistentage have continued to be important, with published proceedings (the latest being the *XVIII. Deutscher Orientalistentag vom 1. bis 5. Oktober 1972 in Lübeck;* hrsg. W. Voigt [*ZDMG* Suppl. 2; Wiesbaden, 1974]). The first International Congress of Orientalists was held at Paris in 1873, and as early as 1905 these went outside Europe (to Algiers); the centennial Congress has appropriately been held at Paris in 1973. In all cases, detailed proceedings have been published (see below). Naturally, these congresses have comprehended the whole of oriental studies, over the geographical area from Muslim North Africa to Japan, and as the size of the congresses and the numbers of orientalists participating have grown, a need has been felt for more specialized, more intimate meetings of Islamic scholars alone. Out of this feeling have grown the Congresses of European Arabic and Islamic Studies, the first of which was held in Cordoba in 1962; eight have so far been held, and the proceedings of most of them published (see below). Other specialized bodies, like the Middle East Studies Association of North America, founded in 1966, hold regular meetings, and in the case of the latter body, publish jointly with the British Society for Middle Eastern Studies a journal, the *International journal of Middle East studies* (1970–). One of the newer disciplines which are influencing Islamic studies, sc. sociology, has received specific attention in the Colloque sur la sociologie musulmane held in Brussels in 1961 (*Actes* [Correspondance d'Orient, 5. Brussels, n.d.]), whilst specific problems in Islamic history have received attention at biennial colloquia held in Oxford since 1965 and, on one occasion, in Philadelphia; the papers presented have been published in book form, beginning with *The Islamic city*, ed. A. Hourani and S. M. Stern (Oxford, 1970). It should also be noted that Islam as a religious phenomenon has always been one aspect of the successive International Congresses for the History of Religions, the first of which was held in Paris in 1900 (*Actes* [Paris, 1901]) and the latest at Lancaster in 1975; in most cases, proceedings have been published (see below).

A comprehensive history of Islamic studies remains to be written. For the present, one may start from W. Barthold's historical section on European orientalism in his *La découverte de l'Asie*, tr. B. Nikitine (Paris, 1947), and from J. Fück's very useful and careful general history, *Die arabischen Studien in Europa bis in den Anfang des 20. Jahrhunderts* (Leipzig, 1955). A sketch of the changing image of Islam as it unfolded to western minds, with penetrating discussion of the different phases of orientalist scholarship, is given by M. Rodinson in his chapter 'The western image and western studies of Islam' in *The legacy of Islam*, 2nd edn., ed. J. Schacht and C. E. Bosworth (Oxford, 1973). For detail on the medieval period, when Islam was a menacing and frightening phenomenon to the West, see N. Daniel, *Islam and the West; the making of an image* (Edinburgh, 1960); R. W. Southern, *Western views of Islam in the Middle Ages* (Cambridge, Mass., 1962); U. Monneret de Villard, *Lo studio dell' Islām in Europa nel XII e nel XIII secolo* (Studi e testi, 110; Vatican City, 1944); and J. Kritzeck, *Peter the Venerable and Islam* (Princeton or. studies, 22; Princeton, 1964). The periods of the Renaissance, Reformation and Enlightenment have also attracted considerable attention, but there has been a concentration on particular aspects rather than on the period as a whole, with special attention to the cultural and literary vehicles for the adumbrating of Europeans' conceptions and misconceptions about Islam. See, for instance, R. Schwoebel, *The shadow of the crescent; the Renaissance image of the Turk, 1453–1517* (Nieuwkoop, 1967); C. D. Rouillard, *The Turk in French history, thought and literature (1520–1660)* (Paris, *c.* 1938); M.-L. Dufrenoy, *L'Orient romanesque en France, 1704–1789* (2v. Montreal, 1946–47); P. Martino, 'Mahomet en France au XVIIe et au XVIIIe siècle', in *Actes du XIVe Congrès International des Orientalistes, Alger, 1905. Troisieme partie: Langues musulmanes* (Paris, 1907), pp. 206–41, and *idem, L'Orient dans la littérature française au XVIIe et au XVIIIe siècle* (Paris, 1906). The Iberian peninsula, alone of western European lands, passed a considerable part of its history under Muslim Arab rule, and this has left profound and lasting effects on later Christian Spanish attitudes and sensibilities; their influence in the academic study of Spanish Islam is examined by J. T. Monroe, *Islam and the Arabs in Spanish scholarship (sixteenth century to the present)* (Medieval Iberian Peninsula texts and studies, 3; Leiden, 1970). Intellectual analysis of the phenomenon of Islam as a faith, by general philosophers and historians of the West as well as by professional orientalists, is skilfully traced in such works as H. Schipperges, *Ideologie und Historiographie des Arabismus* (Sudhoffs Archiv für Geschichte der Medizin und der Naturwissenschaften; Beihefte . . . Hft. 1; Wiesbaden, 1961); A. Hourani, 'Islam and the philosophers of history', *MES* **3**, 1967, pp. 206–68; and J.-J. Waardenburg, *L'Islam dans le miroir de l'Occident* (Maison des sciences de l'homme; Recherches Méditerranéennes, ét., 3; Paris, &c., 1963), this last being a study of the attitudes towards Islam of five great western orientalists, Ignaz Goldziher, C. H. Becker, C. Snouck Hurgronje, D. B. Macdonald and Louis Massignon.

Interest in Islamic studies and their practitioners amongst Islamic peoples themselves is a growth of recent decades, but European orientalists are included incidentally in Khair al-Din al-Ziriklī's biographical dictionary *Al-a'lām* (3rd rev. edn. 11v. in 12. Beirut, *c.* 1970, together with Muslim historical personnages and scholars. Recently there has appeared Najīb al-'Aqīqī's *Al-mustashriqūn* (3rd rev. edn. 3v. Cairo, 1964–65). One aspect of Muslim self-awareness in this century has been a certain reaction, most pronounced amongst Arabs, against the attitudes and techniques of European orientalists and their scholarship. This is exemplified in the Palestinian A. L. Tibawi's 'English-speaking orientalists: a critique of their approach to Islam and Arab nationalism', *MW* **53**, 1963, pp. 185–204, 298–313, also in *IQ* **8**, 1964, pp. 25–45, 73–88; and in the Egyptian Marxist Anouar Abdel-Malik's 'L'orientalisme en crise', *Diogène* **44**, 1963, pp. 109–42 (translated into English as 'Orientalism in crisis', *Diogenes* **44**, 1964, pp. 103–40), cf. the replies by Cahen and Gabrieli in *ibid.* **49**, 1965, pp. 135–8; **50**, 1965, pp. 128–36.

When Gabrieli compiled his chapter 'Orientalismo ed orientalisti' in the original edition of the *Manuale,* it was still possible for him to include a select list of names of European orientalists concerned with Arabic and Islamic studies. It is impossible to compile such a list nowadays, but there are certain sources from which names and addresses may be gleaned. Learned societies like the Société Asiatique, the Royal Asiatic Society, the American Oriental Society and the Deutsche Morgenländische Gesellschaft publish at intervals lists of members at the end of their respective journals. The circulation lists of bodies like the Middle East Studies Association of America, the Association of British Orientalists and the British Society for Middle Eastern Studies would also provide such information, though these are not generally accessible in print. The names of many Islamic scholars whose interests lie mainly in the classical period appear in the *Répertoire des médiévistes* (Lille, 1954; rev. edns. Poitiers, 1960 and 1971).

Hence the compilation of an exhaustive biographical dictionary of orientalists past and present would be an arduous and protracted task. Certain general works exist, like the very outdated one of G. Dugat, *Histoire des orientalistes de l'Europe du XIIe au XIXe siècle* (2v. Paris, 1868–70), and the very useful ones of Barthold and Fück mentioned above. However, the approach has more usually been through the orientalists of separate countries. For Germany, Fück's book is especially important, and see for the more recent period, R. Paret's *The study of Arabic and Islam at German universities; German orientalists since Theodor Nöldeke* (Wiesbaden, 1968). For Russia, we have the second half of Barthold's book, more recently, I. Yu. Krachkovsky's *Ocherki po istorii russkoi arabistiki* (Moscow, &c., 1950), German translation by O. Mehlitz, *Die russische Arabistik; Umrisse ihrer Entwicklung* (Leipzig, 1957) and N. A. Smirnov's *Ocherki istorii izucheniya Islama v SSSR* analysed in detail, with an introduction by A. K. S. Lambton, under the title *Islam and Russia* (London, 1956). Also of value here are the *Brief reviews* put out by the Nauka Publishing House, Central Department of Oriental Literature, under the title *Fifty years of Soviet oriental studies* (Moscow, 1968). The following are relevant to our present purpose: *Soviet orientalology and studies in the history of colonialism* and *History and economy of the Arab countries*. For Britain, there are four short monographs in a series published during the Second World War for publicity-cultural propaganda purposes: B. Lewis, *British contributions to Arabic studies* (London, 1941); A. J. Arberry, *British contributions to Persian studies* (London, 1942); *idem, British orientalists* (London, 1943); and H. Bowen, *British contributions to Turkish studies* (London, 1945). The biography of a great Scottish Old Testament scholar and Arabist, *The life of William Robertson Smith*, was written by J. S. Black and G. Chrystall (London, 1912); Arberry studied a pioneer orientalist in his *Asiatic Jones; the life and work of Sir William Jones (1746–1794), pioneer of Indian studies* (London, &c., 1946), and gave vignettes of several British orientalists, almost all Cambridge ones, in his *Oriental essays* (London, 1960). Arabic studies at Cambridge were surveyed by Arberry in his inaugural lecture, *The Cambridge School of Arabic* (Cambridge, 1948), and Islamic orientalism in Scotland by W. Montgomery Watt in his Edinburgh inaugural lecture, *Islamic studies in Scotland; retrospect and prospect* (Univ. of Edinburgh, Inaugural lecture No. 27; Edinburgh, 1965).

Few orientalists have deemed themselves important enough on the general scene of history and literature to write their own autobiography or memoirs, unless they have had eventful lives outside the strictly academic sphere, such as in diplomacy or the armed forces, as was the case with Sir E. Denison Ross in his *Both ends of the candle* (London, 1943) and Vincent Monteil in his *Soldat de fortune* (Paris, 1966). One must, however, exempt from this general rule such work as the classic study of one formative period in an orientalist's life, E. G. Browne's *A year amongst the Persians* (London, 1893 and later editions), and the delightful, semi-autobiographical book by Krachkovsky, *Among Arabic manuscripts; memories of libraries and men*, tr. T. Minorsky (Leiden, 1953); and Arberry concluded his *Oriental essays* by a chapter on himself.

The main source of biographical material for a dictionary of orientalists of the recent past would probably have to depend largely on obituary notices and appreciations in learned journals and even in newspapers. However, there are in some cases certain other sources available. One useful source of material lies in the studies frequently prefixed to bibliographies of the persons concerned, such as the study of E. Littmann by R. Paret and A. Schall, *Ein Jahrhundert Orientalistik. Lebensbilder . . . und Verzeichnis seiner Schriften, zum 80. Geburtstag zusammengestellt von R.P. und A.S.* (Wiesbaden, 1955). Biographical notices may be prefixed to works posthumously published, such as the studies of Joseph Marquart and his career written by H. H. Schaeder and Barthold and prefixed to Marquart's *Wehrot und Arang; Untersuchungen zur mythischen und geschichtlichen Landeskunde von Ostiran* (Leiden, 1938). Memorial volumes likewise often contain a memoir of the dedicatee, such as that in *Iran and Islam, in memory of the late Vladimir Minorsky*, ed. C. E. Bosworth (Edinburgh, 1971), and the memorial volume *Louis Massignon*, ed. Jean-François Six (Paris, 1970), treats of various aspects of the French scholar's career as remembered by various friends and colleagues. Another work devoted to his biography is G. Basetti-Sani, *Louis Massignon; orientalista cristiano*. Milan, 1971. Material like this in *Festschriften* and memorial volumes can best be tracked down with the aid of the 'List of sources' prefixed to J. D. Pearson's *Index Islamicus* (Cambridge, 1958 and supplements).

There have not as yet been many secondary studies on great orientalists and their work. Waardenburg's *L'Islam dans le miroir de l'Occident* has been mentioned above. The collective work, *Historians of the Middle East*, ed. B. Lewis and P. M. Holt (London, 1962), contains some studies of specific orientalists and their attitudes towards scholarship, including articles on G. Weil, Henri Lammens, Sir John Malcolm and Sir Percy Sykes; full-length studies of specific figures and their works, like Camille Hechaïmé's *Louis Cheikho et son livre 'Le christianisme et la littérature chrétienne en Arabie avant l'Islam': étude critique* (Publs. de l'Inst. de Lettres Orientales, Beyrouth; Recherches, 38; Beirut, 1967), are regrettably rare.

## List of the International Congresses of Orientalists

1. Paris, 1873 – *Compte-rendu*. 3v. Paris, 1874–76 (repr. Nendeln, 1967).
2. London, 1874 – *Transactions*. London, 1876 (repr. Nendeln, 1968).
3. St. Petersburg, 1876 – *Travaux*. 2v. St. Petersburg, &c., 1879–80 (repr. Nendeln, 1967).
4. Florence, 1878 – *Atti*. 2v. Florence, 1880–81 (repr. Nendeln, 1968).
5. Berlin, 1881 – *Verhandlungen*. 2v. 1881–82 (repr. Nendeln, 1968).
6. Leiden, 1883 – *Actes*. 4v. Leiden, 1884–85.
7. Vienna, 1886 – *Berichte und Verhandlungen*. 5v. in 2. Vienna, 1888–89 (repr. Nendeln, 1968).
8. Stockholm and Christiana, 1889 – *Actes, 2e à 4e partie*. (All publ.) 4v. Leiden, 1891–93.
9. London, 1892 – *Transactions*. 2v. London, 1893 (repr. Nendeln, 1968).
10. Geneva, 1894 – *Actes*. 4v. in 2. Leiden, 1895–97 (repr. Nendeln, 1968).
11. Paris, 1897 – *Actes*. 5v. in 2. Paris, 1898–99 (repr. Nendeln, 1968).
12. Rome, 1899 – *Actes*. 3v. Florence, 1901–2 (repr. Nendeln, 1968).
13. Hamburg, 1902 – *Verhandlungen*. Leiden, 1904.

14. Algiers, 1905 – *Actes* and *Recueil de mémoires*. 3v. and Suppl. in 5. Paris, 1906–8 (repr. Nendeln, 1968).
15. Copenhagen, 1908 – *Actes*. Copenhagen, 1909 (repr. Nendeln, 1968).
16. Athens, 1912 – *Actes*. Athens, 1912 (repr. Nendeln, 1968).
17. Oxford, 1928 – *Proceedings*. Oxford, 1929 (repr. Nendeln, 1968).
18, Leiden, 1931 – *Actes*. Leiden, 1932.
19. Rome, 1935 – *Atti*. Rome, 1938.
20. Brussels, 1938 – *Actes*. Louvain, 1940.
21. Paris, 1948 – *Actes*. Paris, 1949.
22. Istanbul, 1951 – *Proceedings*. 2v. Istanbul, &c., 1953–57.
23. Cambridge, 1954 – *Proceedings*. London, 1956.
24. Munich, 1957 – *Akten*. Wiesbaden, 1959.
25. Moscow, 1960 – *Trudy*. 5v. Moscow, 1962–63.
26. New Delhi, 1964 – *Proceedings*. 4v. Delhi, &c., 1966–70.
27. Ann Arbor, 1967 – *Proceedings*. Wiesbaden, 1971.
28. Canberra, 1971 – In preparation.
29. Paris, 1973 – *Actes*. Paris, 1975.
30. Mexico City, 1975.

List of the Congresses of Arabic and Islamic Studies

1. Cordoba, 1962 – *Actas*. Madrid, 1964.
2. Cambridge, 1964 – Never published.
3. Ravello, 1966 – *Atti*. Naples, 1967.
4. Coimbra and Lisbon, 1968 – *Actas*. Leiden, 1971(5).
5. Brussels, 1970 – *Actes*. (Correspondance d'Orient, 11.) Brussels, 1971.
6. Visby, Stockholm, 1972 – Stockholm & Leiden, 1975.
7. Göttingen, 1974.
8. Aix-en-Provence, 1976.

List of the International Congresses for the History of Religions

1. Paris, 1900 – *Actes*. 2 pts. Paris, 1901.
2. Basel, 1904 – *Verhandlungen*. Basel, 1905.
3. Oxford, 1908 – *Transactions*. 2v. Oxford, 1908.
4. Leiden, 1912 – *Actes*. Leiden, 1913.
5. Lund, 1927 – *Actes*. Lund, 1930.
6. Brussels, 1935 – Never published.
7. Amsterdam, 1950 – *Proceedings*. Amsterdam, 1951.
8. Rome, 1955 – *Atti*. Florence, 1956.
9. Tokyo and Kyoto, 1958 – *Proceedings*. Tokyo, 1960.
10. Marburg, 1960 – *X. Internationaler Kongress* . . . Marburg, 1961.
11. Claremont, 1965 – *Proceedings*. 3v. Leiden, 1968.
12. Stockholm, 1970 – *Proceedings*. Supplement to *Numen* **31**. Leiden, 1975.
13. Lancaster, 1975.

# Institutions

J. D. PEARSON

Chapter 6 of Gabrieli (Didattica e propedeutica islamica, antica e moderna) is not superseded by this chapter. No attempt has been made to bring up to date the information given there on education and schools in Muslim countries. Nor has a revised list of *madrasas* been compiled. Also to give, as Gabrieli did, an alphabetical list by town of institutions of higher learning, research establishments, learned societies and the like would require a whole volume and is manifestly impossible within the confines of the present work. We content ourselves, therefore, with giving references to books and articles which might be used in the compilation of such a reference work.

The *International directory of institutes and societies interested in the Middle East*, by F. Ljunggren and C. L. Geddes (Amsterdam, 1962), though antiquated and studded with errors and misprints, is not without value. A new edition was promised some years ago, but this has not yet seen the light of day.

Of the three main guides to the universities of the world, the *Commonwealth universities yearbook* is most conveniently used for our purpose. The index entries 'Islamic studies, Middle Eastern studies, Oriental studies, Arabic' and similar entries will direct to departments, teaching and research appointments in the universities of Australia, Bangladesh, Canada, Ceylon, Ghana, India, Malaya, Malta, Nigeria, Pakistan, the United Kingdom, South Africa and the Republic of Ireland. From the other two reference books *American universities and colleges* and *International handbook of universities*, information on Arab Islamic studies can be extracted only at the expense of much labour. The same may be said of the international handbooks *World of learning* and *Minerva*.

Earlier works on these studies may be traced through *Index Islamicus*, section I.b, *passim*, through *Abstracta islamica* (VII – E), for an earlier period through *Annuaire du monde musulman*, which, regrettably, has not appeared since 1955, and earlier still, from the various issues of *Revue du monde musulman*.

A series of articles on *Les études islamiques dans le monde* appeared in *REI* between 1965 and 1970:

I. *REI* **33**, 1965, pp. 187–97
'Note liminaire' (H. Laoust).
'Les études islamiques à Oxford' (D. S. Richards and S. M. Stern).
'Note sur l'Orientalisme en Algérie' (A. Lézine).
'Le classement des documents Max van Berchem à Genève' (J. Sourdel-Thomine).

II. *REI* **34**, 1966, pp. 195–214
'Les études islamiques à Bruxelles et Gand' (A. Abel).
'Les études arabes et islamiques à la Faculté des Lettres d'Aix-en-Provence' (A. Adam).
'Les études arabes à la Faculté des Lettres de Bordeaux' (D. Sourdel).

'L'enseignement des langues et de la civilisation islamiques à Strasbourg' (T. Fahd).
III. *REI* **35**, 1967, pp. 231–9
'L'enseignement des études arabes à l'Université de Louvain' (G. Ryckmans).
'L'Institut cultural hispano-arabe de Madrid' (R. Arié).
'L'Institut égyptien d'études islamiques de Madrid.'
IV. *REI* **36**, 1968, pp. 167–9
'L'étude du monde islamique à l'Université de Michigan, Ann Arbor, Michigan' (O. Grabar).
V. *REI* **36**, 1968, pp. 331–5
'Les études arabes et islamiques à l'Université de Barcelone' (J. Vernet Ginés).
'L'école d'études arabes de Madrid (Institut Miguel Asín).'
VI. *REI* **37**, 1969, pp. 161–6
'Les études islamiques en Bulgarie' (B. A. Cvetkova).
'Les études islamiques à Haidarabad-Deccan' (M. Hamidullah).
VII. *REI* **37**, 1969, pp. 351–61
'Les études islamiques en Roumanie' (M.-M. Alexandrescu-Dersca Bulgaru).
VIII. *REI* **38**, 1970, pp. 173–5
'Les études islamiques à Édimbourg' (P. Cachia).

The Middle East Studies Association of the U.S.A. has published two editions of *Graduate and undergraduate programs and courses in Middle East studies in the United States, Canada and abroad* (*MESA bull.*, special supplement 1970 and 1972).

The same organization has also published at various times in its *Bulletin* articles on research facilities in Middle Eastern countries. The following have appeared up to now:

Iran. *MESA bull.* **3**, iii (addenda in **6**, i; **6**, ii; **6**, iii; **7**, i; **7**, iii)
Algeria. **4**, i
U.A.R. **4**, ii (addenda in **5**, ii)
Morocco. **4**, iii (addenda in **7**, iii)
Turkey. **5**, i (addenda in **6**, i; **6**, ii; **7**, ii; **9**, ii)
Tunisia. **6**, i
Lebanon. **6**, iii
Israel. **7**, i (addenda in **7**, iii)
Sudan. **7**, ii (addenda in **9**, ii)
Syria. **8**, i
Yemen. **8**, iii
Afghanistan. **9**, i

## I. UNITED KINGDOM

In addition to the information tabulated in *Commonwealth universities yearbook*, which may be supplemented from the Calendars issued by the several universities, The British Society for Middle Eastern Studies began in the first issue of its *Bulletin* (1974), a series of contributions by representatives of 'Middle Eastern studies in British universities'.

## II. FRANCE

CAHEN, Cl. & PELLAT, Ch., 'Les études arabes et islamiques'. (In *Cinquante ans d'orientalisme en France (1922–1972)*, *JA*, numéro spécial, 256, 1973, pp. 89–107.)

Arabic and Islamic studies are pursued in a variety of institutions in France. In Paris facilities are provided at the Institut National des Langues et Civilisations Orientales (formerly École des Langues Orientales Vivantes) as well as at four or five of the new universities, at the École Pratique des Hautes Études, and elsewhere. In the provinces these subjects are cultivated in the universities of Aix, Bordeaux, Lyons and Strasbourg. One must add the Centre National de Recherche Scientifique, especially for the Arabic section of the Institut de Recherche et d'Histoire des Textes and the French institutes overseas, Institut Français d'Études Arabes in Damascus and Institut Français d'Archéologie Orientale in Cairo, not forgetting the contributions of French scholars to studies in the former colonies.

## III. GERMANY

BÜREN, R., *Gegenwartsbezogene Orientwissenschaft in der Bundesrepublik Deutschland. Gegenstand, Lage und Förderungsmöglichkeiten. Mit einem von der Dokumentationsleitstelle Moderner Orient erstellten Verzeichnis von Institutionen mit gegenwartsbezogener Forschung zu der Region Vorderer und Mittlerer Orient*, ed. M. D. Ahmed and I. Otto. Göttingen, 1974.

This work, sponsored by the Volkswagen Foundation, studies how far the Near and Middle East forms the subject of research, teaching, study and documentation in university and other institutions in West Germany. The major part of the book is taken up by a list arranged by location of institutions concerned with contemporary study of the Near and Middle East in the BDR. It contains 161 entries, with information tabulated under a maxim of 34 heads about organizations from Aachen to Würzburg with interests in Oriental and Islamic studies; social sciences in the broader sense; the natural and applied sciences and medicine; economic sciences; interdisciplinary and international co-operation.

## IV. UNITED STATES

Regular information can be obtained from the *MESA bulletin*, particularly its *Graduate and undergraduate programs and courses in Middle East studies in the United States, Canada and abroad*, which has already been mentioned.

# Arabic manuscripts: general

J. D. PEARSON

## I. PALAEOGRAPHY

GROHMANN, A., *Arabische Paläographie.* (Öster. Akad. Wiss., phil.-hist. Kl., Denkschriften 94, Abh., 1–.) Vienna, 1967–.
(i) Einleitung, die Beschreibstoffe, die Schreibgeräte, die Tinte. 1967.
(ii) Das Schriftwesen. Die Lapidarschrift. 1971.

The first volume of Grohmann's monumental work contains in the introduction chapters on previous works on Arabic palaeography by Islamic writers and on the development of the study of the subject in the Western world. Also provided are discussions on the many types of material which have received writing (beginning with papyrus and ranging through materials of vegetable origin such as palm-leaves, bark, wood, linen, cotton and paper, and those of animal origin, silk, leather, parchment, bone, to clay, ostraca, stone, glass and metal) and on the various tools of the writer's trade, from pens, implements for cutting and sharpening them, to sand used in blotting, paste, and utensils for holding these commodities, to whetstones, polishing stones, scissors, rulers, and wiping cloths. A further section deals with ink.

The second volume (1971) is concerned with the scripts, mainly Kufic, used in epigraphy. It is hoped that a third will deal with the whole subject of writing on soft materials.

## II. EXAMPLES OF SCRIPTS

MORITZ, B., *Arabic palaeography; a collection of Arabic texts from the first century of the Hidjra till the year 1000.* (Publs. Khedivial Library, Cairo, 16.) Cairo, 1905.

ARBERRY, A. J., *Specimens of Arabic and Persian palaeography*; selected and annotated. London, 1939.

VAJDA, G., *Album de paléographie arabe.* Paris, 1958.

-MUNAJJID, Ṣalāḥ al-Dīn, *Le manuscrit arabe jusqu'au Xe siècle de l'Hégire.* Vol. 1: *Spécimens.* Cairo, 1960.

## III. LISTS OF COLLECTIONS AND CATALOGUES

### (a) General

VAJDA, G. & DURANTET, M., *Répertoire des catalogues et inventaires de manuscrits arabes.* Paris, 1949.

HUISMAN, A. J. W., *Les manuscrits arabes dans le monde; une bibliographie des catalogues.* Leiden, 1967.

SEZGIN, F., *Geschichte des arabischen Schrifttums.* Leiden, 1967–.
(i) (pp. 706–69); Bibliotheken und Sammlungen arabischer Handschriften.
(iii) (pp. 392–410); Nachträge.

PEARSON, J. D., *Oriental manuscripts in Europe and North America; a survey.* (Bibliotheca Asiatica, 7.) Zug, 1971.
pp. 189–345: Arabic, Persian, Turkish.

UTAS, B., 'Notes on some public and semi-public libraries in the Near and Middle East containing Persian and other Moslem manuscripts'. *Acta Or.* **33**, 1971, pp. 169–92.

The earlier repertory of Vajda and Durantet is now virtually superseded by that of Huisman, though the former contains material which may still be of some interest in section B: 'Recherches de bibliothèques et notices de fonds non catalogués'.

Huisman included notices of Karshuni and Christian Arabic MSS., as well as of Hebrew manuscripts in Arabic characters which, naturally enough, were not mentioned in the lists appended by Sezgin to his *GAS*. These latter, however, occasionally give information on collections not as yet catalogued.

Pearson's work, restricted to Europe and North America, attempts to give information on all collections of manuscripts, whether catalogued or not.

### (b) Individual Countries

GABRIELI, G., *Manoscritti e carte orientali nelle biblioteche e negli archivi d'Italia; dati statistici e bibliografici delle collezioni, loro storia e catalogazione.* Florence, 1930.

Supplemented by:

—— 'Documenti orientali nelle biblioteche e negli archivi d'Italia'. *Accademie e biblioteche* **7**, 1933–34, pp. 287–304.

AKADEMIYA NAUK SSSR, INSTITUT NARODOV AZII, *Vostokovedenye fondy krupneyshikh bibliotek Sovetskogo Soyuza; stat'i i soobshcheniya.* Moscow, 1963.

Translated as:

TVERITINOVA, A. S., *Selections from the holdings in Oriental studies in the great libraries of the Soviet Union. Articles and notes.* Honolulu, 1967.

'AWWĀD, Gūrgīs, 'Al-makhṭūṭāt al-'arabiyya fī dūr al-kutub al-amīrikiyya'. *Sumer* **7**, 1951, pp. 237–77.

VANDEWOUDE, E. & VANRIE, A., *Guide des sources de l'histoire d'Afrique du Nord, d'Asie et d'Océanie conservées en Belgique.* (Guide des sources de l'hist. des nations, III/i.) Brussels, 1972.

### (c) Individual Libraries

SUTTON, S. C., *A guide to the India Office Library with a note on the India Office Records.* 2nd edn. London, 1967.

Arabic MSS., pp. 32–5.

TAYLOR, F., 'The Oriental manuscript collections in the John Rylands Library'. *Bull. of the John Rylands Library* **54**, 1972, pp. 449–78.

Arabic: 802 papyri, 1483 paper fragments, 857 codices.

GABRIELI, G., *La Fondazione Caetani per gli studi musulmani. Notizia della sua istituzione e catalogo dei suoi mss. orientali*. Rome, 1926.

BEESTON, A. F. L., 'The Oriental manuscript collections of the Bodleian Library'. *Bodl. Lib. record* **5**, 1954–55, pp. 73–9.

BESE, L., 'Die orientalische Sammlung der Bibliothek der Ungarischen Akademie der Wissenschaften'. (In K. Schubart-Engelschall *ed., Orientalische Bibliotheken und Sammlungen*, Berlin, 1970, pp. 69–72.)

Arabic: 130 MSS. The catalogue is to be published in seven volumes.

GUBOGLU, M., *Manuscrisele orientale din biblioteca Academiei Romîne cu inventarul lor*. (An. Acad. Rom., Mem. Sect. Ist., ser. 3, tom XXVIII, mem. 4, pp. 77–126.) Bucharest, 1946.

## IV. UNION CATALOGUES

VOORHOEVE, P., *Handlist of Arabic manuscripts in the Library of the University of Leiden and other collections in the Netherlands*. Leiden, 1957.

ZAKŁAD ORIENTALISTYKI POLSKIEJ AKADEMII NAUK, *Catalogue des manuscrits arabes*, par W. Dembski, sous la direction de A. Zajączkowski. (Catalogue des manuscrits orientaux des collections polonaises, tome 5, 1ère partie.) Warsaw, 1964.

The union catalogue of Arabic manuscripts in Germany will form volume 17 of the series 'Verzeichnis der orientalischen Handschriften in Deutschland' and will be compiled by R. Sellheim and others.

## V. BOOKSELLERS' CATALOGUES

Very good descriptions of manuscripts, sometimes accompanied by illustrations, occur in the catalogues produced for sale by booksellers such as Harrassowitz, and by auctioneers such as Sotheby, whose series 'Bibliotheca Philippica' contains much material of interest to the Arabist. A list of manuscripts described in such sources would be of great value to the Arabist.

## VI. THE INSTITUTE OF ARABIC MANUSCRIPTS

Founded around 1946 the Maʿhad (Iḥyāʾ) al-Makhṭūṭāt al-ʿArabiyya (Institut des Manuscrits Arabes), a department of ALECSO, the Arab League Educational, Cultural and Scientific Organization, has microfilmed many thousands of Arabic manuscripts in collections in Asia, Africa and Europe. A series of catalogues of these, *Fihris al-makhṭūṭāt al-muṣawwara* was published in four volumes (eight parts), by various authors between 1957 and 1964. Since 1955 the Institute has published a review, *Majallat Maʿhad al-Makhṭūṭāt al-ʿArabiyya* (*Revue de l'Institut des Manuscrits Arabes*) which regularly publishes catalogues of MSS., articles based on individual or groups of MSS., and criticisms of published works. A monthly newsletter, *Akhbār al-turāth al-ʿarabī*, has been issued in duplicated typescript since 1971.

A former director of the Institute, Ṣalāḥ al-Dīn al-Munajjid, set out its objectives in a pamphlet presented to the XXIVth International Conference of Orientalists in 1957: *Activités de l'Institut des Manuscrits Arabes* (Cairo, 1957). Munajjid is also the author of *A dictionary of Arabic manuscripts edited between 1954–1960, 1961–1965* and *1966–1970* as well as of a code of rules for cataloguing Arabic MSS. and the volume of palaeographical specimens mentioned above. He has also edited many manuscripts from various collections:

*Muʿjam al-makhṭūṭāt al-maṭbūʿa* . . . Beirut.
1954–1960. Published 1962.
1961–1964. 1967.
1966–1970. 1973.

*Qawāʿid fahrasat al-makhṭūṭāt al-ʿarabiyya*. Beirut, 1973.

The Service des Manuscrits Arabes of the Syrian Ministry of Culture and National Guidance (Wizārat al-Thaqāfa wa-al-Irshād al-Qawmī) has published since 1968 a *Bulletin bibliographique* of microfilms of its Arabic MSS.: *Nashra maktabiyya li-al-makhṭūṭāt al-ʿarabiyya al-muṣawwara* . . .

# Illuminated Arabic manuscripts

E. M. F. JACHIMOWICZ

On first perusal of the following bibliography of illuminated Arabic manuscripts the reader may find it strange that the titles listed seldom refer directly to Arabic book illumination or Arabic miniatures. In most cases the references are to Persian book painting and miniatures or simply to Islamic painting in general. This touches on a problem which has occupied students of Islamic art for many decades, and which must be considered here briefly in order to justify the arrangement of this bibliography.

The key question which has been the cause of much dispute and controversy amongst art historians and has caused some confusion to the admirers of Islamic pictorial art is this: is one justified in speaking about Arab art? Has there ever been such a thing as genuine Arab art, or was it not rather the case that the Arabs, in the course of their conquests of neighbouring countries, which had ancient and highly developed artistic traditions of their own, like Persia, and lacking such traditions themselves, adopted these foreign styles of art? The problem in the case of book illumination was whether a distinction should be made between Arab and Persian miniature painting, or whether there are no real grounds for assuming the existence of a true Arab style of miniature art. This controversy is reflected in some of the titles in this bibliography.

Without going any deeper into this problem here, one has to bear in mind when using the following bibliography that the titles referring to Persian miniatures may also contain references to Arab paintings. Hence, illuminations contained in Arabic manuscripts are referred to throughout as Arab. This criterion was chosen as being the most convenient for the compilation of a bibliography. It gives a fairly clear idea of the limitations of the scope of the latter so far as subject is concerned, and so avoids the tricky questions of style and provenance of the illuminations.

A bibliography of such a highly specialized subject is bound to intersect with those of related fields, with subjects for instance such as Persian, Moghul, Turkish and Byzantine book painting, Islamic art in general, exhibition catalogues, and various others such as medicine, pharmacology, astronomy and astrology, navigation, cosmology, music and mechanics, all of which may contain references to miniatures, paintings and iconography.

The most important bibliographical works on this subject are Creswell's *Bibliography of painting in Islam*, Holter's *Die islamischen Miniaturhandschriften vor 1350*, and the Supplementary List to the latter by Buchthal, Kurz and Ettinghausen. These are bibliographies only, but practically all the works listed below contain substantial bibliographical sections. The difficulty in compiling this particular bibliography was that the majority of the titles are of articles and accounts to be found in a very wide range of periodicals. Some of them were found in places where one would scarcely have thought of looking for literature on this subject.

As to the arrangement of the bibliography, it has been done in one particular way, but other methods of arrangement might have been used equally well. This particular system attempts to show clearly the varied contexts in which one may find literature on Arabic book painting.

The General Section contains a group of titles which are general surveys on Islamic art, but also contains works and bibliographical notes on Arabic book illumination in particular. This group deserves special attention because some of the best general studies on Arabic miniature art appear as chapters or sections in the works listed here. This is followed by general surveys which deal solely with Arabic book illumination. These are very few in number. The last heading within the General Section includes various kinds of catalogues. The reason for listing so many of these is that they are not just descriptive lists, but very often contain general notes on their subject, together with many valuable bibliographical notes.

The second section is entitled 'Individual Studies' because the works listed here are all on particular manuscripts and specialized topics. Such is the case with the titles relating to the schools of Arabic book illumination. Opinions among scholars differ considerably regarding the geographical and historical limitations of these schools. Next come various studies on individual manuscripts. This section is divided into several sub-sections for those works of literature and science which were embellished with miniatures and illuminations. The studies on Qur'an illuminations are listed separately. Apart from very rare exceptions, Qur'an manuscripts do not contain miniatures and therefore the illumination is normally confined to *'unwāns*, frontispieces, medallions, sūra headings and colophons, &c.

The first group of titles in the third section relates to comparisons between styles of Arabic illuminations and those of neighbouring cultural areas. The mutual influences between these are obvious and, therefore, this field of research has always been popular with art historians, both Islamic and non-Islamic. The titles in the second group deal with the iconographic details of the miniatures with reference to the corresponding texts, and as historic sources for various aspects of medieval Islamic culture.

A final heading has been added to cover 'Works on various topics containing references to Arabic illuminated manuscripts'. The list under this heading is somewhat tentative.

## I. GENERAL

### *General surveys on Islamic art and Islamic painting, with sections on Arabic book illumination*

A.A., *Zum Schrift- und Buchwesen des Orients. Nebst vermischten Beiträgen aus dem Gesamtgebiete der Schrift- und Buchgeschichte.* Leipzig, 1938.

AHLENSTIEL-ENGEL, E., *Arabische Kunst.* Breslau, 1923.

AMJAD, Ali S., 'Muslim painting'. *Pakistan Qtly* **2**, iv, 1952, pp. 8–13, 63–4.

ANAND, Mulk Raj, *Persian painting.* (Criterion miscellany, 25.) London, [1931].

ARNOLD, T. W., 'Taswīr'. (In *EI*[1].)

—— *Painting in Islam; a study of the place of pictorial art in Muslim culture.* Oxford, 1928.

ARNOLD, T. W. & GROHMANN, A., The Islamic book; a contribution to its art from the seventh to the eighteenth century. Florence, 1929. German edition: *Denkmäler islamischer Buchkunst*. Munich, 1929.

BACHHOFER, L., 'Zur islamischen Buchkunst'. *Pantheon* **5**, 1930, pp. 45–9.

BADAWĪ, 'Abd al-Raḥmān, 'The contribution of the Arabs to Islamic art'. *RSO* **39**, 1964, pp. 261–85.

BETZ, G., *Orientalische Miniaturen*. Brunswick, 1965.

BINYON, L., *The spirit of man in Asian art*. Cambridge, Mass., 1935.

BLAUENSTEINER, K., 'Zur Entwicklung der Bildform in der islamischen Miniaturmalerei'. *Graphische Künste* N.F. **1**, 1936, pp. 41–56.

BLOCHET, E., 'Les écoles de peinture en Perse'. *Rev. arch.* 4e sér., **6**, 1905, pp. 121–48.

—— 'Les miniatures des manuscrits musulmans'. *Gazette des beaux-arts* 3e pér., **17**, 1897, pp. 281–96; **18**, 1897, pp. 105–18.

—— *Musulman painting, XIIth–XVIIth century*, trans. by C. Binyon. London, 1929.

—— 'Les origines de la peinture en Perse'. *Gazette des beaux-arts* 3e pér., **34**, 1905, pp. 115–30.

BRAUN, E. W., 'Das Kunstgewerbe im Kulturgebiete des Islam'. (In G. Lehnert, *Illustrierte Geschichte des Kunstgewerbes*, vol. 2, Berlin, 1909.)

BURGOIN, J., *Précis de l'art arabe*. Paris, 1892.

CHRISTIE, A. H., 'The development of ornament from Arabic script'. *Burlington magazine* **40**, 1922, pp. 287–92; **41**, 1922, pp. 34–41.

DENIKÉ, B., *Zhivopis' Irana*. Moscow, 1938.

DIEZ, E., *Iranische Kunst*. Vienna, 1944.

—— *Die Kunst der iranischen Völker*. Berlin, 1917.

DIMAND, M. S., *A handbook of Mohammedan art*. 3rd edn. New York, 1958.

—— 'Islamic miniature painting and book illumination'. *Bull. of the Metropolitan Museum of Art* **28**, 1933, pp. 166–71.

—— 'Islamic miniature paintings and drawings'. *Bull. of the Metropolitan Museum of Art* **35**, 1940, pp. 240–2.

—— 'Oriental miniatures'. *Bull. of the Metropolitan Museum of Art* **20**, 1925, pp. 124–8.

DU RY, C. J., *Art of Islam*, trans. by A. Brown. New York, 1972.

ERDMANN, K., 'Über die Anfänge der islamischen Kunst'. *OLZ* **57**, 1962, pp. 5–9.

ETTINGHAUSEN, R., 'Interaction and integration in Islamic art'. (In G. E. von Grunebaum *ed.*, *Unity and variety in Muslim civilisation*, Chicago, 1955, pp. 107–31.)

FAGO, V., *Arte araba. I: L'arte araba nella Siria e in Egitto*. Rome, 1909.

FALKE, O. von, 'Zur Entwicklungsgeschichte des muhammedanischen Ornaments'. *Kunstgewerbeblatt* N.F. **5**, 1894, pp. 169–77.

FARÈS, Bishr, *Essai sur l'esprit de la décoration islamique*. Cairo, 1952.

FARMER, H. G., *Islam*. (Musikgeschichte in Bildern, 3.) Leipzig, 1966.

GABRIELI, F., 'La miniatura orientale musulmana'. *Emporium* **68**, 1928, pp. 231–41.

GABRIEL-ROUSSEAU, *L'art decoratif musulman*. Paris, 1934.

GAYET, A., *L'art arabe*. Paris, 1893.

GRAY, B., *Persian painting*. London, 1930.

—— *Persian painting, from miniatures of the XIII–XVI centuries*. London, 1948.

GRUBE, E. J., *Islamic painting*. New York, 1972.

HOLTER, K., 'Islamische Miniaturen; Probleme und Forschungen'. *WZKM* **52**, 1953, pp. 116–24.

HUART, C., *Les calligraphes et les miniaturistes de l'orient musulman*. Paris, 1908 (repr. Osnabrück, 1972).

İPŞİROĞLU, Mazhar S., *Das Bild in Islam; ein Verbot und seine Folgen*. Vienna, 1971.

IVANOV, V., 'Peinture et poésie en Orient'. *Orient* **4**, 1957, pp. 7–16.

KOTOV, G., 'Arabskoe iskusstvo'. (In *Bol'shaya Sovyetskaya Entsiklopediya* **3**, 1926, pp. 207–12.)

KUBIČKOVA, V., 'O knize v zemích Islámu. III: Miniatura'. *Novy Orient* **9**, 1954, pp. 122–3.

KÜHNEL, E., *Islamische Kleinkunst*. (Bibliothek für Kunst- und Antiquitätensammler, 25.) Berlin, 1925. English edition: *Islamic arts*, trans. from the 2nd German edition by K. Watson. London, 1970.

—— 'Die islamische Kunst'. (In A. Springer *ed.*, *Handbuch der Kunstgeschichte* **6**, Leipzig, 1929.)

—— *Die Kunst des Islam*. Stuttgart, 1962.

—— *Kunst und Kultur der arabischen Welt*. Heidelberg, 1943.

—— 'La miniatura dell'arte islamica'. (In *Encyclopedia Italiana* **23**, 1934, pp. 374–6.)

—— *Miniaturmalerei im islamischen Orient*. (Die Kunst des Ostens, 7.) Berlin, 1922; 2nd edn. 1923. French edition: *La miniature en Orient*, trans. by P. Budry. Paris, 1924.

—— *Persische Miniaturmalerei; 13. Jahrhundert bis 17. Jahrhundert*. Berlin, 1959.

—— 'Das Schriftornament in der islamischen Kunst'. *Buch und Schrift* **4**, 1931.

LANCI, M., 'Delle calligrafiche fantasie'. (In *Seconda opera cufica* (2), 1846, pp. 209–49.)

LAVOIX, H., 'Les peintures musulmans'. *Revue de l'Orient, de l'Algérie et des colonies* N.S. **9**, 1859, pp. 353–69.

LOREY, E. de, 'Peinture musulmane ou peinture iranienne'. *RAA* **12**, i, 1938, pp. 20–31.

MARTIN, F. R., *The miniature painting and painters of Persia, India and Turkey, from the eighth to the eighteenth century*. 2v. London, 1912.

MARZŪK, Muḥammad 'Abd al-'Azīz, *Al-Islām wa-al-funūn al-jamīla*. Cairo, 1944.

MASSÉ, H., 'L'imagerie populaire de l'Iran'. *Arts asiatiques* **7**, 1960, pp. 163–78.

MASSIGNON, L., 'Les méthodes de réalisation artistique des peuples de l'Islam'. *Syria* **2**, 1921, pp. 47–53, 149–60.

—— 'Remarks on Moslem art'. *Verve* **1**, iii, 1938, pp. 16–27.

MIGEON, G., *Manuel d'art musulman.* Vol. 2: *Les arts plastiques et industriels.* 2nd edn. Paris, 1927.

MUNTHE, G., *Islams Konst.* Stockholm, 1929.

OTTO-DORN, K., *Kunst des Islam.* (Also English and French editions.) Baden-Baden, 1964.

PEDERSEN, J., *Islams Kultur.* Copenhagen, 1928.

POPE, A. U., *An introduction to Persian art since the seventh century A.D.* London, 1930.

POPE, A. U. & ACKERMAN, P. *eds., A survey of Persian art from prehistoric times to the present* . . . (Published under the auspices of the Asia Inst., Pahlavi Univ., Shiraz.) 9v. Oxford, 1938–39 (repr. 14v., vols. 1–13 2nd edn., London, 1965–67).

Contributions in vol. III:

IX. Painting and the art of the book:

48. Book painting:

Arnold, T. W. A: 'The origins', pp. 1809–19.

B. 'The influence of poetry and theology on painting', pp. 1904–10.

Behzad, H. Taherzade H. 'The preparation of the miniaturist's materials', pp. 1921–7.

Binyon, L. 'The qualities of beauty in Persian painting', (F.), pp. 1911–17.

Kuhnel, E. C: 'History of miniature painting and drawing', pp. 1829–97.

Laurie, A. P. G: 'The pigments and medium', pp. 1918–20.

Monneret de Villard, U. 'The relations of Manichaean art to Iranian art', (B.), pp. 1820–8.

49. Massignon, L. 'The origins of the transformation of Persian iconography by Islamic theology. The Schi'a School of Kufa and its Manichaean connections', pp. 1928–36.

50. Ettinghausen, R. 'Manuscript illumination', pp. 1937–74.

PRISSE D'AVENNES, *L'art arabe d'après les monuments du Kaire.* Paris, 1877 (repr. Dordrecht, &c., 1974).

RIEFSTAHL, R. M., 'La décoration du livre oriental'. *Art et décoration* **32**, 1912, pp. 33–46.

RODENBERG, J., 'Die arabische Schrift als Ornament'. *Buch und Schrift* **2**, 1928, pp. 63–6.

—— *Buchkunst des Morgenlandes.* Leipzig, 1948.

ROSS, E. D., 'The origins of Persian painting'. *Apollo* **12**, 1930, pp. 315–22.

SACS, J., 'La miniatura musulmana'. *Museum* **7**, 1927, pp. 165–83.

SAKISIAN, A., 'Coexistent schools of Persian miniature painting'. *Burlington magazine* **76**, 1940, pp. 144–55.

—— *La miniature persane du XIIe au XVIIe siècle.* Paris, 1929.

SALLES, G., 'Les arts musulmans'. (In L. Réau, *Histoire universelle des arts* **4**, Paris, 1939, pp. 1–102.)

SCHULZ, P. W., 'Die islamische Malerei'. *Orientalisches Archiv* **1**, 1910–11, pp. 12–15, 79–82.

—— *Die persisch-islamische Miniaturmalerei.* 2v. Leipzig, 1914.

STCHOUKINE, I., *Les miniatures persanes*. Paris, 1932.
—— *La peinture iranienne sous les derniers 'Abbasides et les Il-Khâns*. Bruges, 1936.

-SUFYĀNĪ, Abū al-'Abbās Aḥmad b. Muḥammad, *Ṣinā'at tasfīr al-kutub wa-ḥill al-dhahab; L'art de la dorure et de la reliure*. Publié par Prosper Ricard, avec une introduction et un index des termes techniques. 2nd edn. Paris, 1920.

TAYMŪR PĀSHĀ, Aḥmad, *Al-taṣwīr 'inda al-'Arab*, ed. by Z. M. Ḥasan. Cairo, 1942.

Comments on the above:

Muṣṭafā, Muḥammad, 'Al-taswīr 'inda al-'Arab'. *Al-Risāla*, June 29, 1942, pp. 659 f.

-Munajjid, Ṣalāḥ al-Dīn, 'Al-taṣwīr 'inda al-'Arab'. *Al-Risala*, Sept. 7, 1942, pp. 864–6.

Jawād, Muṣṭafā, 'Al-taṣwīr 'inda al-'Arab'. *Al-Thaqāfa*, Nov. 2, 1943, pp. 11–14.

Reply:

Zakī, M. H., 'Ḥawla al-taṣwīr 'inda al-'Arab'. *Al-Thaqāfa*, Nov. 23, 1943, p. 15.

Final article:

Jawād, Muṣṭafā, 'Naẓarāt fī al-taṣwīr 'inda al-'Arab'. *Al-Thaqāfa*, Oct. 10, 1944, pp. 14–17.

TISSERANT, E., *Specimina codicum Orientalium*. Bonn, 1914.

TRESSAN, de, 'La peinture en Extrême Orient. III: La peinture musulmane; Mésopotamie-Perse-Inde musulmane'. *L'art et les artistes* **8**, 1913, pp. 39–56.

WIASMITINA, M., *L'art des pays de l'Islam*. Kiev, 1930.

ZAKĪ, Muḥammad Ḥasan, *Aṭlas al-funūn al-zukhrūfiyya wa-al-taṣāwīr al-islāmiyya*. Cairo, 1956.
—— *Al-fann al-islāmī fī Miṣr*. Cairo, 1935.
—— *Fī al-funūn al-islāmiyya*. Cairo, 1938.
—— *Funūn al-Islām*. Cairo, 1948.
—— 'Imḍa'āt al-fannānīn fī al-Islām'. *Al-Thaqāfa* **1**, No. 40, 1939, pp. 22–5.
—— 'Al-kitāb fī al-funūn al-islāmiyya'. *Al-Kitāb* **1**, 1946, pp. 255–63.
—— 'Tadhhīb al-makhṭūṭāt fī al-fann al-islāmī'. *Al-Thaqāfa* **1**, No. 42, 1939, pp. 25–8.
—— 'Al-taṣwīr wa-a'lām al-muṣawwirīn fī al-Islām'. (In I. M. Zaki and others eds., *Nawāḥīn majīda min al-thaqāfa al-islāmiyya*, Cairo, 1938.)

## II. BIBLIOGRAPHIES ON PAINTING IN ISLAM

CRESWELL, K. A. C., *A bibliography of painting in Islam*. (Publs. de l'I.F.A.O.; Art islamique, 1.) Cairo, 1953.
—— *A provisional bibliography of painting in Muhammadan art*. London, 1922 (privately printed).

HOLTER, K., 'Die islamischen Miniaturhandschriften vor 1350'. *ZB* **54**, 1937, pp. 1–34.

BUCHTHAL, H. and others, 'Supplementary notes to K. Holter's check list of Islamic illuminated manuscripts before 1350'. *AI* **7**, ii, 1940, pp. 147–64.

## III. MUSEUMS, LIBRARIES, ARCHIVES, COLLECTIONS, EXHIBITIONS INCLUDING SPECIMENS OF ARABIC ILLUMINATED MANUSCRIPTS (CATALOGUES, HAND LISTS, DESCRIPTIONS, GUIDES)

ARNOLD, T. W., 'Arabic and Persian manuscripts lent by the Secretary of State for India'. *J. of Indian art* **15**, 1912, pp. 87–90.

BALLOT, M.-J., *Les collections de l'Orient musulman. Musée du Louvre.* Paris, 1928.

BARRETT, D., 'Persian art of the 9th–19th century at the British Museum'. *Oriental art* **2**, 1949, pp. 53–6.

BENOIST D'AZY, M., 'La miniature à l'Exposition des Arts de l'Iran'. *L'art et les artistes* N.S. **36**, 1938, pp. 325–30.

BERLIN. KÖNIGLICHE MUSEEN, KUNSTGEWERBE-MUSEUM, *Katalog der Sonderausstellung orientalischer Buchkunst, Handschriften und Miniaturen aus den Ländern des Islams und aus Ost-Turkestan, Februar–März 1910.* Berlin, 1910.

BERLIN. STAATLICHE MUSEEN, ISLAMISCHE ABTEILUNG, *Sonderausstellung islamischer Buchkunst aus Privatbesitz, August–November 1938.* Berlin, 1938.

BIBLIOTHEQUE NATIONALE, *Les arts de l'Iran, l'ancienne Perse et Bagdad.* Catalogue rédigé par H. Corbin [and others]. Paris, 1938.

BINYON, L., *Asiatic art in the British Museum.* Paris, 1925. (Also in French, forming vol. 6 of the series *Ars asiatica* (1925).)

BINYON, L. and others, *Persian miniature painting, including a critical and descriptive catalogue of the miniatures exhibited at Burlington House, January–March, 1931.* London, 1933.

BLOCHET, E., *Catalogue de la collection de manuscrits orientaux arabes, persans et turcs formée par M. Charles Schefer et acquisée par l'État.* Paris, 1900.

—— *Les enluminures des manuscrits orientaux – turcs, arabes, persans – de la Bibliothèque Nationale.* Paris, 1926.

—— 'Inventaire et description des miniatures des manuscrits orientaux de la Bibliothèque Nationale à Paris'. *Revue des bibliothèques* 8e année, pp. 1–32, 134–51, 246–62, 315–32, 391–414, 441–55; 9e année, pp. 35–72, 135–53, 227–68, 326–38; 10e année, pp. 165–96, 290–308. Also published separately, Paris, 1900.

—— 'Mussulman manuscripts and miniatures as illustrated in the recent exhibition at Paris'. *Burlington magazine* **2**, 1903, pp. 132–44; **3**, 1903, pp. 276–85.

—— 'Notices sur les manuscrits persans et arabes de la Collection Marteau, à la Bibliothèque Nationale'. *Notices et extraits des manuscrits de la Bibliothèque Nationale* **41**, 1923, pp. 91–398.

—— *Peintures de manuscrits arabes, persans et turcs de la Bibliothèque Nationale.* Paris, 1911.

—— *Les peintures des manuscrits orientaux de la Bibliothèque Nationale.* Paris, 1914–20.

—— 'Les peintures orientales de la collection Pozzi'. *Bull. de la Société Française de Réproductions de Manuscrits à Peintures* **12**, 1928.

BRITISH MUSEUM, *Guide to an exhibition of Persian art in the Prints and Drawings Gallery*. London, 1931.

COOMARASWAMY, A. K., 'Early Arabic and Persian paintings'. *Bull. of the Museum of Fine Arts, Boston* **21**, No. 126, 1923, pp. 49–53.

—— *Les miniatures orientales de la collection Goloubew au Museum of Fine Arts de Boston*. (*Ars asiatica*, 13.) Brussels, 1929.

COTT, P. B., 'Recent accessions of Near Eastern miniature paintings'. *Worcester Art Museum annual* **1**, 1935–36, pp. 32–48.

DAVID, M., 'L'art iranienne à la Bibliothèque Nationale'. *Beaux arts* N.S. **75**, No. 285, 17 juin 1938, pp. 1–2, 11.

DAY, F., 'Muhammedan manuscripts'. *Bull. of the Metropolitan Museum of Art* **9**, 1914, pp. 152–62.

DIMAND, M. S., 'Dated specimens of Mohammedan art in the Metropolitan Museum of Art. Pt. 2'. *Metropolitan Museum studies* **1**, 1928–29, pp. 208–32.

—— 'The exhibition of Islamic painting and book illumination in the Metropolitan Museum of Art'. *Apollo* **19**, 1934, pp. 200–5.

—— *A guide to an exhibition of Islamic miniature painting and book illumination, the Metropolitan Museum of Art*. New York, 1933–34.

—— 'New accessions of Islamic art'. *Bull. of the Metropolitan Museum of Art* **16**, 1958, pp. 227–35.

EASTMAN, A. C., 'Islamic miniature painting'. *Parnassus* **5**, 1933, pp. 22–3.
On an exhibition at the Metropolitan Museum of Art.

EDHEM, Fehmi & STCHOUKINE, I., *Les manuscrits orientaux illustrés de la Bibliothèque de l'Université de Stamboul*. (Mém. de l'Inst. Fr. d'Arch. de Stamboul, 1.) Paris, 1933.

FARMER, H. G., 'Arabic musical manuscripts in the Bodleian Library'. *JRAS* 1925, pp. 639–54.

GRATZL, E., *Katalog der Ausstellung von Handschriften aus dem islamischen Kulturkreis im Fürstensaal der K. Hof- und Staatsbibliothek*. Munich, 1910.

GRUBE, E. J., *Muslim miniature paintings from the XIII to XIX century from collections in the United States and Canada; catalogue of the exhibition*. Venice, 1962.

GUILLAUME, G., 'Miniatures iraniennes de la collection Henri Vever'. (Thesis at the École du Louvre.) *Bull. des musées de France* **8**, viii, pp. 135–7.

HAMARNEH, Sami, 'Medical manuscripts at the Zahiriyah National Library'. *Viewpoints* **6**, iv, 1966.

HITTI, P. K., 'The Arabic and Islamic manuscripts of the Garrett collection'. *Princeton Univ. Lib. chronicle* **4**, 1942, pp. 116–22.

HOLTER, K., 'Les principaux manuscrits à peintures de la Bibliothèque Nationale de Vienne. Deuxième partie: Section des manuscrits orientaux'. *Bull. de la Société Française de Reproductions de Manuscrits à Peintures* **20**, 1937, pp. 85–150.

JANC, Z., *Islamski rukopisi iz jugoslowenskich kolektsiya*. Belgrade, 1956.

JAROSŁAWIECKA-GASIOROWSKA, M., 'Les principaux manuscrits à peintures du Musée des Princes Czartoryski, à Cracovie. (Miniatures orientales)'. *Bull. de la Société Française de Reproductions de Manuscrits à Peintures* **18**, 1935, pp. 168–84.

JEAN, R., 'Une collection d'art asiatique; la collection Victor Goloubew'. *Les arts* **145**, 1914, pp. 10–31.

KARABACEK, J. von, *Katalog der Buchkunst-Ausstellung, K.K. Hofbibliothek*. Vienna, 1916.

—— *Katalog der Miniaturen-Ausstellung, K.K. Hofbibliothek*. 4th edn. Vienna, 1902.

KOHLHAUSEN, H., *Islamische Kleinkunst*. (Führer durch das Hamburgische Museum für Kunst und Gewerbe, 12.) Hamburg, 1930.

KRACHKOVSKAYA, V. A., 'Musulmanskoe iskusstvo v sobranii Khanenko'. *ZKV* **2**, 1925, pp. 50 ff.

KRACHKOVSKII, I. Y., 'Opisanie sobraniya koranov privezennykh iz Trapezunta akademikom F.I. Uspenskim'. *Bull. de l'Académie des Sciences* 6 sér., **11**, 1917, pp. 346–50.

KRÄMER, J., *Ausstellung. Persische Miniaturen und ihr Umkreis; Buch- und Schriftkunst arabischer, persischer, türkischer und indischer Handschriften aus dem Besitze der früheren Preussischen Staats- und der Tübinger Universitätsbibliothek*. Tübingen, 1956.

KRONICK, D. A. & EHRENKREUTZ, A. S., 'Some highlights of Arabic medicine, A.D. 700–1400. (Catalogue of an exhibition of books and manuscripts from the collection of Dr. Lutfi M. Sa'adi)'. *University of Michigan medical bull.* **22**, 1956, pp. 215–26.

KÜHNEL, E., 'Die Ausstellung muhammedanischer Kunst in München 1910'. *Münchener Jahrbuch der bildenden Kunst* **5**, 1910, pp. 209–51.

—— *Ausstellung von Meisterwerken muhammedanischer Kunst. Amtlicher Katalog*. Munich, 1910.

—— 'Die Buchkunst auf der muhammedanischen Ausstellung in München 1910'. *Kunst und Kunsthandwerk* **13**, 1910, pp. 486–504.

—— 'Islamische Buchkunst; zur Sonderausstellung im Berliner Kunstgewerbemuseum'. *Cicerone* **2**, 1910, pp. 121–2.

—— 'Kunstgewerbemuseum. Ausstellung islamischer Buchkunst'. *Amtliche Berichte aus dem Königlichen Kunstsammlungen* **31**, 1910, pp. 186–7.

LEWIS, J. F., *Paintings and drawings of Persia and India, with some others; illuminated manuscripts in Persian, Arabic, Ethiopic, Sanscrit, Armenian, Hindi, Burmese, etc., from the XVth to the XIXth century, from the collection of John Frederick Lewis*. Philadelphia, 1923.

LINDESIANA, *List of manuscripts and examples of metal and ivory bindings. Exhib. to the Bibliographical Society at the Grafton Galleries*. Aberdeen, 1898.

LOREY, E. de, 'New light on Islamic paintings; emphasis on the picture in the new Paris exhibition'. *Art news* June 11, 1938, pp. 8–11.

LOUVRE, *Les accroissements des musées nationaux français. Le Musée du Louvre depuis 1914; dons, legs et acquisitions*. 2v. Paris, &c., 1919–20.

MARTEAU, G. & VEVER, H., *Miniatures persanes exposées au Musée des Arts Décoratifs*. 2v. Paris, 1912.

MARTIN, F. R., 'Miniaturen und Buchkunst'. (In F. Sarre *ed.*, *Die Ausstellung von Meisterwerken muhammedanischer Kunst in München*, vol. 1, Munich, 1912.)

MAYER, A. L., 'Ausstellung von Miniaturmalereien aus dem islamischen Kulturkreis in München 1910'. *Monatshefte für Kunstwissenschaft* **3**, 1910, pp. 331–9.

MÉLAN, A., 'Les arts de l'Iran à la Bibliothèque Nationale'. *Cahiers de France* **1**, 1938, pp. 76–8.

MENDEL, G., 'L'exposition des arts musulmans à Munich'. *Revue de l'art ancien et moderne* **28**, 1910, pp. 253–68, 351–66.

MIGEON, G., 'L'exposition d'art oriental de la Bibliothèque Nationale'. *Gazette des beaux-arts* 5e pér., **9**, 1925, pp. 317–30.

—— 'Exposition des arts musulmans à Munich'. *Les arts* **108**, 1910, pp. 1–34.

MIGEON, G. and others, *Exposition des arts musulmans, Pavilion de Marsan; catalogue déscriptif*. 2nd edn. Paris, 1903.

MINASSIAN COLLECTION, 'Rare examples of Islamic art in the Minassian collection'. *Art news* Dec. 3, 1939.

MINGANA, A., 'Brief notes on some of the rarer or unique Arabic and Persian-Arabic manuscripts in the John Rylands Library'. *Bull. of the John Rylands Library* **6**, 1921–22, pp. 522–30.

MÖLLER, J. H., *Catalogus librorum tam manuscriptorum quam impressorum qui jussu divi Augusti ducis Saxe-Gothani a beato Seetzenio in Oriente emti in Bibliotheca Gothana asservantur*. 2 pts. Gotha, 1825–26.

—— *Paläographische Beiträge aus den herzoglichen Sammlungen in Gotha*. Fasc. 1. Ehrfurt, 1842.

MONNERET DE VILLARD, U., 'Codici magrebini decorati della Biblioteca Vaticana'. *AION* N.S. **3**, 1949, pp. 83–91.

MONTANDON, M., 'L'art musulman à l'exposition de Munich 1910'. *L'art décoratif* **25**, 1911, pp. 61–108.

O'CONNOR, V. C., *An Eastern library; with two catalogues of its Persian and Arabic manuscripts*, comp. by Khan Sahib Abdul Muqtadir and Abdul Hamid. Glasgow, 1920.

ÖSTERREICHISCHE NATIONALBIBLIOTHEK, *Buchkunst des Morgenlandes; Katalog der Ausstellung im Prunksaal, Juni–Oktober 1953*, ed. by F. Unterkircher and others. Vienna, 1953.

ÖSTERREICHISCHES MUSEUM FÜR KUNST UND INDUSTRIE, *Ausstellung islamischer Miniaturen, Textilien und Kleinkunst*. Veranstaltet gemeinsam mit dem Verein der Freunde Asiatischer Kunst und Kultur und dem Kulturbund. Vienna, 1935. (With an introduction on Islamic miniature painting by E. Wellesz and K. Blauensteiner, pp. 5 ff.)

OSLER, W., *Bibliotheca Osleriana*. Oxford, 1929.

PAPYRUS ERZHERZOG RAINER, *Führer durch die Ausstellung*, ed. by J. van Karabacek. Vienna, 1894.

PAULL, F. V., 'The Goloubew collection of Persian and Indian paintings'. *Bull. of the Museum of Fine Arts, Boston* **13**, 1915, pp. 1–16.

PIERPONT MORGAN LIBRARY, *The animal kingdom; illustrated catalogue of an exhibition of manuscript illumination, book illustrations, drawings, cylinder seals and bindings, Nov. 19, 1940–Feb. 28, 1941*. New York, 1940.

RESCHER, O., 'Arabische Handschriften des Top Kapú Seraj (Privatbibliothek S.M. des Sultans)'. *RSO* **4**, 1911–19, pp. 695–733.

—— 'Über arabische Handschriften der Aja Sofia'. *WZKM* **26**, 1912, pp. 63–95.

RICE, D. T., 'The Paris exhibition of Iranian art, 1938'. *AI* **5**, 1938, pp. 216–20.

RIEFSTAHL, R. M., *Catalog of an exhibition of Persian and Indian miniature paintings forming the private collection of Dikran Khan Kelekian, New York City. From November 25, 1933–January 31, 1934.* New York, 1933.

—— *Catalogue of Persian and Indian miniature paintings forming the private collection of D. K. Kelekian.* Detroit, 1934.

RITTER, H., 'Arabische Handschriften in Anatolien und Istanbul. Philologica XIII'. *Oriens* **2**, 1949, pp. 236–314.

ROLAND-MARCEL, P. R., *Bibliothèque Nationale. Catalogue des manuscrits à peintures – estampes – médailles – monnaies – objects d'art – livres et cartes, exposés du 19 mai au 19 juin 1925.* Paris, 1925.

—— 'L'exposition orientale de la Bibliothèque Nationale'. *La renaissance de l'art français* **8**, 1925, pp. 259–66.

ROSEN, V., 'Remarques sur les manuscrits orientaux de la collection Marsigli à Bologne'. *Atti della R. Accademia dei Lincei, 3 ser., mem. sci. mor. stor. filol.* **12**, pp. 163–205.

SAKISIAN, A. B., 'L'exposition de miniature et d'enluminure musulmanes du Metropolitan Museum of Art de New York'. *Syria* **15**, 1934, pp. 276–81.

—— 'L'exposition des arts de l'Iran à la Bibliothèque Nationale'. *Journal des débats* 2 juillet, 1938, p. 3.

SAMMLUNG F. u. M. SARRE, *Katalog der Ausstellung im Städelschen Kunstinstitut.* Frankfurt/Main, 1932.

SARRE, F., 'Neuerwerbungen der islamischen Kunstabteilung'. *Amtliche Berichte aus den Königlichen Kunstsammlungen* **35**, 1913, col. 63–74.

SCHROEDER, E., *Persian miniatures in the Fogg Museum of Art.* Cambridge, Mass., 1942.

SEMENOV, A. A., 'Litsevnie rukopisi Bukharskoi Tsentral'noi Biblioteki. (Les manuscrits à miniatures de la Bibliothèque Centrale de Boukhara)'. *Iran* **2**, 1928, pp. 89–92.

SIMSAR, Muḥammad Aḥmad, *Oriental manuscripts of the John Frederick Lewis collection in the Freer Library of Philadelphia; a descriptive catalogue.* Philadelphia, 1937.

STCHOUKINE, I., 'Les manuscrits illustrés musulmans de la Bibliothèque du Caire'. *Gazette des beaux-arts* 6e pér., **13**, 1935, pp. 138–58.

STEINBRUCKER, C., 'Die Miniaturen in der islamischen Kunstabteilung der staatliche Museen in Berlin'. *Islamica* **6**, 1934, pp. 267–82.

STOCKHOLM. NATIONALMUSEUM, *Oriental miniatures and manuscripts in Scandinavian collections.* (Exhibition catalogue.) Stockholm, 1957.

TIETZE, H., *Die illuminierten Handschriften der Rossiana in Wien-Lainz.* Leipzig, 1911.

UNTERKIRCHER, F., *Verzeichnis der illuminierten Handschriften der Handschriftensammlung der Österreichischen Nationalbibliothek. Orientalische Handschriften.* Vienna, 1958.

VAJDA, G., 'Les manuscrits arabes datés de la Bibliothèque Nationale de Paris'. *Bull. inf. Inst. de Recherche et d'Hist. des Textes* **7**, 1958, pp. 47–69.

VILLARD, M., 'Two private collections at the Asiatic Galleries'. *Parnassus* **5**, No. 7, 1933, pp. 18–20, 29.

WARNER, G., *Descriptive catalogue of illuminated manuscripts in the library of C. W. Dyson Perrins*. 2v. London, 1920.

WATELIN, L. C., 'L'exposition orientale à la Bibliothèque Nationale'. *L'amour de l'art* **6**, 1925, pp. 277–8.

WEISSBERGER, H., 'The Metropolitan stages show of Islamic paintings'. *Art news* Oct. 21st, 1933, pp. 1, 14–15.

WELLESZ, E., 'Three exhibitions of Oriental art'. *Burlington magazine* **91**, 1949, pp. 258–61.

WIET, G., 'Deux manuscrits égyptiens à l'exposition d'art persan de Londres'. *BIE* **13**, 1930–31, pp. 91–6.

—— 'L'exposition d'art persan à Londres'. *Syria* **13**, 1932, pp. 65–93.

—— *L'exposition persane de 1931, Institut Français d'Archéologie Orientale*. Cairo, 1933.

—— *Les miniatures de la collection de Son Excellence Chérif Sabry Pacha*. (With Arabic text.) Cairo, 1943.

M. H. DE YOUNG MEMORIAL MUSEUM, *Exhibition of Islamic art*. San Francisco, 1937.

ZAKĪ, Muḥammad Ḥasan, *Moslem art in the Fouad I University Museum*. Vol. 1. Cairo, 1950.

## IV. GENERAL WORKS ON ARAB BOOK ART

ETTINGHAUSEN, R., *Arabische Malerei*. (Also English and French editions.) Geneva, 1962.

FULTON, A. S., 'Arabic medieval manuscripts'. *BM qtly* **11**, 1937, pp. 81–3.

KRACHKOVSKII, I. Y., *Among Arabic manuscripts*. Leiden, 1953. Also in Russian (Moscow, 1948) and French (Algiers, 1954).

LEVEY, M., 'Medieval Arabic bookmaking and its relations to early chemistry and pharmacology'. *Transactions of the American Philosophical Society* N.S. **52**, iv, 1962, pp. 1–79.

-MUNAJJID, Ṣalāḥ al-Dīn, *Le manuscrit arabe jusqu'au siècle de l'Hégire*. Vol. 1: *Spécimens*. Cairo, 1960.

PEDERSEN, J., *Den arabiske Bog*. Copenhagen, 1946.

SAYYID, Fu'ād, *Fihris al-makhṭūṭāt al-muṣawwara*. I: *Ma'had iḥyā' al-makhṭūṭāt al-'arabiyya*. Cairo, 1954.

## V. SCHOOLS OF BOOK ILLUMINATION

(a) *The 'Baghdād School' (Mesopotamian School)*

DENIKÉ, B., 'Arabo-mesopotamskaya shkola miniatyury'. *Novy Vostok* **3**, 1923, pp. 387–98.

FARÈS, Bishr, 'Distinction de deux tendances syrienne et iranienne dans la miniature de l'École de Bagdad'. (In *Actes du XXIe congrès des Orientalistes, Paris, 1948*, Paris, 1949, pp. 332–3.)

KÜHNEL, E., 'Die bagdader Malerschule auf der Ausstellung iranischer Kunst in Paris 1938'. *Pantheon* **18**, i, 1939, pp. 203–7.

—— 'Die bagdader Malerschule'. *Sitzb. der Kunstgeschichtlichen Gesellschaft Berlin* 1939, pp. 6–9.

LOREY, E. də, 'Le miroir de Bagdad'. *L'illustration* **96**, 1938.

—— 'La peinture musulmane; l'École de Bagdad'. *Gazette des beaux-arts* 6e pér., **10**, 1933, pp. 1–13.

WIET, G., 'Paintings of the Baghdad School'. *Graphis* **10**, No. 51, 1954, pp. 38–47.

ZAKĪ, Muḥammad Ḥasan, 'Madrasat Baghdād fī al-taṣwīr al-islāmī'. *Sumer* **11**, 1955, pp. 15–46.

(b) *Egypt in general*

MOUSA, Ahmad, *Zur Geschichte der islamischen Buchmalerei in Ägypten*. (Diss. Berlin.) Cairo, 1931.

(c) *Fāṭimid painting*

ETTINGHAUSEN, R., 'Early realism in Islamic art'. (In *Studi orientalistici in onore di Giorgio Levi della Vida* **1**, Rome, 1936, pp. 250–73.)

—— 'Painting in the Fatimid period; a reconstruction'. *AI* **9**, 1942, pp. 121–24.

ZAKĪ, Muḥammad Ḥasan, *Kunūz al-Fāṭimiyyīn*. Cairo, 1937.

(d) *Painting under the Ṭulūnids*

ZAKĪ, Muḥammad Ḥasan, *Les Tulunides*. Paris, 1933.

(e) *Mamlūk painting*

HOLTER, K., 'Die frühmamlukische Miniaturenmalerei'. *Die graphischen Künste* N.F. **2**, 1937, pp. 1–14.

(f) *Pre-Mongol School in Persia*

DUDA, D., 'Die Buchmalerei der Galā'iriden. Part 1'. (Diss. Vienna.) *Der Islam* **48**, 1971, pp. 28–76.

SAKISIAN, A. B., 'L'école de miniature prémongole de la Perse orientale'. *RAA* **7**, iii, 1931, pp. 156–62.

Reviewed by M. Jirmounsky in *Gazette des beaux-arts* 6e pér., 1932, p. 127.

SAKISIAN, A. B., 'Une école de peinture prémongole dans la Perse orientale'. *Gazette des beaux-arts* **7**, 1923, pp. 16–30.

## VI. STUDIES ON INDIVIDUAL MANUSCRIPTS AND MINIATURES

(a) *Manuscripts of the 'Maqāmāt' of al-Ḥarīrī*

BORISOV, A., *Miniatyury 'Knigi Makâm' al-Khariri*. Leningrad, 1938.

BUCHTHAL, H., 'Three illustrated Ḥarīrī manuscripts in the British Museum'. *Burlington magazine* **77**, 1940, pp. 144–52.

GRABAR, O., 'The illustrated Maqāmāt of the thirteenth century; the bourgeoisie and the arts'. (In A. Hourani and S. M. Stern *eds.*, *The Islamic city*, Oxford, 1970, pp. 208–22.)

—— 'The illustrations of the Maqāmāt'. (In *Trudy XXV Mezhdunarodn. Kongr. Vostokovedov, Moskva 1960* **2**, Moscow, 1963.)

—— 'A newly discovered illustrated manuscript of the Maqāmāt of Ḥarīrī'. *AO* **5**, 1963, pp. 97–109.

HOLTER, K., 'Die Galen-Handschrift und die Makamen des Hariri der Wiener Nationalbibliothek'. *Jahrbuch der kunsthistorischen Sammlungen in Wien* Sondernummer 104, N.F. **9**, 1937, pp. 1–48.

KARABACEK, J. von, 'Eine arabische Bilderhandschrift des XIV. Jahrhunderts'. *Mitteilungen des k.k. österr. Museums für Kunst und Industrie* **3**, 1870, pp. 261–3.

KRACHKOVSKAYA, V. A., 'Miniatyury "Makâm" al-Kharīrī Leningradskoi rukopisi C.23 Instituta Narodov Azii Akademii Nauk SSSR'. *Filologiya stran Vostoka* 1962, pp. 171–84.

LOREY, E. de, 'Les séances de Hariri'. *Verve* **1**, iii, 1938.

MAYER, L. A., 'A hitherto unknown Damascene artist'. *AI* **9**, 1942, p. 168.

(b) *Manuscripts of 'Kalīla wa Dimna'*

A.A., 'Bidpai, forefather of fables'. *Verve* **1**, 1938.

AVERY, M., 'Miniatures of the Fables of Bidpai and of the life of Aesop in the Pierpont Morgan Library'. *Art bulletin* **23**, 1941, pp. 103–16.

BUCHTHAL, H., 'Indian fables in Islamic art'. *JRAS* 1941, pp. 317–24.

DAVID-WEILL, J., 'Sur quelques illustrations de Kalila et Dimna'. (In O. Aslanapa *ed.*, *Beiträge zur Kunstgeschichte Asiens in memoriam Ernst Diez*, Istanbul, 1963, pp. 256–63.)

WALZER, S., 'An illustrated leaf from a lost Mamluk Kalīlah wa-Dimnah manuscript'. *AO* **2**, 1957, pp. 503–5.

—— 'The Mamluk illuminated manuscripts of Kalīla wa-Dimna'. (In R. Ettinghausen *ed.*, *Aus der Welt der islamischen Kunst; Festschrift E. Kühnel*, Berlin, 1959, pp. 195–206.)

(c) *Manuscripts of the Materia Medica of Dioscurides*

BONNET, E., 'Étude sur les figures de plantes et d'animaux peintes dans une version arabe manuscrite de la matière médicale de Dioscuride'. *Janus* **14**, 1909, pp. 294–303.

BUCHTHAL, H., 'Early Islamic miniatures from Baghdad'. *Journal of the Watters Art Gallery* **5**, 1942, pp. 18–39.

DAY, F., 'Mesopotamian manuscripts of Dioscurides'. *Bull. of the Metropolitan Museum of Art* N.S. **8**, 1950, pp. 274–80.

DUBLER, L. E., 'Die "Materia Medica" unter den Muslimen des Mittelalters'. *Sudhoffs Archiv für Geschichte der Medizin* **43**, 1959, pp. 329–50.

FARÈS, Bishr, 'Un herbier arabe illustré du XIVe siècle'. (In G. C. Miles *ed.*, *Archaeologica orientalia in memoriam Ernst Herzfeld*, New York, 1952, pp. 84–8.)

GRAY, B., 'Persian miniatures'. *BM qtly* **9**, 1934–35, pp. 88–91.

GRUBE, E. J., 'Materialen zum Dioscurides arabicus'. (In R. Ettinghausen *ed.*, *Aus der Welt der islamischen Kunst; Festschrift für E. Kühnel*, Berlin, 1959, pp. 163–94.)

LECLERC, L., 'De la traduction arabe de Dioscurides et des traductions arabes en général'. *JA* 6e sér., **9**, 1867.

MEYERHOF, M., 'Die Materia Medica des Dioskurides bei den Arabern'. *Quellen und Studien zur Geschichte der Naturwissenschaft und der Medizin* **3**, iv, 1933, pp. 72–84.

ÜNVER, A. Suheyl, *İstanbul'da Dioscurides eserleri*. Istanbul, 1944.

(d) *Manuscripts of the Treatise on automata by al-Jazarī*

AĞA-OĞLU, Mehmet, 'On a manuscript by al-Jazarī'. *Parnassus* **3**, vii, 1931, pp. 27–8.

ANET, C. & COOMARASWAMY, A. K., 'Dr. F. R. Martin and oriental painting; "Le traité des automates" '. *Burlington magazine* **23**, 1913, pp. 49–50.

BORN, W., 'Early European automatons'. *The connoisseur* **100**, 1937.

COOMARASWAMY, A. K., 'An Arabic treatise on automata'. *Bull. of the Museum of Fine Arts, Boston* **22**, 1924.

—— 'The treatise of al-Jazarī on automata; leaves from a manuscript of the Kitāb fī maʻrifāt al-ḥiyal al-handasīya in the Museum of Fine Arts, and elsewhere'. *Museum of Fine Arts, Boston. Communications to the Trustees* **6**, 1924, pp. i and 23.

CRESWELL, K. A. C., 'Dr. F. R. Martin's manuscript "Treatise on automata" '. *Yearbook of oriental art and culture* **1**, 1925, pp. 33–40.

DAVIDSON, J. L., 'Persian art at the Brooklyn Museum'. *Parnassus* **7**, v, 1635, pp. 18–19.

GLIDDEN, H. W., 'A note on the Automata of al-Djazarī'. *AI* **3**, 1936, pp. 115–16.

HOLLIS, H., 'Page from an automata manuscript'. *Bull. of the Cleveland Museum of Art* **33**, 1946, pp. 85–7.

MAYER, L. A., 'Zum Titelblatt der Automata Miniaturen'. *OLZ* **35**, 1932, pp. 165–6.

RIEFSTAHL, R. M., 'The date and provenance of the automata miniatures'. *Art bull.* **11**, No. 2, 1929, pp. 206–14.

STCHOUKINE, I., 'Un manuscrit du traité d'al-Jazarī sur les automates du VIIe siècle de l'Hégire'. *Gazette des beaux-arts* 6e pér., **11**, 1934, pp. 134–40.

WIEDEMANN, E., 'Beiträge zur Geschichte über Trinkgefässe und Tafelaufsätze nach al-Ǧazari und den Benu Musà'. *Der Islam* **8**, 1918.

—— 'Über die Abbildung eines Affenführers und seiner Affen bei al-Ǧazarī'. *Der Islam* **13**, 1923, pp. 107–8.

—— 'Über Musikautomaten bei den Arabern'. (In *Centenario Amari* **2**, Palermo, 1910, pp. 164–85.)

—— 'Über Schalen, die beim Aderlass verwendet werden und Waschgefässe nach al-Ǧazarī'. *Archiv. für Geschichte der Medizin* **11**, 1918, pp. 22–43.

WIEDEMANN, E. & HAUSER, F., *Über die Uhren im Bereich der islamischen Kultur*. (Abh. der Kaiserlichen Leopoldinisch-Carolinischen Deutschen Akademie der Naturforscher, Nova Acta 100, No. 5.) Halle, 1915.

—— 'Über eine Palasttüre und Schlosser nach al-Ǧazarī'. *Der Islam* **11**, 1921, pp. 213–51.

WITTEK, P., 'Datum und Herkunft der Automaten-Miniaturen'. *Der Islam* **19**, 1931, pp. 177–8.

(e) *Manuscripts of the 'Kitāb al-aghānī'*

FARES, Bishr, 'L'art sacré chez un primitif musulman'. *BIE* **36**, 1955, pp. 619–77.

—— 'De la figuration en Islam; un document inédit'. *Revue des arts* 30 mars, 1951.

—— 'Une miniature nouvelle de l'école de Bagdad datée 614 Hég./1217–18 figurant le prophète Muḥammad'. *BIE* **28**, 1947, pp. 259–62.

—— *Une miniature religieuse de l'école arabe de Baghdad.* (Mémoires présentés à l'Institut d'Égypte, 51.) Cairo, 1948.

—— *Vision chrétienne et signes musulmans autour d'un manuscrit arabe illustré au XIIIe siècle.* (Mémoires présentés à l'Institut d'Égypte, 56.) Cairo, 1962.

KÜHNEL, E., 'Une miniature religieuse de l'école de Bagdad'. *Oriens* **4**, 1951, pp. 171–3.

Review of FARÈS: Une miniature religieuse . . . above.

RICE, D. S., 'The Aghānī miniatures and religious painting in Islam'. *Burlington magazine* **95**, 1953, pp. 128–34.

STERN, S. M., 'A new volume of the illustrated Aghānī manuscript'. *AO* **2**, 1957, pp. 501–3.

(f) *Manuscript of Ibn al-Durayhim's 'Kitāb manāfi' al-ḥayawān'*

LOREY, E. de, 'Le bestiaire de l'Escurial'. *Gazette des beaux-arts* 6e pér., **14**, 1935, pp. 228–38.

(g) *Manuscripts of al-Qazwīnī's ''Ajā'ib al-makhlūqāt'*

KÜHNEL, E., 'Das Qazwini-Fragment der Islamischen Abteilung'. *Jahrbuch der Preussischen Kunstsammlung* **64**, 1943, pp. 59–72.

MASSÉ, H., *Le livre des merveilles du monde.* Paris, 1944.

RUSKA, J., 'Kazwīnīstudien'. *Der Islam* **4**, 1913, pp. 14–66, 236–62.

(h) *Manuscripts of al-Ṣūfī's 'Kitāb ṣuwar al-kawākib'*

SCHJELLERUP, H. C. F. C., *Description des étoiles fixes composée au milieu du Xe siècle de notre ère par l'astronome persan Abd-al-Rahman Al-Sufi.* Traduction littérale de deux manuscrits arabes de la Bibliothèque Royale de Copenhague et de la Bibliothèque Impériale de St. Pétersbourg, avec des notes. St. Petersburg, 1874.

UPTON, J., 'A manuscript of "The book of the fixed stars" by 'Abd ar-Raḥmān as-Ṣūfī'. *Metropolitan Museum studies* **4**, 1933, pp. 179–97.

WELLESZ, E., 'An early al-Ṣūfī manuscript in the Bodleian Library in Oxford'. *AO* **3**, 1959, pp. 1–26.

(i) *Manuscripts of al-Jāḥiẓ's Zoology*

LÖFGREN, O., 'Unbekannte arabische Texte in der Ambrosiana'. *Orientalia Suecana* **13**, 1963, pp. 122–34.

LÖFGREN, O. & LAMM, C. J., *Ambrosian fragments of an illuminated manuscript containing the Zoology of al-Ǧāḥiẓ. The miniatures; their origin and style.* (Uppsala Universitets Årsskrift, 5.) Uppsala, 1946.

(j) *Manuscripts of the Pseudo-Galenic 'Kitāb al-tiryāq'*

FARÈS, Bishr, 'Décoré dans un atelier arabe au XIIe siècle; le Livre de la thériaque. Manuscrit arabe conservé à la Bibliothèque Nationale de Paris'. *Presse medicale* **61**, 1953, pp. 938–40.

—— *Le Livre de la thériaque; manuscrit arabe à peintures de la fin du XIIe siècle conservé à la Bibliothèque Nationale de Paris.* (Publs. de l'I.F.A.O.; Art islamique, 2.) Cairo, 1953.

KARWATH, J., 'Zwei pharmazeutische Kostbarkeiten der Wiener Nationalbibliothek; der griechische Dioskurides . . . und der arabische Galen'. *Pharmazeutische Monatshefte* **4**, 1924.

MEYERHOF, M., 'Joannes Grammatikos (Philoponos) von Alexandrien und die arabische Medizin'. *Mitteilungen des deutschen Instituts für ägyptische Altertumskunde in Kairo* **2**, 1932.

—— 'La version arabe d'un traité perdu de Galien'. *Byzantion* 1926, pp. 413–42.

(k) *Manuscripts of Ibn al-Ahnaf's 'Kitāb al-bayṭara'*

BJÖRK, G., 'Griechische Pferdheilkunde in arabischer Überlieferung'. *Le monde oriental* **30**, 1936, pp. 1–12.

FRÖHNER, R., *Die Pferdheilkunde des Aḥmad ibn Ḥasan ibn al-Ahnaf.* Berlin, 1936.

SBATH, P., *Manuscrit arabe sur la pharmacopée hippiatrique.* Cairo, 1932.

(l) *Manuscripts of 'Bayād wa-Riyād'*

MONNERET DE VILLARD, U., 'Un codice arabo-spagnolo con miniature'. *Bibliofilia* **43**, 1942, pp. 209–23.

NYKL, A. R., *Historia de los amores de Bayād y Riyād; una chantefable oriental en estilo persa (Vat. Ar. 368) con diez facsimiles.* New York, 1941.

(m) *Arabic version of Rashīd al-Dīn's 'Jāmiʿ al-tawārīkh'*

JAHN, K., *Die Chinageschichte des Rašīd ad-Dīn.* Übersetzung, Kommentar, Facsimiletafeln. Unter sinologischem Beistand von Herbert Franke. (Österr. Akad. d. Wiss., Phil.-hist. Kl., Denkschriften, 105.) Vienna, 1971.

MORLEY, W. H. & FORBES, D., 'Letters . . . on the discovery of part of the second volume of the "Jāmiʿ al tawārīkh", supposed to be lost'. *JRAS* **6**, 1841, pp. 11–41.

(n) *Manuscript of al- Ṣuyūṭī's 'Al-wasā'il 'ilā maʿrifat al-awā'il'*

FULTON, A. S., 'A Mamluk Arabic manuscript (Or. 12012)'. *BM qtly* **16**, 1952, pp. 93–4.

(o) *Manuscript of Ibn Faḍlallāh al-'Umarī*

RICE, D. S., 'A miniature in an autograph of Shihāb al-Dīn Ibn Faḍlallāh al-'Umarī'. *BSOAS* **13**, 1951, pp. 856–67.

(p) *Manuscript of an apocryphal Arabic Gospel*

BAUMSTARK, A., 'Erbe christlicher Antike im Bildschmuck eines arabischen Evangelienbuches des XIV. Jh.'. *Oriens Christianus* **35**, 1938, pp. 1–38.

REDIN, E. K., 'Miniatyury apokrificheskago arabskogo Evangeliya dyetstva Christa, Laurentsienskoi Biblioteky vo Florentsii'. *ZVO* **7**, 1895, pp. 55–71.

(q) *Manuscript of Barlaam and Joasaph*

LEROY, J., 'Un nouveau manuscrit arabe-chrétien illustré du roman de Barlaam et Joasaph'. *Syria* **32**, 1935, pp. 101–22.

(r) *Manuscript of al-Zahrāwī's surgical treatise*

HAMARNEH, Sami K., 'Drawings and pharmacy in al-Zahrāwī's 10th century surgical treatise'. *United States National Museum bull.* **228**, 1961, pp. 81–94.

(s) *Manuscript of al-Ghafiqī's pharmacology*

MEYERHOF, M., 'Deux manuscrits illustrés du Livre des simples d'Aḥmad al-Ghāfiqī. Études de pharmacologie arabe tirées de manuscrits inédits, no. III'. *BIE* **20**, 1940, pp. 133–52, 157–62; **23**, 1940–41, pp. 13–30, 89–101.

(t) *Early fragments from Fustat, Fayyum and Damietta*

GRAY, B., 'A Fatimid drawing'. *BM qtly* **12**, 1938, pp. 91–6.

—— 'Islamic charm from Fostat'. *BM qtly* **9**, 1935, pp. 130–1.

GRUBE, E. J., 'Three miniatures from Fusṭāṭ in the Metropolitan Museum of Art in New York'. *AO* **5**, 1963, pp. 89–95.

KARABACEK, J. von, 'Ein arabisches Reiterbild des X. Jahrhunderts'. *Mitteilungen aus der Sammlung der Papyrus Erzherzog Rainer* **5**, 1892, pp. 123–6.

RICE, D. S., 'A drawing of the Fatimid period'. *BSOAS* **21**, 1958, pp. 31–9.

—— 'The oldest illustrated Arabic manuscript'. *BSOAS* **22**, 1959, pp. 207–20.

WIET, G., 'Un dessin du XIe siècle'. *BIE* **19**, 1936–37, pp. 223–7.

—— 'Une peinture du XIIe siècle'. *BIE* **26**, 1944, pp. 109–18.

## VII. ICONOGRAPHY

ARNOLD, T. W., 'The Caesarian section in an Arabic manuscript dated 707 A.H.'. (In *A volume of oriental studies presented to Edward G. Browne*, Cambridge, 1922, pp. 6–7.)

BRONSTEIN, L., 'Space forms in the Assemblies of al-Ḥarīrī'. *Verve* **1**, 1938.

—— 'Space forms in Persian miniature composition'. *Bull. of the American Institute for Persian Art and Archaeology* **5**, 1935, pp. 15–28.

CAMPOS, J. A. Correia de, 'Representações da fauna na arte árabe'. *Bol. Soc. Geogr. Lisboa* **79**, 1961, pp. 253–60. (With English summary.)

COUCHOUD, P. L., *Mythologie asiatique illustrée*. Paris, 1938.

ETTINGHAUSEN, R., 'Die bildliche Darstellung der Ka'ba im islamischen Kulturkreis'. *ZDMG* **87**, 1934, pp. 111–37.

FARÈS, Bishr, 'Figures magiques'. (In R. Ettinghausen *ed.*, *Aus der Welt der islamischen Kunst; Festschrift E. Kühnel*, Berlin, 1959, pp. 154–62.)

—— 'L'horloge du palais'. *BIE* **40**, 1958–59, pp. 7–9.

—— 'Philosophie et jurisprudence illustrées par les Arabes'. (In *Mélanges Louis Massignon* **2**, Damascus, 1957, pp. 77–109.)

FARMER, H. G., 'A Maghribi work on musical instruments'. *JRAS* 1935, pp. 339–53.

HARTNER, W., 'The pseudoplanetary nodes of the moon's orbit in Hindu and Islamic iconographies; a contribution to the history of ancient and medieval astrology'. *AI* **5**, 1938, pp. 113–54.

HARTNER, W. & ETTINGHAUSEN, R., 'The conquering lion; the life cycle of a symbol'. *Oriens* **17**, 1964, pp. 161–71.

HAUBER, A., 'Planetenkinderbilder und Sternbilder'. *Studien zur deutschen Kunstgeschichte* **194**, 1916, pp. 145 ff.

JANC, Z., 'Minijature u islamskom astrološkom spisu Orijentalnog Instituta u Sarajevu'. *Prilozi Orijent. Filol. Ist.* **6–7**, 1956–57, pp. 139–45. (English summary p. 145.)

MOSTAFA, Muhammad, 'Darstellung des täglichen Lebens in der islamischen Kunst'. *Bustan* **2**, 1960.

PANOFSKY, E. & SAXL, F., 'Classical mythology in medieval art'. *Metropolitan Museum studies* **4**, 1933, pp. 228–80.

PAUTY, E., 'L'architecture dans les miniatures islamiques'. *BIE* **17**, 1934–35, pp. 23–57.

PONZI, E., 'Per l'iconografia dell'operazione cesarea'. *Rivista di storia delle scienze mediche* **19**, (anno 28), 1937, pp. 77–84.

RICE, D. S., 'Deacon or drink; some paintings from Samarra re-examined'. *Arabica* **5**, i, 1958, pp. 15–33.

SAXL, F., 'Beiträge zu einer Geschichte der Planetendarstellungen im Orient und im Okzident'. *Der Islam* **3**, 1912, pp. 151–77.

SIDDIQI, Abdul Sattar, 'Construction of clocks and Islamic civilisation'. *IC* **1**, 1927, pp. 246–51.

VALENTINER, W. R., 'The front plane relief in medieval art'. *Art quarterly* (*Detroit Institute of Arts*) **2**, 1939, pp. 154–77.

WHISHAW, B. & ELLEN, M., 'Animate life in early Arabic art'. *Nineteenth century* **67**, 1910, pp. 1068–76.

WITTKOWER, R., 'Marvels of the East; a study in the history of monsters'. *Journal of the Warburg and Courtauld Institutes* **5**, 1942, pp. 159–97.

## VIII. QUR'ĀN ILLUMINATION AND RELATED STUDIES

ABBOTT, N., 'Maghribī Koran manuscripts of the seventeenth to the eighteenth centuries (in the possession of Dr. and Mrs. Paul Hudson, Ohio State University)'. *American journal of Semitic languages and literatures* **55**, 1938, pp. 61–5.

—— *The rise of the North Arabic script and its ḳur'ānic development, with a full description of the Kur'ān manuscripts in the Oriental Institute.* (Univ. of Chicago Oriental Inst. Publs., 1.) Chicago, 1939.

BARANI, Syed Hasan, 'Some remarkable illuminated manuscripts of the Qur'ān in my library'. *Indo-Iranica* **4**, i, 1950–51, pp. 35–6.

COOMARASWAMY, A. K., 'Leaf of a Koran'. *Bull. of the Museum of Fine Arts, Boston* **18**, 1920, p. 52.

DEVERDUN, G. & GHIATI, Muḥ. b. Abdeslem, 'Deux taḥbīs almohades'. *Hespéris* **41**, 1954, pp. 411–23.

ETTINGHAUSEN, R., 'A signed and dated Seljuq Qur'ān'. *Bull. of the American Institute of Persian Art* **4**, 1935, pp. 92–102.

GOTTHEIL, R., 'An illustrated copy of the Koran'. *REI* **5**, 1931, pp. 21–4.

GUTHRIE, A., 'A manuscript Qur'ān in the Glasgow University Library'. *Glasgow Univ. Or. Soc. transactions* **15**, 1953–54, pp. 36–43.

IQBAL, M., 'Some specimens of the calligraphy of the Qur'ān from the Library of Meshed'. (In *Woolner commemoration volume*, Lahore, 1940, pp. 109–12.)

JANÉR, F., 'El-Koran; códice árabe llamado de Muley Cidan, rey de Marruecos, conservado en la Biblioteca del Escorial. Descripción y consideraciones'. *Museo Español de Antiguedades* **3**, 1874, pp. 409–32.

KARABACEK, J. von, *Ein Koranfragment des IX. Jahrhunderts.* (Zur orientalischen Altertumskunde, 6.) Vienna, 1913.

KRACHKOVSKAYA, V. A., 'Redkaya rukopis' Korana XVI veka'. *KSINA* **47**, 1961, pp. 38–42.

—— 'Un rare manuscrit de Coran du XVI siècle'. (In *Trudy XXV Mezhdunarodn. Kongr. Vostokovedov, Moskva, 1960* **2**, Moscow, 1963, pp. 105–10.)

KRACHKOVSKII, I. Y., 'Rukopis' Korana v Pskove'. *Comptes rendus de l'Académie des Sciences de Russie* (*Doklady Rossiiskoi Akademii Nauk*) 1924, pp. 165–8.

LEVI DELLA VIDA, G., *Frammenti coranici in carattere cufico.* (Studi e testi, 132.) Vatican, 1947.

LÉVI-PROVENÇAL, E., 'Note sur un Cor'an royal du XIVe siècle'. *Hespéris* **1**, 1921, pp. 83–6.

McALLISTER, H. E., 'Acquisitions of leaves from early Korans'. *Bull. of the Metropolitan Museum of Art* **36**, 1941, pp. 165–8.

—— 'Leaves from three early Korans'. *Bull. of the Metropolitan Museum of Art* **32**, 1937, pp. 264–5.

MINGANA, A., 'Notes upon some of the Kuranic manuscripts in the John Rylands Library'. *Bull. of the John Rylands Library* **2**, 1914–15, pp. 240–50.

MORITZ, B., *Arabic palaeography; a collection of Arabic texts from the first century of the Hidjra till the year 1000.* (Veröff. der Bibliothek des Khediven, 16.) Cairo, 1905.

-NAQSHABANDĪ, Nāṣir, 'Al-maṣāḥif al-karīma fī ṣadr al-Islām'. *Sumer* **12**, 1956, pp. 33–7.

NÖLDEKE, T. and others, *Geschichte des Qorans.* 3v. Leipzig, 1936.

RICE, D. S., *The unique Ibn al-Bawwāb manuscript in the Chester Beatty Library, Dublin*. Dublin, 1955.

STERN, S. M., 'A manuscript from the library of the Ġaznawid Amīr 'Abd al-Rashīd'. (In R. Pinder-Wilson *ed.*, *Paintings from Islamic lands*. (Oriental studies, 4.) Oxford, 1969.)

## IX. ARABIC BOOK ILLUMINATION IN RELATION TO FOREIGN STYLES

(a) *Relation to Byzantine art* (*including Hellenistic*)

BLOCHET, E., 'Peintures de manuscrits arabes à types byzantins'. *Rev. arch.* 4e sér., **9**, 1907, pp. 193–223. Also published separately, Paris, 1907.

BUCHTHAL, H., ' "Hellenistic" miniatures in early Islamic manuscripts'. *AI* **7**, 1940, pp. 125–33.

DUTHUIT, G., *Byzance et l'art du XIIe siècle*. Paris, 1926.

GASIOROWSKI, S. J., *Malarstwo minjaturowe grecko-rzymskie*. Cracow, 1928.

GRABAR, O., 'Islamic art and Byzantium'. *Dumbarton Oaks papers* **18**, 1964, pp. 67–88.

SCHLUMBERGER, G., *Un empereur byzantin au dixième siècle; Nicéphore Phocas*. Paris, 1890.

—— *L'épopée byzantine à la fin du Xe siècle*. 3v. Paris, 1896–1905.

WEITZMANN, K., *Ancient book illumination*. Cambridge, Mass., 1959.

—— 'The Greek sources of Islamic scientific illustrations'. (In G. C. Miles *ed.*, *Archaeologica orientalia in memoriam Ernst Herzfeld*, New York, 1952, pp. 244–66.)

(b) *Relations to Syrian Christianity*

ARNOLD, T. W., *The Old and New Testaments in Muslim religious art*. London, 1932.

BUCHTHAL, H., 'The painting of the Syrian Jacobites in its relation to Byzantine and Islamic art'. *Syria* **20**, 1939, pp. 136–50.

JERPHANION, G. de, 'L'influence de la miniature musulmane sur un évangéliaire syriaque illustré du XIIIe siècle (Vat. Syr. 559)'. *CRAIBL* 1939, pp. 482–509.

—— 'Un nouveau manuscrit syriaque illustré de la Bibliothèque Vaticane'. *OCP* **5**, 1939.

KÜHNEL, E., 'Christliche Motive in der persischen Malerei'. (In *Kunstgeschichtliche Studien für H. Kauffman*, Berlin, 1956, pp. 120–7.)

PROKHOROV, B., *Khristianskiya drevnosti*. St. Petersburg, 1862.

(c) *Relation to Coptic art*

WEITZMANN, K., 'An early Copto-Arabic miniature in Leningrad'. *AI* **10**, 1943, pp. 119–34.

ZAKĪ, Muḥammad Ḥasan, 'Ba'ḍ al-ta'thīrāt al-qibṭiyya fī al-funūn al-islāmiyya'. *Bull. de l'Association des Amis de l'Art Copte* **3**, 1937, pp. 83–104.

(d) *Relation to Armenian art*

SAKISIAN, A. B., 'Thèmes et motifs d'enluminure et de décoration arméniennes et musulmanes'. *AI* **6**, 1939, pp. 66–87.

(e) *Relation to Slavonic art*

GRABAR, A., 'Influences musulmanes sur la décoration des manuscrits slaves balkaniques'. *Revue des études slaves* **27**, 1951, pp. 124–35.

STASSOF, W., *L'ornement slave et oriental*. St. Petersburg, 1887.

*Relation to Sassanian and Manichaean art*

ARNOLD, T. W., *Survivals of Sasanian and Manichaean art in Persian painting*. Oxford, 1924.

—— 'The survival of Sasanian motifs in Persian painting'. (In *Studien zur Kunst des Ostens (Festschrift J. Strzygowski)*, Vienna, &c., 1923, pp. 95–7.)

—— 'La survivance possible dans les manuscrits arabes du XIVe siècle de motifs offerts par les fresques et les peintures manichéennes'. (In *Actes du Congrès d'Histoire de l'Art, Paris, 1921*, Paris, 1923, pp. 273–6.)

BORISOV, A. Y., *Ob odnom illyustrirovannom astrologicheskom traktate sasanidskogo vremeni*. (III. International Congress of Persian Art, Leningrad, 1935.) Moscow, &c., 1939, pp. 31–3.

## X. WORKS ON VARIOUS TOPICS, CONTAINING REFERENCES TO ARABIC ILLUMINATED MANUSCRIPTS

ARNOLD, T. W. & GUILLAUME, A., *The legacy of Islam*. 9th edn. London, 1965.

BERGSTRÄSSER, G., *Ḥunain ibn Isḥāq; über die syrischen und arabischen Galenübersetzungen*. (Abh. f. d. Kunde des Morgenlandes 17, ii.) Leipzig, 1925.

BROCKELMANN, C., *Der Islam von seinen Anfängen bis zur Gegenwart*. (Weltgeschichte, ed. J. von Pfluck-Hartung **1**.) Berlin, 1910.

BROWNE, E. G., *Arabian medicine*. Cambridge, 1921.

BUZURG IBN SHAHRIYĀR, *Kitab 'adjā'ib al-Hind, barruhu wa-baḥruhu wa-djazā'iruhu*, ed. by P. A. van der Lith, trans. by M. Devic. Leiden, 1883–6.

FARMER, H. G., 'Some musical manuscripts identified'. *JRAS* 1926, pp. 91–3.

—— *The sources of Arabian music*. Leiden, 1940.

—— 'The structure of the Arabian and Persian lute in the Middle Ages'. *JRAS* 1939, pp. 41–51.

GUILMAIN, J., 'Zoomorphic decoration and the problem of the sources of Mozarabic illumination'. *Speculum* **35**, 1960, pp. 17–38.

GUNDEL, W., *Dekane und Dekansternbilder*. Gluckstadt, &c., 1936.

HAMMER, J. von, 'Über die Sternbilder der Araber, und ihre eigenen Namen für einzelne Sterne'. *Fundgruben des Orients* **1**, 1809, pp. 1–15; **2**, 1811, pp. 235–8.

HITTI, P. K., *History of the Arabs*. London, 1937, and various other editions.

HODGSON, M. G. S., 'Islam and image'. *History of religions* **3**, 1964, pp. 220–60.

HOURANI, G. F., *Arab seafaring in the Indian Ocean in ancient and early medieval times*. Princeton, 1951.

IBN ḤUDHAYL AL-ANDALUSĪ, 'Alī, *La parure des chevaliers et l'insigne des preux*. (Arabic text of *Ḥilyat al-fursān wa-shi'ār al-shuj'ān*.) Ed. by L. Mercier. Paris, 1922; French translation, Paris, 1924.

LADREIT DE LACHARRIÈRE, J., 'Un manuel arabe de science hippique'. *Bull. Com. de l'Afrique Française. Renseignements coloniaux*, 1926, pp. 59–62.

MANN, T., *Der Islam einst und jetzt*. (Monographien sur Weltgeschichte, 32.) Bielefeld, &c., 1914.

MAYER, L. A., *Mamluk costume*. Geneva, 1952.

MEYERHOF, M., 'Arabian pharmacology in North Africa, Sicily, and the Iberian Peninsula'. *Ciba Symposia* **6**, v, vi, 1944, pp. 1868–72.

—— 'The background and origins of Arabian pharmacology'. *Ciba Symposia* **6**, v, vi, 1944, pp. 1847–56.

—— 'Die literarischen Grundlagen der arabischen Heilmittellehre'. *Ciba Zeitschrift* **8**, 1942, pp. 2957–94.

—— *Le monde islamique*. (Bibliothèque générale illustré, 3.) Paris, n.d.

—— 'Pharmacology during the Golden Age of Arabian medicine'. *Ciba Symposia* **6**, v, vi, 1944, pp. 1957–67.

—— 'The sources of the history of Arabian medicine'. *Ciba Symposia* **6**, v, vi, 1944, pp. 1873–6.

SINGER, C., 'The herbal in antiquity'. *Journal of Hellenic studies* **47**, 1927.

ÜNVER, A. S., *Selçuk tababeti 10–14cü asĭrlar; binalar ve minyatürler*. Ankara, 1940.

WIEDEMANN, E., 'Über Leuchtfeuer bei den Muslimen'. *Archiv für Geschichte der Naturwissenschaften und der Technik* **2**, 1910, pp. 151–4.

# Arabic Papyri

C. WAKEFIELD

The following bibliography is an attempt to provide a comprehensive guide to the literature on Arabic papyri. The kernel of the bibliography comprises five titles by Adolf Grohmann chosen for their extensive documentation of editions, collections and other relevant literature; they are arranged in chronological order. Some duplication will be found of the bibliographical citations provided by these titles, but each contains some significant material not present in the others. The second part of the bibliography aims to supplement this coverage by listing materials published since the appearance of the last item in 1966.

By the words Arabic papyri is to be understood not only writings in Arabic on papyrus, but also such writings on those other materials customarily handled by papyrologists, viz. leather, bone, fragments of pottery, &c. For a discussion of the scope of Arabic papyrology reference may be made to two articles by Claude Cahen in *Arabica* **5**, 1958, pp. 301–3, and *Arabica* **15**, 1968, pp. 104–6. These two articles also contain reviews of items 3 and 4 cited below. It should be stated in this regard that the scope of the present bibliography does not embrace reference to Arabic papers from the Cairo Geniza.

## A. Basic List

1. GROHMANN, A., *Überblick über die bisherigen Veröffentlichungen arabischer Stücke.* (Corpus papyrorum Raineri 3, Series Arabica, tom. 1, pars 1, pp. 14–17.) Vienna, 1924.

—— *Übersicht über die veröffentlichten Protokolle.* (Corpus papyrorum Raineri 3, Series Arabica, tom. 1, pars 2, pp. xiii–xv.) Vienna, 1924.

These two articles give a chronological survey of the literature of the previous 100 years, since the publication of Silvestre de Sacy's first study in 1825.

2. GROHMANN, A., Article 'Kirṭās' in *The encyclopaedia of Islām, Supplement,* pp. 117–18. Leiden, &c., 1938.

The bibliography which concludes the article brings up to date the listing in the two foregoing titles.

3. GROHMANN, A., *Einführung und Chrestomathie zur arabischen Papyruskunde.* Bd. 1. (Československý ústav orientální v Praze; Monografie Archivu orientálního, 13.) Prague, 1954.

A detailed work giving much useful information on the finds of Arabic papyri, writing materials, language and script, with copious references to the literature in the footnotes. Chapter 3 reviews the papyrus collections, indicating catalogues and editions. Only vol. 1, the Einführung, was published.

4. GROHMANN, A., *Arabische Papyruskunde.* (Hdb. d. Orientalistik, Abteilung 1, Ergänzungsband 2, Halbband 1, ii.) Leiden, &c., 1966.

Based on a format similar to that of the *Einführung,* this manual, representing Grohmann's latest survey of Arabic papyrology, provides much new information and bibliographical data on catalogues and editions.

## B. Supplement

1. For further periodical articles in European languages *Index Islamicus* and *Supplements* cover the years 1906–.
2. Some additional information on the collections may be found in the article by A. Dietrich in *Bibliotheca Orientalis* **25**, 1968, p. 81 (a review of Grohmann's *Arabische Papyruskunde*), and in J. D. Pearson's *Oriental manuscripts in Europe and North America; a survey.* (Bibliotheca Asiatica, 7.) Zug, 1971.
3. ABBOTT, N., *Studies in Arabic literary papyri, vol. 2: Qur'ānic commentary and tradition.* (Univ. of Chicago, Or. Inst. publs., 76.) Chicago, 1967.

Vol. 1 is cited by Grohmann; a third volume is projected entitled 'Language and literature'.

4. GROHMANN, A., *Arabische Paläographie.* Teil 1. (Öster. Akad. Wiss., phil.-hist. Kl., Denkschriften, Bd. 94, Abh. 1.) Vienna, 1967.

The first part of a projected three-part work on Arabic palaeography of which two parts have appeared to date. Part 1 has an exhaustive study of papyrus and other writing materials, writing implements and inks. Part 2 of the work deals with monumental inscription.

5. The small body of literature published in Arabic has concerned itself mainly with the palaeography of Arabic papyri. Among more recent studies may be cited:

SHABBŪḤ, Ibrāhīm, 'Baʿḍ mulāḥaẓāt ʿalā khaṭṭ al-bardiyyāt al-ʿarabiyya al-miṣriyya'. *Abḥāth al-Nadwa al-Duwaliyya li-Ta'rīkh al-Qāhira* **1**, 1970, pp. 15–47.

-MUNAJJID, Ṣalāḥ al-Dīn, *Dirāsāt fī ta'rīkh al-khaṭṭ al-ʿarabī mundhu bidāyatihi ilā nihāyat al-ʿaṣr al-umawī*, pp. 37–9, 115–19. Beirut, 1972.

# Archives

DEREK HOPWOOD

Other sections of this guide deal with manuscripts, papyri and library holdings. This paper attempts to be a guide to those collections specifically described as archival, usually administrative, diplomatic and juridical records, accounts and private correspondence. Such records are scattered through the world in public record offices, in libraries, in mosques, churches and monasteries, in local administrative centres or still in private hands. The items listed here fall roughly into three categories: guides to the archival holdings of an institution, a region or country; published collections of or selections from specific archives; books or articles listing available archives in various locales on certain topics. Items in this paper are listed under the country *in* which the archives are to be found with a cross-references to the country *to* which they refer. For example, 'Turkish documents from English archives' would be listed under Britain with a reference under Turkey. As not all the items have been seen, however, it may be that on occasion the main entry is misplaced.

The importance of archives has long been recognized but only recently have several major efforts been made to locate and collect them. Guides to the major Western collections have been published, for example to the Public Record Office or the United States Archives, but the archives of the Middle East are less well known. In particular the Ottoman archives remain a largely unexplored field, yet their importance to Middle Eastern history is indisputable. The Egyptian archives have only recently begun to be utilized for certain areas of research. Political and national considerations often hinder access to archive collections, not only in the Middle East but elsewhere, and especially in the Soviet Union where few Western scholars have been able to consult the archives.

Several bodies are now concerned with preserving and cataloguing archives. The International Council on Archives has been preparing several series of guides to the archival materials of many countries concerning the history of South America, Africa and Asia. These guides aim to contain inventories and indexes of archive collections and will be issued according to the countries holding the collections. At the time of writing this project has only just begun and more information may be obtained from the Interdocumentation Company of Leiden, Holland.

The British Academy's Committee on Oriental Documents has been established to promote the editing and publication of such documents of historical and archival importance in Oriental languages as are to be found in British archives and private collections. A conference of scholars met recently (1974) in Paris to discuss the location and importance of Arabic archival material. A volume containing their findings was published in 1976.

The private papers of officials and others who lived and worked in the Middle East can often provide valuable additional information to that found in public archives. In Great Britain, at least, a determined effort was made to collect such papers from forgotten corners of attics before they were lost for ever. As the period of colonialism and imperialism passed, as men grew old, so there was an urgent need to gather in their memories, either written or oral. Some oral records projects have been undertaken but mainly several important private papers collections have been established, notably the Sudan Archive in Durham, the Colonial Records Project at Rhodes House, Oxford, and the Middle Eastern Private Papers Collection at St. Antony's College, Oxford. The Historical Manuscripts Commission in London makes a continuing effort to locate valuable papers and the London School of Economics is listing British political archives. Professor J. D. Pearson is at present (1977) editing a guide to documents and manuscripts in the British Isles relating to the Near and Middle East which was compiled some years ago by M. D. Wainwright and N. Mathews.

Several journals, *Archivum, Archives, American Archivist*, may be consulted for the most recent information. The *Index Islamicus* lists articles on archives, but not separately and they have to be searched for under the history of the country concerned. The following work may be usefully consulted for general information:

BADR, Aḥmad, *Dalīl dūr al-maḥfūẓāt wa-al-maktabāt wa-marākiz al-tawthīq wa-al-maʿāhid al-bibliyūghrāfiyya fī al-duwal al-ʿarabiyya; Directory of archives, libraries, documentation centres and bibliographical institutions in Arabic-speaking countries; Répertoire des archives, bibliothèques, centres de documentation et institutions bibliographiques en pays arabes*. Cairo, 1965.

## I. MIDDLE EAST

*General*

The Bulletin of the Middle East Studies Association of North America has published a valuable series of articles on research facilities in various Middle Eastern countries. The articles are listed here under the relevant country. In addition to information on general research facilities, they often contain useful data on the local archives. The journal *Archivum* (UNESCO) has numerous references to archives in Arab countries, in particular in volume 5. There are articles in the *Encyclopedia of Islam*[2] under 'Daftar' and 'Diplomatic' which are relevant.

BADR, Ahmed, *Répertoire des archives, bibliothèques, centres de documentation et institutions bibliographiques en pays arabes*. Cairo, 1965.

BERQUE, J. *et al.*, *Les arabes par leurs archives*. (Colloque internat. du C.N.R.S., 555.) Paris, 1976.

BRAVMANN, M. M., 'The state archives in the early Islamic era'. *Arabica* **15**, 1968, pp. 87–9.

DAVIDSON, R. H., 'Archives in the Near East, with special reference to Ottoman history'. *News from the Center* **4**, Fall 1968, pp. 2–11.

LEWIS, B., 'Sources for the economic history of the Middle East'. (In M. A. Cook *ed.*, *Studies in the economic history of the Middle East*, Oxford, 1970, pp. 78–92.)

ROEMER, H. R., 'Christliche Klosterarchive in der islamischen Welt'. (In *Der Orient in der Forschung; Festschrift für O. Spies*, Wiesbaden, 1967, pp. 543–56.)

SAUVAGET, J., *Introduction to the history of the Muslim East; a bibliographical guide,* based on the second edition by C. Cahen. Berkeley, 1965.

Pp. 16–21 'Archives'; pp. 193–201 'Sources of Ottoman history; archives'.

STERN, M. *ed., Documents from Islamic chanceries.* Oxford, 1965.

SEE ALSO

GREAT BRITAIN, Owen, Yapp.

OTTOMAN EMPIRE, Lewis (*Ottoman archives as a source for the history of Arab lands*).

YUGOSLAVIA, Bajraktarević, Korkut.

*Egypt*

The archives in Egypt are among those best described in the Middle East. Several scholars have devoted much attention to describing and publishing them, from the early days of Deny and Rustum to the more recent work of Shaw, Rivlin and Crecelius. But as archive collections have been moved and recatalogued so the information contained in the earlier works becomes out of date. Even Rivlin's guide of 1970 must be supplemented by Schölch's and Crecelius's articles. The extensive collections of the Cairo Geniza documents are scattered through several libraries, but Shaked's bibliography is an attempt to locate them and Goitein's works are indispensable for Geniza scholarship.

CRECELIUS, D., 'The organization of *waqf* documents in Cairo'. *IJMES* **2**, 1971, pp. 266–77.

A useful survey which should be read in conjunction with his as yet unpublished paper 'On archival sources for demographic studies of the Middle East', which despite its title deals only with Egypt.

DENY, J., *Sommaire des archives turques du Caire.* Cairo, 1930.

EGYPT, *Documents diplomatiques concernant l'Égypte de Méhémet Ali jusqu'en 1920* réunis par L'Association Égyptienne de Paris. Paris, 1920.

GOITEIN, S. D., *A Mediterranean society.* 2v. Berkeley, &c., 1967, 71.

HUNTER, F. R., 'The Cairo archives for the study of élites in modern Egypt'. *IJMES* **4**, 1973, pp. 476–88.

ḤUSAYN, Muḥammad A., *Al-wathā'iq al-ta'rīkhiyya.* Cairo, 1954.

Chapter 7: ''Al-arshīfāt wa-al-wathā'iq al-miṣriyya'. Pp. 109–12 list sources.

NAHOUM, H., *Recueil de firmans impériaux adressés aux valis et aux khédives d'Egypte, 1006 H.–1322 H. (1597 JC–1904 JC).* Cairo, 1934.

RAYMOND, A., *Artisans et commerçants au Caire au XVIII^e siècle.* 2v. Damascus, 1973.

Pp. xxi–xxvi contain a description of the archival sources in Cairo. Works by E. Driault and G. Douin also have useful information about archives.

RICHARDS, D. S., 'Arabic documents from the Karaite community in Cairo'. *JESHO* **15**, 1972, pp. 105–62.

RIVLIN, H. A., *The Dar al-Wathā'iq in 'Ābdīn Palace of Cairo as a source for the study of the modernization of Egypt in the nineteenth century.* Leiden, 1970.

ROEMER, H. R., 'Arabische Herrscherurkunden aus Ägypten'. *OLZ* **61**, 1966, pp. 325–34.

—— 'Documents et archives de l'Égypte islamique'. *MIDEO* **5**, 1958, pp. 237–52.
—— 'Über Urkunden zur Geschichte Ägyptens . . . in islamischer Zeit'. *ZDMG* **107** (N.F. 32), 1957, pp. 519–38.

RUSTUM, A., *A calendar of state papers from the Royal Archives of Egypt relating to the affairs of Syria.* 4v. and index. Beirut, 1940–43.
'An exhaustive list'.

SCHÖLCH, A., Review of Rivlins 'Dār al-Wathā'iq'. *MES* **8**, 1972, p. 125.

SHAW, S. J., 'Cairo's archives and the history of Ottoman Egypt'. *Report on Current Research* (Middle East Institute, Washington). Spring, 1956.
—— 'Dār al-Maḥfūẓāt al-'umūmiyya' in *EI*².
This article lists some published collections from the archives of Ottoman Egypt.

SHAYYAL, Gamel el-Din, 'The Fatimid documents as a source for the history of the Fatimids and their institutions'. *Bull. Fac. Arts Alexandria* **8**, 1954, pp. 3–12.

STERN, S. M., *Fāṭimid decrees; original documents from the Fāṭimid Chancery.* London, 1964.

WIET, G., 'Petits papiers du consulat de France au Caire'. *Orient* **8**, 1958, pp. 79–108.

WILLIAMS, J. A., 'Research facilities in the U.A.R.'. *MESA bull.* **4**, ii, 1970, pp. 47–54.

SEE ALSO
GREAT BRITAIN, Deighton.
ITALY, Marro, Sammarco.
OTTOMAN EMPIRE, Adali, Altundağ, Bonelli, Shaw (*Ottoman archives*), Shaw (*Turkish source materials*).
U.S.S.R., Cataui.

*Sudan*

ABŪ SALĪM, Muḥammad I., *Al-murshid ilā wathā'iq al-Mahdī.* Khartoum, 1969.
A comprehensive calendar of the Mahdi's writings.

BAKHIET, Gaafar, *British administration and Sudanese nationalism.* Unpublished Ph.D. thesis, Cambridge, 1965.

BECHTOLD, P. K., 'Research facilities in the Sudan'. *MESA bull.* **7**, ii, 1973, pp. 23–31; Addendum in **9**, ii, 1975, pp. 30–5.

HILL, R. L., 'Mahdist MSS & lithographs (in the School of Oriental Studies, Durham)'. *Durham Philobiblon* **2**, vi, 1961, pp. 47–8.

HOLT, P. M., 'The archives of the Mahdia'. *SNR* **36**, 1955, pp. 71–80.
—— 'Mahdist archives and related documents'. *Archives* **28**, 1961–62, pp. 193–200.
—— *The Mahdist state in the Sudan.* 2nd edn. Oxford, 1970.
Pp. 267–75: 'The Mahdist Documents'.
—— 'The source materials of the Sudanese Mahdia'. *St. Antony's Papers* No. 4, *M.E. Affairs* **1**, pp. 107–19.

O'FAHEY, R. S., 'Arabic documents from Darfur'. *Bull. Int. Cttee on urgent anthrop. & ethnol. res.* **12**, 1970, pp. 117–18.

*Palestine*

As this guide deals with the Arab world, references to Israel as such are not included. However, some collections may contain material which is relevant to Arab affairs in Palestine and are therefore mentioned here.

BRINNER, W. M., 'Research facilities in Israel'. *MESA bull.* **7**, i, 1973, pp. 42–8.

ESHEL, Benzion, *Records of the Chief Secretary's Office 1918–1925*. Jerusalem, 1966.

In Hebrew with short introduction in English.

ISRAEL ARCHIVES ASSOCIATION, *Guide to the Archives in Israel*. Jerusalem, 1966.

In Hebrew.

SEE ALSO

ITALY, Pratesi, Roncaglia.

OTTOMAN EMPIRE, Heyd.

U.S.A., Kaganoff.

*Lebanon*

BAZ, Selim, *Pièces diplomatiques relatives aux événements de 1860 au Liban*. Beirut, 1974.

CHEVALLIER, D., *La société du Mont Liban à l'époque de la révolution industrielle en Europe*. Paris, 1971.

Pp. xiv–xvi discuss the archives in Beirut.

DAYR MĀR YŪḤANNĀ, *Maḥfūẓāt Dayr Mār Yuḥannā al-Ṣābīgh*.

DAYR AL-MUKHALLIṢ, *Maḥfūẓāt Dayr Mār al-Mukhalliṣ*. Sidon.

HOURANI, A. H., 'Historians of Lebanon'. (In B. Lewis and P. M. Holt *eds.*, *Historians of the Middle East*, Oxford, 1962.)

Pp. 242–5 contain a note on Lebanese archives.

HUDSON, M. C., 'Research facilities in Lebanon'. *MESA bull.* **6**, iii, 1972, pp. 17–25.

*Syria*

HUMPHREYS, S., 'Opportunities and facilities for research in Syria'. *MESA bull.* **8**, i, 1974, pp. 16–21.

MANDAVILLE, J., 'The Ottoman court records of Syria and Jordan'. *JAOS* **86**, 1966, pp. 311–19.

RUSTUM, Asad, *Al-uṣūl al-ʿarabiyya li-taʾrīkh Sūriya fī ʿahd Muḥammad ʿAlī Bāshā*. 5v. (in 4). Beirut, 1930–33.

'A collection of Arabic sources drawn from family papers and the archives of religious courts'. Rustum has also published several short works based on archival material; see the Hourani article noted under Lebanon, above.

SEE ALSO

EGYPT, Rustum.

*Jordan*

ABIDI, A. H. H., 'Select Arabic source material for the modern political history of Jordan'. *Int. studies* **4**, 1963, pp. 317–28.

SEE ALSO
SYRIA, Mandaville.

*Iraq*

KHAN, Rasheeduddin. 'Arabic source material for the political history of modern Iraq'. *Int. studies* **2**, 1961, pp. 298–316.

PÉROTIN, Y., *Organization of archives – Iraq.* (UNESCO.) Paris, 1970.

SEE ALSO
INDIA, Kumar, Sluglett.

*Arabia, Bahrain, Kuwait, Aden*

'Textes historiques sur le réveil arabe au Hedjaz'. *RMM* **46**, 1921, pp. 1–22; **47**, 1921, pp. 1–27; **50**, 1922, pp. 74–100; **57**, 1924, pp. 158–67.

SEE ALSO
GREAT BRITAIN, Introductory paragraph, Bidwell.

## II. NORTH AFRICA

JULIEN, C.-A., *History of North Africa from the Arab Conquest to 1830*, trans. by J. Petrie. London, 1970.

Pp. 353–421 contain a detailed survey of the sources for North African history.

LE TOURNEAU, R., 'Les archives musulmanes en Afrique du Nord'. *Archivum* **4**, 1954, pp. 175–8.

SEE ALSO
FRANCE, Cooke, France Ministère de la Guerre.
ITALY, Aumenier, Giglio.
SPAIN, Brunschvig.

*Morocco*

AGUILERA PLEGUEZUELO, J., 'Varios documentos referentes a la embajada marroquí al Papa Léon XIII'. *Tamuda* **1**, 1953, pp. 265–71.

ANON, 'La Bibliothèque Générale et archives'. *Bull. signalétique*, vol. ii, Rabat, 1963.

AYACHE, G., 'La question des archives historiques marocaines'. *Hespéris-Tamuda* **2**, 1961, pp. 311–26.

—— 'L'utilisation et l'apport des archives historiques marocaines'. *Hespéris-Tamuda* **7**, 1966, pp. 69–85.

—— 'Une source inutilisée pour l'histoire du Maroc: les archives marocaines'. (In *Trudy XXV Mezhdunarod. Kong. Vostokovedov, Moscow 1960* **2**, Moscow, 1963, pp. 23–6.)

BAUDRY, J., 'Une ambassade au Maroc en 1767. Documents inédits'. *Rev. quest. hist.* N.S. **36** (80), 1906, pp. 181–98.

BERQUE, J., 'Petits documents d'histoire sociale marocaine; les archives d'un cadi rural'. *RA* **94**, 1950, pp. 113–24.

BRISSAC, P. de C., 'Quelques documents inédits sur le Maroc (1670–1680)'. *Hespéris* **37**, 1950, pp. 97–116.

BROWN, K. and others, 'Research facilities in Morocco'. *MESA bull.* **4**, iii, 1970, pp. 55–67; Addendum in **7**, iii, 1973, pp. 47–52.

KETTANI, Mohammed I., 'Les sections d'archives et de manuscrits des bibliothèques marocaines'. *Hespéris-Tamuda* **9**, 1968, pp. 459–68.

NALLINO, M., 'Documenti arabi sulle relazioni tra Genova e il Marocco nella seconda metà del secolo XVIII'. *RSO* **21**, 1946, pp. 51–76.

ROUX, A., 'Quelques documents manuscrits sur les campagnes de Moulay el Hassan'. *Hespéris* **22**, 1936, pp. 90–3.

SEE ALSO

EUROPE, Castries, Guillen, Miège.

FRANCE, Grillon, Yver.

GERMANY, Guillen (*L'Allemagne*), Guillen (*Les sources*).

SPAIN, Aledo, Arribas Palau, Garcia Figueras, Ricard.

SWEDEN, Zetterstéen.

*Algeria*

Most of the French archives dealing with the pre-1962 period were removed to the Archives d'Outre Mer at Les Fenouillères at Aix-en-Provence. Therefore, some of the articles listed below are out of date as to the location of the material referred to.

BOYER, P., 'Notice sur les archives départementales d'Alger'. *RA* **101**, 1957, pp. 393–6.

BRAIBANT, C., 'Inventaire des archives de l'Amirauté d'Alger'. *RA* **63**, 1922, pp. 39–84.

COUR, A., 'Deux documents sur les relations du gouvernement d'Alger avec les indigènes de Blida en janvier 1836'. *RA* **51**, 1907, pp. 107–15.

DELVOUX, A., *Archives du Consulat Général de France à Alger*. Algiers, 1865.

DENY, J., 'A propos du fonds arabe-turc des archives du Gouvernement Général de l'Algérie'. *RA* **62**, 1921, pp. 375–8.

—— 'Documents turcs inédits relatifs à l'Algérie des années 1754 à 1829'. *JA* 11 ser. **3**, 1914, pp. 708–9.

—— 'Les registres de solde des Janissaires conservés à la Bibliothèque Nationale d'Alger'. *RA* **61**, 1920, pp. 19–46, 212–60.

ESQUER, G., 'Les sources de l'histoire de l'Algérie'. (In *Histoire et historiens de l'Algérie*, Paris, 1931.)

'A survey of archives, libraries and bibliographies relevant to Algeria'.

ESQUER, G. & DERMENGHEM, E., *Répertoire* (Archives du Gouv. Générale de l'Algérie). Algiers, 1953.

GRAMMONT, H. de, *Correspondance des Consuls d'Alger (1690–1742)*. Algiers, &c., 1890.

KOERNER, F., 'Sources de l'histoire contemporaine de l'Algérie conservées à Oran (1830–1955)'. *Rev. hist. civ. Maghreb* **9**, 1970, pp. 95–103.

LESPÈS, R., 'Quelques documents sur la corporation des Mozabites d'Alger depuis les premiers temps de la conquête (1830–38)'. *RA* **66**, 1925, pp. 197–218.

NOUSCHI, A., 'Archives de l'ex-Gouvernement Générale de l'Algérie, série HH'. *CT* **9**, 1961, 36, pp. 1–79.

PÉROTIN, Y., *Algérie: archives publiques.* (UNESCO.) Paris, 1964.

A summary of archival material in Algeria and a proposal for the future organization of archives.

PESTEMALDJOGLOU, 'Contributions à l'histoire de la colonisation de d'Algérie. La Série M des Archives départementales d'Oran'. *RA* **82**, 1938, pp. 138–57.

PLANTET, E., *La correspondance des Deys d'Alger avec la cour de France* (*1579–1833*). 2v. Paris, 1898.

ROY, B., 'Deux documents inédits sur l'expédition algérienne de 1628 contre les Tunisiens'. *RT* 1917, pp. 183–204.

ZARTMAN, I. W., 'Research facilities in Algeria'. *MESA bull.* **4**, i, 1970, pp. 42–50.

SEE ALSO

FRANCE, Ageron, Bourgin, Bourgin & Dillaye, Hassenforder, Heggoy, Yacono.

ITALY, Veccia Vaglieri.

*Tunisia*

BACQUENCOURT, M. de & GRANDCHAMP, P., 'Documents divers concernant Don Philippe d'Afrique, prince tunisien, deux fois rénegat (1646–86)'. *RT* 1938, pp. 55–77, 289–311.

GANDOLPHE, M., 'Extraits de l'ouvrage "Documenti sulla storia di Tunis", da G. Niculy detto Limberi'. *RT* 1919, pp. 507–13.

GANIAGE, J., *Les origines du protectorat français en Tunisie 1861–88.* Paris, 1959.

Pp. 702–22 contain information on archives in Tunisia and Europe.

GHALLOUSSI, Béchir, 'Archives du Sahel au XIX siècle'. *CT* **8**, 1960, pp. 97–108.

GRANDCHAMP, P., 'Documents concernant la course dans la Régence de Tunisie de 1764 à 1769 et de 1783 à 1843'. *CT* **5**, 1957, pp. 269–340.

—— 'Documents relatifs à la fin de l'occupation espagnole en Tunisie (1567–1574)'. *RT* 1914, pp. 3–13.

—— *Documents relatifs à la révolution de 1864 en Tunisie.* 2v. Tunis, 1935.

—— 'Documents turcs relatifs aux relations entre Tunis et la Toscane (1626–1703)'. *RT* 1940, pp. 109–14.

HANNEZO, G., 'Documents inédits concernant la Tunisie'. *RT* 1921, pp. 80–2, 143–5, 217–19; 1922, pp. 265–72.

HEGGOY, A. A., 'The National Archives and research libraries of Tunis'. *Maghreb digest* **5**, iii, 1967, pp. 5–9.

MANTRAN, R., 'Documents turcs relatifs à l'armée tunisienne'. *CT* **4**, 1956, pp. 359–72.

—— *Inventaire des documents d'archives turcs du Dar el-Bey* (*Tunis*). Paris, 1961.

MARTEL, A., *Les confins Saharo-Tripolitains de la Tunisie 1881–1911*. 2v. Paris, 1965.
Pp. iii–xvii on archival material.

MZALI, Mohammed S. & PIGNON, J., 'Documents sur Khérédine'. *RT* 1934, pp. 177–225, 347–96; 1935, pp. 50–80, 209–33, 289–307; 1936, pp. 223–54; 1937, pp. 209–52, 409–32; 1938, pp. 79–153; 1940, pp. 71–107, 251–302.

PLANTET, E., *La correspondance des Beys de Tunis et des Consuls de France avec la Cour (1577–1830)*. 3v. Paris, 1893–99.

RACCAGNI, M., 'Research facilities in Tunisia'. *MESA bull.* **6**, i, 1972, pp. 30–6.

SEE ALSO
ALGERIA, Roy.
FRANCE, Grandchamp, Martel.
U.S.A., Triulzi.

*Libya*

BONO, S., 'Fonti inedite di storia della Tripolitania'. *Libia* **1**, ii, 1953, pp. 117–21.

MURABET, M., *A bibliography of Libya, with particular reference to sources available in libraries and public archives in Libya*. La Valetta, 1959.

TOSCHI, P., *Le fonti inedite della storia della Tripolitania*. Rome? 1934.
Lists archival material preserved in Tripoli in the various consulates and elsewhere, and also relevant material in Paris, London and Italy.

WARD, P., *A survey of Libyan bibliographical resources*. 2nd edn. Tripoli, 1970.

SEE ALSO
SWEDEN, Zetterstéen.

## III. NON-ARAB COUNTRIES

*Ottoman Empire – Turkey*

ADALI, Hasan, 'Documents pertaining to the Egyptian question in the Yildiz collection of the *Başbakanlik Arşivi*, Istanbul'. (In P. M. Holt *ed.*, *Political and social change in modern Egypt*, London, 1968, pp. 52–8.)

ALTUNDAĞ, Şinasi, 'Ottoman archival materials on nineteenth century Egyptian history'. (In P. M. Holt *ed.*, *Political and social change*, pp. 49–51.)

BAJRAKTAREVIĆ, F., 'Glavni Carigradski arhiv i ispisi iz njega. (Les Archives Centrales de Constantinople et leurs extraits.)' *Prilozi Orijent. Filol. Ist.* **6–7**, 1956–57, pp. 283–98. (French résumé pp. 298–9.)

BAYERLE, G., 'Towards a classification of Ottoman *tapu* registers'. *Acta or.* **32**, 1970, pp. 15–19.

BONELLI, L., 'Una collezione di firmani ottomani riguardanti l'Egitto dal 1597 al 1904'. *OM* **15**, 1935, pp. 42–4.

FEKETE, L., 'Über Archivalien und Archivwesen in der Türkei'. *Acta or. hung.* **3**, 1953, pp. 179–206.

HEYD, U., *Ottoman documents on Palestine 1552–1615; a study of the firman according to the Mühimme Defteri*. Oxford, 1960.

—— 'The Mühimme Defteri (Register of Decrees): a major source for the study of Ottoman administration'. (*Akten 24 Int. Cong. Or. 1957*, Wiesbaden, 1959, pp. 389–91.)

LEWIS, B., 'Başvekalet Arşivi' in *EI*².

—— 'The Ottoman archives as a source for the history of Arab lands'. *JRAS* 1951, pp. 139–55.

—— 'Studies in the Ottoman archives'. *BSOAS* **16**, 1954, pp. 469–501.

PETROSYAN, Y. A., 'Tsennye publikatsii turetskikh arkhivnykh materialov'. *Problemy vostokoved.* 1959, i, pp. 158–9.

REYCHMAN, J. & ZAJACZOWSKI, A., *Handbook of Ottoman-Turkish diplomatics.* The Hague, 1968.

SAUVAGET, J., *Introduction to the history of the Muslim East.* Berkeley, 1965.
Pp. 193–201 provide a useful list of works published on the Ottoman archives and of documents published. There is also some information on European archives.

SERTOĞLU, Midhat, *Muhteva bakimindan Başvekâlet Arşivi.* Ankara, 1955.

SHAW, S. J., 'The Ottoman archives as a source for Egyptian history'. *JAOS* **83**, 1963, pp. 447–52.

—— 'Turkish source materials for Egyptian history'. (In P. M. Holt *ed.*, *Political and social change*, pp. 28–48.)

WITTEK, P., 'Les archives de Turquie'. *Byzantion* **13**, 1936, pp. 691–9.

—— 'Zu einigen frühosmanischen Urkunden'. *WZKM* **53**, 1957, pp. 300–13; **54**, 1957, pp. 240–55; **55**, 1959, pp. 122–41; **56**, 1960, pp. 267–84.

SEE ALSO

ALGERIA, Deny (*A propos du fonds*), Deny (*Documents*), Deny (*Registres*).

EGYPT, Deny, Nahoum, Shaw (*Cairo's archives*), Shaw (*Dār al-Maḥfūẓāt*).

EUROPE, Davidson.

FRANCE, Spiridonakis.

GREAT BRITAIN, Heywood, Kurat.

SWEDEN, Zetterstéen.

TUNISIA, Grandchamp (*Documents turcs*), Mantran (*Documents turcs*), Mantran (*Inventaire*).

## IV. INDIA

KUMAR, R., 'The records of the Government of India on the Berlin Baghdad railway question'. *Hist. J.* **5**, 1962, pp. 70–9.

LOW, D. A. and others, *Government archives in South Asia; a guide to national and state archives in Ceylon, India and Pakistan.* Cambridge, 1969.

SLUGLETT, P., *Britain in Iraq 1914–1932.* (St. Antony's Middle East monographs, 4.) Oxford, 1976.
Contains information on Indian archives relevant to Iraq.

## V. EUROPE

*General*

CASTRIES, H. de, *Les sources inédits de l'histoire du Maroc de 1530 à 1843.* 26v. Paris, 1905–.

This is a multi-volume work in two series which is still in course of publication. The contents consist of materials from the archives of England, France, Holland, Spain and Portugal, preceded by studies by experts in the field.

DAVIDSON, R. H., 'European archives as a source for later Ottoman history'. *Report on current research* (M.E. Inst.) Washington, 1958, pp. 33–45.

GUILLEN, P., 'Les sources européennes sur le Maroc (fin XIXe – début XXe siècles)'. *Hespéris-Tamuda* **7**, 1966, pp. 87–96.

MIÈGE, J.-L., *Le Maroc et l'Europe 1830–1894.* 4v. Paris, 1961–63.

Volume 1 has much material on relevant archives.

THOMAS, H., *Guide to the diplomatic archives of Western Europe.* Philadelphia, 1959.

SEE ALSO

LEBANON, Baz.

LIBYA, Toschi.

TUNISIA, Ganiage, Martel.

*Belgium*

VANDEWOUDE, É. & VANRIE, A., *Guide des sources de l'histoire d'Afrique du Nord, d'Asie et d'Océanie conservées en Belgique.* Bruxelles, 1972.

*France*

Sauvaget (*op. cit.*) discusses the French Archives on p. 196. The Foreign Ministry Archives in Paris contain correspondence from Morocco, Tunisia and Iran. An *État numérique* (1936) is a catalogue classified according to country. The bulk of the archives from Algeria have been transferred to Aix-en-Provence and are discussed in the article by Heggoy.

The correspondence of several notable figures in Algerian history was published in the series 'Collection de documents inédits sur l'histoire de l'Algérie après 1830'. The first series was 'Correspondance générale', the second 'Documents divers'.

AGERON, C.-R., *Les algériens musulmans et la France (1871–1919).* 2v. Paris, 1968.

Pp. 1247–57 contain useful information on archives.

BOURGIN, G., 'Les documents de l'Algérie conservés aux Archives nationales'. *RA* **50**, 1906, pp. 157–84.

BOURGIN, G. & DILLAYE, M., 'Inventaire du fond de l'Algérie aux Archives Nationales (F80 suite)'. *RA* **69**, 1928, pp. 249–305; **70**, 1929, pp. 68–113; **72**, 1931, pp. 332–4.

COOKE, J. J., 'The Army Archives at Vincennes'. *MW* **61**, January 1971, pp. 35–8.

For the study of North African history in the colonial period.

DOCUMENTATION FRANÇAISE, *Les archives nationales.* (Doc. Fr. Illustrée 250–1.) Paris, 1969.

FRANCE, Ministère de la Guerre, *L'Afrique du Nord; Bibliographie militaire des ouvrages français ou traduits en français et des articles.* 4v. Paris, 1930.

Still useful.

GRANDCHAMP, P. *ed.*, *Le citoyen Louis Guiraud proconsul de la R.F. à Tunis (1796); correspondance et documents inédits.* Tunis, 1919.

The editor published several articles in the *Revue Tunisienne* dealing with Tunisian documents.

GRILLON, P. *ed.*, *Un chargé d'affaires au Maroc; la correspondance du consul Louis Chénier 1767–1782.* Paris, 1970.

HASSENFORDER, 'Inventaire des archives historiques du musée du Val-de-Grâce concernant l'Algérie'. *RA* **99**, 1955, pp. 379–416.

HEGGOY, A. A., 'Some useful French depositories for the study of the Algerian revolution'. *MW* **58**, 1968, pp. 345–7.

MARTEL, A., 'Sources inédits de l'histoire tunisienne. Les Papiers Nyssen aux Archives Nationales'. *CT* **5**, 1957, pp. 349–80.

SPIRIDONAKIS, B. G., *Empire ottoman; inventaire des mémoires et documents aux Archives du Ministère des Affaires éstrangères* [sic] *de France.* Thessaloniki, 1973.

YACONO, X., *Les bureaux arabes et l'évolution des genres de vie indigènes dans l'ouest du Tell algérois.* Paris, 1953.

YVER, G., 'Documents relatifs à la guerre franco-marocaine de 1844'. *RA* **5**, 1910, pp. 62–83.

SEE ALSO

ALGERIA, Delvoux, Esquer (*Les sources*), Grammont, Plantet.

EGYPT, Wiet.

TUNISIA, Plantet.

*Great Britain*

The British Academy Committee on Oriental Documents is sponsoring the publication of documents in Oriental languages in British archives (see article in *Bulletin of British Society for Middle Eastern Studies* **1**, i, 1974, pp. 18–19; also Heywood, below). The Bahrain Court Records are at present being listed and it is hoped to edit the Arabic material from the Aden Residency. Most archival material from Aden has been deposited in the India Office Library.

BIDWELL, R. *ed.*, *Affairs of Kuwait.* 2v. *Affairs of Arabia.* 2v. (F.O. Confidential Print.) London, 1971.

COOK, C. *ed.*, *Sources in British political history 1900–51.* 3v. London, 1975–.

DEIGHTON, H. S., 'Some English sources for the study of modern Egyptian history'. (In P. M. Holt *ed.*, *Political and social change*, pp. 59–67.)

GIUSEPPE, M. S., *Guide to the contents of the Public Record Office* (H.M.S.O.). 3v. London, 1963–68.

HEYWOOD, C., *Turkish documents from English Archives 1660–1703.* (To be published.)

KURAT, A. N., 'Some Turkish records and materials in the Public Record Office (London) and English Libraries'. *Ankara Üniv. Dil ve Tarih-Coğ. Fak. Derg.* 7, 1949, pp. 25–7.

OWEN, E. R. J. *ed.*, *A list of the locations of records belonging to British firms and to British businessmen active in the Middle East 1800–1950.* (St. Antony's College, Oxford.)

A duplicated list.

PUGH, R. B., *The Records of the Colonial and Dominion Offices* (H.M.S.O.). London, 1964.

This is P.R.O. Handbooks No. 3 and there are also No. 4 *List of Cabinet Papers 1880–1914*, No. 6 *List of Papers of the Committee of Internal Defence to 1914*, No. 11 *Records of the Cabinet Office to 1922*, No. 13 *Records of the Foreign Office 1782–1939.*

SUTTON, S. C., *A Guide to the India Office Library* (H.M.S.O.). London, 1967.

YAPP, M. E., 'The India Office Records as a source for the economic history of the Middle East'. (In M. A. Cook *ed.*, *Studies in the economic history of the Middle East*, London, 1970.)

*Germany*

AMERICAN HISTORICAL ASSOCIATION, *A catalogue of files and microfilms of the German Foreign Ministry Archives 1867–1920.* (Committee for the study of War Documents), 1959.

GUILLEN, P., *L'Allemagne et le Maroc.* Paris, 1967.

—— 'Les sources allemandes sur le Maroc'. *Ann. Afr. Nord* 1963, pp. 1023–38.

Survey of archives in Germany and elsewhere.

KENT, G. O., *A catalogue of files and microfilms of the German Foreign Ministry Archives 1920–45.* (Historical Office, Department of State), 1962.

*Italy and the Vatican*

AUMENIER, V. & MIÈGE, J.-L., 'Sources italiennes sur l'Afrique du Nord'. *Ann. Afr. Nord* 1964, pp. 713–26; 1966, pp. 793–811.

Detailed survey of Archives in Italy.

GIGLIO, C. *ed.*, *Inventario delle fonti manoscritte relative alla storia dell' Africa del Nord esistenti in Italia.* (Ist. di Storia ed Istituzioni dei Paesi Afro-Asiatici della Univ. di Pavia.) Leiden, 1971–.

Vol. 1. *Gli archivi storici del soppresso Ministero dell' Africa Italiana e del Ministero degli Affari Esteri dalle origini al 1922.*

Vol. 2. *Gli archivi storici del Ministero della Difesa (Esercito, Marina, Aeronautica) dalle origini al 1922.*

Vol. 3. *Gli archivi pubblici della campania e in particolare l'Archivio di Stato di Napoli dalle origini al 1922.*

Other volumes are promised: 'I tomi successivi saranno dedicati agli Archivi di Stato e agli Archivi pubblici e privati che possiedono materiale relativo all' Africa del Nord'.

Most of the material deals with Libya with smaller sections on other parts of North Africa.

JENKINSON, H. & BELL, H. E., *Italian archives during the war and at its close.* London, 1947.

MARRO, G., 'Ibrahim Pacha dans les archives privées du consul Drovetti'. *Cahiers hist. ég.* **1**, 1948, pp. 66–77.

PRATESI, R., 'La questione dei Luoghi Santi; nuovi documenti, 1757. *Studia Orientalia* (Cairo) **1**, 1956, pp. 135–43.

RONCAGLIA, M., 'Note di storia di Terra Santa. Documenti inediti del Museo Correr (Venezia)'. *Studia Orientalia* (Cairo) **2**, 1957, pp. 35–51.

SAMMARCO, A., 'I documenti diplomatici concernenti il regno di Mohammed 'Alī e gli archivi di stato italiani'. *OM* **9**, 1929, pp. 287–96.

VALENSIN, G., 'Per un archivo bibliografico coloniale'. *Atti del congresso di studi coloniali* **1**, ii, 1931, pp. 203–10.

VECCIA VAGLIERI, L., 'Documenti vaticani relativi ad Algeri 1825–1830'. *OM* **10**, 1930, pp. 495–514, 575–88.

SEE ALSO

LIBYA, Bono.

MOROCCO, Nallino.

TUNISIA, Grandchamp (*Documents turcs relatifs aux relations entre Tunis et la Toscane*).

*Spain*

A short note on archives will be found in Pearson, J. D., *Oriental manuscripts in Europe and North America.* Zug, 1971, p. 278.

ALARCON Y SANTON & GARCIA DE LINARES, R., *Los documentos árabes diplomaticos del Archivo de la Corono de Aragón.* Madrid and Granada, 1940.

ALEDO, Marqués de, 'Unos documentos inéditos para la historia de la guerra de Africa (enero–abril 1860)'. *Boletin de la Real Acad. de la Hist.* **131**, 1952, pp. 31–62.

ARRIBAS PALAU, M., 'Documentos sobre Marruecos en el Archivo Histórico Nacional de Madrid'. *Hespéris-Tamuda* **9**, 1968, pp. 65–72.

BOSCH VILÁ, J., 'Los documentos árabes del archivo catedral de Huesca'. *RIEI* **5**, 1957, pp. 1–48.

BRUNSCHVIG, R., 'Documents inédits sur les relations entre la Couronne d'Aragon et la Berbérie orientale au XIVe siècle'. *AIEO* **2**, 1936, pp. 235–65.

GARCIA FIGUERAS, T., 'Documents espagnols sur le siège d'Arzila en 1508'. *Hespéris* **23**, 1936, pp. 3–8.

GONZALEZ PALENCIA, A., 'Documentos árabes del Cenete (Siglos XII–XV)'. *And.* **5**, 1940, pp. 301–82; **6**, 1941, pp. 477–80.

—— 'Los documentos árabes diplomaticos del archivo de la Corona de Aragón'. (In *Atti 19 Cong. Int. Or.* 1935, Rome, 1938, pp. 534–7.)

HOENERBACH, W., *Spanisch-islamische Urkunden aus der Zeit der Nasriden und Moriscos*, hrsg. und übers. Bonn, 1965.

KARAS, M., 'Materialy Arkhiva toledskikh mosarabov ot XII–XIII vekov'. *Vopr. ist.* **10**, 1950, pp. 95–103.

MARIN, F., *Guia historica y descriptiva de los archivos, bibliotecas y museos.* Madrid, 1966.

RICARD, R., 'Documentos sobre las relaciones de Andalacia con las plazas portuguesas de Marruecos (1541)'. *And.* **13**, 1948, pp. 275–92.

SANCHEZ BELDA, L., *Guia del Archivo Historico Nacional.* Madrid, 1955.

SECO DE LUCENA, L. *ed.*, *Documentos arábigo-granadinos; edición crítica del texto árabe y traducción al español con introducción, glosarios e índices.* Madrid, 1961.

SEE ALSO

TUNISIA, Grandchamp (*Documents relatifs à la fin de l'occupation espagnole*).

*Sweden*

ZETTERSTÉEN, K. V., 'The Oriental documents in the Swedish State Archives'. (In *Goldziher memorial volume* **1**, Budapest, 1948, pp. 191–208.)

Describes the author's largely unpublished catalogue, which includes Tripolitanica, Turcica and Maroccana.

*U.S.S.R.*

CATTAUI, R., 'L'importance des documents russes pour la connaissance du règne de Mohamed Aly'. *BIE* **18**, 1936, pp. 177–89.

GRIMSTED, P. K., *Soviet archives and manuscript collections: a bibliographical introduction.* Reprinted from the *Slavic Review* **24**, i, March 1965.

VALKA, S. N., *Tsentral'ny Gosudarstvenny istoricheskii Archiv SSSR v Leningrade.* Leningrad, 1956.

*Yugoslavia*

BAJRAKTAREVIĆ, F., *Dubrovačka Arabica.* (*Les documents arabes aux archives d'état à Dubrovnik.*) Belgrade, 1962.

BAJRAKTAREVIĆ, S., *Ottenfelsova orijentalistička zbirka u zagrebačkom Državnom arhivu.* Zagreb, 1959.

KALEŠI, H., *Najstariji vakufski documenti u Jugoslaviji na arapskom jeziku. Die ältesten Waqf-Urkunden in Jugoslawien in arabischer Sprache.* Priština, 1972.

KORKUT, Besim, *Arapski dokumenti u Državnom archivu u Dubrovniku.* 3v. Sarajevo, 1960–69.

Articles are regularly published in the journal *Prilozi za orijentalni filologiyu.* See also:

NURUDINOVIĆ, B., *Bibliografija jugoslovenske orijentalistike; Bibliography of Yugoslav orientalistics, 1945–1960.* Sarajevo, 1968.

## VI. U.S.A.

ECKHOFF, M. G. & MAVRO, A. P., *List of Foreign Service post records in the National Archives* (Record Group 84, The National Archives.) Washington, 1967.

HAMER, P. M., *A guide to archives and manuscripts in the United States.* Yale, 1961.

KAGANOFF, N. M., *A preliminary survey of the manuscript collections found in the American Jewish Historical Society*. Pt. 1. New York, 1967.

Contains references to several collections of papers dealing with Palestine.

NATIONAL ARCHIVES, *Material in the National Archives relating to the Middle East*. (Reference Information Papers, 44, May 1955.)

TRIULZI, A., 'Una fonte ignorata per la storia della Tunisia; i dispacci dei consoli americani a Tunìsi, 1797–1867'. *OM* **51**, 1971, pp. 653–78.

VAN TYNE, C. H., *Guide to the Archives of the United States in Washington*. Washington, 1907.

# Arabic epigraphy

A. D. H. BIVAR

## I. BIBLIOGRAPHIES (see also the chapter on 'Scientific Expeditions')

CRESWELL, K. A. C., *A bibliography of the architecture, arts and crafts of Islam.* Cairo, 1960; *Supplement.* Cairo, 1973.
The chapter on calligraphy and palaeography, 'Specimens on stone', is on pp. 675–714 of the original volume, pp. 215–22 of the supplement.

DANI, A. H., *Bibliography of the Muslim inscriptions of Bengal (down to A.D. 1538.* Dacca, 1957. (Suppl. *JAS Pakistan* **2**, 1957.)

MILES, G. C., 'Epigraphy'. *AI* **8**, 1941, pp. 105–8.
A full list of the Arabic inscriptions of Iran.

WIET, G., *L'exposition persane de 1931.* (I.F.A.O.) Cairo, 1933.
P. 137 contains a 'Liste chronologique des inscriptions buyides'. P. 10 illustrates a wooden door bearing an inscription of the Buyid 'Aḍud ad-Daula, apparently now in the museum at Persepolis.

## II. GENERAL TREATISES

COMBES, E. and others, *Répertoire chronologique de l'epigraphie arabe.* Cairo, 1931–.
Short texts with bibliography of the Arabic inscriptions known at the time of publication of each fascicule, arranged in chronological order. The earlier volumes are now seriously out of date.

GROHMANN, A., *Arabische Paläographie,* Teil 2. (Öster. Akad. Wiss., phil.-hist. Kl., Denkschriften **94**, Abh. 2.) Vienna, &c., 1971.
An elaborate treatment in the tradition of formal scholarship, but not very convenient to use. The Bibliography will presumably come in the following volume. Many inscriptions on hard materials are discussed and illustrated, with copious footnotes. The earlier vol. 1 dealt with preliminary matters.

SCHIMMEL, A.-M., *Islamic calligraphy.* Leiden, 1970.
An easy general treatment with useful bibliography and many references to epigraphic materials.

## III. UMAYYADS

-HAWARY, Hassan Mohammed, 'The most ancient Islamic monument known, dated A.H. 51 (A.D. 652)'. *JRAS* 1930, pp. 322–33.

KESSLER, C., ''Abd al-Malik's inscription in the Dome of the Rock; a reconsideration'. *JRAS* 1970, pp. 2–14.

MILES, G. C., 'Early Islamic inscriptions near Ṭā'if'. *JNES* **7**, 1948, pp. 236–42.

SHARON, M., 'An Arabic inscription of the time of the Caliph Abd al-Malik'. *BSOAS* **29**, 1966, pp. 367–72.

## IV. ABBASIDS AND CONTEMPORARY DYNASTIES

KURAISHI, Muhammad Hamid, 'A Kufic Sarada inscription from the Peshawar Museum'. *Epigraphia Indo-Moslemica* 1925–26, pp. 27–8.

MEGAW, A. H. S., 'A Muslim tombstone from Paphos'. *JRAS* 1950, pp. 108–9.

## V. LATER PRE-MONGOL DYNASTIES: EGYPT AND EASTWARDS

BIVAR, A. D. H., 'Seljuqid ziyārats of Sar-i Pul (Afghanistan)'. *BSOAS* **29**, 1966, pp. 57–63.

FLURY, S., 'Le décor épigraphique des monuments de Ghazna'. *Syria* **6**, 1925, pp. 61–90.

—— 'The Kufic inscriptions of Kisimkazi mosque, Zanzibar, 500 H. (A.D. 1107)'. *JRAS* 1922, pp. 257–64.

GROHMANN, A., 'The origin and early development of floriated Kufic'. *AO* **2**, 1957, pp. 103–63.

MILES, G. C., ''Ali b. 'Īsā's pilgrim road; an inscription of the year 304 H. (A.D. 916–17)'. *BIE* **36**, 1953–54, pp. 477–87.

—— 'Early Islamic tombstones from Egypt in the Museum of Fine Arts, Boston'. *AO* **2**, 1957, pp. 215–26.

—— 'Inscriptions on the minarets of Saveh, Iran'. (In *Studies in Islamic art and architecture in honour of Professor K. A. C. Creswell*, Cairo, 1965, pp. 163–78.)

SOURDEL-THOMINE, J., 'Le coufique alépin de l'époque seljoukide'. (In *Mélanges Louis Massignon* **3**, pp. 301–17.)

—— 'Deux monuments d'époque seljoukide en Afghanistan'. *Syria* **30**, 1953, pp. 108–36.

—— 'Stèles arabes de Bust (Afghanistan)'. *Arabica* **3**, 1956, pp. 285–306.

VOLOV, L., 'Plaited Kufic on Samanid epigraphic pottery'. *AI* **6**, 1966, pp. 107–33.

WIET, G., 'Nouvelles inscriptions fatimides'. *BIE* **24**, 1942, pp. 145–58.

## VI. AFRICA

DEVERDUN, G., *Inscriptions arabes de Marrakech.* (Publs., IHEM, 60.) Rabat, 1956.

ROSSI, P., *Le epigraphi musulmane del Museo di Tripoli.* Tripoli, 1953.

ROY, B. and others, *Inscriptions arabes de Kairouan.* 2v. (Publs., IHET, **2**, i–ii.) Tunis, 1950–58.

SAUVAGET, J., 'Les epitaphes royales de Gao'. *And.* **14**, 1949, pp. 123–41. Also in *Bull. de l'Inst. Français d'Afrique Noir* **12**, 1950, pp. 418–40.

ZBISS, M., *Corpus des inscriptions arabes de Tunisie.* 1: *Inscriptions de Tunis et de sa banlieue.* Tunis, 1955; *Inscriptions de Monastir.* Tunis, 1960.

## VII. AL-ANDALUS

LÉVI-PROVENÇAL, E., *Inscriptions arabes d'Espagne.* Leiden, 1931.

NYKL, A. R., 'Arabic inscriptions in Portugal'. *Ars Islamica* **11–12**, 1946, pp. 167–83.

# Muslim numismatics

A. D. H. BIVAR

A full bibliography of the valid studies (since Gabrieli) in the numismatics of Islam would extend to a considerable length. An attempt is here made to reduce its bulk by listing first the recent bibliographical surveys, which taken together provide an all but comprehensive coverage of earlier publications; and by adding to these direct references to a select list of publications, especially some of the most recent. A number of standard items from the earlier literature are also included, so that practical use can as far as possible be made independently of the present selection, without need of constant resort to the larger bibliographies.

Surveys of the numismatic literature fall into two classes. In the first are those chiefly designed for the working numismatist, which allow rapid reference to modern and reliable information on the coins themselves. In this application, convenient arrangement and indexing, together with strict selection, are more important than sheer extent. In the second category are works primarily interesting to the bibliographer. In this class the work of Mayer is probably unequalled, since it lists numerous rarities and bibliographical curiosities, often unobtainable except in the larger centres, or superseded for purposes of current work, and so little known. Such items often throw special light on the history of the subject, or on numismatic essays undertaken in remote regions. They can be helpful too in tracing reproductions of particular coins, and following their history in the collections. However, for current numismatic research Mayer's arrangement is not always convenient. Loss of time can result through looking up entries which are not locally available. The single alphabetical order of authors, and large undivided headings in the dynastic index are not always helpful for the rapid retrieval of specific information. The present essay will adopt the opposite emphasis, and cater rather for the numismatist than the specialist bibliographer, historiographer or antiquarian.

The traditional classification of Islamic coinage is according to dynasties. A similar arrangement would naturally be applicable to much of the pertinent literature. Since the present section is compiled as a revision of Gabrieli, the contributor's first instinct is to adopt the enumeration which he followed, that of 'Fraehn's classes', customarily indicated by Roman numerals. It should be pointed out, however, that this system is today inadequate and largely obsolete. One of the difficulties is that the complete tabulation of Fraehn's system is now rather inaccessible. A modified version is found in Codrington's *Manual*,[1] which is itself now antiquated. The greater problem is that coinages have since been discovered to which Fraehn allotted no place, and which are not easily placed in the system. The contributor charged with maintaining a comprehensive bibliography of Islamic coinage at the present day would find it most satisfactory

[1] O. Codrington, *A manual of Musalman numismatics* (Royal Asiatic Society Monographs VII), London, 1904; repr. Amsterdam, 1970.

to follow the numbering of Zambaur,[2] the most complete and logical list currently available, which moreover has the advantage of possessing its own elaborate indexes. The facility of ready reference to Zambaur's work is valuable in itself, since his dynastic tables contain a note against the name of each ruler and dynasty known by him to have issued surviving coins, and each section is followed by a bibliography. As his full repertoire of numbering is too detailed to be convenient for a short working list such as the present, the system adopted here is to subdivide merely according to the chapter-headings adopted by Zambaur, which are indicated, as are Fraehn's classes, by Roman numerals. In a few cases, where Zambaur's chapters bring together widely separated materials, it has seemed best further to divide them into two or three arbitrary sections (designated [a], [b], &c.).

The steady accretion in recent decades of studies on the numismatics of Islam has tended to show that the arrangement by dynasties, natural enough at first sight, presents serious inconveniences at the more detailed level. It is liable to mask the disturbed periods of dynastic change when the evidence of coinage is especially valuable since it provides a continuous record. In circumstances of dynastic struggle, mint-cities are known to have changed hands as often as four times in a single year. Yet the traditionally-arranged catalogues, especially where the dynasties in question originated in different geographical areas, can wholly obscure the sequence of events in such situations. Moreover, they tend to neglect, or even omit, the important anonymous issues that bridge the gaps in certain of the interregna, and also make it far from convenient to arrange the extensive municipal and autonomous copper issues of certain periods and regions. Provided that the volume of material available for study is sufficiently large, the arrangement of future catalogues in the form of a continuous mint-history may well prove the most satisfactory procedure. In recent work, such an arrangement is being increasingly employed, and its special advantages are likely to result in wider adoption, even though the number of entries in this section is still comparatively small.

At the same time, provision has to be made for other principles of compilation. The catalogues of particular museums are most conveniently listed under their location, whichever the dynasty or dynasties covered. Contributions dealing with specialized aspects of numismatic evidence such as mint technology, metrology and weights, or iconography, are most conveniently listed under special headings, though each individual coin discussed in such connections could find its place in a dynastic classification. The selection of items included under such heads is naturally limited, in a list of the present scope.

The theoretical analysis of hoards and casual finds represents a special branch of numismatic research. Such deposits can contain the issues of one, or of many dynasties. Their contents can cover a wide, or narrow, span of years. In other fields of numismatics, where the recorded evidence of hoards is very plentiful, systematic study of such deposits has produced rich results, of interest from different viewpoints. In the case of the Islamic coinage, ample hoard evidence has been recorded from Sweden, and in recent years from Eastern Europe and the USSR, but the number of recorded hoards of Middle Eastern origin is so far rather small, and this section of the bibliography relatively brief. It is likely

[2] E. von Zambaur, *Manuel de généalogie et de chronologie pour l'histoire de l'Islam*, Hanover, 1927 (rep. Bad Pyrmont, 1955), pp. x–xii.

to expand considerably with the application of modern methods, and throw light on the nature of local 'coin-populations', and circulation areas. Casual finds and excavation material are for the time being allotted to the same heading as the hoards. Yet between hoards and excavation material there exists a difference of character. The former, on the one hand, usually come to light in sealed containers, are composed of issues of high intrinsic character (gold or silver), and are generally in an excellent state of preservation. Since the coins were deliberately hidden, in locations that were not obvious, their discovery, even in the course of excavations, depends largely on chance. Yet the greater part of the coinage typically found in excavations consists rather of lower denominations, the pieces having been lost or abandoned. These are issues of base metal – copper or potin – and are generally recovered in poor preservation, often heavily corroded from contact with the soil. Such material is none the less valuable for its relation to local conditions, and to the local authorities. In the same way gold and silver reflect the conditions and policies of the great dynastic centres, which were often, in the case of the 'Abbāsid Caliphate, for example, situated at a great distance from the site of an individual coin-find.

Inevitably, in classifying the literature of numismatics, with its numerous aspects of interest outlined above, conflicting principles of arrangement tend to overlap. A fully comprehensive bibliography requires some further indexing. Since the arrangement is classified, an index of authors is necessary. An index of dynasties may also be useful, covering the items not themselves arranged dynastically. The addition of an index of mint-cities, as included in many coin-catalogues, would require much laborious searching of comprehensive articles, and is here hardly justified.

One final bibliographical source for numismatics needs to be mentioned, the evidence of the Arabic historical writers themselves. It is not true, as Rosenthal asserted,[3] that the Arab historians never made use of numismatic evidence, or cited accurate descriptions of coins. Besides the important mint treatises (Section I), there are several authors, in particular Ibn 'Idharī and al-Mas'ūdī, who make repeated reference to the legends and dates upon coins and seals. These notices are however too scattered to be easily assembled in a list of the present character, and need first to be collected in article form, before they can be made easily available to the student.

A collective work of recent appearance calls for special notice, the Festschrift published in honour of George C. Miles.[4] Not only does it include the bibliography of that author's writings. The 34 articles by leading authorities include 18 concerned with aspects of Muslim numismatics, not separately included in the following analysis.

## I. BIBLIOGRAPHICAL SURVEYS

ZAMBAUR, E. von, *Die Münzprägungen des Islams*. Wiesbaden, 1968, pp. 16–25. The most convenient bibliography down to 1942 for the working numismatist.

[3] Franz Rosenthal, *A history of Muslim historiography*, Leiden, 1952, p. 113: 'Coins were not used by Muslim historians as sources of historical information . . .'.

[4] Dickran K. Kouymjian (ed.), *Near Eastern numismatics, iconography, epigraphy and history: studies in honour of George C. Miles*. Beirut, 1974.

An alphabetical index of authors, cross-referenced by dynasties, while the body of the work provides an index of mints.

MILES, G. C., 'Islamic and Sassanian numismatics: retrospect and prospect'. (In *Congrès International de Numismatique*, Paris, 6–11 juillet 1953. Tom. I., *Rapports*, Paris, 1953, pp. 129–44.)

Supplements the bibliography of Zambaur down to 1953.

—— 'Islamic numismatics: a progress report'. (In *Congreso internazionale di numismatica*, Rome, 11–16 Settembre 1961, Vol. I: *Relazioni*, Roma, 1961, 181–92.)

A further supplement down to 1961.

—— 'Oriental numismatics'. (In *A survey of numismatic research 1960–1965*, Bd. 2, Copenhagen, 1967. Publications of the International Numismatic Commission.)

A further bibliographical supplement down to 1967.

MITCHELL BROWN, H. W., 'Oriental numismatics'. (In *A survey of numismatic research 1966–1971*. Vol. 2, New York, 1973, pp. 315–46.)

MAYER, L. A., *Bibliography of Moslem numismatics, India excepted*. 2nd edn. London, 1954.

Probably the fullest bibliography of Muslim numismatics, arranged in alphabetical order of authors, and indexed by dynasties. This is not a very convenient aid for the numismatist, since it is time-wasting. The subject-index has large, undivided entries which are laborious to look up. Many of the items so traced turn out to be rarities or bibliographical curiosities that are either unobtainable, or of little interest to the practical worker. For the specialist bibliographer, however, the range is unequalled.

GRIERSON, P., *Bibliographie numismatique*. (Cercle d'études numismatiques, Travaux, 2.) Brussels, 1966.

pp. 141–5: 'Les monnaies musulmanes'.

pp. 146–50: 'Les Indes' (some references relevant to Indo-Muslim numismatics).

p. 156: 'Les déneraux, les jetons et les méreaux'.

The author is a medievalist but not an Islamist. None the less this is a very useful working selection of titles especially relevant to the history of the Crusades, and of relations between Islam and medieval Europe. It contains entries of interest from the viewpoint of economic history.

SINGHAL, C. R., *Bibliography of Indian coins*, Pt. 2: Muhammadan and later series. Bombay, 1952.

A comprehensive listing of periodical articles, without critical evaluation. It is less thorough in its coverage of major catalogues and larger works.

KOUYMJIAN, Dickran K. *ed.*, *Near Eastern numismatics, iconography, epigraphy and history; studies in honor of George C. Miles*. Beirut, 1974.

This Festschrift contains a bibliography of the works of George C. Miles on pp. xvii–xxv.

CARSON, R. A. G. & MITCHELL, H. W., 'John Walker 1900–1964'. *NC* 7 ser., **5**, 1965, 255–64.

Obituary of Dr. John Walker, Keeper of Coins and Medals at the British Museum, with a full bibliography of his works, being mainly studies in Muslim numismatics.

BIVAR, A. D. H., 'Richard Bertram Whitehead 1879–1967'. *NC* 7 ser., **7**, 1967, 282–6.

The bibliography of R. B. Whitehead's works which accompanies this obituary includes a number of contributions to Indo-Muslim numismatics.

*Numismatic Literature.* American Numismatic Society, New York, 1947/9–.

A periodical survey of numismatic bibliography, with especially full sections devoted to Muslim numismatics.

## II. STUDIES OF PARTICULAR MINTS

ABARQUBĀD

MILES, G. C., 'Abarqubadh, a new Umayyad mint'. *Amer. Num. Soc. Mus. notes* **4** (1950), p. 115.

ĀMUL

STERN, S. M., 'The coins of Āmul'. *NC* 7 ser., **7**, 1967, 205–78.

ANBĪR

BALOG, P., 'An Umayyad dirhem struck in 79 H. at Anbīr in Juzjān, Khurasan'. *AION* **30** (N.S. **20**, 1970), pp. 555–8.

KIRMĀN

MILES, G. C., 'Some new light on the history of Kirman in the first century of the Hijra'. (In J. Kritzeck and R. B. Winder *eds.*, *The world of Islam; studies in honour of Philip K. Hitti*, London, 1959, pp. 85–98.)

MAWṢIL (MOSUL)

ROTTER, G., 'The Umayyad fulūs of Mosul'. *Amer. Num. Soc. Mus. notes* **19** (1974), pp. 165–97.

ʿOMĀN

BIVAR, A. D. H. & STERN, S. M., 'The coinage of Oman under Abū Kālījār the Buwayhid'. *NC* 1958, pp. 147–56.

VASMER, R., 'Zur Geschichte und Münzkunde von ʿOmān im X. Jahrhundert'. *ZN* **37** (1927), pp. 274–87.

RAYY

MILES, George C., *The numismatic history of Rayy* (Numismatic studies No. 2). American Numismatic Society, New York, 1935.

The classic history of an Islamic mint, so far without an equal on this scale.

WĀSIṬ

LINDER WELIN, Ulla S., 'Wasit, the mint-town'. (In *Kong. Humanistiska Vetenkapssamfundets i Lund Arsberättelse* 1955–56, pp. 126–69.)

## III. STUDIES ARRANGED BY DYNASTIES

### Studies covering the Coinage of several Dynasties

MILES, G. C., *Rare Islamic coins* (ANS Numismatic Notes and Monographs, 118). New York, 1950.

ZAMBAUR, E. von, 'Contributions à la numismatique orientale'. *Num. Z.* **36** (1904), pp. 43–122; **37** (1905) pp. 113–98.

—— 'Nouvelles contributions à la numismatique orientale'. *Num. Z.* **48** (1914), pp. 115–90.

#### ARAB-BYZANTINE

(See entry under IV. MUSEUMS, London.)

#### ARAB-SASSANIAN

BIVAR, A. D. H., 'Fresh evidence on the "Sijistan barbarous" series of Arab-Sasanian dirhams'. *JNSI* **30** (1968), pp. 52–7.

MILES, George C., 'Two unpublished Arab-Sasanian dirhems of 'Abdallāh b. Umayya'. *Amer. Num. Soc. Mus. notes* **14** (1968), pp. 155–7.

WALKER, J., 'Some new Arab-Sassanian coins'. *NC* 6 ser., **12**, 1952, pp. 106–10.

A notable article which includes a remarkable issue bearing the portrait of Yazīd b. al-Muhallab, issued at Juzjān in 84 H.

(See also entry under D. MUSEUMS, London.)

### i. Caliphates

GRIERSON, P., 'The monetary reforms of 'Abd al-Malik'. *JESHO* **3**, 1960, pp. 241–64.

MILES, George C., *The coinage of the Umayyads of Spain.* 3v. (Hispanic numismatic series, 1.) New York, 1950.

### iii. Spain

PRIETO Y VIVES, A., *Los reyes de taifas; estudio historic-numismatico de los Musulmanes españoles en el siglo V de la Hégira* (XI de J.C.). Madrid, 1926.

VIVES Y ESCUDERO, A., *Monedas de las dinastías arábigo-españolas.* Madrid, 1893.

(See also under IV. MUSEUMS, New York.)

### iv. Africa and Mediterranean

#### (a) NORTH AFRICA AND THE ISLANDS

BEL, A., 'Contributions à l'étude des dirhems de l'époque almohade'. *Hespéris* **16**, 1933, pp. 1–68.

EUSTACHE, D., *Corpus des dirhams Idrissites et contemporains.* (Etudes sur la numismatique et l'histoire du Maroc, I.) Rabat, 1970–71.

HAZARD, H. W., *The numismatic history of late medieval North Africa.* (Numismatic studies, 8.) New York, 1952.

MILES, George C., *The coinage of the Emirs of Crete.* (Numismatic notes and monographs, 160.) New York, 1970. With a bibliography of 11 items.

WALKER, John, 'The coins of the Amīrs of Crete'. *NC* 6 ser., **13**, 1953, pp. 125–30.

(b) EAST AFRICAN COINAGES

CHITTICK, H. N., 'A coin hoard from near Kilwa'. *Azania* **2**, 1967, pp. 194–8.

FREEMAN-GRENVILLE, G. S. P., 'Coin finds and their significance for East African chronology'. *NC* 1971, pp. 283–301.

—— 'Coins from Mogadishu'. *NC* 1963, pp. 179–200.

—— 'Coinage in East Africa before Portuguese times'. *NC* 1957, pp. 151–79.

—— 'A new hoard and some unpublished variants of the coins of the Sultans of Kilwa'. *NC* 1954, pp. 220–4.

MITCHELL, H. W., 'Fakhr al-Dunya and Nasir al-Dunya; notes on two East African topics'. *NC* 1970, pp. 253–7.

WALKER, J., 'Some new coins from Kilwa'. *NC* 1939, pp. 223–6.

—— 'The history and coinage of the Sultans of Kilwa'. *NC* 1936, pp. 43–81.

## V. EGYPT AND SYRIA

(a) EARLIER DYNASTIES AND GENERAL

BALOG, P., 'Études numismatiques de l'Egypte musulmane'. *BIE* **33**, 1952, pp. 1–42; **34**, 1951–52, pp. 17–55; **35**, 1954, pp. 401–29.

—— 'Quatre dinars du Khalife Fatimite al-Mountazar li-amr-illah ou bi-amr-illah'. *BIE* **33**, 1952, pp. 375–8.

—— 'The history of the dirhem in Egypt from the Fatimid conquest until the collapse of the Mamlūk Empire (358–922 A.H. = A.D. 968–1517)'. *Rev. num.* 6, no. **3**, 1961, pp. 109–46.

—— 'Notes on some Fatimid round-flan dirhems'. *NC* 7 ser., **1**, 1961, pp. 175–9.

GATEAU, A., 'Sur un dinar fatimide'. *Hespéris* **32**, 1945, pp. 69–72.

GRABAR, O., *The coinage of the Tulunids.* (Numismatic notes and monographs, 139.) New York, 1957.

MILES, George C., *Fatimid coins in the collection of the University Museum, Philadelphia, and the American Numismatic Society.* (Numismatic notes and monographs, 121.) New York, 1951.

TROUSSEL, M., 'Notes sur quelques monnaies fātimites'. *Receuil des notices et mémoires de la Société Historique et Géographique de Constantine* **70**, 1951, pp. 67–71.

(b) MAMLUK DYNASTY

BALOG, Paul, *The coinage of the Mamlūk Sultans of Egypt and Syria.* (Numismatic studies, 12.) New York, 1964.

With a full bibliography including 11 items additional to Mayer's *Bibliography*.

—— 'The coinage of the Mamlūk Sultans: additions and corrections'. *Amer. Num. Soc. Mus. notes* **16** (1970), pp. 113–71.

ALLAN, J. W., 'Mamlūk sultanic heraldry and the numismatic evidence: a reinterpretation'. *JRAS* 1970, pp. 99–112.

MITCHELL, H. W., 'Notes on some Mamlūk dirhems'. *Amer. Num. Soc. Mus. notes* 1970, pp. 179–84.

## vi. ARABIA

BATES, M. L., 'Notes on some Isma'īlī coins from Yemen'. *Amer. Num. Soc. Mus. notes* **18** (1972), pp. 149–62.

LOWICK, N. M., 'Some unpublished dinars of the Ṣulayhids and Zuray'ids'. *NC* 7 ser., **4**, 1964, pp. 261–70.

SCANLON, G. T., 'Leadership in the Qarmatian sect'. *Bull. IFAO* **58**, 1958, pp. 29–48.

SHAMMA, Samir, 'A hoard of fourth century dinars from Yemen'. *Amer. Num. Soc. Mus. notes* **17** (1971), pp. 235–9.

STERN, S. M., 'Some unrecognised dirhems of the Zaydīs of the Yemen'. *NC*, 6 ser., **9**, 1949, pp. 180–8.

### vii. 'Irāq and Mesopotamia

WALKER, J., 'A rare coin of the Zanj'. *JRAS* 1933, pp. 651–5.

### ix. Caucasus and Caspian Regions

ALBUM, S., 'Notes on the coinage of Muhammad ibn al-Husayn al-Rawwadi'. *Rev. num.*[6] **14** (1972), pp. 99–104.

AMEDROZ, H. F., 'On a dirham of Khusru Shah of 361 H.'. *JRAS* 1905, pp. 471–84.

BYKOV, A. A., 'Daisam ibn Ibrākhīm al-Kurdī i ego monety'. *Epigrafika Vostoka* **10** (1955), pp. 14–37.

MILES, G. C., 'The coinage of the Bāwandids in Tabaristan'. (In C. E. Bosworth ed., *Iran and Islam; in memory of the late Vladimir Minorsky*, Edinburgh, 1971, pp. 443–60.)

STERN, S. M., 'The early Ismā'īlī missionaries in North-West Persia and in Khurāsān and Transoxania'. *BSOAS* **23**, 1960, pp. 56–90.

Publishes and comments on an unrecorded dirhem of Wahsūdān b. Muḥammad struck at Jalālābād in 343 H.

TORNBERG, C. J., 'Ueber muhammedanische Revolutions-Münze'. *ZDMG* **22**, 1869, pp. 700–7.

VASMER, R., 'Zur Chronologie der Ǧastāniden und Sallāriden'. *Islamica* **3**, 1927, pp. 165–8, 483–5.

### x. Iran and Transoxania

DAVIDOVICH, E. A., 'Numismaticheskii material dlya khronologii i genealogii sredneaziatskikh karakhanidov'. ('Numismatic materials for the genealogy and chronology of the Central Asian Qarakhanids'), *Numismaticheskii sbornik*, Moscow, 1957, pp. 91–119.

HENNEQUIN, G., 'Grandes monnaies Sāmānides et Ghaznavides de l'Hindū-Kush, 331–421 A.H. Étude numismatique et historique'. *Annales islamologiques* **9** (1970), pp. 127–77.

MILES, G. C., 'The coinage of the Kākwayhid dynasty'. *Iraq* **5** (1938), pp. 89–104.

—— 'Notes on Kākwayhid coins'. *Amer. Num. Soc. Mus. notes* **9** (1960), pp. 231–6.

—— 'A hoard of Kākwayhid dirhems'. *Amer. Num. Soc. Mus. notes* **12** (1966), pp. 165–93.

—— 'Coinage of the Ziyārid dynasty of Ṭabaristan and Gurgān'. *Amer. Num. Soc. Mus. notes* **18** (1972), pp. 119–37.

—— 'Another Kakwayhid note'. *Amer. Num. Soc. Mus. notes* **18** (1972), pp. 139–48.

VASMER, R., 'Zur Münzkunde der Qarāḥāniden'. *MSOS* **33**, 1930, pp. 83–104.

—— 'Über die Münzen der Saffariden und ihrer Gegner in Fars und Hurasan'. *Num. Z.* **63**, 1930, pp. 131–62.

WALKER, J., *The coinage of the second Saffarid dynasty in Sistan.* (Numismatic notes and monographs, 72.) New York, 1936.

### xi. Seljūqs and Atabegs

LOWICK, N. M., 'A gold coin of Rusūltegīn, Seljuk ruler in Fars'. *NC* 7 ser., **8**, 1968, pp. 225–30.

—— 'Seljuq coins'. *NC* 1970, pp. 241–51.

### xii. Mongols

BURN, R., 'Coins of the Ilkhanis of Persia'. *JRAS* 1933, pp. 831–44.

Ilkhanid coins from excavations at Abū Sudaira near Kish, Iraq.

JUNGFLEISCH, M., 'Un fels curieux frappé à Tabrīz'. *BIE* **34**, 1953, pp. 97–103.

### xiii. Persia after the Mongols

BURN, R., 'Coins of the Jahanshāh Karā Koyūnlū and some contemporary rulers'. *NC* 5 ser., **18**, 1938, pp. 173–97.

CODRINGTON, H. W., 'Coins of some kings of Hormuz'. *NC* 4 ser., **14**, 1914, pp. 156–67.

RABINO DI BORGOMALE, H. L., 'Coins of the Jalā'ir, Ḳarā Ḳoyūnlī, Musha'sha' and Aḳ-Ḳoyūnlī dynasties'. *NC* 6 ser., **10**, 1950, pp. 94–139.

With full bibliography.

—— *Coins, medals and seals of the Shahs of Iran.* Vol. I, Text. Hertford, 1941; Vol. II, Album. Oxford, 1951.

With bibliographies in both volumes.

SMITH, J. M., *The history of the Sarbadar dynasty. A.D. 1336–1381, and its sources.* Brussels, 1971.

### xv. South Asia

(a) early dynasties

BULLIET, R. W., 'A Mu'tazilite coin of Maḥmūd of Ghazna'. *Amer. Num. Soc. Mus. notes* **15** (1969), pp. 119–29.

(b) later sultanates

RAO, D., 'On some new and rare Bahmani coins'. *JNSI* **22** (1960), pp. 217–20.

KAUS, Hormuz, 'Coins of the Qutb Shahi dynasty of Golconda'. *Numis. circular* **63**, 5, 1955, pp. 209–16.

—— 'The copper coins of the Barīd Shahi Kings of Bidar'. *JNSI* **7**, 1945, pp. 51–3.

SPEIGHT, E. E., 'Coins of the Bahmani kings of the Deccan'. *IC* **9** (1935), pp. 268–307.

WRIGHT, N. H., 'The coinage of the Sulṭāns of Mâlwa'. *NC* 5 ser., **11**, 1931, pp. 291–312; 1932, pp. 13–53.
—— *The coinage and metrology of the Sultans of Delhi*. Delhi, 1936.

## IV. CATALOGUES OF MUSEUMS

*Berlin*
NÜTZEL, H., *Katalog der orientalischen Münzen*. (Königliche Museen zu Berlin.) 2v. Berlin, 1898–1902 (unfinished).
Includes (i) The Eastern Caliphate and (ii) Spain and North Africa.

*Bombay*
SINGHAL, C. R., *Catalogue of the coins in the Prince of Wales Museum, Bombay; The Sulṭans of Gujarat* (ed. G. V. Acharya). Bombay, 1936.

*Copenhagen*
ØSTRUP, J., *Catalogue des monnaies arabes et turques du Cabinet Royale des Médailles du Musée Nationale de Copenhague*. Copenhagen, 1938.

*Hyderabad, Deccan*
ABDUL WALI KHAN, Mohammad, *Bahmani coins in the Andhra Pradesh Government Museum, Hyderabad*. (Andhra Pradesh Government Museum ser., 7.) Hyderabad, 1964.

*Istanbul*
ARTUK, Ibrahim & CEVRIYE, *Istanbul arkeoloji Müseleri Teshirdeki Islâmî Sikkeler Kataloğu*. (Catalogue of the Islamic coins from the exhibition of the Istanbul Archaeological Museum.) 2v. Istanbul, 1971–.

*Kabul*
SOURDEL-THOMINE, D., *Inventaire des monnaies musulmanes anciennes du Musée de Caboul*. Damas, 1953.

*Lahore*
WHITEHEAD, R. B., *Catalogue of the coins in the Punjab Museum, Lahore*. Vol. III: *Coins of Nadir Shah and the Durrani dynasty*. Oxford, 1934.

*London*
WALKER, J., *A catalogue of the Arab-Sasanian coins*. London, 1941 (repr. 1967).
—— *A catalogue of the Arab-Byzantine and post-reform Umaiyad coins*. London, 1956.

*Lucknow*
BROWN, C. J., *Catalogue of the coins in the Provincial Museum, Lucknow: Coins of the Mughal emperors* (in two volumes). Oxford, 1920.

*New York*
MILES, G. C., *Rare Islamic coins*. (Numismatic notes and monographs, 118.) New York, 1950.
—— *Coins of the Spanish Mulūk al-Ṭawā'if*. (Hispanic numismatic series, 3.) New York, 1954.

*Paris*

LAVOIX, H., *Catalogue des monnaies musulmanes de la Bibliothèque Nationale.* 3v. Paris, 1887–96 (unfinished).

Includes (i) The Eastern Caliphate, (ii) Spain and North Africa and (iii) Egypt and Syria.

*Tunis*

FARRUGIA DE CANDI, J., 'Monnaies fâtimides du Bardo'. *RT* N.S. **7**, 1936, pp. 334–72; **8**, 1937, pp. 89–136.

## V. HOARDS, FINDS AND EXCAVATIONS

ALBUM, S., 'An Umayyad hoard from Afghanistan'. *Amer. Num. Soc. Museum notes* **17** (1971), pp. 241–6.

ANDERSON, W., 'Der Münzfund von Vaabina'. *Annales Litterarum Societatis Esthonicae* 1937, i, pp. 1 ff.

BALOG, P., 'Three hoards of Mamlūk coins'. *Amer. Num. Soc. Museum notes* **16** (1960), pp. 173–8.

EUSTACHE, D., 'Monnaies musulmanes trouvées à Volubilis'. *Hespéris* **48**, 1956, pp. 133–97.

JUNGFLEISCH, M., 'Le problème des trouvailles de monnaies anciennes'. *BIE* **35** (1952), pp. 69–75.

LOWICK, N. M. & NISBET, J. D. F., 'A hoard of dirhams from Ra'ṡ al-Khaimah'. *NC* 7 ser., **8**, 1968, pp. 231–40.

MILES, G. C., *Excavation coins from the Persepolis region.* (Numismatic notes and monographs, 143.) New York, 1959.

—— *The Athenian Agora.* Vol. 10: *The Islamic coins.* Princeton, 1962.

SOURDEL-THOMINE, D., 'Un trésor de dinars gaznavides et salǧūqides découvert en Afghanistan'. *BEO* **18**, 1963–64, pp. 197–219.

TROUSSEL, M., 'Le trésor monétaire de Tiddis'. *Receuil des notices et mémoires de la Societe Archéologique du Département de Constantine* **66** (1948).

LINDER WELIN, U. S., 'Ein grosser Fund arabischer Münzen aus Stora Velinge, Gotland'. *Nordisk num. arsskrift* 1941.

—— 'Some rare Samanid dirhams and the origin of the word "mancusus" '. (In *Atti del Congresso Internazionale di Numismatica 1961* **2**, Rome, 1965.)

## VI. ICONOGRAPHY

ALTEKAR, A. S., 'A bull and horseman type coin of the Abbasid Caliph al-Muqtadir biliah [*sic*] Ja'far'. *JNSI* **7**, 1945, pp. 75–8.

BALOG, P., 'Apparition prématurée de l'écriture nashky sur un dinar de l'imam fatimite al-Moustaly-billah'. *BIE* **31**, 1949, pp. 181–5.

BAHRAMI, Mehdi, 'A gold medal in the Freer Gallery of Art'. (In G. C. Miles *ed.*, *Archaeologia Orientalia in memoriam Ernst Herzfeld*, Locust Valley, N.Y., 1952, pp. 5–20.)

DE SHAZO, A. S. & BATES, M. L., 'The Umayyad governors of al-'Irāq and the changing annulet patterns on their dirhams'. *NC* 1974, pp. 110–18.

MILES, G. C., 'Mihrāb and 'Anazah; a study in early Muslim iconography'. (In G. C. Miles *ed.*, *Archaeologia Orientalia in memoriam Ernst Herzfeld*, Locust Valley, N.Y., 1952, pp. 156–71.)

—— 'A portrait of the Buyid prince Rukn al-Daulah'. *Amer. Num. Soc. Museum notes* **11** (1964), pp. 283–93.

—— 'The earliest Arab gold coinage'. *Amer. Num. Soc. Museum notes* **13** (1967), pp. 205–29.

—— 'The iconography of Umayyad coinage'. *AO* **3**, 1959, pp. 207–13.

A detailed review of J. Walker's *A catalogue of the Arab-Byzantine and post-reform Umaiyad coins*, London, 1956 (above).

WALKER, J., 'Is the caliph bare-headed on Umaiyad coins?'. *NC* 5 ser., **16**, 1936, pp. 321–3.

—— 'Islamic coins with Hindu types'. *NC* 6 ser., **6**, 1946, pp. 121–8.

—— 'A unique medal of the Seljuk Ṭughrilbeg'. (In *Centennial publication of the American Numismatic Society*, New York, 1958, pp. 691–5.)

## VII. METROLOGY AND WEIGHTS

BALOG, P., 'Les jetons fāṭimites en verre'. *RBN* **107**, 1961, pp. 171–83.

ETTINGHAUSEN, R., 'An Umaiyad pound weight'. *Journal of the Walters Art Gallery* **2**, 1939, pp. 73–6.

HINZ, W., *Islamische Masse und Gewichte umgerechnet ins metrische System.* (Hdb. Orientalistik. Ergänzungband I, Heft 1.) Leiden, 1955.

JUNGFLEISCH, M., 'Jetons (ou poids?) en verre de l'Imam el-Montazer'. *BIE* **33**, 1952, pp. 359–74.

LAUNOIS, A., 'Estampilles et poids faibles en verre Omeyyades et Abbasides au Musée Arabe du Caire'. *Mélanges islamologiques* **3**, 1976, pp. 1–83.

MILES, G. C., *Early Arabic glass weights and stamps.* (Numismatic notes and monographs, 111.) New York, 1948.

—— *Early Arabic glass weights and stamps; a supplement.* (Numismatic notes and monographs, 120.) New York, 1951.

—— *Contributions to Arabic metrology I.* (Numismatic notes and monographs, 141.) New York, 1958.

—— *Contributions to Arabic metrology II.* (Numismatic notes and monographs, 150.) New York, 1963.

—— 'On the varieties and accuracy of eighth-century Arab coin-weights'. *Eretz-Israel* **7**, 1963 (= L. A. Mayer memorial volume), pp. 78–87.

## VIII. TECHNOLOGY OF COINAGE

BALOG, P., 'Etudes numismatiques de l'Egypte musulmane; période Fatimite et Ayoubite. Nouvelles observations sur la technique de monnayage'. *BIE* **33**, 1950, pp. 1–30.

BACHARACH, J. L. & AWAD, H. A., 'The problem of obverse and reverse in Islamic numismatics'. *NC* **13**, 1973, pp. 183–91.

JUNGFLEISCH, M., 'Les points sécrets en numismatique: une innovation due aux Arabes (?)'. *BIE* **28**, 1947, pp. 101– .

LOWICK, N. M., 'A Sāmānid/Kakwayhid mule'. *Amer. Num. Soc. Mus. notes* **14**, 1968, pp. 159–62.

MAYER, L. A., 'A Fatimid coin-die'. *Quarterly of the Department of Antiquities of Palestine* **1**, 1931.

MILES, G. C., 'Note on a die engraver of Isfahan'. *AI* **5**, 1938, pp. 100–3.

A Buyid coin with miniature signature of the die-engraver.

TOLL, C., 'Minting technique according to Arabic literary sources'. *Orientalia suecana* **19–20**, 1970–71, pp. 125–39.

## IX. ARAB SOURCES ON COINAGE

EUSTACHE, D., 'La question des monnaies d'après El-Balādhurī'. *Hespéris-Tamuda* **9**, 1968, pp. 74–107.

—— 'Études de numismatiques et de métrologie musulmanes'. *Hespéris-Tamuda* **10**, 1969, pp. 95–189.

KĀMILĪ, Manṣūr b. Barʿa, *Kashf al-asrār al-ʿilmiyya bi-dār al-ḍarb al-misriyya*, ed. ʿAbd al-Raḥmān Fahmī. Cairo, 1966.

A technical treatise on the operation of the Ayyubid mint at Cairo.

MAQRĪZĪ, Aḥmad b. ʿAlī, *Shudhūr al-ʿuqūd fī dhikr al-nuqūd*, transl. and annot. A. L. Mayer. 1. *Intro.* London, 1933.

# Arabic printing and book production

YASIN H. SAFADI

## I. INTRODUCTION

Bibliographical material for the history of Arabic printing is not to be found in a few comprehensive reference books. C. F. Schnurrer's *Bibliotheca Arabica*, which is probably the only bibliography on this subject was produced more than 150 years ago and is out of date. Bibliographical information on Arabic typography is derived mainly from the many historical, political, biographical, sociological and other relevant studies on the Arab world which conceal within their shell valuable information on this topic. More concentrated information is, of course, available in the histories and records of individual firms of printers, and in the biographies and autobiographies of the pioneers in this field and of the founders of publishing houses and major booksellers. It is also important to note that actual records of the main Arabic newspapers, journals and certain institutions provide basic documentary facts. The most notable of those institutions that have relevant but unpublished records and documents are:

ʿĀBIDĪN. *Maḥfūẓāt ʿĀbidīn.*

DAYR MĀR YUḤANNĀ. *Maḥfūẓāt Dayr Mār Yuḥannā al-Ṣābigh.*

DAYR AL-MUKHALLIṢ. *Maḥfūẓāt Dayr al-Mukhalliṣ.*

BŪLĀQ. *Maḥfūẓāt al-Maṭbaʿa al-Amīriyya bi-Būlāq.*

QALʿA. *Maḥfūẓāt al-Qalʿa.*

MUKHALLIṢIYYA. *Maḥfūẓāt al-Rahbāniyya al-Mukhalliṣiyya.*

MĀRŪNIYYA. *Sijillāt al-Risāla al-Mārūniyya.*

A few travelogues are listed and although relevant information in such accounts is often fortuitous, it is generally precise and fairly reliable.

Several works that relate primarily to the establishment of the Arabic press and the development of journalism are also relevant in varying degrees to the history of Arabic printing. Such works were initially included in this study, but have been excised for reasons of economy and they feature in Dr. Hopwood's study on periodical publications which is published in this volume and to which reference is recommended.

An earnest attempt has been made to examine most of the bibliographical items listed in order to assess their relevance in whole or in part, and in order to provide specific collation or reference. Where Arabic works are mentioned their titles are given in transliteration. Book entries are listed alphabetically under main author headings. Articles considered particularly useful are listed analytically under authors. Articles published in runs are listed under their titles with the name of the periodical publication as a main heading; so are articles that are considered too brief, insubstantial or anonymous. When fragmentary information is given throughout runs of periodicals, reference is made to the relevant year or number, otherwise relevant pagination is noted fully. Anonymous works other than articles are listed under title. When a secondary title in a European language is available for an Arabic work, it is mentioned as a descriptive note; alternatively, an adequate description in English is inserted as required. In the case of joint authorship, the principal author only is noted; works consisting of contributions by numerous authors are listed under the editor or attributable body if ascertainable, otherwise under a collective title.

## II. A BRIEF HISTORY

The importance of paper manufacture in relation to the history of printing is obvious, and although in this case space does not allow for a comprehensive account, a brief sketch of the history of paper manufacture should be useful. It is generally agreed that paper was invented in China early in the second century A.D. Emperor Ts'ai Lun is recorded to have proclaimed its manufacture in A.D. 105. The manufacture of paper improved and expanded rapidly, so much so that paper replaced most other materials for writing purposes in China and neighbouring regions early in the fifth century. It subsequently spread to the Muslim Empire and was introduced through Samarkand in A.D. 751 after the capture of a number of Chinese prisoners during a battle. It soon spread to Baghdad, Damascus, Mecca and other towns. The earliest dated Arabic paper is part of the Rainer Collection and is dated A.D. 874. It later spread through Egypt along the Maghrib and into Spain where the earliest noted date for its manufacture is A.D. 1150. Soon afterwards, during the early part of the same century, paper manufacture passed into Europe through Constantinople, Sicily and Italy, and later by the route through Spain. The first paper mill in Europe was founded in 1157 by Jean Montgolfer. Damascus together with Mambij or Manbij continued, however, to be the main supplier of paper to Europe for more than three centuries. Hence the early names of paper such as *Charta Damascena*, *Bambyx* or *Bambycina*, which was later corrupted by proximity of phonology into *Bombycina*, i.e. paper of cotton, which led to a misconception and the currency of the term cotton paper until it was eventually corrected in the early fifteenth century by a German scholar.

This very brief outline of the history of paper manufacture is not only important because paper was the forerunner of printing and its main essential material, but because it also serves to establish the main routes of transition of the earliest forms of printing, namely block-printing. The earliest extant block-printed book is the *Prajnâ Pâramitâ*, more famed as the Diamond Sutra, which is exhibited by the Department of Oriental Manuscripts and Printed Books of the British Library. It bears the statement *printed on 11 May 868*. Late ninth and early tenth century Arabic block-prints are also extant in the Rainer Collection. Block-printing of money, amulets, calendars, &c., was also noted from the late ninth century in other parts of the Muslim world. There are several extant specimens of Arabic block-prints on vellum, paper and calico. Among the earliest and probably the most significant is a block-printed Quranic fragment available in the Rainer Collection, *c.* tenth century. A later Quranic fragment, *c.* fourteenth century, block-printed on vellum is in the collection of the University of Pennsylvania Museum. The earliest dated block-print in Europe, however, dates back to 1423. This method gave way to lithography and to printing from movable type.

Movable type was invented in China between 1040–1048, and the earliest extant printed book is Korean. It is dated 1361 and was exhibited in Paris in 1900. In Europe experiments on printing from movable type were first carried out by Gutenberg in 1436; in 1454 the first dated document printed by this method was produced and it is attributed to the press of Gutenberg, Fust and Schöffer. All early printed works produced from movable type, however, were in Latin. The first dated vernacular book was the German *Der Edelstein* which was printed in 1461. Soon afterwards the evolution of printing from movable type accelerated and spread widely throughout Europe.

Arabic printing from movable type was first used in Europe, probably in the last decade of the fifteenth century, but no specimens of Arabic printing from movable type dating back to the fifteenth century are extant. Important centres in Italy, France, the Netherlands, Germany, and Spain began to produce Arabic works printed from movable type early in the sixteenth century. Religious motives and particularly missionary efforts are among the most important factors that led to the publication of early Arabic books in Europe.

A notion that has gained considerable currency is that the Qur'ān is the earliest Arabic text to have been printed from movable type in Arabic characters. Preliminary research inclines one to accept this notion, but there are no extant copies of this edition which apparently were all destroyed in a fire. It has been claimed that this Qur'ān edition was printed in Venice in 1499 at the 'Paganini' press, which makes it, if only by a hair's breadth, the only truly Arabic incunabulum; although others attribute to it dates ranging from 1509 to 1538. The first extant Arabic book printed from movable type, a book on Christian prayer entitled *Kitāb ṣalāt al-sawāʿī*: '*Horologium breve*' or '*Septem horae canonicae*' pp. 240, was printed in 1514 at Fano by Gregorio de Gregoriis. Its printing was probably sponsored by Pope Julius II for distribution among the Christian Arabs of the Near East. Miroslav Krek states that it may have been printed on the press of the Soncinati operating at that time in Pesaro and Fano. It is slightly puzzling that Gregorio de Gregoriis, who is known to have operated mainly in Forli and Venice, should have printed this work in Fano. According to P. K. Hitti only three or four copies of this book are known to exist, but this author estimates that at least nine copies are extant. A polyglot psalter, *Mazmūr ʿibrī, yūnānī, ʿarabī*: '*Psalterium hebraeum, graecum, arabicum, etc.*' pp. 184, was printed soon afterwards in 1516 at Genoa by Petrus Paulus Porrus. From this tentative beginning, Arabic printing became gradually more widespread in Europe in a relatively short time; but the cursive character outline of Arabic letters and the comparatively complex orthographic structure caused many difficulties at first in cutting Arabic type and obtaining an acceptable degree of elegance and readability. These difficulties, which mainly fall within the sixteenth century period of this development, were encountered by many pioneers who took up the challenge with varying degrees of success. *al-Qawāʿid al-ʿArabiyya*: '*Grammatica arabica*' by Guillaume Postel was printed in Paris, *c.* 1538, with primitively cut Arabic characters, and it illustrates the problems that were being encountered at that point of time. *al-Alifbāʾ al-ʿArabiyya*: '*Alphabetum arabicum*' by Jacob Christmann was also printed in Arabic characters in 1582, and it marks a definite advance. al-Ṣāliḥī's *Kitāb al-Bustān fī ʿAjāʾib al-Arḍ wa al-Buldān*: '*Libro del Giardino, etc.*' pp. 212, was published in Rome in 1585, and demonstrates a typographically greater degree of success than most of the attempts preceding it. Whilst satisfactory solutions to the various difficulties were being sought, an escape from the typographical problems of Arabic script was obtained by printing Arabic in less cursive and more manageable alphabets such as Roman, Hebrew and Syriac, and Arabic printed in Syriac characters became known as Karshūnī. *Fann taʿallum al-lugha al-ʿarabiyya bi-suhūla*: '*Arte para legeramente saber la lengua araviga*' by Pedro d'Alcalà was printed in Granda in 1505, and although printed almost entirely in Roman characters it contains a small amount of Arabic script all individually cut, and thus ranks as the earliest printed book containing Arabic characters produced in Spain.

The establishment of La Stamperia Orientale Medicea in Rome in 1584 by Cardinal Fernando de' Medici was very significant for the history of Arabic printing in general, for he entrusted the management of the new press to the famous orientalist Giovanni Battista Raimondi who recruited the services of the Parisian printer and type designer Robert Granjon; they both devoted great efforts to the advancement of Arabic typography and succeeded in solving most of its outstanding problems. This development was soon augmented by the work of Le Bé who succeeded in cutting a new fine and elegant Arabic type in 1591 for the Typografia Medicea in Rome which began to produce excellent editions in cursive yet elegant Arabic type. The most noted and earliest editions are:

*Al-Injīl al-Muqaddas*: '*Evangelium Sanctum . . .*'

*Kitāb nuzhat al-mushtāq*: '*De geographia universali . . .*'

*Al-qānūn fī al-ṭibb*: '*Libre quinque canonis medicinae Abu Ali principis filii Sinae . . .*'

Arabic printed books from Europe, most of them on Christian religion, began to arrive in the Lebanon and Syria, and a few filtered through to neighbouring Arab countries.

Some priests who came from the Near East to study and train in Rome's Eastern colleges were able to obtain sufficient experience in printing and a few of them later possessed their own presses and must be considered a main factor in introducing printing to the Arab world. In 1610 a press with Syriac type was imported from Rome and set up at Qazḥayyā in Lebanon, and several works were produced in Karshūnī. In 1706 the Arab pioneer in printing, al-Shammās ʿAbd Allāh Zākhir (1680–1748), established a press at Aleppo for the Patriarch al-Dabbās with Arabic type which he designed and cut himself, wherewith a book of psalms in Arabic script was published. He later moved to Lebanon where he set up a press with redesigned Arabic type at Mār Yuḥannā al-Ṣābigh in 1733. Egypt was introduced to printing in 1798 during the French occupation. Later the Būlāq printing press was established by Muḥammad ʿAlī in 1815, and was destined to play a great role in consolidating the development of Arabic typography in Egypt and the Arab world. Printing soon spread to the Maghrib, Iraq and Palestine between 1820 and 1830, to Yemen in 1877 and to Hijaz in 1882. Since the late nineteenth century many private and official presses have been established throughout the Arab world, and although its invention was late in reaching certain Arab countries, the technology of printing has been widely and firmly established and has reached a very high standard.

Even a very brief history such as this cannot escape the need for a special reference to the history of printing in Turkey, for most of the formative stages through which Arabic printing had passed fall within the time span of the Ottoman Empire. Although printing was one of the earliest aspects of Western civilization to be introduced into the Ottoman Empire, it was not to be fully assimilated until the eighteenth century. The Ottoman Sultans were not easily induced to allow printing to be used widely and freely. When the early Jewish refugees from Spain sought permission to establish printing presses in Turkey, Sultan Bayazid II (1482–1512) consented only on the condition that they would not print in Arabic characters, hence they printed books only in Hebrew and European languages. A Jewish press was established in Istanbul in 1494 and this was followed by others set up in various cities. Other minority groups followed the Jews' example; in 1567 an Armenian press was also established in Istanbul by Apkar of Sivas, and in 1627 Nicodemus Metaxas imported Greek type from England and succeeded in establishing a press there. But despite these early successes printing in Arabic characters continued to be prohibited, until under the growing cultural and social influences of Europe upon the Ottoman Empire, printing was eventually consolidated after several temporary setbacks. The restriction on printing in Arabic characters was not finally removed until the early eighteenth century, and it was initially due to the persistent efforts of Sa'id Çelebi, who served as Turkish Ambassador in Paris in 1721 and became very interested in printing, and Ibrahim Müteferrika, who was destined to take charge of the first Turkish press which was established in July 1727. Presses, type and typographical experts were imported from Europe, and the first Turkish book was printed in 1729. The press was closed in 1742, but re-opened again in 1794, followed by rapid development. In 1883 official records listed 54 presses in Istanbul, and by 1908 this number had increased to 99. A bibliography published in 1890 lists more than 4000 books, mainly Turkish, printed in Arabic characters. With the rise of Kemal Atatürk and his westernizing plans, Turkish became romanized and divorced itself, typographically speaking, from the course and development of Arabic printing.

'ABD AL-KARĪM, Aḥmad 'Izzat, *Ta'rīkh al-ta'līm fī 'aṣr Muḥammad 'Alī.* Cairo, 1938.

'ABD AL-RAḤĪM, Aḥmad, *Anwā' al-khuṭūṭ al-mawjūda li-al-ṭab' fī maṭba'at Būlāq*. Cairo, n.d.

'ABDUH, Ibrāhīm, *Ta'rīkh al-ṭibā'a wa-al-ṣiḥāfa fī Miṣr khilāl al-ḥamla al-farānsiyya, 1798–1801*. 2nd edn. Cairo, 1949.

A history of printing and the press in Egypt during the French occupation.

—— *Ta'rīkh al-Waqā'i' al-Miṣriyya, 1828–1942*. 3rd edn. Cairo, 1946.

A history of the gazette *al-Waqā'i'* including a history of the Būlāq press.

ABILA, R., *Qānūn al-maṭbū'āt al-lubnānī*. Beirut, 1942.

-AHRĀM, *Jarīdat al-Ahrām*. Cairo.

A daily newspaper. Particularly relevant are the following issues: 1 September 1876, 7 October 1876, 7 July 1881, 31 October 1893, 5 June 1902, 8 June 1908, 25 May 1952.

'ALĪ, Muḥammad Kurd, *Khiṭaṭ al-Shām*. 6v. Damascus, 1925–28.

Particularly relevant are **4**, pp. 88–98; and **6**, pp. 185–95.

'AQQĀD, 'Abbās Maḥmūd, *Ḥarakat al-ta'līf fī al-'ālam al-'arabī*. Cairo, 1953.

ARTIN, Ya'qūb, 'Étude statistique de la presse égyptienne'. *BIE* sér. 4, **6**, 1904, pp. 89–98.

'ĀṢIM, 'Alī Ḥusayn, *Al-ṭibā'a al-ḥadītha*. 6v. Cairo, 1958–62.

BABINGER, F. C. H., *Zur Geschichte der Papiererzeugung im Osmanischen Reiche*. Berlin, 1931.

—— *Stambuler Buchwesen im 18. Jahrhundert*. Leipzig, 1919.

BAHJAT, Muḥammad Amīn, *Taqrīr 'an ma'raḍ al-ṭibā'a bi madīnat Leipzig*. Cairo, 1932.

BANDINI, A. M., *La stamperia Mediceo-Orientale* . . . ed. by G. Palagi. Florence, 1878.

BAṬṬĪ, Rufā'īl, 'Ta'rīkh al-ṭibā'a al-'irāqiyya'. (Histoire de la presse en Mésopotamie.) *Lughat al-'Arab* **4**, 1926, pp. 147–52, 197–206, 276–80, 471–3, 591–5; **5**, 1927, pp. 271–6, 334, 529–34.

BELIN, F. A., 'Note nécrologique et littéraire sur Marcel, 1776–1854'. *JA* sér. 5, **3**, 1854, pp. 553–62.

Relevant material on printing in Arabic and other oriental languages while Marcel was Director of the Imprimerie Nationale de l'Armée in Egypt.

BIANCHI, T. X., *Catalogue des livres turcs, arabes et persans, imprimés à Constantinople depuis l'introduction de l'imprimerie en 1726–1728 jusqu'en 1820*. Paris, 1821.

—— For the period 1820 to 1863, including Būlāq, *see*: *JA* sér. 4, **2**, 1845, pp. 24–61; **20**, pp. 244–50; sér. 5, **13**, pp. 519–55; **14**, pp. 287–98; **15**, pp. 323–46; sér. 6, **2**, pp. 217–71.

—— 'Catalogue général des livres arabes, persans et turcs imprimés à Boulac, depuis l'introduction de l'imprimerie dans ce pays'. *JA* sér. 4, **2**, 1845, pp. 24–63.

BIBLIOTHÈQUE NATIONALE, *Le livre*. Paris, 1972.

With illustrations and plates.

BILLAWSKI, J., *Książka w świecie Islam*. Wroclaw, 1961.

On the book in the Muslim world. Chapters 8, 9 and 10 are particularly relevant.

BIRGE, J. K., 'The printing of books in Turkey in the 18th century'. *MW* **33**, 1943, pp. 292–4.

BOCKWITZ, H., *Beiträge zur Kulturgeschichte des Buches*. Leipzig, 1956.

—— *Zu Karabačeks Forschungen über das Papier im islamischen Kulturkreise*. Leipzig, 1940.

BONOLA, F., *Bey*, 'Note sur l'origine de l'imprimerie arabe en Europe'. *BIE* sér. 5, **3**, ii, 1909, pp. 74–80.

—— 'Una visita a Mohamed Ali nel 1822. La prima stamperia et il primo giornale'. *RIE* **2**, 1905, pp. 146–51.

Le BOSPHORE ÉGYPTIEN.

Particularly relevant are the following issues: 20 December 1886, 15 and 16 July 1887, 4 December 1887, 13 January 1888, 16 October 1889, 16 November 1889, 10 December 1892.

BROCCHI, G. B., *Giornale delle osservazioni fatte nei viaggi in Egitto, nella Siria e nella Nubia*. 6v. Bassano, 1841–43. (**1**, pp. 172–5; **2**, pp. 370–1; **3**, pp. 110–331 and 274–81.)

—— *Giornale estero in Egitto nella Siria e nella Nubia*. Bassano, 1841.

BROCKHAUS, H., 'Die Transcription des arabischen Alphabets'. *ZDMG* **17**, 1863, pp. 441–543.

BROWNE, W. G., *Travels in Africa, Egypt and Syria*. London, 1799.
Chapters 26 and 28 are of some relevance.

BURCKHARDT, J. L., *Travels in Syria and the Holy Land*. London, 1822.
Page 22 has a reference to printing of Arabic in Syriac characters.

-BUSTĀNĪ, Fu'ād Afrām, ''Abd Allāh Zākhir'. *Al-Kitāb* **2**, 1948, pp. 386–98.

—— 'Al-Shammās 'Abd Allāh Zākhir'. *al-Masarra* July 1948.

-BUSTĀNĪ, Salīm, *Ta'rīkh Napoléon Bonaparte fī Miṣr wa Sūriyya*. Alexandria, 1913. With plates.

CAIRO. DĀR AL-KUTUB, *Nubdha ta'rīkhiyya fī aṣl Dār al-Kutub al-Miṣriyya wa ta'sīsihā wa ḥarakat a'mālihā wa maṭbū'ātihā*. Cairo, 1927.

CAIRO. DĀR AL-MANĀR, *Fihris maṭbū'āt Dār al-Manār*. Cairo, 1949.

CANIVET, R. G., 'L'imprimerie de l'Expédition d'Égypte, les journaux et les procès-verbaux de l'Institut (1798–1801)'. *BIE* sér. 5, **3**, 1909, pp. 1–22.

—— 'L'expédition d'Égypte. La Bibliothèque de l'expédition'. *BIE* **4**, 1906, pp. 113–27.

CARRET, J. M., *Voyageurs et écrivains français en Égypte*. Cairo, 1932.
Particularly vol. 1.

CARTER, T. F., *The invention of printing in China and its spread westward*. New York, 1955.
Particularly relevant are pp. 3–10, 32–5, 119–201; bibl. 255–78.

—— 'Islam as a barrier to printing'. *MW* **33**, 1943, pp. 213–16.

—— 'The westward movement of the art of printing'. *YOAC* **1**, 1924–25, pp. 19–28.

CENTRO PER LE RELAZIONI ITALIANO-ARABE, *Studi arabistici e arte tipografica araba in Italia dal XV al XX secolo; Al-dirāsāt al-'arabiyya wa fann al-ṭibā'a al-'arabiyya fī Iṭāliyā* . . . Algiers, 1973.
A history of Arabic printing in Italy from the fifteenth century to the present.

CEVDET PAŞA (JAWDAT *Pasha*), *Ta'rīkh-i Cevdet*. 12v. Istanbul, 1854–84.
A history of the Ottoman Empire from 1774–1826. *See also* translation by 'Abd al-Qādir al-Dunā, pp. 81–4, on firmans relating to printing.

CHARON, C., *Histoire des patriarcats melkites*. 3v. Rome, 1909.

CHAUVIN, V., *Bibliographie des ouvrages arabes ou relatifs aux arabes, publiés dans l'Europe chrétienne de 1810 à 1885*. 2v. Liège, 1892–1909.

—— 'Notes pour l'histoire de l'imprimerie à Constantinople'. *ZB* **24**, 1907, pp. 255–62.

CHEIKHO, L., *Al-ādāb al-'arabiyya fī al-qarn 19*. Beirut, 1908–10.
Particularly relevant: pt. 1, pp. 2–14, 69–70; pt. 2, pp. 3–7, 63–4.

—— 'Ta'rīkh fann al-ṭibā'a fī al-mashriq'. *Al-Mashriq* **3**, 1900, pp. 78–85, 124–81, 251–7, 359–62, 501–8, 670, 706–16, 804–8, 839–44, 998–1003, 1030–3, 1054; **4**, 1901, pp. 86–90, 224–9, 319–25, 471–4, 520–4, 877–81; **5**, 1902, pp. 69–76, 423–9, 840–4.

CLAIR, C., *A chronology of printing*. London, 1969.
Useful notes on printing in Arabic characters from 1514 to 1815. Particularly relevant are notations under the years 1514, 1591, 1616, 1720, 1815, and the index.

LE COURIER DE L'ÉGYPTE. Cairo, 1789–1800.
Particularly relevant are Nos. 63, 67, 109.

DASŪQĪ, Ibrāhīm, *Maqāla shukriyya li-al-ḥaḍra al-Ismā'īliyya 'ala inshā' dār al-wirāqa bi-Būlāq*. Cairo, 1288.
On the establishment of a paper factory at Bulaq.

DÉHÉRAIN, H., *Histoire de la nation égyptienne*. Vol. 5. Paris, 1937.

DEHIF, Cheikh, 'Un project de réforme de l'écriture arabe'. *RMM* **11**, 1910, pp. 448–50.

DEMEERSEMAN, A., 'Une étape importante de la culture islamique; une parente de l'imprimerie arabe et tunisienne, la lithographie'. *IBLA* **16**, 1953, pp. 347–89.

DENY, J., *Sommaire des archives turques du Caire*. Cairo, 1930.

-DIMASHQĪ, Muḥammad Munīr 'Abduh, *Namūdhaj min al-a'māl al-khayriyya fī idārat al-ṭibā'a al-Munīriyya*. Cairo, 1930.
History of the Munīriyya Press.

DUPONT, P., *Histoire de l'imprimerie*. Vol. 2. Paris, 1854.

DVORAK, R., *Rapport et note technique de la Commission de la réforme et de l'amélioration du caractère arabe de l'Imprimerie Nationale de Boulaq*. Cairo, 1906.

—— 'Sind türkische Dichterausgaben zu vokalisieren?'. *ZDMG* **42**, 1888, pp. 102–12.

EATON, T., *The history of the book*. Champaign, 1963.

EDMOND, C., *Pseud.* (Edmond Chojecki), *L'Égypte à l'exposition universelle de 1867*. Paris, 1867.

EGYPT. GOVERNMENT COMMITTEE OF TECHNICAL ADVICE ON PRINTING. *Notes on papermaking in Egypt*. Cairo, 1919.

EGYPT. WIZĀRAT AL-MĀLIYYA. *Lā'iḥat al-ṭibā'a*. Cairo, 1931.
Issued by the Egyptian Government.

ENCYCLOPAEDIA OF ISLAM, *1927–34, and new edition, 1960–*.
Brief, but useful notes under countries.

ERSOY, Osman, *Türkiyeye matbaanın girişi*. Istanbul, 1959.

FERRETTE, J., 'Méthode simplifiée pour imprimer l'arabe avec les points voyelles'. *JA* sér. 5, **14**, 1859, pp. 298–327.

FORNI, G., *Viaggio nell' Egitto et nell' alta Nubia*. 2v. Milan, 1859.
Especially vol. 1, chapter XII.

FRANCE, *Annuaire de la République Française pour l'an VII*. Cairo.

FRIEDBERG, B., *Histoire de la typographie hébraique en Italie, Espagne, Portugal, Turquie et l'Orient depuis le commencement*. Paris, 1935.

FURAYḤA, Anīs, 'Ḥurūf al-hijā' al-'arabiyya'. *Al-Abḥāth* **5**, i, 1952, pp. 1–32.

GEISS, A., *L'histoire de l'imprimerie en Égypte. Époque contemporaine.*
Unpublished and in typescript. It is located in the holdings of La Bibliothèque de l'Institut Français d'Archéologie Orientale in Cairo.
*See also BIE* sér. 5, **1**, 1907, pp. 133–57; and **2**, 1908, pp. 81–4.

—— 'Observations à la suite de la note de M. Bonola Bey'. *BIE* sér. 5, **3**, ii, 1909, pp. 81–4.

GERÇEK, Selim Nuzhet, *Türk matbaacılığı*. Istanbul, 1928.
A history of two hundred years of Turkish printing. With plates. In Ottoman Turkish.
—— *Türk matbaacılığı*. Istanbul, 1939–.
Similar work as above, but enlarged and printed in roman script. 3v.
Vol. 1: *Müteferrika matbaası*.
Vol. 2: *Mühendishane ve Üsküdar matbaaları*.
Vol. 3: *Darüttibaa ve Takvimhane matbaaları*.
*Türk taşbasmacılığı*. Istanbul, 1939.
On printing in Turkey, with particular reference to lithography. With plates.

-GHAḌBĀN, ʻĀdil, 'Mustaqbal al-kitāb al-maṭbuʻ'. *Al-Kitāb* **9**, 1950, pp. 5–10.
—— 'Al-ṣiḥāfa al-miṣriyya fī niṣf qarn'. *Al-Kitāb* **9**, 1950, pp. 676–81 and 771–5.

GRANJON, *Granjon's specimen of Arabic type*.
Available at the British Library at 622. h.s (2).

GUBERNATIS, A. de, *Matériaux* (pp. 189–218). Rome, 1890–1910.

GUIGNES, J. de, *Essai historique sur l'origine des caractères orientaux de l'imprimerie royale*. Paris, 1787.

ḤĀJJ, al-Ab, *Ṣafḥa min ta'rīkh al-Rahbāniyya al-Bāsiliyya*. Beirut, 1948.

HAMMER-PURGSTALL, J. de, *Histoire de l'Empire Ottoman*, tr. by J. Hellert. 18v. Paris, 1835–43.
Vol. 14, and particularly p. 197, on firmans relating to printing are relevant.
—— 'Liste des ouvrages imprimés à Constantinople en 1841–44'. *JA* 1843–46, sér. 4, **1** (1843), pp. 247–66; **3** (1845), pp. 211–24; **8** (1846), pp. 253–82.

HARTMANN, M., 'Das Buchwesen und die türkischen Drucke der Sammlung'. *MSOS* **7**, ii, 1904, pp. 69–103.
—— 'Notice sur le développement du livre et des bibliothèques en pays musulmans'. *RMM* **1**, 1906, pp. 453–6.
—— 'Zum Bibliothekswesen in dem islamischen Ländern'. *ZB* **16**, 1899, pp. 186–9.
—— 'Zum chinesischen Umschrift des arabischen'. *T'oung – pao, ou Archives concernant l'histoire, les langues, ... de l'Asie Orientale* **2**, viii, 1907, pp. 704–8.
—— *Zur literarischen Bewegung und zum Buch und Bibliothekswesen in den islamischen Ländern*. Halle, 1905.

ḤASAN, Aḥmad Muḥammad & FIELDMAN, W., *Majmūʻat al-qawānīn wa-al-lawā'iḥ al-maʻmūl bihā fī Miṣr*. 2 pts. Cairo, 1926.
For laws relating to printing.

ḤASAN, Zakī Muḥammad, 'Al-kitāb fī al-funūn al-islāmiyya'. *Al-Kitāb* **2**, 1946, pp. 255–63.

ḤĀTŪM, Dimitriyūs, *Al-maṭbaʻa al-Shuwayriyya bayn al-ams wa al-yawm*. Beirut, 1951.

ḤIDR, ʻAbd al-Raḥmān, *Qānūn al-maṭbūʻāt wa al-maṭābiʻ wa taʻdīlātuhā*. Baghdad, n.d.
On law relating to printing in Iraq.

-HILĀL, 'Ta'rīkh al-ṭibāʻa'. *Al-Hilāl* Dec. 1897, pp. 249–54.
A brief history of printing in the Arab world. With illustration.

—— 'Ta'rīkh al-nahḍa al-'ilmiyya al-akhīra fī Miṣr wa-al-Shām'. *Al-Hilāl* March 1901, pp. 319–23.
On printing in Egypt and Syria.

ḤILMĪ, Ibrāhīm, 'Al-ṭibā'a fī Dār al-Salām wa al-Najaf wa Karbalā'. (Les imprimeries dans la Basse-Mésopotamie)'. *Lughat al-'Arab* **2**, 1912–13, pp. 303–9.
—— 'Al-ṭibā'a'. *Lughat al-'Arab* **2**, 1912–13, pp. 223–31.
On printing in Iran, Turkey and Syria.

HITTI, P. K., 'The first book printed in Arabic'. *PULC* **4**, 1942, pp. 5–9, 942–3.

-ḤUṢRĪ, Sāṭi', *Ḥawliyyāt al-thaqāfa al-'arabiyya*. 5v. Cairo, 1949–54.
—— *Taqārīr 'an ḥālat al-ma'ārif fī Sūriyya*. (With illustrations.) Damascus, 1944.

ḤUSNĪ, Ḥusayn, *Unmūdhaj min maṣnū'āt al-maṭba'a al-Saniyya*. Cairo, n.d.

IBRĀHĪM, 'Abd al-Laṭīf, *Min al-wathā'iq al-'arabiyya; dirāsāt fī al-kutub wa-al-maktabāt al-islāmiyya*. Cairo, 1962.
On the history of book production and libraries in the Muslim world. With illustrations.

-IMĀM, Ibrāhīm, *Fann al-ikhrāj al-ṣuḥufī*. Cairo, 1957.

INSTITUT D'ÉGYPTE, *Bulletin de l'Institut Égyptien*. 1859–1918, Alexandria. Continued 1918 – as *Bulletin de l'Institut d'Égypte*, Cairo.
—— *Index des communications et mémoires publiés*, par J. Ellul.
—— *Mémoires ou travaux originaux de l'Institut Égyptien*. Paris, &c., 1862–1916.

IRAQ, *Fihrist al-qawānīn wa-al-anẓima wa-al-bayānāt . . . 1917–1927*. Baghdad, 1929.
An index of laws and regulations issued by the Ministry of Justice in Iraq, 1917–27.

ISKĀRŪS, Tawfīq, 'Ta'rīkh al-ṭibā'a fī Wādī al-Nīl'. *Al-Hilāl* **22**, 1913–14, pp. 105–12 and 426–33.
On printing in Egypt.

JESSUP, H. H., *Fifty-three years in Syria*. London, 1910.
Particularly, pp. 25, 27, 219–20, 362, 433–7, 505, 542, 590, 603, 625, 694, 741, 753, 778–9, 815. On printing in Syria.

JUM'A, Ibrāhīm, *Qiṣṣat al-kitāba al-'arabiyya*. Cairo, 1947.

KREK, M., *Typographia Arabica*. Brandeis University Library, Waltham, 1971.
The development of Arabic printing as illustrated by extant specimens of Arabic type. With illustrative specimens, catalogue captions and notes relating to the exhibition held at the Rapaporte Treasure Hall.

LANE, E. W., *An account of the manners and customs of the modern Egyptians*. London, 1836, and numerous later edns.
Written in Egypt during the years 1833–35. With some useful general information on printing.

LAROQUE, J. de, *Voyage au Liban et Syrie*. Paris, 1776.

LEBANON, *Qānūn al-maṭbū'āt wa qānūn niqābat al-ṣiḥāfa al-lubnāniyya*. Beirut, 1949.

LEVI DELLA VIDA, G., 'An Arabic block print'. *SM* **59**, 1944, pp. 473–4.

LEWIS, B., *The emergence of modern Turkey*. London, 1961.
Particularly relevant for the history of printing in Turkey are: pp. 7, 41, 46–7, 50–2, 63, 184, 286, 421–5.

LIMONGELLI, S., *L'arte italiana nella stamperia nationale d'Egitto*. Cairo, 1911.
Particularly relevant is the chapter: Le memorie del Forni furono scritte durante la sua dimora in Egitto dal 1815–40.

LINDSAY, A. W., *Letters on Egypt, Edom and the Holy Land*. London, 1839.
Vol 1, Letter 3, on Bulaq printing press.

LUSHINGTON, C., *Narrative of a journey from Calcutta to Europe by way of Egypt, 1827–1828*. London, 1829.
Chapter XIII, lithographic press in Egypt.

MAḤMŪD, ʿIṣām Muḥammad, *Maṭbūʿāt al-Mawṣil mundhu 1861–1970*. Mosul, 1971.
On printing and publishing in Mosul, Iraq.

-MAJALLA AL-MAṬBAʿIYYA, *Le bulletin typographique*. Cairo, 1888–89.
Discontinued after five issues.

-MAKKĪ, Muḥammad Ṭāhir, *Taʾrīkh al-khaṭṭ al-ʿarabī wa ādābuhu*. Cairo, 1939.
On the evolution of the Arabic characters and type forms.

-MAṬBAʿA AL-AMIRĪKĀNIYYA. *Al-ʿīd al-miʾawī li naql al-Maṭbaʿa al-Amirīkaniyya ilā Bayrūt, 1834–1934*. Beirut, 1934.
Particularly relevant for the history of the American Press in Beirut.

-MAṬBAʿA AL-KĀTHŪLĪKIYYA, *Catalogue de l'Imprimerie Catholique*. 4 pts. Beirut, 1883–1908.
Including:
*Catalogue spécial et spécimens des caractères de l'Imprimerie Catholique.*

-MAṬBAʿA AL-MĀRŪNIYYA, *Namādhij ḥurūf al-Maṭbaʿa*. Aleppo, 1938.
Specimens of Arabic type used by al-Mārūniyya Press.

MAṬBAʿAT BŪLĀQ, *Lāʾiḥat al-ṭibāʿa li al-maṭbaʿa al-Amīriyya bi-al-Qāhira*. Cairo, 1914.
On the American Press in Cairo.

MAṬBAʿAT AL-MAʿĀRIF, *Maṭbaʿat al-Maʿārif wa aṣdiqāʾuhā mundhu nashʾatihā ila al-ān, 1890–1931*. Cairo, 1931.
History of al-Maʿārif Press in Cairo.

MATTEI, S. C., 'Tipografia orientale in Italia'. *Il Bibliofilo. Giornale dell arte antica in estampe* (Florence), **4**, 1883, pp. 120–1, 145–9.

MAZZONI, G., *Avviamento allo studio critico delle lettre italiane*. Verona, 1892.
Another edn.: *Il edizione interamente rifatta. Con appendici di P. Rajna e G. Vandelli*. Florence, 1907.

MERRUAU, P., *L'Égypte contemporaine*. Paris, 1858.
Particularly pp. 88–90.

MICHAUD, J. F., *Correspondance d'Orient*. 7v. Paris, 1835. Another edn.: Brussels, 1841.
Vol. 3, lettre 54, pp. 56–62: L'Imprimerie Impériale; vol. 6, lettre 152, pp. 290–303: L'Imprimerie de Boulac.

MINGANTI, P., 'Semplificazione dei caratteri di stampa per l'arabo nella Repubblica Araba Unita'. *OM* **40**, 1960, pp. 656–60.

MUBĀRAK, ʿAlī, *Al-khiṭaṭ al-tawfīqiyya*. 4v. Cairo, 1305–6/1887–88.
Particularly: vol. 2, pt. 7, pp. 49–50; pt. 9, pp. 45–.

-MUHAYDĪ, Muḥammad Ṣāliḥ, *Taʾrīkh al-ṭibāʿa wa-al-nashr bi-Tūnis*. Tunis, 1965.
On the history of printing in Tunisia. With plates.

MUKHLIṢ, Rushdī, ʿAl-ṣiḥāfa wa-al-maṭābiʿ fī al-Ḥijāzʾ. *Umm al-Qurā* Nos. 207 and 211, Rajab 1347/1929.
On the history of printing in the Hijaz.

-MUQTAṬAF, *Majallat al-Muqtaṭaf*. Cairo.
Nineteen brief articles on printing have been located; although they are on the whole insubstantial, they may be relevant to certain aspects of this study: **1**, 1876, p. 136; **2**, 1877, p. 261; **6**, 1881, pp. 65–8, 130–4, 193–5, 241–4; **7**, 1882–83, pp. 136, 385–92, 465–76, 529–37; **9**, 1884–85, pp. 172–3, 252; **22**, 1898, p. 636; **24**, 1900, pp. 97–101; **28**, 1903, pp. 269–70, 281–6; **29**, 1904, pp. 29–33, 567–8; **35**, 1909, p. 921; **74**, 1929, pp. 253–6; **96**, 1940, pp. 145–53; **99**, 1941, p. 73.

—— *Al-kitāb al-dhahabī li yūbīl al-Muqtaṭaf al-khamsīnī, 1876–1926*. Cairo, 1926.
Golden Jubilee publication commemorating the 50 years 1876–1926.

NAṢR ALLĀH, Yūsuf, *L'imprimerie au Liban*. [Beirut] *c*. 1949.

NICHOLSON, R. A., *A literary history of the Arabs*. Cambridge, 1930 (repr. London, 1969).
Particularly pp. 468–9.

NIQĀBAT AṢḤĀB AL-MAṬĀBIʿ BI-DIMASHQ, *Ḥaqāʾiq maṭmūsa wa ḥuqūq mahḍūma* . . . Damascus, 1937.
Report on printing submitted to the Syrian Parliament in 1937.

PERON, A., 'Lettre sur les écoles et l'imprimerie du pacha d'Égypte'. *JA* sér. 4, **2**, 1843.

PEARSON, J. D., *Index Islamicus, 1906–55*. Cambridge, 1958, pp. 21, 26, 27.

—— *Supplement, 1956–60*. Cambridge, 1962, p. 12.

—— *Supplement, 1961–65*. Cambridge, 1967, p. 12.

—— *Supplement, 1966–70*. London, 1972, pp. 16, 18.

—— *Supplement. 1971–72*. London, 1973, p. 3.

PINTO, O., 'Una rarissima opera araba stampata a Roma nel 1585'. *Studi Bibliografici*, Balzano (7–8 October 1965), pp. 47–51.

RAḌWĀN, Abū al-Futūḥ Aḥmad, *Taʾrīkh maṭbaʿat Būlāq wa lamḥa fī taʾrīkh al-ṭibāʿa fī buldān al-sharq al-awsaṭ*. Cairo, 1953.

-RĀFIʿĪ, ʿAbd al-Raḥmān, *ʿAṣr Muḥammad ʿAlī*. Cairo, 1947.
With useful reference to the history of printing in Egypt.

—— *Muṣṭafa Kāmil*. Cairo, 1939.
Particularly pp. 143, 254.

-RAHBĀNIYYA, AL-BĀSILIYYA, 'Al-Shammās ʿAbd Allāh Zākhir'. *Nashrat al-Rahbāniyya al-Bāsiliyya al-Ḥalabīya* Nos. 9 and 10, 1948.
A biography of al-Shammās with particular reference to his contribution to the advancement of Arabic printing.

PAPYRUS ERZHERZOG RAINER, *Führer durch die Austellung*, ed. by J. von Karábacek. Vienna, 1894.
With illustrations. With an article on the earliest extant Arab block-printing of the Qurʾān, *c*. tenth century.

RASMUSSEN, B. H., *The transition from manuscript to printed book*. London, 1962.

RAINAUD, J. T., 'De la gazette arabe, turque, imprimée en Égypte'. *JA* **8**, 1831, pp. 238–49.

—— 'Notice des ouvrages arabes, persans et turcs imprimés en Égypte'. *JA* **8**, 1831, pp. 333–53.

—— 'Histoire de la lithographie en Égypte'. *Revue de l'art graphique en Égypte* Février 1933.

RIBERA, S., *Bibliófilos y bibliotecas en la España musulmana*. Saragossa, 1896.

ROCHLIN, S. A., 'Early Arabic printing at the Cape of Good Hope'. *BSOAS* **7**, 1933, pp. 49–54.

RONZEVALLE, S., 'L'imprimerie catholique de Beyrouth et son oeuvre en Orient, 1854–1903'. *Relations d'Orient* (1903), fasc. Suppl. 143.

ROWNTREE, J. H., *The process of lithography*. Cairo, 1913.

ṢĀBĀṬ, Khalīl, *Qiṣṣat al-ṭibā'a*. Cairo, 1957.

—— *Ta'rīkh al-ṭibā'a fī al-sharq al-'arabī*. Cairo, 1958; 2nd edn. Cairo, 1966.

History of Arabic printing in the Middle East. With facs.

SAINT-JOHN, J. A., *Egypt and Mohammed Ali* (or *Travels in the valley of the Nile*). 2v. London, 1834.

Especially vol. 2, pp. 402–3 on lithography.

SALTINI, G. E., 'Della stamperia orientale Medicea . . .'. *Giornale storico archeologico* (Tuscany) **4**, 1860, pp. 258–96.

SĀMĪ, Amīn, *Taqwīm al-Nīl*. Cairo, 1916–36.

On historical events in Egypt. Useful for the history of printing, particularly vol. 1, iii, pp. 156–9, 356–7; vol. 3, ii, pp. 382, 438, 579, and iii, pp. 1156–69, 1235–350, 1447–8.

SARHANK, Ismā'īl, *Ḥaqā'iq al-akhbār 'an duwal al-biḥār*. Cairo, 1312–14/ 1894–6.

SARKĪS, Yūsuf Ilyās, *Mu'jam al-maṭbū'at al-'arabiyya wa al-mu'arraba*. (*Dictionnaire encyclopédique de bibliographie arabe*.) 2v. and 2 supp. pts. Cairo, 1928–31.

SAUVAGET, J., 'Suggestions pour une réforme de la typographie arabe'. *REI* 1951, pp. 127–32.

ṢĀWĪ, Aḥmad Ḥusayn, *Ṭibā'at al-ṣuḥuf wa ikhrājuhā*. Cairo, *c*. 1965.

On the printing of newspapers in the Arab world. With illus.

SCHNURRER, C. F., *Bibliotheca Arabica*. Halle, 1811.

In Latin and Arabic. With notations on early Arabic printed books. Although it is still a valuable bibliography in this field, it has long been out of date.

SCHWAB, M., *Les incunables orientaux et les impressions orientales au commencement du xvi*[e] *siècle. Avec marques typographiques*. Paris, 1883.

SERJEANT, R. B., 'Al-adab al-'aṣrī fī al-janūb al-gharbī li shibh jazīrat al-'arab'. (On the modern literature of S.W. Arabia. With a section on printing in Yemen.) *Al-Adab wa al-fann* **2**, 1944, pp. 22–34; **3**, 1945, pp. 13–24.

SHANĪṬĪ, Maḥmūd, *Al-kitāb al-ʿarabī bayn al-māḍī wa-al-ḥāḍir*. Cairo, 1963.
History of Arabic printing and book production, with particular reference to Egypt. With illus. and facs.

SHUKRĪ, Muḥammad Fu'ād and others, *Binā' dawlat Miṣr; Muḥammad ʿAlī*. Cairo, 1948.
Based on John Bowring's Report on Egypt and Candia. With reference to Arabic printing in Egypt.

SHURBAJĪ, Muḥammad Jamāl al-Dīn, *Qā'ima bi awā' il al-maṭbūʿāt al-ʿarabiyya al-maḥfūẓa bi Dār al-kutub ḥatta sanat 1862*. Cairo, 1963.
On early Arabic printed books in the holdings of Dār al-Kutub, including those printed in Europe.

STEINBERG, S. H., *Five hundred years of printing*. London, 1959.
Relevant pp. 36–79. Useful for general background reference, bibl. 271–8.

TANĀḤĪ, Ṭāhir Aḥmad, *Ḥayāt Khalīl Maṭrān*. Cairo, n.d.
Relevant, pp. 251–62.

TARĪḤĪ, ʿAbd al-Mawla, ʿAl-maṭbūʿāt al-ḥadītha fī al-Najaf'. *Lughat al-ʿArab* 7, 1929, pp. 464–71.

TARRĀZĪ, Philippe de, *Khazā'in al-kutub al-ʿarabiyya fī al-khāfiqayn*. (Histoire des bibliothèques arabes.) 4v. Beirut, 1947–51.

TŪNIJĪ, Muḥammad & ḤAFYĀN, Aḥmad, *Al-ṭibāʿa wa risālatuhā al-qawmiyya fī ʿālaminā al-ʿarabī*. Aleppo, 1955.
On printing in the Arab world.

TURKEY, *Qanūn al-ṣiḥāfa al-ʿUthmāniyya al-jadīd*. Zahle, 1909.
The Ottoman law of 1907. Translated from the Turkish by Jamil Maʿlūf.

ṬŪSŪN, ʿUmar, *Al-baʿthāt al-ʿilmiyya fī ʿahd Muḥammad ʿAlī wa ʿAbbās al-awwal wa Saʿīd*. Alexandria, 1934.

—— *Al-ṣanā'iʿ wa al-madāris fī ʿahd Muḥammad ʿAlī*. 2nd edn. Alexandria, 1932.
Both contain brief but useful information relevant to printing.

VACCARI, A., 'I caratteri arabi della Typographia Savariana'. *RSO* **10**, 1923–25, pp. 37–47.

VOLNEY, C. F. de, *Thalāthat aʿwām fī Miṣr wa barr al-Shām*. (Translated into Arabic from the French by Idwār al-Bustānī.) Beirut, 1949.

—— *Voyage en Syrie et en Égypte pendant les années 1783–84 et 1785*. Paris, 1787.
Particularly relevant are: t. 2, pp. 174–84, 190.

-WAQĀ'Iʿ AL-MIṢRIYYA.
Particularly relevant are the following issues: 3, 4, 10, 11, 28, 34, 41, 44–7, 61–4, 66, 68, 72, 85, 96, 185, 328, 341, 349, 358, 360, 365, 370, 372, 373, 375, 378, 379, 384, 385, 396, 405, 410, 411, 426, 429, 433, 434, 442, 443, 446, 447, 450, 501, 535, 537, 540, 542, 619.

WEIL, G., 'Die ersten Drücke der Türken'. *ZB* **24**, 1907, pp. 49–61.

# Libraries

J. P. C. AUCHTERLONIE

This chapter is divided into four parts. Parts I–III deal with printed catalogues, accessions lists and descriptions of Arab-Islamic holdings and also include a section on current Arab bibliographies. Excluded, however, are annual reports, library guides and the like, while manuscript catalogues, periodicals and archival material are all covered elsewhere in this volume.

A particular problem was presented by library catalogues listing material on individual subjects such as the Palestine question or Islam. In the end it was decided not to include them in this chapter, but to place them in the chapter on Bibliographies.

## I. WESTERN LIBRARIES WITH ARABIC AND ISLAMIC COLLECTIONS

As many libraries treat Arab-Islamic collections as integral parts of general Oriental holdings, several catalogues of Oriental printed books are listed. On the whole, however, catalogues dealing principally with Western printed books such as the Library of Congress catalogues have not been included.

Under each country there are two alphabetical sequences: the first, under author, is for entries dealing with more than one library; the second, under the name of the library, is for entries dealing with specific libraries or collections.

In all cases, the vernacular form of the library's name has been preferred.

### General

HAMIDULLAH, M., 'Islamic sections in the Western and Oriental libraries'. (In *Proc. 8th All-India Or. Conf.* 1935, pp. 207–18.)

LJUNGGREN, F. & GEDDES, C. L., *An international directory of institutes and societies interested in the Middle East.* Amsterdam, 1962.

Based on a questionnaire, it often fails to provide any information at all, particularly on the Middle East, but where replies have been forthcoming, it provides useful details of library holdings.

PEARSON, J. D., *Oriental and Asian bibliography.* London, 1966.

Part III, pp. 163–222, contains a detailed survey of Orientalist libraries in Great Britain, the U.S.A. and the U.S.S.R. It is less complete for European collections.

—— *Oriental manuscripts in Europe and North America.* Zug, 1972.

The introduction, pp. i–lxxvii, contains a comprehensive and well-balanced survey of academic institutions which deal with Asia. It includes brief details of library holdings with references.

## Western Libraries by Country

*Austria*

ÖSTERREICHISCHE NATIONALBIBLIOTHEK, 'Die Bestände der Österreichischen Nationalbibliothek aus dem islamischen Kulturbereich', by H. Loebenstein. *Bustān* **4**, iv and **5**, i, 1963–64, pp. 96–120.

*Bulgaria*

NARODNA BIBLIOTEKA (Sofia), 'Orientalistikata v Sofiiskata Narodna Biblioteka', by B. Nedkov. (In *Festschrift N. V. Mikhov*, Sofia, 1948, pp. 226–39.)

*Canada*

INSTITUTE OF ISLAMIC STUDIES, McGILL UNIVERSITY (Montreal), 'The library', by M. Mazzaoui. (In *Special collections in Canadian libraries* (Canadian Lib. Assn. Occ. Papers, 56), 1967, pp. 1–28.)

—— *Guide to Arabic sources*, compiled by J. Gutkowski. Montreal, 1973.

*France*

ÉCOLE DES LANGUES ORIENTALES VIVANTES (Paris), *Catalogue de la bibliothèque*. Tome 1: Linguistique [1ère partie, philologie; 2ème partie, langue arabe]. Paris, 1897.

3533 title entries with author index.

—— 'Vergangenheit und Gegenwart der Bibliothek', by G. Lecomte. (In K. Schubart-Engelschall *ed.*, *Orientalistische Bibliotheken und Sammlungen*, Berlin, 1970, pp. 105–11.)

KAISERLICHE UNIVERSITÄTS- UND LANDESBIBLIOTHEK (Strasbourg), *Katalog; Arabische Litteratur*, by J. Euting. Strasbourg, 1877.

*Germany*

BEHN, W., 'The Islamic Union Catalogue in Germany'. *MELA Notes* **2**, 1974.

WAGNER, E., 'Der Zentralkatalog der Orientalia'. *Z. Bibliothekswesen u. Bibliog.* **17**, 1970, pp. 18–25.

This union catalogue began in Mainz in 1957 and is now maintained in Berlin. It contains the post-1957 accessions of the major German Orientalist libraries (nine in all, including the Deutsche Staatsbibliothek in East Berlin); it includes all works in Oriental languages and all translations from Oriental languages, but excludes Afro-Asiatic publications in European languages. Arabic titles make up about a quarter of the total of 50,000 cards. It is hoped to publish the catalogue eventually.

DEUTSCHE MAROKKO-BIBLIOTHEK, 'Studien und Mitteilungen', by G. Kampffmeyer. *MSOS* **14**, 1911, pp. 1–85; **18**, 1915, pp. 131–88.

DEUTSCHE MORGENLÄNDISCHE GESELLSCHAFT, *Katalog der Bibliothek*, Leipzig, 1880–1; 2nd edn., Leipzig, 1900.

—— *Zugangsverzeichnis der Bibliothek*, 1931–.

Earlier accessions (1848–1930) are listed in the *ZDMG*.

DEUTSCHE STAATSBIBLIOTHEK (Berlin), *Katalog der Handbibliothek der Orientalischen Abteilung*. Leipzig, 1929.

—— 'Die Orientalische Abteilung', by G. Weil. *ZB* **37**, 1920, pp. 57–66. Also in *Festschrift Adolf von Harnach*, Berlin, 1921, pp. 298–302.
—— 'Die Orientalische Abteilung', by G. Auster. (In H. Kunze *ed.*, *Deutsche Staatsbibliothek, 1661–1961* **1**, Leipzig, 1961, pp. 275–317.)
—— 'Der Plan für die Einrichtung der Orientalischen Abteilung . . . und ihre heutige Funktionen', by K. von Schubart-Engelschall. *ZB* **83**, 1969, pp. 129–35.
—— 'Fünfzig Jahre Orientalische Abteilung', by K. Schubart-Engelschall. (In K. Schubart-Engelschall *ed.*, *Orientalistische Bibliotheken und Sammlungen*, Berlin, 1970, pp. 1–15.)
DEUTSCHE VORDERASIENINSTITUT, 'Verzeichnis der Bücherei. 1 Teil'. *Beiträge zur Kenntnis des Orients* **14**, 1917, pp. 183–264; **15**, 1918, pp. 121–74.

*Great Britain*

COLLINSON, R., *Directory of libraries and special collections on Asia and North Africa*. London, 1970.

Coverage limited to the British Isles. Includes many references to public library collections and has a good subject index.

LIBRARY ASSOCIATION. UNIVERSITY, COLLEGE AND RESEARCH SECTION, 'A note on the regional library groups'. (In B. C. Bloomfield *ed.*, *Acquisition and provision of foreign books by National and University libraries in the United Kingdom*, London, 1972, p. 165.)

UNION CATALOGUE OF ASIAN PUBLICATIONS, ed. D. Hall. 4v. London, 1971; 1971 suppl. London, 1974.

Covers almost all books from Asia bought by British libraries from 1965 to 1970, and also books from Africa, in Arabic and Ethiopic script. The exceptions are: (a) the acquisitions of S.O.A.S. and the Bodleian Library (included, however, in the Supplement; (b) scientific works; (c) works published in the U.S.S.R.; (d) periodicals.

A supplementary sequence to cover the accessions of all British libraries from 1970 to 1975 was planned in annual volumes, but after the publication of the volume for 1971, the sequence was suspended. It is now planned to issue a cumulation for 1965–75 on microfiche, with annual supplements and five-year cumulations to follow.

BRITISH MUSEUM (London) (now BRITISH LIBRARY, REFERENCE DIVISION), *Catalogue of Arabic books in the British Museum*, by A. G. Ellis. 2v. London, 1894–1901 (repr. London, 1967).
—— *Indexes*, by A. S. Fulton. London, 1935.
—— *Supplementary catalogue, 1901–1926*, by A. S. Fulton and A. G. Ellis. London, 1926.
—— *Second supplementary catalogue, 1926–1957*, by A. S. Fulton and M. Lings. London, 1959.

A third supplementary catalogue of Arabic books, ed. by Yasin Safadi, is in the press.

—— *The catalogues of the British Museum; Oriental printed books and manuscripts*, by F. C. Francis, London, 1959. (Rev. edn. of article in *J. Doc.* **7**, 1951.)
—— 'The Department of Oriental books and manuscripts', by K. Gardner. *J. Asian Studies* **18**, 1959, pp. 310–18.

DURHAM UNIVERSITY, CENTRE FOR MIDDLE EASTERN AND ISLAMIC STUDIES, *Middle East Datafile*. High Wycombe, 1975–76.

Quarterly accessions list of the Documentation Centre, published commercially by University Microfilms. Many of the documents listed are available on microfiche to subscribers.

EDINBURGH UNIVERSITY, *Fihrist al-kutub al-ʿarabiyya wa-al-fārsiyya wa-al-urdiyya al-mawjūda fī kutubkhāna Jāmiʾat Idinburg*, by M. Badr, Edinburgh, 1908.

Only Gabrieli is certain of the existence of this work.

INDIA OFFICE (London), 'The India Office Library; its history, resources and function', by R. Datta. *Library q.* **36**, 1966, pp. 99–148.

—— 'The India Office Library', by N. N. Gidwani. *Quest* **63**, 1969, pp. 36–8.

—— *The India Office Library*, by S. C. Sutton. 2nd edn. London, 1967.

ROYAL ASIATIC SOCIETY (London), *Catalogue of printed books published before 1932*. London, 1942.

ROYAL EMPIRE SOCIETY (London) (now ROYAL COMMONWEALTH SOCIETY), *Subject catalogue*, by E. Lewin. 4v. London, 1930–37 (repr. London, 1967).

—— *Subject catalogue*. (*Supplement*.) 7v. Boston, 1971.

—— *Biographical catalogue*. London, 1961.

SCHOOL OF ORIENTAL AND AFRICAN STUDIES (London), *Catalogue*. 28v. Boston, 1963.

—— *First supplement*. 16v. Boston, 7968.

—— *Second supplement*. 16v. Boston, 1974.

The original work contains 550,000 cards, in author, title and subject sequences. The first supplement contains 190,000 cards. Works in both Oriental and Western languages are included.

—— *Monthly list of titles added to the catalogue*. 1951–.

—— 'The school of Oriental and African Studies Library', by J. D. Pearson. (In B. C. Bloomfield *ed.*, *Acquisition and provision of foreign books by National and University libraries in the United Kingdom*, London, 1972, pp. 147–55.)

—— 'The Library of the School of Oriental and African Studies', by B. C. Bloomfield. (In D. A. Clarke *ed.*, *Acquisitions from the Third World*, London, 1975, pp. 245–65.)

The most recent of several articles on S.O.A.S.

*Hungary*

UNGARISCHE AKADEMIE DER WISSENSCHAFTEN (now MAGYAR TUDOMÁNYOS AKADÉMIA, Budapest), 'Die Goldziher-Sammlung'. *Ungarisches Jahrbuch* **13**, 1933, pp. 371–2.

—— 'Die Orientalische Sammlung', by L. Bese. (In K. Schubart-Engelschall *ed.*, *Orientalistische Bibliotheken und Sammlungen*, Berlin, 1970, pp. 69–72.)

*Italy*

PINTO, O., 'Manoscritti e stampati orientali nelle biblioteche governative italiane'. *RSO* **24**, 1949, pp. 161–8.

ACCADEMIA NAZIONALE DEI LINCEI (Rome), 'Libri donati all'Accademia da . . . Leone Caetani'. *Rendiconti* ser. 5, **75**, 1916, pp. 1255–73.

—— 'Orientalismo e orientalisti nella Biblioteca dei Lincei', by F. Gabrieli. *Almanacco dei Bibliotecari Italiani* 1958, pp. 43–6.

BIBLIOTECA AMBROSIANA (Milan), *Catalogo dei libri a stampa e elenco sommario dei mss. del Dr. Griffini, legati alla Biblioteca Ambrosiana*, by A. Codazzi. Milan, 1926.

ISTITUTO UNIVERSITARIO ORIENTALE (Naples), 'Sviluppo e funzionalità della Biblioteca', by P. Sbriziolo. (In *Convegno di Studi sulle Bibl. Univ., 1960*, Naples, 1962, pp. 51–5.)

*Poland*

REYCHMAN, J., 'Zbiory orientaliow w Polsce, 18 w'. *Stud. Kaz. Piekarskiego.* Wroclaw, 1951, pp. 283–94.

UNIWERSYTET WARSZAWSKI, 'Dzialalność Antoniego Muchlinskiego w Bibliotece', by A. Mrozowska. *Przegl. or.* **36**, 1960, pp. 432–5.

—— 'Z dziejòw najstarszego zasobu orientalistycznego Biblioteki', by A. Mrozowska. *Przegl. or.* **31**, 1959, pp. 277–88.

*Rumania*

GUBOGLU, M., 'L'importance des matériaux documentaires orientaux existant dans les archives, bibliothèques et collections roumaines'. *Studia et acta orientalia* **2**, 1959, pp. 107–18.

*Spain*

ACADEMIA DE LA HISTORIA (Madrid), 'Libros árabes adquiridos para la Academia', by F. Codera y Zaidín. *Bol. de la R. Acad. Hist.* **58**, 1911, pp. 181–7.

BIBLIOTECA NACIONAL (Madrid), 'Un important fonds européen; la section "Africa" ', by M. de Epalza. *Rev. hist. maghrébine* **1**, 1971, pp. 81–2.

DIRECCIÓN GENERAL DE PLAZAS Y PROVINCIAS AFRICANAS (Madrid), 'El archivo y biblioteca', by M. Asunción del Val. *RABM* **65**, 1958, pp. 123–8.

*Sweden*

UNIVERSITETSBIBLIOTHEK UPPSALA, 'Samling av Arabiska 1500- och 1600-Talstryck', by B. Lewin. (In *Festschrift A. Grape*, Uppsala, 1945, pp. 577–604.)

*U.S.S.R.*

BENDIK, A. I., 'Library collections and the systematization of information on Orientology in the U.S.S.R.'. (In J. D. Pearson *ed., Papers on Oriental library collections*, Zug, 1971, pp. 120–6.)

BENDIK, A. I. & GRIVNIN, V. S., 'Orientalia in USSR libraries'. *Unesco bull. lib.* **15**, 1961, pp. 322–6.

GRIŠINA, A. M., 'A system of bibliographical information on Asian and African studies (USSR)'. *Unesco bull. lib.* **27**, 1974, pp. 87–91.

LITERATURA O STRANAKH AZII I AFRIKI. EZHEGODNIK. Moscow, 1961–.

Irregular. Includes all books published in the Soviet Union on Asia and Africa.

NOVAYA SOVETSKAYA I INOSTRANNAYA LITERATURA PO STRANAM ZARUBEZHNOGO VOSTOKA. Moscow, 1953–68.

The monthly list of Oriental accessions of seven Soviet libraries. Continued as:

NOVAYA LITERATURA PO STRANAM AZII I AFRIKI. Moscow, 1969–.

This lists the Oriental and African accessions to ten Soviet libraries.

TVERITINOVA, A. S., *Vostokovednye fondy krupneyshikh bibliotek Sovetskogo Soyuza; stat'i i soobshcheniya*. Moscow, 1963.

GOSUDARSTVENNAYA PUBLICHNAYA BIBLIOTEKA IM. SALTYKOVA-SHCHEDRINA (Leningrad), *Literatura v yazykakh stran Azii i Afriki*, 1956?–.

Accessions list.

GOSUDARSTVENNAYA PUBLICHNAYA ISTORICHESKAYA BIBLIOTEKA (Moscow), 'Vostochnye fondy'. *Sovetskoe vostokovedenie* 1956, pp. 199–205.

GOSUDARSTVENNAYA RESPUBLIKANSKAYA BIBLIOTEKA GRUZINSKOI SSR (Tbilisi), 'Khranyashchiesya v nei vostochnye fondy', by A. K. Kavkasidze. (In K. Schubart-Engelschall *ed.*, *Orientalistische Bibliotheken und Sammlungen*, Berlin, 1970, pp. 73–87.)

LENINGRADSKII GOSUDARSTVENNYI UNIVERSITET, 'Biblioteka Vostochnogo Fakul'teta'. *Vostokovedenie v Leningradskom Univ.* 1968, pp. 177–88.

*U.S.A.*

'AWWĀD, Gūrgīs, *Jawla fi dūr al-kutub al-amrīkiyya*. Baghdad, 1951.

Concentrates on libraries with Middle Eastern collections.

EL-HADI, Mohammed Mohammed, *Arabic library resources in the United States; an investigation of their evolution, status and technical problems*. Ph.D. thesis. Illinois, 1964.

A valuable survey covering books, manuscripts and periodicals. For a summary in Arabic of this thesis, see: *'A. al-M.* **6**, iii, 1964, pp. 19–23.

HAZARD, H. W., *Bibliographical resources and needs in the social sciences relating to the Near and Middle East; a working paper*. New York, 1957.

MATTA, Ṣ., 'Arabic library resources in American research libraries and P.L.480'. *College and Research Libs.* 1964, pp. 472–4.

MIDDLE EAST LIBRARIANS ASSOCIATION, 'Association of Middle East Librarians'. *Unesco bull. lib.* **27**, 1973, pp. 295–6.

PARTINGTON, D. H., 'Arabic library collections; a study of the PL480 program by the Committee on the Middle East'. *MESA bull.* **9**, i, 1975, pp. 12–29.

POLLOCK, J. W., 'Directory of library collections on the Middle East'. *MESA bull.* **8**, i, 1974, pp. 22–44.

Lists major collections in the United States and Canada.

STEVENS, R., 'United States research library acquisitions in India, Pakistan and the U.A.R.'. *Unesco bull. lib.* **17**, 1963, pp. 178–80.

YAMAK, Labib Zuwiyya, 'Middle Eastern resources in American research libraries'. *MESA bull.* **2**, i, 1968, pp. 1–4.

AMERICAN GEOGRAPHICAL SOCIETY (New York), *Research catalog.* 15v. Boston, 1962.

AMERICAN MEDICAL LIBRARY (Chicago), 'The collection of Arabic medical literature', by C. F. Mayer. *Bull. Med. Lib. Assn.* N.S. **30**, 1942, pp. 96–104.

AMERICAN ORIENTAL SOCIETY (Boston), *Catalog of the Library,* by E. Sprout. New Haven, Conn., 1930.

CALIFORNIA UNIVERSITY (Los Angeles), *Books acquired for the Near Eastern collection.* 19?–.

CHICAGO UNIVERSITY, ORIENTAL INSTITUTE, *Catalog.* 16v. Boston, 1971.

280,000 cards in author and LC classified sequences. Special emphasis on the Middle East.

—— *Books acquired by the Oriental Institute Library.* 19?–.

COLUMBIA UNIVERSITY (New York), 'The Near Eastern Collection', by I. Mendelsohn. *Columbia Univ. q.* **32**, 1940, pp. 283–99.

HARTFORD THEOLOGICAL SEMINARY (Connecticut), 'The Müller Semitic Library', by D. B. Macdonald. *Hartford Sem. record* **4**, 1894, pp. 174–9.

—— 'The Arabic collection', by E. de W. Root. *Connecticut Lib. Assn. bull.* **10**, ii, 1943, pp. 10–11.

HARVARD UNIVERSITY, *Catalog of Arabic, Persian and Ottoman Turkish Books.* 5v. Cambridge, Mass., 1968.

Vols. 1–3 with 31,000 cards deal with the Arabic collection in separate author, title and subject sequences.

—— 'Middle East collections in Harvard libraries', by Labib Zuwiyya Yamak. *Harvard lib. bull.* **16**, 1968, pp. 313–25.

HOOVER INSTITUTE OF WAR, REVOLUTION AND PEACE (Stanford Univ.), *Catalog of the Arabic collection.* Boston, 1970.

18,900 cards.

LIBRARY OF CONGRESS, *Accessions list; Middle East* [P.L.480]. Cairo, 1963–.

Annual cumulations are also published.

—— 'Orientalia'. *Quarterly journal of current acquisitions.* Washington, 1943–.

Deals with Asian accessions.

MARY WASHINGTON COLLEGE (Fredericksburg, Va.), *A bibliography of books, periodicals and recordings pertaining to Asia,* by C. H. Quenzell. Fredericksburg, 1966.

MICHIGAN UNIVERSITY (Ann Arbor), *Asia Library; list of new acquisitions.* Ann Arbor, 1961–.

Plans are now under way to publish in fully catalogued format the library's Asian accessions. Annual listings in microform are envisaged.

MINNESOTA UNIVERSITY (Minneapolis), *Current accessions in the Middle East Library.* Minneapolis, 1970–.

NEW YORK CITY, *Libraries in New York City with collections of materials on Asia and notes on other sources of information.* New York, 1962.

NEW YORK PUBLIC LIBRARY, *Dictionary catalog of the Oriental collection.* 16v. Boston, 1960.

318,000 cards for 65,000 volumes. The Arabic collection is the largest in the U.S.A. The catalogue also contains works in Western languages on Oriental subjects and numerous analytical entries for articles. A supplement is planned.

—— *List of works in the NYPL relating to Arabic poetry*, by C. Pratt under the direction of R. Gottheil. New York, 1908.

SYRACUSE UNIVERSITY (New York), *A survey of Asian materials . . . with some recommendations.* New York, 1961.

This university does not have a specific programme in Middle Eastern studies.

UTAH UNIVERSITY (Salt Lake City), *Middle East Library catalogue series.* Vol. 1: *Arabic collection.* Salt Lake City, 1968.

Partial coverage of Arabic monographs in a sizeable work.

WASHINGTON UNIVERSITY (St. Louis), *Bibliography of materials concerning the Middle East and North Africa* . . . by A. Carvely. St. Louis, 1970.

*Yugoslavia*

JUGOSLAVENSKA AKADEMIYA (Zagreb), 'Kratak osrvt na istorijat Orijentalne zbirke', by S. Bajraktarević. *Prilozi Orijent. Filol. Ist.* **2**, 1951, pp. 315–17.

*Private Libraries*

BERCHEM, M. van, 'Max van Berchem library', by G. Wiet. *JRAS* 1926, pp. 308–10; *Hespéris* **5**, 1925, pp. 443–4; *RSO* **11**, 1926–28, p. 120; *Der Islam* **16**, 1927, pp. 167–8.

Now in the Bibliothèque Publique in Geneva.

LITTMANN, E., *The library of Enno Littmann, 1875–1958, with an autobiographical sketch*; intr. Maria Höfner. (Brill catalogue No. 307.) Leiden, 1959.

MALVEZZI, A., 'La "collezione orientale" di Aldobrandino Malvezzi', by G. Finazzo. *Africa* [Rome] **21**, 1966, pp. 289–98.

RICE, D. S., *The library of the late Prof. D. S. Rice.* N.pl., n.d.

SILVESTRE DE SACY, A. I., Baron, *La bibliothèque de . . . Silvestre de Sacy*, by R. Merlin. 3v. Paris, 1842–47.

Contained about 850 volumes.

WIDMANSTETTER, J. A., 'Die Bücherei des Orientalisten Johann Albrecht Widmanstetter', by H. Striedl. *Serta Monacensia* 1952, pp. 200–44.

## II. NON-ARABIC SPEAKING ASIAN AND AFRICAN COUNTRIES WITH ARABIC COLLECTIONS

This section deals with collections of Arabic material only.

*China*

BOUVAT, L., 'Une bibliothèque de mosquée chinoise'. *RMM* **4**, 1908, pp. 516–21.

*India*

ASIATIC SOCIETY OF BENGAL (Calcutta), *Catalogue of the Arabic books and manuscripts*, by Mirza Ashraf 'Ali. Calcutta, 1904.

RAMPUR STATE LIBRARY, *Fihrist-i kutub-i 'arabī*. 2v. Rampur, 1902–28.

*Nigeria*

IBADAN UNIVERSITY, 'The Arabic collection', by K. Mahmud. *Libri* **14**, 1964, pp. 97–107.

*Pakistan*

MIDDLE EAST RESEARCH LIBRARY OF THE AMERICAN FRIENDS OF THE MIDDLE EAST (Lahore), *Catalogue of books and periodicals*. Lahore, 1962.

*Turkey*

ISTANBUL ÜNIVERSITESI KÜTÜPHANESI, *Arapça basmalar kataloğu*, by F. E. Karatay. (Ist. Univ. yay., 501.) 2v. Istanbul, 1951–53.

## III. LIBRARIES AND BIBLIOGRAPHICAL SERVICES IN THE ARAB WORLD

(a) History of Arab-Islamic libraries.
(b) Bibliographical services in the Arab World.
(c) Libraries in the Arab World.

### (a) History of Arab-Islamic Libraries

'AWWĀD, Gūrgīs, *Khazā'in al-kutub al-qadīma fī al-'Irāq mundhu aqdam al-'uṣūr ḥattā 1000 A.H. (A.D. 1591)*. Baghdad, 1948.

BADRĪ, 'Abd al-Rāziq Shākir, 'Maktabāt Sāmarrā', qadīmuhā wa ḥadīthuhā'. *'A. al-M.* **6**, i, 1964, pp. 30–3.

BASHIRUDDIN, S., 'Fate of sectarian libraries in mediaeval Islam'. *Libri* **17**, 1967, pp. 149–62.

ECHE, Y., *Les bibliothèques arabes publiques et semi-publiques en Mésopotamie, en Syrie et en Égypte au Moyen Age*. Damascus, 1967.

GHANEM, I. E., *Zur Bibliotheksgeschichte von Damascus, 1154–1516*. Bonn, 1969. [Doctoral thesis.]

GOTTSCHALK, W., 'Die Bibliotheken der Araber im Zeitalter der Abbasiden'. *ZB* **47**, 1930, pp. 1–6.

GROHMANN, A., 'Bibliotheken und Bibliophilen im islamischen Orient'. (In *Festschrift der Nationalbibliothek in Wien hrsg. zur Feier des 200 jährigen Bestehens des Gebäudes*, Vienna, 1926, pp. 431–42.)

ḤAMĀDA, Muḥammad Māhir, *Al-maktabāt fī al-Islām*. Beirut, 1970.

ḤAMDĪ, 'Umar Ḥasan, *Al-maktaba fī al-'ālam al-'arabī; tā'rīkhuhā wa-ṭuruq al-'amal bihā*. Cairo, 1959.

Includes an introduction to librarianship.

HEFFENING, W. & KRENKOW, F., 'Kitabkhāna'. *EI*[1] **2**, pp. 31–3.

HUSSEIN, S. V., 'Organisation and administration of Muslim libraries (786–1492)'. *Qtly. J. Pakistan Lib. Assn.* **1**, 1960, pp. 8–11.

IBRĀHĪM, 'Abd al-Laṭīf, *Dirāsāt fī al-kutub wa-al-maktabāt al-islāmiyya min al-wathā'iq al-'arabiyya.* Cairo, 1962.

IMAMUDDIN, S. M., *Hispano-Arab libraries.* Karachi, 1961.

This study was previously published as two separate articles in the *JPHS* **7**, 1959.

INAYATULLAH, S., 'Bibliophilism in mediaeval Islam'. *IC* **12**, 1938, pp. 155–69. Also in *Pakistan lib. rev.* **3**, ii, 1961, pp. 29–45.

KABĪR, M., 'Libraries and academies during the Buwaihid period, 946–1055'. *IC* **33**, 1959, pp. 31–3.

KHUDA BAKHSH, S., 'The Islamic libraries'. *Nineteenth century* **15**, 1902, pp. 135–9.

MACKENSEN, R. S., 'Arabic books and libraries in the Umaiyad period'. *AJSL* **52**, 1935–36, pp. 245–53; **53**, 1936–37, pp. 239–50; **54**, 1937, pp. 41–61.

—— 'Supplementary notes'. *AJSL* **56**, 1939, pp. 149–57.

—— 'Background to the history of Moslem libraries'. *AJSL* **51**, 1934–35, pp. 114–25; **52**, 1935–36, pp. 22–3, 104–10.

—— 'Four great libraries of mediaeval Baghdad'. *Lib. Q.* **3**, 1932, pp. 279–99.

—— 'Moslem libraries and sectarian propaganda'. *AJSL* **51**, 1934–35, pp. 83–113.

MAḤFŪẒ, Ḥusayn 'Alī, *Khazā'in kutub al-Kāẓimiyya qadīman wa-ḥadīthan.* Baghdad, 1958.

MAHMUD, K., 'The influence of the Holy Quran on the development of libraries'. *Nigerian J. Islam* **1**, ii, 1971, pp. 11–22.

MEYERHOF, M., 'Über einige Privatbibliotheken im fatimidischen Ägypten'. *RSO* **12**, 1929–30, pp. 286–90.

PADOVER, S. K., 'Muslim libraries'. (In J. W. Thompson *ed.*, *The medieval library*, Chicago, 1939, pp. 347–68 (repr. New York, 1957).)

PINTO, O., 'Le biblioteche degli Arabi nell'età degli Abbasidi'. *Bibliofilia* **30**, 1928, pp. 139–65.

This article was translated into English as:

'Libraries of the Arabs during the time of the Abbasides'. *IC* **3**, 1929, pp. 210–43. Also in *Pakistan lib. rev.* **2**, 1959, pp. 44–72.

PLUMBE, W. J., 'The libraries of medieval Islam'. *Malayan lib. J.* **2**, iv, 1962, pp. 130–5.

QASIMI, A. S., 'Libraries in the early Islamic world'. *J Univ. Peshawar* **6**, 1958, pp. 1–15.

RIBERA Y TARRAGÓ, J., *Bibliófilos y bibliotecas en la España musulmana.* Saragossa, 1896. Also in *Disertaciones y opúscolos* (Madrid), **1**, 1928, pp. 189–228.

ROY CHOUDHURY SASTRI, M. L., 'Library in Islam'. *BPP* **61**, 1941, pp. 65–70.

SHALABĪ, Aḥmad, *History of Muslim education.* Beirut, 1954; translated into Arabic as: *Tā'rīkh al-tarbiyya al-islāmiyya.* Cairo, 1966.

Chapter 2 deals with the organization and administration of medieval Islamic libraries.

SHAFI, M., 'Libraries and learning in the Islamic world'. *Pakistan lib. rev.* **3**, ii, 1961, pp. 28–36.

SHANĪṬĪ, Maḥmūd (Sheniti, Mahmoud), *Al-kitāb al-'arabī bayn al-māḍī wa-al-ḥāḍir*. Cairo, n.d.

SOURDEL, D., 'Dār al-Ḥikma' and 'Dār al-'Ilm'. *EI*² **2**, pp. 126–7.

-ṬABBĀKH, Muḥammad Rāghib, 'Dūr al-kutub fī Halab qadīman wa ḥadīthan. *RAAD* **15**, 1937, pp. 244–30.

TARRAZI, P. de, *Khazā'in al-kutub al-'arabiyya fī al-khāfiqayn*. 4v. Beirut, 1947–51.

Contains predominantly historical material, but also touches on librarianship and modern Arab libraries.

WEIL, G., 'Arabische Verse über das Ausleihen von Büchern'. *Islamica* **2**, 1926, pp. 556–61.

WEISWEILER, M., 'Avicenna und die iranischen Fürstenbibliotheken seiner Zeit'. (In *Avicenna commem. vol.*, 1956, pp. 47–63.)

WIET, G., 'Recherches sur les bibliothèques égyptiennes aux Xe et XIe siècles'. *Cah. civ. méd.* **6**, 1963, pp. 1–11.

## (b) Bibliographical Services in the Arab World

In the past, bibliographical activities in the Arab world have been relatively poorly organized, mainly due to socio-economic factors. Small editions, local markets, temporary and underground publishers, unevenly enforced deposit laws and a lack of qualified staff often prevented central institutions from monitoring current publications effectively. National libraries therefore turned to other, more feasible, projects, such as manuscript catalogues, special subject lists and support for teaching programmes. In the last decade, however, it has become increasingly possible for Arab countries to contemplate some sort of national coverage, and several national bibliographies have indeed appeared, though with varying regularity. Plans for others have received government approval and it seems likely that the trend towards the central control of book production will continue.

Side by side with increasing national bibliographical consciousness, there have been attempts to institute co-operative projects among the Arab states. So far, the Institute of Arab Manuscripts (Ma'had al-Makhṭūṭāt al-'Arabiyya) remains the most enduring monument to these endeavours, but the most recent schemes,[1] if implemented, could bring about a radical improvement in Arab bibliography on both national and supra-national levels. For the moment, however, an overall picture of the situation can be gained from the following works:

### GUIDES TO BIBLIOGRAPHICAL SERVICES

'ABD AL-RAḤMĀN, 'Abd al-Jabbār, *Dalīl al-marāji' al-'arabiyya wa-al-mu'arraba*. (*Guide to Arabic reference books.*) Basra, 1970.

Contains a short chapter, pp. 82–6, on current Arab bibliographies.

[1] 'Meeting of experts on book development in the Arab countries, 1972'. Briefly reported in the *Unesco bull. lib.* **26**, 1972, p. 348; *final report*. Unesco, 1972. Also: 'Meeting of the Directors of National Libraries in countries of the Maghreb [Tunisia, Algeria, Morocco]'. *Unesco bull. lib.* **27**, 1973, p. 188.

AMAN, Muhammad, 'Bibliographical activities of the Arab countries of North Africa'. *Int. lib. rev.* **2**, 1970, pp. 263–74.

—— 'Bibliographical services in the Arab countries'. *College & Research Libs.* **3**, 1970, pp. 249–59.

Both these articles are useful, if incomplete, and not entirely free from inaccuracies.

AVICENNE, P., *Bibliographical services throughout the world.* Unesco, 1972. [Also available in French.]

Gives uneven coverage to Algeria, Bahrein, Iraq, Jordan, Kuwait, Lebanon, Libya, Mauritania, Morocco, Qatar, Sa'udi Arabia, Sudan, Syria and Tunisia.

BIBLIOGRAPHY, DOCUMENTATION, TERMINOLOGY. Unesco, 1961–.

Bi-monthly, this serial continually updates Avicenne. Available in English, French, Spanish and Russian editions.

DĀGHIR, Yūsuf As'ad (Dagher, Joseph A.), 'L'état actuel de la bibliographie dans le monde arabe'. *Arabica* **5**, 1958, pp. 47–55.

'ĪSĀ, Aḥmad (Issa, Ahmad), 'Lights on some bibliographical activities in UAR'. (In K. Schubart-Engelschall *ed.*, *Orientalistische Bibliotheken und Sammlungen*, Berlin, 1970, pp. 112–14.)

UNESCO, *Guide to national bibliographical information centres; Guide des centres nationaux d'information bibliographique.* 3rd edn. Unesco, 1970.

Less complete and up to date than Avicenne, this gives information on Egypt, Iraq, Jordan, Qatar, Sa'udi Arabia, Sudan and Tunisia.

UNESCO BULLETIN FOR LIBRARIES, Unesco, 1947–.

Quarterly. Supplements Avicenne and Unesco's own *Bibliography, documentation, terminology.* Contains many short notices on individual libraries, reference works and bibliographical projects.

GENERAL BIBLIOGRAPHIES

(*See also the section headed 'Journals' in Part 4.*)

DALĪL AL-KITĀB AL-MIṢRĪ (Egyptian books in print), Cairo, 19?–.

Published by al-Hay'a al-Miṣriyya al-'Āmma li-al-Kitāb, this useful work is arranged by subject with author and title indexes. The bibliographical information it contains is not always accurate.

-MAKTABA, Harissa, Lebanon, 1956–57.

Ran for two complete issues and covered books published in Jordan, Iraq, Syria and Lebanon.

-NASHRA AL-'ARABIYYA LI-AL-MAṬBŪ'ĀT (Bulletin of Arab Publications), Cairo, 1970–.

Published annually by the Arab League in two parts. Part 1 acts as the national bibliography for all books published in Algeria, Bahrein, Iraq, Jordan, Kuwait, Lebanon, Libya, Sudan, Syria and Tunisia, and includes books published by the Palestine Liberation Organization. Part 2 covers Egypt and is substituted by the corresponding volume of Al-Nashra al-Miṣriyya li-al-Maṭbū'āt. The first volume for 1970 appeared in 1973.

BIBLIOGRAPHY OF THE MIDDLE EAST, Damascus, 1969–.

LA REVUE BIBLIOGRAPHIQUE DU MOYEN-ORIENT, Damascus, 1968–.

Annual. Both purport to be complete and classified lists, but there are innumerable gaps, classification is haphazard and presentation is poor. Romanization and author headings are particularly weak. I have not been able to establish the date of first issue with certainty.

NATIONAL BIBLIOGRAPHIES

(For para-national bibliographies, see the section above, and the section headed 'Journals' in Part 4. For the accessions lists and catalogues of individual libraries, see section (c).)

*Algeria*

-BIBLIYŪGHRĀFIYYA AL-JAZĀ'IRIYYA (Bibliographie de l'Algérie), Algiers, 1963–.

Meant to appear every six months, but publication is irregular. Vols. 1–3 covered serials and monographs alternately, but from vol. 4 on, both are listed in the same volume. Uses a classified arrangement (by UDC?).

*Egypt*

-NASHRA AL-MIṢRIYYA LI-AL-MAṬBŪ'ĀT (Egyptian publications bulletin), Cairo, 1956–.

Quarterly till 1959, then annual. Cumulations have appeared as follows: 1956–60, 1961–62, 1961–65, 1966–67, 1966–71.

Although published with a two-year delay, this is an excellent bibliographical tool; it is classified by Dewey, has good indexes for authors, titles and publishers, and separate sections for school texts and juvenilia.

NASHRAT AL-ĪDĀ' AL-SHAHRIYYA (Legal deposit monthly bulletin), Cairo, 1969–.

Is identical in structure to the national bibliography. Both are issued by the Dār al-Kutub.

*Iraq*

-NASHRA AL-'IRĀQIYYA LI-AL-MAṬBŪ'ĀT (Iraqi bulletin for publications), Baghdad, 1963–.

Appears spasmodically, published by the Maktaba al-Markaziyya. Classified by Dewey.

A cumulated edition for 1963–67 has been published, namely:

-BIBLIYŪGHRĀFIYYA AL-MUJAMMA'A AL-'IRĀQIYYA.

NASHRAT AL-ĪDĀ' AL-QĀNŪNĪ LI-AL-MAṬBŪ'ĀT AL-'IRĀQIYYA (Monthly deposit bulletin), Baghdad, 1971–.

*Jordan*

RISĀLAT AL-MAKTABA (Rissalat al-Maktaba; Message of the library), Amman, 1965–.

One issue per year contains the national bibliography. A cumulated bibliography for 1971–75, and a retrospective volume for 1900–70 have been published by Maḥmūd al-Akhras; both are entitled *al-Bibliyūghrāfiyā al-Filasṭīniyya al-Urdunniyya* (*Palestine-Jordan Bibliography*).

*Kuwait*

BIBLIYŪJRĀFIYĀ MUKHTĀRA ʻAN AL-KUWAIT WA-AL-KHALĪJ AL-ʻARABĪ (Al-silsila al-bibliyūjrāfiyya, 2). Comp. by Thurayā Muḥammad Qābīl. Kuwait, 1970.

SELECTED BIBLIOGRAPHY ON KUWAIT AND THE ARABIAN GULF (Bibliographic ser., 1). Comp. by Soraya M. Kabeel (Thurayā Muḥammad Qābīl). Kuwait, 1969.

These two works perform the function of a national bibliography; they are to be formalized later, on the promulgation of a legal deposit law.

*Lebanon*

-NASHRA AL-BIBLIYŪGHRĀFIYYA AL-LUBNĀNIYYA LI-AL-INTĀJ AL-FIKRĪ WA-AL-ṬIBĀʻĪ FĪ LUBNĀN (Bulletin bibliographique libanais des oeuvres intellectuelles et des imprimés au Liban), Beirut, 1964–65, 1971–72.

Only two annual issues were originally published due to the poor response of the Lebanese book trade; two further issues for 1971 and 1972 have been published on roneographed stencils, but the Bulletin's future remains uncertain.

*Libya*

-BIBLYŪGHRĀFIYYA AL-WAṬANIYYA AL-LĪBIYYA (National bibliography of the Libyan Arab Republic), Tripoli, 1972–.

The first annual volume in 1972 gave retrospective coverage to books 1951–71 and to periodicals 1827–1971; subsequent volumes give current coverage. In 1973 the English subtitle was changed to *The Arab bibliography of Libya*. For a description of this publication see:

SCHLÜTER, H., 'Nationale Bibliographie Libyens'. *Z. Bibliothekswesen u. Bibliog.* **22**, 1975, pp. 47–9.

*Morocco*

-BIBLIYŪGHRĀFIYYA AL-WAṬANIYYA AL-MAGHRIBIYYA (Bibliographie nationale marocaine), Rabat, 1963–.

Previously issued as a part of *Hespéris*, 1921–53 and 1962; a cumulated edition covering 1921–62 was published in three volumes by the Bibliothèque Générale in Rabat. For descriptions of the national bibliography see:

AUERBACH, W., 'The national bibliography of Morocco'. *Africana lib. J.* **3**, 1971, pp. 7–13.

HARIKI, G., 'La bibliographie nationale marocaine'. *Hespéris-Tamuda* **7**, 1966, pp. 97–100.

BULLETIN DU DÉPÔT LÉGAL, Rabat, 1968–.

*Syria*

-NASHRA AL-MAKTABIYYA BI-AL-KUTUB AL-ṢĀDIRA FĪ AL-J. ʻA. S., Damascus, 1972–.

Published by the Wizārat al-Thaqāfa wa-al-Irshād al-Qawmī.

*Tunisia*

-BĪBLIYŪGHRĀFIYĀ AL-QAWMIYYA AL-TŪNISIYYA (Bibliographie de la Tunisie), Tunis, 1969–.

Divided into two parts – official and non-official publications – and issued twice yearly.

## (c) Libraries in the Arab World

This section has tried to include the relevant material in Western languages, but has been selective as regards Arabic. In particular, only a representative cross-section of articles from *ʿĀlam al-Maktabāt* has been indexed.

The arrangement of entries is the same as in Part 1, with one exception; in the second sequence, libraries are listed under the town in which they are situated rather than their own name. As for the libraries themselves, I have preferred the Arabic form of the name, where this was clear and consistent.

### GUIDES TO ARAB LIBRARIES

BADR, Aḥmad, *Dalīl dūr al-maḥfūẓāt wa-al-maktabāt wa-marākiz al-tawthīq wa-al-maʿāhid al-bibliyūghrāfiyya fī al-duwal al-ʿarabiyya; Directory of archives, libraries, documentation centres and bibliographical institutions in Arabic speaking countries; Répertoire des archives, bibliothèques, centres de documentation et institutions bibliographiques en pays arabes.* Cairo, 1965.

Published in separate French, Arabic and English editions. Gives much information on Egypt, but is weak on North Africa and the Arabian Peninsula. Sponsored by Unesco.

DĀGHIR, Yūsuf Asʿad, *Fahāris al-maktabāt al-ʿarabiyya fī al-khāfiqayn.* Beirut, 1947.

Unfortunately, I have not been able to see this work.

—— *Répertoire des bibliothèques du Proche et du Moyen-Orient.* Paris, 1951.

Though now out of date, it contains useful information not in Badr. Covers Iran and Turkey as well as the Arab World.

-HUṢRĪ, Ṣāṭiʿ, *Ḥawliyyāt al-thaqāfiyya.* Cairo, 1949–62.

A section in each of the first five numbers was devoted to the libraries of the Arab World.

KĀẒIM, Midḥat, *Dalīl al-maktabāt; Library directory.* Cairo, 1954.

A brief introduction to librarianship is followed by a detailed list of Egyptian libraries, and more cursory notes on libraries in other countries.

KHALAF ALLĀH, Muḥammad Aḥmad, *Dirāsāt fī al-maktaba al-ʿarabiyya.* Cairo, 1958.

Lectures on source materials in Arabic, including details of the major libraries.

MIDDLE EAST STUDIES ASSOCIATION BULLETIN, New York, 1967–.

Contains a series of articles on research facilities in individual Arab countries, with details on libraries.

### GENERAL

ʿABD AL-HĀDĪ, Muḥammad Fatḥī, *Al-maktabāt wa-dirāsātuhā fī al-ʿālam al-ʿarabī; qāʾima bibliyūjrāfiyya.* Cairo, 1972. *Mulḥaq.* Cairo, 1973.

A comprehensive bibliography of 1577 books, articles and theses (almost entirely in Arabic) covering every aspect of librarianship.

AITKEN, B. M. W., 'Some impressions of books and publishing in the Middle East'. *RCAJ* **53**, 1966, pp. 158–65.

BIELAWSKI, J., 'Ksiegozbiory jako wyraz kultury swiate muzulmanskiego'. *Przegl. Or.* **34**, 1960, pp. 131–44.

CARTER, M. D., 'Special libraries in the Near East'. *Sp. libs.* **42**, 1951, pp. 245–8, 267–8.

Describes a few libraries in Egypt.

CHANDLER, G., *Libraries in the East; an international and comparative study.* London, 1971.

Chapters 2–3 deal with major libraries in Lebanon and Egypt.

—— 'Near, Middle and Far Eastern libraries'. *Int. lib. rev.* **3**, 1971, pp. 187–228.

A shortened version of his monograph listed above.

HARTMANN, M., 'Das Bibliothekswesen in den islamischen Ländern'. *ZB* **16**, 1899, p. 186.

HARVEY, J. F. & LAMBERT, B., 'Librarianship in six South-West Asian countries'. *Int. lib. rev.* **3**, 1971, pp. 15–34.

Devotes one page to the A.U.B., otherwise deals with non-Arab countries.

HATHORN, V., 'Middle East library workshop'. *Wilson Lib. bull.* June 1969.

HOLLOWAY, M. F., 'Patterns of library service in the Middle East'. *Lib. trends* **8**, 1959, pp. 192–208.

HEINTZE, I., 'Resa till bokliga Arabien'. *Biblioteksbladet* **50**, 1965, pp. 353–7.

On libraries in Lebanon and Egypt.

KALIA, D. R., *Report on a mission to some of the Arab states (Syria, Lebanon and Jordan).* ASFEC, 1957.

KENT, A. & LANCOUR, H., *Encyclopedia of library and information science.* New York, 1968–.

An authoritative work to be completed in 18 volumes, it contains articles on libraries in all the Arabic-speaking countries; these range in extent from 9 lines on Aden by Nasser Sharify to 14 pages on Egypt by Muḥammad M. Aman.

KENT, F. L., 'Libraries in the developing countries; the Arab World'. *Libri* **14**, 1964, pp. 168–75.

KENT, F. L. & ABU HAIDAR, Fawzi, 'Library development in the Arab World'. *Rev. int. doc.* **29**, 1962, pp. 3–7.

KHOURY, Y. K., 'Bibliographical activities of Unesco in the Arab World'. (In E. Bishop and J. Waller *eds.*, *International co-operation in orientalist librarianship*, Canberra, 1972, pp. 213–29.)

SHANĪṬĪ, Maḥmūd, 'Unesco and library and related services in Arab-speaking countries'. *Unesco bull. lib.* **20**, 1966, pp. 219–25.

SIMSOVA, S. & MACKEE, M., *A handbook of comparative librarianship.* 2nd edn. London, 1975.

Includes a guide to sources on librarianship throughout the world, with 25 pages being devoted to the Middle East. Although neither complete nor wholly accurate, the listings do provide a useful checklist.

THOMPSON, L. S., 'Awakening library consciousness in the Middle East'. *Library q.* **24**, 1954, pp. 154–68.

UNESCO, 'Arab States Conference on the exchange of publications, Damascus (1957)'. *Unesco bull. lib.* **11**, 1957, pp. 293–4.

—— *Meeting of experts on the national planning of documentation and library services in Arab countries, Cairo (1973). Main working document.* Paris, 1973.
Comprehensive survey of the present state of documentation and library services in the Arab World. A follow-up conference took place in 1974 and was reported as:
—— 'National planning of documentation and library services in Arab countries, Cairo, 1974'. *Unesco bull. lib.* **28**, 1974, pp. 182–7.
—— 'Report on regional seminar on bibliography, documentation and exchange of publications in the Arab-speaking states, Cairo, 1962'. *Unesco bull. lib.* **17**, 1963, pp. 137–45; also in *'A. al-M.* **4**, v, 1962, pp. 6–16.
—— 'Summary report of the regional seminar on library development in Arabic-speaking states'. *Unesco bull. lib.* **14**, 1960, pp. 117–23.
ANON, 'Library development in the Middle East'. *Leads* **10**, ii, 1967.
—— 'Notice sur le developpement du livre et des bibliothèques en pays musulmans'. *RMM* **1**, 1906, pp. 453–6.
—— 'Special libraries in the Middle East'. *Sp. libs.* **48**, 1957.

*Algeria*
LEBEL, G., 'La lecture publique en Algérie'. *Cah. des bibs. fr. en Algérie* 1956, pp. 45–59.

*Egypt*
AGWANI, M. S., 'A preliminary note on libraries and archives in Egypt and Libya'. *Int. studies* **1**, 1959, pp. 201–3.
AMAN, Muḥammad Muḥammad, 'Egyptian university libraries'. *Int. lib. rev.* **2**, 1970, pp. 175–81.
—— 'Libraries abroad; libraries in the U.A.R.'. *J. lib. hist.* **4**, 1969, pp. 158–68.
'AWWĀD, Tawfīq (Awad, Tewfiq), 'School libraries in the Arab Republic of Egypt'. *Unesco bull. lib.* **26**, 1972, pp. 214–17.
BURGEMEISTER, B., 'Entwicklungsprobleme der Universitätsbibliothek Kairo und des wissenschaftlichen Bibliothekswesen der V.A.R.'. *ZB* **79**, 1965, pp. 321–6.
EL-DIB, B., 'Report from Egypt'. *Lib. J.* **77**, 1952, pp. 20–33.
On library provision and service.
FAIR, E. M., 'Impressions of librarianship in Cairo'. *Lib. Cong. inf. bull.* **10**, 1951, p. 41.
JAMĪ'AT MAKTABĀT AL-QĀHIRA, *Dalīl maktabāt al-Qāhira.* Cairo, 1950.
KIRK, A., *United Arab Republic; proposed national press for scientific production.* Paris (Unesco) [1965].
LAVER, M., *Library services and development in Egypt.* Thesis, Univ. of Pittsburgh, 1964.
LITTMANN, E., 'Ein arabisches Lied über die Ägyptische Bibliothek in Kairo'. (In *Festschrift G. Leyh*, 1937, pp. 309–11.)
McCARTHY, S. A., 'Egyptian libraries'. *Lib. J.* **80**, 1955, pp. 106–8.
MATTA, S., 'In search of the Nile; the challenge to libraries in Egypt'. *Wilson Lib. bull.* **44**, 1970, pp. 1040–5.
NATIONAL INFORMATION AND DOCUMENTATION CENTRE, Cairo, *Directory of scientific and technical libraries in the U.A.R.* Cairo, 1970.
A detailed guide.

SABET, A. A., 'The library movement in Egypt'. *Unesco bull. lib.* **10**, 1956, pp. 182–3.

SARINGULYAN, M., 'The libraries of Egypt'. *Bibliotekar'* (*USSR*) **1**, 1957, pp. 67–70.

'UMAR, 'Abd al-Mun'im Muḥammad, 'Al-maktabāt al-'āmma wa-dawruhā fī al-tawjīh al-qawmī'. *'A. al-M.* **4**, ii, 1962, pp. 6–7.
Deals mainly with Egyptian problems.

YOUSSEF, F., *Public library organisation in Egypt*. Thesis, Univ. of Minnesota, 1964.

ZAFAR NADVI, S. A., 'Some libraries of Cairo'. *MW* **28**, 1938, pp. 223–30.

AIN SHAMS, JĀMI'AT 'AIN SHAMS, *Qā'ima bibliyūghrāfiyya bi-muqtanayāt al-Maktaba min al-rasā'il al-'ulyā allatī ijāzathā al-jāmi'āt al-miṣriyya wa-al-jāmi'āt al-ajnabiyya li-abnā' al-J. 'A. M. ḥattā 1968*. Cairo, 1969.
—— *Sijill al-ḥāṣilīn 'alā darajatay al-mājistīr wa-al-dūkturāh, 1950–68*. Cairo, *c*. 1969.

ALEXANDRIA, ALEXANDRIA LIBRARY, 'À propos de l'incendie de la Bibliothèque d'Alexandrie par les Arabes', by F. Laloë. *RA* **66**, 1925, pp. 95–107.
—— *The Alexandrian Library, glory of the Hellenic world; its rise, antiquities and destructions*, by E. A. Parsons. London, 1952.
Chapter 18, pp. 371–412, deals with alleged burning of the library by the Arabs.
—— 'The burning of the books at the Library of Alexandria and elsewhere', by Jurjī Zaydān. Extracted from his book, *Tā'rīkh al-tamaddun al-islāmī*, part 3, and translated into English in *The Alexandria Library*, by E. A. Parsons (see above), pp. 413–21.
—— 'The destruction of the Alexandrian Library', by S. Niazi. *J. Pakistan Hist. Soc.* **16**, 1968, pp. 163–74.
—— 'L'incendie de la Bibliothèque d'Alexandrie par les Arabes', by M. Casanova. *CRAIBL*, 1923, pp. 161–71.
—— 'The Library of Alexandria, notes on current work', by E. A. Parsons. *Private libs.* **4**, 1962, pp. 10–13.
Reviews the literature on the subject from 1952 to 1962.
—— *Maktabat al-Iskandariyya; ta'sīs wa-iḥrāquhā*, by Gūrgīs 'Awwād. Baghdad, 1955.
—— 'A note on the alleged destruction of the Alexandria Library by the Arabs', by Mohammed Awad. *JWH* **8**, 1964, pp. 213–14.
—— 'Observation sur le sort de la Bibliothèque d'Alexandrie en réponse à sa Béatitude Kyrillos Macaire', by Magdi Bey. *Bull. Soc. Géog. du Caire* **7**, 1907–12, pp. 553–70.
—— 'Sull'incendio della Biblioteca di Alessandria', by G. Furlani. *Aegyptus* **5**, 1924, pp. 205–12.
—— 'Sur la fin probable de la Bibliothèque d'Alexandrie', by T. D. Maschonas. *Cah. d'Alex.* **4**, 1967, pp. 205–12.
—— 'Über die Sage von der Verbrennung der alexandrinischen Bibliothek durch die Araber', by L. Krehl. (In *Atti 4th Int. Cong. Or. 1878*. 2v. Florence, 1880–1, p. 436 (repr. Nendeln, 1968.)

ALEXANDRIA, AL-MAKTABA AL-BALADIYYA, *Fahāris*, ed. Aḥmad Abū ʿAlī, 4 pts. Alexandria?, 1926–29.
Two supplements appeared in 1955.

ASYUT, JĀMIʿAT ASYŪT, 'Land-grant colleges in the Muslim world'. (In W. R. Collings, *Academic librarianship in the international milieu*, Manhattan, Kan., 1968, pp. 32–47.)
Deals with Asyut University Library and Atatürk U. L., Erzerum.

CAIRO, AL-AZHAR, *Fihris al-kutub al-mawjūda bi-al-Maktaba al-Azhariyya ilā 1952*. 6v. Cairo, 1946–52. Supplement in two parts up to 1962.
The first edition listed works up to 1945. All parts include manuscripts.
—— *Qāʾima . . . li-al-rasāʾil al-jāmiʿiyya allatī ujīzat li-nayl darajāt al-dirāsāt al-ʿulyā li-kulliyyat uṣūl-al-dīn, al-sharīʿa, al-lugha al-ʿarabiyya*. Cairo, 1968.

CAIRO, DĀR AL-KUTUB, *Arab Republic of Egypt; mechanisation of the catalogues of the National Library*, by A. E. Jeffrey. Paris (Unesco), 1971.
—— *Catalogue de la section européenne*. Vol. 1: Égypte. [No more published.] Cairo, 1892; 2nd edn. 2v. Cairo, 1899–1901; 3rd edn. Cairo, 1957, published as: *Egypt: subject catalogue.*
—— *Dār al-Kutub fī ʿahd al-thawra, 1952–62*. Cairo, 1962.
—— *Fihrist al-khizāna al-Taymuriyya*. 4v. Cairo, 1947–50.
—— *Fihrist al-kutub al-ʿarabiyya al-maḥfūẓa bi-al-Kutubkhāna al-Khidāwiyya al-Miṣriyya*. 7v. in 8. Cairo, 1889–92.
Lists all holdings including manuscripts up to 1891.
—— *Fihrist al-kutub al-ʿarabiyya al-mawjūda bi-Dār al-Kutub li-ghāyat 1932*. 8v. in 9. Cairo, 1925–42.
From vol. 2 onwards appendices and supplements update earlier parts. Arranged on a subject basis, but deals only with the humanities and the Islamic sciences. Separate catalogues have been published for the Persian and Turkish books held by Dār al-Kutub.
—— *Fihris Maktabat Mukarram al-mawjūda bi-Dār al-Kutub*. Cairo, 1933.
Also known as Maktabat Makram.
—— *Fihris maktabat Qawala*. 4v. Cairo, 1931–33.
—— 'Al-Khizāna al-Zakiyya aw majmūʿat kutub Aḥmad Zakī Bāshā al-Miṣriyya', by Muḥammad Kurd ʿAlī. *Al-Muqtabas* **8**, 1914, pp. 393–404.
—— *Nashrat Dār al-Kutub al-Miṣriyya*. Cairo, 1948–.
Accessions list.
—— *Nashra dawriyya; Bulletin des additions; Bulletin of additions*. Cairo, 1928–?
An accessions list issued separately in English, French and Arabic. Has long ceased publication.
—— *National Library, Cairo, 1952–64*, by ʿAbd al-Munʿim ʿUmar. Cairo, 1964.
—— *Qāʾima bi-ʿawāʾil al-matbūʿāt al-ʿarabiyya al-maḥfūẓa bi-Dār al-Kutub*, comp. by Jamāl al-Dīn Shurbājī. Cairo, 1962.
CAIRO, JĀMIʿAT AL-QĀHIRA, *Fihris al-kutub wa-al-makhṭūṭāt al-mahfūẓa fī Khizānat al-amīr Ibrāhīm Hilmī*. Cairo, 1933.
—— *Al-rasāʾil al-ʿilmiyya li-darajatay al-mājistīr wa-al-duktūrāh*. Cairo, 1958.
Contains English and Arabic texts.

CAIRO, MAKTABAT AL-HĀMĪ BĀSHĀ, *Fihrist al-kutub allatī kānat fī tarikat al-marḥūm al-Hāmī Bāshā*. Bulaq, 1278/1861.

CAIRO, MAKTABAT MUKHTĀR BEY, *Fihrist Maktabat al-maghfūr lahu Mukhtār Bey*, by Muṣṭafā Muḥarram Mukhtār. Cairo, 1936.

CAIRO, MANAGEMENT INFORMATION CENTRE, 'Management information centre in the U.A.R.', by El-Radi. *Unesco bull. lib.* **23**, 1969, pp. 109–10.

CAIRO, AL-MATḤAF AL-MIṢRI, *Catalogue de la Bibliothèque du Musée Egyptien du Caire*, par D. Abou-Ghazi et El-Mohsen El-Khachab. Cairo, 1966–.

CAIRO, NATIONAL INFORMATION AND DOCUMENTATION CENTRE, 'Dirāsāt al-usus al-'ilmiyya wa-al-'amaliyya fī inshā' markaz bibliyūghrāriyya fī Miṣr'. *'A. al-M.* **4**, vi, 1962, pp. 10–13.

—— 'La division de documentation scientifique et technique du Caire', par A. Pérez-Vitoria. *Rev. doc.* **26**, 1959, pp. 97–100.

—— *A mechanized information retrieval system for the Documentation Centre in Cairo*, by V. Laiko. Paris (Unesco), 1969.

CAIRO, UNITED STATES INFORMATION LIBRARY, 'The U.S. Information Libraries in Athens and Cairo'. *Stechert-Hafner Book News* **21**, 1967, pp. 117–19.

CAIRO, WIZĀRAT AL-TARBIYYA, *Fihris al-funūn li-al-kutub al-muḍāfa fī sana . . .* Cairo, 19?–.

Annual accessions list.

—— *Ministry of Education Library. Catalogue of additions 1965–66, subject catalogue and subject index*, prepared by 'Abd al-Moneim Fahmi, Girgis Rizk Dawood and Sobhy Antoun Wahba. Cairo, 1969.

*Iraq*

'AWWĀD, Gūrgīs, 'Khazā'in kutub al-'Irāq al-'āmma'. *Sumer* **2**, 1946, pp. 213–34.

COX, P. H., 'A librarian's memories of a working tour in Iraq'. *Eastern librarian* **3**, 1968, pp. 9–15.

DARWĪSH, Muḥammad Fahmī, *Dalīl al-Jumhūriyyat al-'Irāqiyya li-sana 1960*. Baghdad, 1960.

Contains a chapter by Gūrgīs 'Awwād on Iraqi libraries, pp. 536–44.

DIETZE, J., 'Bibliotheken in Iraq – Eindrücke und Einsichten'. *ZB* **84**, 1970, pp. 336–42.

DUJAYLĪ, Kāẓim, 'Maktabāt al-Najaf'. *Lughat al-'Arab* **3**, 1914, pp. 593–600.

EL-KINDILCHIE, A. I., 'Academic libraries in Iraq'. *Int. lib. rev.* 1973, pp. 463–70.

-NĀṢIRĪ, Nihād 'Abd al-Majīd, *Al-khidmāt al-maktabiyya fī al-Jumhūriyya al-'Irāqiyya*. Baghdad, 1961.

QAZANCHI, F. Y. M., 'Academic libraries in Iraq'. *Al-Mustansiriyya Univ. rev.* **1**, 1969–70, pp. 158–67; also in *Unesco bull. lib.* **25**, 1971, pp. 91–3 [Abridged version].

-SĀMARRĀ'Ī, Amīr Rashīd, *Al-Maktaba al-Sha'biyya al-'Irāqiyya*. Baghdad, 1973.

ANON, 'Unesco technical assistance to Iraqi libraries'. *Unesco bull. lib.* **8**, vii, 1954, E 73.

BAGHDAD, MAKTABAT AL-AWQĀF AL-ʿĀMMA, *Fihrist al-makhṭūṭāt al-ʿarabiyya*, by ʿAbd Allah al-Jabbūrī. Vols. 2–4. Baghdad, 1974.

—— *Maktabat al-awqāf al-ʿāmma: tāʾrīkhuhā wa-nawādir makhṭūṭātihā*, by ʿAbd Allāh Jabbūrī. Baghdad, 1969.

BAGHDAD, JĀMIʿAT BAGHDĀD, AL-MAKTABA AL-MARKAZIYYA, *Majāmīʿ al-kutub al-ʿarabiyya al-mawjūda fī al-Maktaba al-Markaziyya, 1959–64* [later 1965 and 1966]: *fihrist mawḍūʿī*. 4v. Baghdad, 1964–66. Annual supplements 1966–.

Mimeographed subject list of accessions in Arabic. A Western language catalogue also exists:

—— *A list of books in the Central library as represented in the shelf list, 1959–65*. Baghdad, 1965.

Other catalogues for special forms are:

—— *Catalogue of the map collection*. Baghdad, 1968.

—— *Fihrist al-kharāʾiṭ*. Baghdad, 1968. Supplement, 1971.

—— *Fihris mawḍūʿī bi-al-maṭbūʿāt al-ḥukūmiyya*. Baghdad, 1969.

—— *A list of theses and dissertations of Iraqis kept in the Central library*. Baghdad, 1967. Supplement, 1969.

—— *Uṭrūḥāt al-ʿIrāqiyyīn al-mūdaʿa ladā al-Maktaba al-Markaziyya*. Baghdad, 1970. Supplements 1, 2. Baghdad, 1971–72.

—— 'Some remarks on the Central Library', by Hisham al-Shawaf. (In K. Schubart-Engelschall *ed.*, *Orientalistische Bibliotheken und Sammlungen*, Berlin, 1970, pp. 116–16.)

MOSUL, AL-MAKTABA AL-ʿĀMMA, 'Mosul Public Library'. *Unesco bull. lib.* **10**, 1956, p. 236.

*Jordan*

AKHRAṢ, Maḥmūd & SHURAYHA, H., *Jamʿiyyat al-Maktabāt al-Urdinniyya fi 6 sanawāt, 1964–69*. Amman, 1970.

AKHRAṢ, Maḥmūd, *Libraries in Jordan*. Amman?, 1972.

ASALI, Kemal, 'Libraries in Jordan'. *Int. lib. rev.* **6**, 1974, pp. 171–83.

CHANDLER, G. and others, 'The Jordanian library scene, 1973'. *Int. lib. rev.* **6**, 1974, pp. 167–206.

Seven contributions by various authors on Jordanian libraries.

DARWĀZA, Muḥammad ʿIzzat, 'Khazāʾin kutub al-ʿarabiyya'. *RAAD* **4**, 1924, pp. 453–7.

Deals with libraries in Nablus.

ʿAMMĀN, NATIONAL RESOURCES AUTHORITY (Sulṭanat al-Maṣādir al-Ṭabiʿiyya), *Qāʾimat al-iḍāfāt al-jadīda*. Amman, 1968–.

Accessions list.

ʿAMMĀN, ROYAL SCIENTIFIC SOCIETY (Al-Jāmiʿa al-ʿIlmiyya al-Malikiyya), *Qāʾimat al-iḍāfāt al-jadīda*. Amman, 1970–.

Accessions list.

ʿAMMĀN, UNIVERSITY OF JORDAN, *Al-kutub allatī uḍīfat li-majmūʿāt al-maktaba*. Amman, 1970–.

Accessions list, whose title varies. Most commonly used are the above and *Al-kutub allatī ṣunifat aw uʿīda taṣnīfuhā*.

Printed catalogues also exist for the Parliament Library and the Ashrafiyya Mosque Library; an accessions list has also been issued by the Ministry of Information since 1973.

*Kuwait*

BADR, Aḥmad & KALANDER, S., 'Kuwait university libraries'. *Unesco bull. lib.* **24**, 1970, pp. 79–82.

THOMPSON, A., 'Library mission to Kuwait'. *Lib. world* **64**, 1963, pp. 179–84.

ZEHERY, Mohamed H., 'Libraries and librarianship in Kuwait'. *Int. lib. rev.* **7**, 1975, pp. 3–13.

ANON, 'Al-khidmāt al-maktabiyya fī dawlat al-Kuwayt'. *'A. al-M.* **4**, vi, 1962, pp. 27–30.

—— 'Library services in Arabic-speaking states; Kuwait'. *Unesco bull. lib.* **14**, 1960, pp. 124–5.

KUWAIT, JĀMI'AT AL-KUWAYT, *Quarterly accessions list; Al-nashra al-faṣliyya*. Kuwait, 1971.

*Lebanon*

LOMBARD, E., *Liban; évaluation et développement des bibliothèques*. Paris (Unesco), 1965.

BEIRUT, AMERICAN UNIVERSITY OF BEIRUT, *Al-Abḥāth*. Beirut, 1948–.
This journal has contained an annual list of accessions to the A.U.B. Library since 1950.

BEIRUT, DĀR AL-KUTUB AL-WAṬANIYYA, *Nubdha tā'rīkhiyya*, by Ibrāhīm Mu'awwad and Munīr Wahba. Beirut, 1948.

TRIPOLI, KHIZĀNAT ĀL AL-MAGHRIBĪ, 'Description', by 'Abd Allāh Mukhliṣ. *RAAD* **18**, 1943, pp. 123–9.

*Libya*

GALLAL, A. M., 'Libraries in Libya'. *Unesco bull. lib.* **27**, 1973, pp. 257–61.

-KA'ĀK, 'Umar, 'Al-maktabāt fī Lībiyā'. *'A. al-M.* **5**, ii, 1963, pp. 7–8.

MINISTRY OF EDUCATION AND GUIDANCE, *Libyan library development plan*. Tripoli, 1970.

WARD, P., *Survey of Libyan bibliographical sources; Maṣādir al-kutub fi Libiyyā*. Tripoli, 1966.
Arabic and English texts. Supersedes the Oasis Oil Company's *Guide to the libraries of Libya*, 1964.

TRIPOLI, OASIS OIL COMPANY, *Catalogue of the research library*. Tripoli, 1970.

*Mauritania*

TOUPET, C., 'Orientation bibliographique sur la Mauritanie'. *Bull. IFAN* **24**, 1962, pp. 594–613.

NOUAKCHOTT, BIBLIOTHEQUE NATIONALE, *Mauritanie; organisation de la Bibliothèque Nationale*, by A. Heymowski, Paris (Unesco), 1965.

*Morocco*

EL-FASI, M., 'Les bibliothèques au Maroc et quelques-uns de leurs manuscrits les plus rares'. *Hespéris-Tamuda* **2**, 1961, pp. 135–44; also in *Trud. XXV Mezhdunarod. Kong. Vostokovedov, Moskva 1960*, Moscow, 1963, 2, pp. 16–22.

GUASTAVINO GALLENT, G., 'La acción española en los archivos y bibliotecas de la zona norte de Marruecos'. *RABM* **65**, 1958, pp. 148–213.

NEIGEL, 'La Médersa et les bibliothèques de Bou Djad [Boujad]'. *RMM* **24**, 1913, pp. 290–7.

RABAT, CENTRE NATIONALE DE DOCUMENTATION, *Répertoire des Centres services de documentation et des bibliothèques du Royaume du Maroc.* Rabat, 1972.

FEZ, MAKTABAT AL-QARAWIYYĪN, *Barnāmaj al-kutub al-ʿarabiyya*, by A. Bel. (*Catalogue des livres.*) Fez, 1918.

MARRAKESH, MASJID ʿALĪ IBN YŪSUF, 'Un registre d'inventaire et de prêt de la bibliothèque de la mosquée ʿAlī ben Youssef à Marrakech, daté de 1111/1700', by G. Deverdun. *Hespéris* **31**, 1944, pp. 55–9.

RABAT?, BIBLIOTHEQUE DE LA MISSION SCIENTIFIQUE AU MAROC, 'Description'. *RMM* **24**, 1913, pp. 352–5.

RABAT, BIBLIOTHEQUE GÉNÉRALE, *Al-anbāʾ al-bibliyūghrāfiyya al-Maghribiyya; Informations bibliographiques marocaines.* Rabat, 1931–.

Comes out every two weeks in two parts, Arabic and French. Deals mainly with official publications and books about Morocco.

—— *Nouvelles acquisitions.* Rabat, 1970–.

TETUAN, BIBLIOTECA ESPAÑOLA, 'Description', by D. Bacaicoa Arnaiz. *Cuadernos de la Bibl. Española de Tetuán* **1**, 1964, pp. 95–9.

TETUAN, AL-MAKTABA AL-ʿĀMMA, *Catálogo de autores.* Larache, 1941.

—— *Catálogo de autores*, red. por G. Guastavino Gallent. Tetuan, 1946.

These are different editions of the same work.

—— *Catálogo de la sección de raros* (*siglos XVI al XVIII*), red. por G. Guastavino Gallent. Tetuan, 1942.

—— 'Ediciones anteriores a 1800 conservados en la Biblioteca General', by G. Guastavino Gallent. *Tamuda* **5**, 1957, pp. 27–86.

—— *Fahāris* (*Sección árabe: índice y inventarios*). Tangier, 1940.

—— *Fihris al-muʾallifīn wa-al-ʿanāwīn*, by Aḥmad Muḥammad al-Maknasī. (*Catálogo de autores y títulos . . . sección árabe*). Tetuan, 1952.

—— *Inventario provisional de la sección de grabados y cartografía*, red. por G. Guastavino Gallent. Tetuan, 1962 [i.e. 1942].

TETUAN, AL-KHIZĀNA AL-KHALĪFIYYA BI-MAʿHAD MULAY AL-ḤASAN, *Catálogo de autores de la biblioteca, sección europea*, red. por M. Arribas Palau. Tetuan, 1953.

—— *Catálogo de las obras en lenguas árabe y europas.* (*Fihrist al-khizāna al-khalīfiyya*). Tetuan, 1942.

*Palestine*

POHL, J., 'Führer durch die Bibliotheken Palästinas'. *ZB* **55**, 1938, pp. 50–64.

ṬALAS, Muḥammad Asʿad, 'Dūr kutub Filasṭīn wa-nafāʾis makhṭūṭātihā'. *RAAD* **21**, 1946, pp. 49–60.

JERUSALEM, AL-MAKTABA AL-KHĀLIDIYYA, *Barnāmaj*, by Muḥammad b. Maḥmūd al-Ḥabbāl. Jerusalem, 1318/1900.

*Sa'udi Arabia*

BELTRAN, A. A., 'Books in the desert'. *Lib. J.* **81**, 1956, pp. 585–9.

On the Aramco libraries.

CHILDS, J. R., 'Sa'udi Arabian libraries still largely unknown'. *Lib. J.* **75**, 1950, pp. 1276–7, 1382–3.

Again on the Aramco libraries.

SPIES, O., 'Die Bibliotheken des Hidchas'. *ZDMG* **90**, 1936, pp. 83–120.

This volume of the *ZDMG* **90**, 1936, contains other articles by O. Spies on Sa'udi Arabian libraries.

ANON, 'Al-taqrīr al-rasmī li-tanẓīm al-maktaba al-madrasiyya wa-al-'āmma fī al-M. 'A. S.'. *'A. al-M.* **4**, ii, 1962, pp. 25–7.

*Sudan*

'ABD AL-KĀFI, Muḥammad (Kafie, Mohamed Abdel), 'Public library development in the Republic of the Sudan'. *'A. al-M.* **2**, i, 1960, pp. 65–6.

MASSIGNON, L., 'Une bibliothèque saharienne [Shaykh Sidia]'. *RMM* **8**, 1909, pp. 409–18.

OFFOR, R., 'University libraries in the British colonies and the Sudan'. *Libri* **8**, 1954–55, pp. 54–75.

PARKER, J. S., 'Library development in the Sudan'. *Unesco bull. lib.* **27**, 1973, pp. 78–83.

SEWELL, P. H., 'The development of library services in Sudan'. *Unesco bull. lib.* **15**, 1961, pp. 87–90.

KHARTOUM, JĀMI'AT KHARṬŪM, *Classified catalogue of the Sudan collection.* Khartoum, 1970.

Contains 5114 entries with author index.

*Syria*

ZAYYĀT, Ḥabīb, *Khazā'in al-kutub fī Dimashq wa-ḍawāḥihā.* Cairo, 1902.

DAMASCUS, INSTITUT FRANÇAIS, 'The Library', by N. Elisséef. *Unesco bull. lib.* **10**, 1956, p. 235.

DAMASCUS, JĀMI'AT DIMASHQ, *Bulletin mensuel des publications reçues.* Damascus, n.d.

—— 'Description'. *Unesco bull. lib.* **21**, 1967, pp. 343–4.

DAMASCUS, AL-MAKTABA AL-ẒĀHIRIYYA, *Fihrist al-Maktaba al-'Umūmiyya.* Damascus, 1299/1881.

DAMASCUS, MALEK DAHOR LIBRARY, 'La biblioteca araba di Malek Dahor'. *Boll. Min. Aff. Est.* **1**, 1889, pp. 381–90.

*Tunisia*

BULLETIN ÉCONOMIQUE ET SOCIAL DE LA TUNISIE, Tunis, 1949–.

Contains bibliographical information regarding: (a) books received in compliance with the legal deposit laws; (b) official publications; (c) newspapers and serials.

CHANDLER, G., *Tunisie: développement des bibliothèques*. Paris (Unesco), 1964.

-JĪLĀNĪ IBN AL-ḤĀJJ YAḤYĀ, 'Al-maktabāt al-'āmma bi-Tūnis, lamḥa tā'rīkhiyya'. *Majallat al-maktabāt al-'arabiyya* **2**, ii, 1965.

LELONG, M., 'L'effort tunisien pour la diffusion de la culture. (Comités culturelles, Maisons de la Culture, Maisons du Peuple, Bibliothèques)'. *IBLA* **27**, 1964, pp. 43–54.

MASSON, A., 'La lecture publique en Tunisie'. *Bull. bibl. de France* **13**, 1968, pp. 271–4.

PAWLIKOWSKA, E., 'Biblioteki publiczne w Tunizji'. *Bibliotekarz* **38**, iv, 1971, pp. 103–7.

TUNIS, CENTRE DE DOCUMENTATION NATIONALE, *Al-anbā' al-bibliyūghrāfiyya; Informations bibliographiques*. Tunis, 1966–.

Accessions list in two series, Arabic and non-Arabic.

ANON, 'National archives and research libraries of Tunis'. *Maghreb digest* **5**, iii, 1972?, pp. 5–8.

—— 'Statistics of libraries in Tunisia (1965–68)'. *Bib. Doc. Ter.* **11**, 1971, p. 211.

TUNIS, JĀMI' AL-ZAYTŪNA, *Barnāmaj al-'Abdaliyya* [al-Ṣādiqiyya]. 4v. Tunis, 1908–11.

—— *Daftar al-Maktaba al-Ṣādiqiyya*. Tunis, 1292/1875.

—— *Extrait du catalogue des manuscrits et des imprimés . . .* par B. Roy; *histoire* [de la bibliothèque] par B. Roy avec la collaboration de Mohammed bel Khodja et de Mohammed el Hachaichi. Tunis, 1900.

*Yemen*

SANAA, AL-JĀMI' AL-MUQADDAS, *Fihrist kutub al-Khizāna al-Mutawakkiliyya*. Sanaa, n.d.

## IV. LIBRARIANSHIP WITH REGARD TO ARABIC AND THE ARAB WORLD

As in Part III (c), this section has concentrated on European rather than Arabic material; in particular, many library school textbooks in Arabic have been excluded.

### General

-AMĪN, 'Abd al-Karīm, *Al-maktaba al-'āmma; idāratuhā wa-tanẓīmuhā wa-nihāyatuhā wa-ikhtiyār kutubihā*. Baghdad, 1971.

FARSUNI, Fuad, 'Acquisition of Arabic books'. *Risālat al-Maktaba* **10**, i, 1975, pp. 5–18.

ḤARBĪ, Muḥammad Khayrī & FAHMĪ, 'Abd al-Mun'im, 'I'dād wa-ikhtiyār umanā' maktabāt al-buḥūth wa-al-muwaththiqīn fī al-bilād al-nāṭiqa bi-al-lugha al-'arabiyya'. *'A. al-M.* **4**, vi, 1962, pp. 14–20.

Discusses the training of librarians, national bibliographical services and major libraries.

ḤASAN, 'Izzat, *Al-maktaba al-'arabiyya; dirāsa li-ahamiyyat al-kutub fi al-thaqāfa al-'arabiyya*. Damascus, 1970–.

ḤIJĀZĪ, Fu'ād al-Sayyid, *Al-wathā'iq: tanẓīmuhā, ḥafẓuhā, idāratuhā.* Cairo, 1966.

HOPWOOD, D., 'Book acquisition from the Middle East'. (In D. A. Clarke *ed.*, *Acquisitions from the Third World*, London, 1975, pp. 79–84.)

Deals with booksellers and national bibliographical information.

—— 'The Islamic Near East'. (In B. C. Bloomfield *ed.*, *Acquisition and provision of foreign books by National and University Libraries*, London, 1972, pp. 77–80.)

Deals with the general problems of book supply facing Middle Eastern libraries.

KALIA, D. R., 'Encouragement of reading in Arab states'. *Unesco bull. lib.* **14**, 1960, pp. 107–12.

Reviews book production and the rôle of libraries among other things.

KĀẒIM, Midḥat, *Al-taṭawwurāt al-maktabiyya fī al-'ālam al-jadīd.* Cairo, n.d.

-KHAṬĪB, Muḥammad 'Ajjāj, *Lamaḥāt fī al-maktaba wa-al-baḥth wa-al-maṣādir.* Damascus, 1971.

KÜMMERER, E., 'Bericht über eine Beschaffungsreise nach Nordafrika'. *Z. Bibliothekswesen u. Bibliog.* **18**, 1971, pp. 174–8.

McNIFF, P. J., 'Acquisition of library material from the Middle East'. *Lib. resources and technical services* **7**, 1963, pp. 20–5.

-MAHDĪ, Muḥammad, *Al-mawādd al-sam'iyya wa-al-baṣariyya fī al-maktaba.* Cairo, 1961.

PEARSON, J. D., 'Orientalia'. *Q. J. Lib. Congress* **26**, ii, 1969.

—— 'Orientalist libraries today'. *Int. lib. rev.* **2**, 1970, pp. 3–18.

Based on a paper presented to the 1969 SCONUL *Conference on the acquisition of library materials from Asia* (see below).

—— 'Rôle of the library in Oriental studies'. (In *Proc. 23rd Int. Con. Or. Cambridge 1954*, London, 1956, pp. 34–42.)

SA'ĪD, Aḥmad, *Al-maḥfūẓāt wa-al-kutub wa-mabādi' idārat al-aqlām.* Cairo, 1928.

SCONUL GROUP OF ORIENTALIST LIBRARIES, *Conference on the acquisition of library materials from Asia.* London, 1967; follow-up conferences, London, 1968 and 1969.

—— *Newsletter of library development*, 1970.

All the reports contain valuable information on the Middle East.

SMITH, W. C., 'Islamic Near East: intellectual rôle of librarianship'. *Library Q.* **35**, 1965, pp. 283–94.

This is followed, on pp. 294–7, by a discussion and criticism of the article, headed by D. H. Partington.

'UMAR, Aḥmad Anwar, *Majmū'āt al-nasharāt wa-al-quṣāṣāt bi-al-maktabāt.* Baghdad, 1967.

WILDER, D., *Acquisition and control of publications from the Middle East: a report.* New York, 1958.

### Journals

See also the section headed: General biographies (in part 3 (b)).

'ĀLAM AL-MAKTABĀT (Library world), Cairo, 1957–69.

Dealt principally with librarianship. Articles carried a summary in English. Every year a special issue was devoted to a bibliography of current Egyptian publications.

-ʿARABĪ, Kuwait, 1958–.

Occasionally has articles on libraries and library science.

BRITISH SOCIETY FOR MIDDLE EASTERN STUDIES BULLETIN, London, 1974–.

Has much information on British library activities regarding the Middle East.

MAJALLAT AL-KITĀB AL-ʿARABĪ (Arabic book journal), Cairo, 1964–71.

Dealt with librarianship and the history of libraries, though wider in scope than *ʿĀlam al-Maktabāt*. Almost every number had a special subject bibliography, and indexes of periodical articles were also frequently published.

MAJALLAT AL-MAKTABA AL-ʿARABIYYA (The Arab library), Cairo, 1963–?.

This has now ceased publication.

-MAKTABA (The Library), Baghdad, 1960–73.

A trade journal, this dealt with cultural activities in the Arab World, including libraries.

MELA NOTES, Cambridge, Mass., 1973–.

Published by the Middle East Librarians' Association of North America, this is the first Western language journal devoted entirely to Middle Eastern librarianship. Since all its contents are relevant to this bibliography, individual articles have in general not been indexed here.

RISĀLAT AL-MAKTABA (Rissalat al-Maktaba/Message of the library), Amman, 1965–.

Published by Jamʿiyyat al-Maktabāt al-Urdunniyya (Jordan Library Association). Apart from containing the Jordanian national bibliography, this journal gives English abstracts of all its major articles.

ṢAḤĪFAT AL-MAKTABA (Egyptian Library Journal), Cairo, 1969–.

The organ of the Egyptian School Library Association. A successor to *ʿĀlam al-Maktabāt*?

SIJILL AL-THAQĀFĪ, Cairo, 1948–62.

Dealt with cultural activities in Egypt, including libraries. Like *ʿĀlam al-Maktabāt* an annual issue listed a year's book production in Egypt.

Several other librarianship serials exist in the Arab World, notably the organs of the various library associations and national libraries. As their circulations seem to be very limited, however, it has not been possible to give any information about them.

## Cataloguing

AMAN, Muḥammad M., *Arab states author headings*. New York, 1973.

A valuable list of the official names of government institutions and ministries in the various Arab states. Gives the Arabic title and the English and/or French equivalents.

ANDERSON, M. D., 'The alphabetization of Islamic names'. *The indexer* **7**, iii, 1971.

ʿAWDA, Abū al-Futūḥ, *Jadāwil tarqīm asmāʾ al-muʾallifīn al-ʿarab fī al-maktabāt*. Cairo, 1967.

BEESTON, A. F. L., *Arabic nomenclature; a summary guide for beginners*. Oxford, 1971.

BEHN, W., 'Islamic filing'. *The indexer* **10**, 1974.

BRAUN, H., 'Die alphabetische Katalogisierung von Werken in arabischer, persischer und türkischer Sprache'. *Z. Bibliothekswesen u. Bibliog.* **11**, 1964, pp. 9–32.

CENTRAL INTELLIGENCE AGENCY, *Arabic personal names* (*Arabic script personal names – Arabic, Kurdish, Pashto, Persian, Urdu*). Washington, 1964.

Lists all the variant romanizations of Islamic names in alphabetical order, with their equivalent in Arabic script. Also contains a good guide to the structure of Arabic nomenclature.

CHAPLIN, A. H., 'National usages for the entry of names of persons'. (In *Int. conf. cat. principles*, Sevenoaks, 1967.)

EUSTACHE, D., 'Catalogue d'imprimés ou de manuscrits arabes. Choix de la vedette-auteur'. *Bull. bibl. de France* **3**, 1958, pp. 99–111, 619–28.

JIRJĀS, Sulaymān, 'Taḥlīl wa-naqd li-kitāb Mabādiʾ al-fahrasa al-waṣfiyya'. *ʿA. al-M.* **6**, i, 1964, pp. 36–9.

A critical review of Shanīṭī's work on descriptive cataloguing (see below).

—— 'Taʿqīb ḥawl fahrasat asmāʾ al-muʾallifīn al-ʿarab'. *ʿA. al-M.* **4**, iii, 1962, pp. 16–19.

-MUNAJJID, Ṣalāḥ al-Dīn, *Qawāʾid fahrasat al-makhṭūṭāt al-ʿarabiyya*. Beirut, 1973.

ṢABĀḤ, Muḥammad al-Saʿīd, 'Raʾy fī madkhal al-kitāb al-ʿarabī'. *ʿA. al-M.* **4**, iii, 1962, pp. 28–9.

SENGUPTA, B., 'Rendering of Hindu and Muslim names in catalogue entries'. *Ind. lib.* **14**, 1959, pp. 57–63.

SHANĪṬĪ, Maḥmūd & FAHMĪ, ʿAbd al-Munʿim, *Madākhil al-muʾallifīn al-ʿarab, al-qāʾima al-ūlā* (*Entries of Arabic authors, first list to 1215/1800*). Prelim. edn. Cairo, 1961.

SHANĪṬĪ, Maḥmūd & AL-MAHDĪ, Muḥammad, *Qawāʾid al-fahrasa al-waṣfiyya li-al-maktabāt al-ʿarabiyya*. Cairo, 1962.

SHANĪṬĪ, Maḥmūd, 'Cataloguing and classification of Arabic books: some basic considerations'. *Unesco bull. lib.* **14**, 1960, pp. 104–6.

—— 'Problems of standardization in descriptive cataloguing of Arabic materials'. (In E. Bishop and J. Waller *eds.*, *International co-operation in orientalist librarianship*, Canberra, 1972, pp. 49–57.)

—— *Vedette des noms arabes*. Paris?, 1961.

TIBBETTS, G., 'The cataloguing of Arabic books'. *Library Q.* **29**, 1959, pp. 113–32.

WAGNER, E., *Regeln für die alphabetische Katalogisierung von Drucksachen in den islamischen Sprachen*. Wiesbaden, 1961.

—— 'Zur alphabetischen Katalogisierung orientalischer Titel'. *Z. Bibliothekswesen u. Bibliog.* **7**, 1960, pp. 228–32.

Treats principally of the problems of cataloguing Islamic works.

## Classification

'ABD AL-NŪR, 'Abd al-Wahhāb, *Al-taṣnīf al-bibliyūjrāfī li-'ulūm al-dīn al-islāmī.* Cairo, 1973.

'ABD AL-RAḤMĀN, 'Abd al-Jabbār, *Al-maktaba wa-minhaj al-baḥth.* (*The library and research.*) Basra, 1972.

In many ways, a companion to the author's *Dalīl al-marāji' al-'arabiyya wa-al-mu'arraba*; (see above, section 3(b)), this work also contains an interesting chapter on classification.

'ABD AL-SHĀFĪ, Ḥasan, *Al-i'dād al-fannī li-al-kutub fī al-maktabāt; al-fahrasa wa-al-taṣnīf.* Cairo, 1970.

AFSHĀR, Īrāj, 'The need for Persian and Islamic subject headings in basic subject lists'. (In E. Bishop and J. Waller *eds*, *International co-operation in orientalist librarianship*, Canberra, 1972, pp. 210–12.)

AMAN, Muḥammad M., *Analysis of terminology, form and structure of subject headings in Arabic literature and formulation of rules for Arabic subject headings.* Ph.D. thesis, Univ. of Pittsburgh, 1968.

-AMĪN, 'Abd al-Karīm, *Al-taṣnīf wa-al-fahrasa fī 'ilm al-maktaba.* Baghdad, 1963.

-ANṢĀRĪ, 'Abd al-Dā'im, *Al-taṣnīf al-'asharī al-'arabī wa-fahārisuhu al-hijā'iyya.* Cairo, 1967.

'AṬIYYA, 'Alī Imām, *Kashshāf taṣnīf al-maktaba 'alā niẓām Dewey al-mu'addal.* Cairo, 1962.

-BANHĀWĪ, Muḥammad Amīn, *Namādhij bi-ṭāqāt al-fahāris al-'arabiyya li-al-maktabāt.* Cairo, 1971.

CAMBRIDGE UNIVERSITY LIBRARY, *Oriental languages classification.* 2nd edn. Cambridge, 1965.

-DABBĀGH, Jalāl Maḥmūd, *Al-fahrasa al-'amaliyya li-al-kitāb al-'arabī.* Baghdad, 1968.

—— *Ru'ūs al-mawḍū'āt li-kitābat al-abḥāth.* (*Subject headings for research.*) Baghdad, 1969.

DĀGHIR, Yūsuf As'ad, *Dalīl al-a'ārib ilā 'ilm al-kutub wa-fann al-makātib.* (*Manuel pratique de bibliographie et de bibliothéconomie à l'usage des pays du Proche-Orient.*) Beirut, 1947.

Covers bibliographical sources for Arabic studies and also gives an abridged version of Dewey in Arabic.

DEWEY, M., *Mūjaz al-taṣnīf al-'asharī ... mu'addalan li-al-maktabāt al-'arabiyya*, tr. by Maḥmūd Shanīṭī and Aḥmad Kabbāsh. Cairo, 1970.

ECHE, Y., *Essai sur une classification des sciences à l'intention des bibliothèques arabes et arabisantes; avec, exclusivement en arabe, un index alphabétique des matières destiné à guider les recherches à travers la classification.* Damascus, 1937.

HARTZELL, M. E., 'A special library in Arab culture'. *Sp. libs.* **48**, 1957, pp. 56–63.

Deals with the adaptation of Dewey for Islamic subjects by the Aramco library at Dhahran, Sa'udi Arabia.

-IDĀRA AL-MARKAZIYYA LI-AL-IḤṢĀ' (Cairo), *Al-taṣnīf al-'arabī al-muwaḥḥid li-al-sila'; al-aqsām wa-al-abwāb wa-al-fuṣūl.* Cairo, 1965.

INDIAN INSTITUTE OF ISLAMIC STUDIES, *Library classification schedule on Islam and related subjects.* New Delhi, 1974.

KĀẒIM, Midḥat, *Al-taṣnīf niẓām Dewey 'asharī.* Cairo, 1968.

MENOU, M. J., *L'indexation de la documentation scientifique, technique et économique adoptée au développement du Maroc.* Paris (Unesco), 1971.

-NĀṢIRĪ, Nihād 'Abd al-Majīd, *Uṣūl tanẓīm al-maktabāt 'alā ṭarīq Dewey al-'asharī.* Baghdad, 1955.

SHAFI, M., 'Expansion of Dewey Decimal Classification relating to Oriental, Islamic and Pakistani topics'. *Pakistan lib. rev.* **4**, 1962, pp. 42–88.

TIBBETTS, G., 'The classification of Arabic books'. *Library Q.* **29**, 1959, pp. 174–98.

The notation is entirely new, although theoretically the schedule is an expansion of Bliss. There is a good introduction to the theory of classification in Medieval Islam.

'UMAR, Aḥmad Anwar, *Ru'ūs al-mawḍū'āt fī al-fahāris al-hijā'iyya.* Baghdad, 1968.

### Education and Training

AWAD, Awad Tawfik, 'Training and in-service training of librarians in the Arab Republic of Egypt'. *Unesco bull. lib.* **28**, 1974, pp. 268–72.

BIRCH, F. M., 'A library education project in Jordan'. *LA record* **76**, 1974, pp. 129–31.

BONNY, H. V., 'Library training in Iraq'. *Unesco bull. lib.* **12**, 1958, pp. 123–6.

CASSELL, K. A., 'An international woman-assignment; Morocco'. *Wilson lib. bull.* **74**, 1973, pp. 848–51.

On the training of librarians in Morocco.

ḤARBĪ, Muḥammad Khayrī, 'The importance of training for information work in the Arab states'. (In G. Lubbock *ed., International conference on training for information work, Rome, 1971*, Rome, &c., 1972, pp. 185–9.)

KENT, F. L. & ABU HAIDAR, F., 'Professional training of librarians'. *Unesco bull. lib.* **14**, 1960, pp. 100–5.

Reviews the situation in all the Arab countries, except Mauritania, Yemen and the Gulf States.

KENT, F. L., 'Training of librarians and documentalists in Arabic-speaking countries'. *Unesco bull. lib.* **21**, 1967, pp. 301–10.

MASLIAH, M., 'The training of documentalists with a view to the needs of documentation centres and specialized libraries in Tunisia'. (In G. Lubbock *ed., International conference on training for information work, Rome, 1971*, Rome, &c., 1972, pp. 261–6.)

RAFIDI, S., 'The library technician programme in Lebanon'. *Unesco bull. lib.* **27**, 1973, pp. 278–80.

SHARIFI, N., 'Education for librarianship abroad; U.A.R., Iran, Iraq, Lebanon and Syria'. *Lib. trends* **12**, 1963, pp. 227–59.

SRIVASTAVA, A. P., *Iraq; education for library science and documentation, 1968*. Paris (Unesco), 1969.

UNESCO, *Selection and training of research librarians and documentalists in Arabic-speaking countries*. Unesco, 1963. [Working paper.]

—— *World guide to library schools and training courses in documentation; Guide mondial des écoles de bibliothécaires et documentalistes*. Paris, &c., 1972.
Poor coverage of the Arab World.

ANON, 'Library training in Iraq'. *Unesco bull. lib.* **12**, 1958, pp. 123–6.

—— *Report on the Royal Scientific Society course in library science*. Amman, 1974.

# Booksellers for the supply of material on the Arabo-Islamic Near and Middle East

M. DRISKELL

## I. EUROPE

(i) *Denmark*
Ejnar Munksgaard,
6 Norregade,
Copenhagen.

(ii) *France*
J. Gabalda & Cie,
90, rue Bonaparte,
Paris VIe.

Paul Geuthner,
12, rue Vavin,
Paris VIe.

La Guilde,
18, rue de Turbigo,
Paris IIe.

Librairie C. Klincksieck,
11, rue de Lille,
Paris VIIe.

A. Maisonneuve,
11, rue Saint-Sulpice,
Paris VIe.

G. P. Maisonneuve & Larose,
11, rue Victor-Cousin,
Paris Ve.

François Maspero,
1, Place Paul Painlevé,
Paris Ve.

Librairie F. de Nobèle,
35, rue Bonaparte,
Paris VIe.

Librairie Orientale H. Samuelian,
51, rue Monsieur le Prince,
Paris VIe.

Michèle Trochon,
76, rue du Cherche-Midi,
Paris VIe.

(iii) *Germany*
Rudolf Habelt,
Buchhändler und Antiquar,
Bonn 5,
Schliessfach 4.

Otto Harrassowitz,
6200 Wiesbaden,
Postfach 349,
Taunusstrasse 5.

J. C. B. Mohr (Paul Siebeck),
H. Laupp'sche Buchhandlung,
74 Tübingen,
Postfach 2040.

H. F. Rosner,
Munich,
Fasanerstrasse 68F,
8025 Unterhaching/Munich.

(iv) *Great Britain*
Ad Orientem,
2, Cumberland Gardens,
St. Leonard's-on-Sea,
East Sussex TN38 0QR.

Adab Books,
50, Saddler Street,
Durham DH1 3NU.

ASP Distributors,
7, Bishopsthorpe Road,
London SE26.

B. H. Blackwell Ltd.,
Broad Street,
Oxford OX1 3BQ.

E. J. Brill Ltd.,
41, Museum Street,
London WC1A 1LX.

A. R. Bullock,
62, Kelburne Road,
Oxford OX4 3SH.

Collets London Bookshop,
66, Charing Cross Road,
London WC2.

Collets Russian Bookshop,
39, Museum Street,
London WC1.

W. Heffer & Sons Ltd.,
20, Trinity Street,
Cambridge CB2 3NG.

Kegan Paul, Trench, Trubner Ltd.,
39 Store Street,
London, WC1E 7DD.

Luzac & Co. Ltd.,
P.O. Box 157,
46, Great Russell Street,
London WC1B 3PE.

Arthur Probsthain,
41, Great Russell Street,
London WC1B 3PL.

A. Rosenthal,
9–10, Broad Street,
Oxford OX1 3AP.

J. Thornton,
11, Broad Street,
Oxford.

(v) *Italy*
O. P. Sirovich,
4, Piazza Oberdam,
Trieste.

(vi) *Netherlands*
E. J. Brill Ltd.,
Oude Rijn 33a–35,
Leiden.

Antiquariaat Broekema,
Faradaystraat 1,
Amsterdam.

Gé Nabrink's Boekhandel en Antiquariaat,
Korte Korsjespoortsteg 8,
Amsterdam.

M. Nijhoff,
Lange Voorhout 9,
The Hague.

Boekhandel Swets & Zeitlinger,
Keizersgracht 471,
Amsterdam.

(vii) *Spain*
Libreria Julian Barbazan,
Calle de los Libreros 4,
Madrid 13.

## II. U.S.A.

Orientalia Inc.,
61 4th Avenue,
New York 10003.

Paragon Book Gallery,
14 East 38th Street,
New York 10016.

## III. MIDDLE EAST

(i) *Algeria*
Société Nationale d'Édition et de Diffusion,
3, Boulevard Zirout Youcef,
Algiers.

(ii) *Egypt*
Al-Arab Bookshop,
28, Faggalah Street,
Cairo.

Dar al-Ma'arif,
15 Sh. Sabri Abu 'Alam &
1119 Corniche el Nil,
Cairo.

Les Livres de France,
Immeuble Immobilia,
Rue Kasr el Nil,
Cairo.

Trans World Press Agency (Wakālat al-ṣuhuf al-'ālamiyya),
18, Abdel Khalek Sarwat,
Cairo.

(iii) *Iraq*

Makatabat al-Muthanna,
Sh. al-Mutanabbi,
Baghdad.

(iv) *Lebanon*

Byblos,
B.P. 8363,
Rue Madame Curie,
Arts et Metiers,
Beirut.

Dar Assakafa,
P.O. Box 543,
Beirut.

Dar Sader,
B.P. 10,
Beirut.

Librarie du Liban,
Immeuble Esseily,
Place Riad Solh,
B.P. 945,
Beirut.

Librairie Orientale,
B.P. 1986,
Place de l'Étoile,
Beirut.

New Book Publishing House,
B.P. 5264,
Beirut.

Ras Beirut Bookshop,
P.O. Box 2796,
Beirut.

Sulaiman's Bookshop,
Salihah Building, Room 64,
P.O. Box 8258,
Beirut.

(v) *Syria*

Sami Asaad Aintabi,
Farafra Quarter,
Aleppo.

Dar al-Fikr,
P.O. Box 962 (S.A.R.),
Damascus.

J. G. Zakhour,
B.P. 2776,
Damascus.

(vi) *Tunisia*

Maison Tunisienne de l'Édition,
70, Ave. de la Liberté,
Tunis.

Société Nationale de Diffusion,
5, Ave. de Carthage,
Tunis.

# INDEX OF AUTHORS, WITH TITLES OF ANONYMOUS WORKS